The New Best of BetterBaking.com

The New Best of BetterBaking.com

MORE THAN 200 CLASSIC RECIPES
FROM THE BELOVED BAKER'S WEBSITE

Marcy Goldman

whitecap

Whitecap Books

The Best of BetterBaking.com first published in the United States
by Ten Speed Press, Berkeley, CA.

Whitecap Books is known for its expertise in the cookbook market,
and has produced some of the most innovative and familiar titles
found in kitchens across North America. Visit our website
at www.whitecap.ca.

Interior design by Five Seventeen (www.picapica.ca)
Photography by Ryan Szulc (www.ryanszulc.ca),
food styling by Marcy Goldman, and prop styling
by Madeleine Johari (except pages 35, 47, 67, 79, 97,
117, 180, and 221: photography by Maren Caruso
and food styling by Erin Quon and Kim Konecny)
Custom-made clock pictured on page vi
by John Borin (www.johnborin.com)

Printed in China

Library and Archives Canada Cataloguing in Publication

Goldman, Marcy
The new best of betterbaking.com / Marcy Goldman.

ISBN 978-1-77050-002-0

1. Baking. I. Title.

TX763.G643 2009   641.8'15   C2009-902678-3

The publisher acknowledges the financial support of the Government
of Canada through the Book Publishing Industry Development Program
(BPIDP) and the Province of British Columbia through the Book
Publishing Tax Credit.

09   10   11   12   13   5   4   3   2   1

Dedicated, with much love,
to my three sons, Jonathan,
Gideon, and Benjamin

Contents

· ·

· ·

· ·

Preface to the New Edition

· ·

DEAR FELLOW BAKERS AND FRIENDS OF
BETTERBAKING.COM,

Welcome to the BetterBaking.com test kitchen. If you are new, you're in for a treat. If you are a returning baking friend, then I'm delighted to offer you a brand new, photo-packed, recipe-fortified (more than 30 new ones!) cookbook. *The Best of BetterBaking.com* is back—and it's better than ever.

What a difference a new millennium makes, especially in launching a new edition of a very special cookbook—with the words "dot-com" in its title. The first and original edition of this cookbook had its 2002 debut during the relative infancy of the Internet. Years before, in May 1997, my website of the same name first appeared online. The original name of the website was actually Baker Boulanger; BetterBaking .com was its URL (or its Internet address). However, in very short time, BetterBaking.com—or "BB" as it became affectionately known by my visitors and subscribers—became both the unofficial name of my online baking magazine and, later, of my unique cookbook.

It's hard to believe, but the proposal for this cookbook had everyone, including many publishers, claim that it was too ahead of its time. Not to mention the fact that countless agents and editors just said, "No way," when I pitched a classic cookbook based on something as edgy as a web baking magazine. To the naysayers I simply said, "Yes, way!" This was long before the power of positive thinking found its way into such books as *The Secret*. I suppose my vision, born in print, transferred to cyberspace and then back onto the printed page, was not to be detoured. Never stop a baker on a tear.

It's been over a decade since the launch of my website, and almost that same passage of time since the original companion cookbook, *The Best of BetterBaking.com*, was first found in stores and places like Amazon.com. As the Internet has evolved and websites have become beyond commonplace—in fact, most of us rely on the Net for almost any and everything—this glorious new edition, *The New Best of BetterBaking.com*, is finally right on time, and right at home in what is now the comfortable fusion of technology and lifestyle. It represents a handcrafted distillation of my own best original recipes I've created for my website since 1997. It includes both my personal favorites and the most popular recipes (the ones with the most "hits").

Of course, both the Internet and the iBaker (me!) have changed. Today, recipes flit around *even faster* than instant yeast rises. I see people browsing the Internet and taking recipes from collegial sites using their BlackBerries, iPhones, Kindles, laptops, and other electronic readers. "Exotic" ingredients that your local supermarket never used to stock are now readily available, or you can easily order them online. There are many incredible food sites and food blogs, along with incredible culinary websites on which you can find baking related resources. YouTube, Craigslist, Facebook, and Twitter also all carry tales of baking and sharing. Who knows what's next?

One thing that doesn't change: great baking from superb recipes will always be part of whatever new order there is, regardless of the delivery system. That said, I am ever most proud to offer a print cookbook—a real paper, smear-me-with-batter, douse-me-with-vanilla, chock-full-of-new-recipes cookbook—to tuck under your arm and take into your kitchen.

There is just something so beautiful about a book. No buttons to press or click, or mouse to scroll with, nothing to plug in or upload. Just open the book and bake. Here is a special recipe collection just for you, from me, inspired by the flavors of life—a special sweetness that is sans rival.

As always, I wish you happy baking, and sweet times, in the kitchen and in life.

Warmly,

Marcy Goldman

Marcy Goldman
www.BetterBaking.com

Acknowledgments

· ·

A NEW EDITION OF A BOOK means there are new and old friends to thank. Here's where the gratitude should be warmly parlayed.

I would probably never have published a book, let alone a second one, if not for the many newspaper and magazine editors who have allowed me to "guest" in their food pages. Many of the recipes in this book were inspired by the creative work that is part and parcel of feature food writing. My thanks to my editors at *Bon Appétit*, the *Chicago Tribune*, the *Detroit Free Press*, the *Los Angeles Times and Syndicate*, the *Montreal Gazette*, the *New York Times*, *Newsday*, *Pastry Art and Design Magazine*, *Cook's Illustrated*, *Fine Cooking*, *Costco Connection*, and the *National Post*, among other fine papers. Thank you to Bonnie Benwick, food editor at the *Washington Post*, for all that ink online and off, in one of the finest papers I know. Many thanks to Martha Stewart Living Radio (Sirius) for inviting me so often, to drop by and talk baking.

One of the biggest thank you's goes to Ellen Fuss, my test kitchen manager and editor, who also flew up to Montreal to actually handhold and play sous chef during the photo shoot for this book. Once a stranger, she is now family. Not only did she head the cyberspace test kitchen, she did extra duty in

ingredient checking (for the American side of the border), completed acres of editing (both of my website and the book manuscript), and has a fine eye for detail and accuracy, skills so valuable in a test kitchen.

A heartfelt, collective hug and thanks to the BetterBaking.com testing teams of both editions of this book, including Heidi Cooney, Ellen Gold, Janet Goldstein, Marla Gottlieb, Ann Harste, Christian Hudon, Regina Joskow, Whynter Lamarre, Leone Lamb, Jillian Montcarz, Laurie Rosenthal, Wendy Serfaty, Nancy Schofer, Linda Sidel, and Amy Stromberg. My test-kitchen sisters-in-the-trenches took time from their personal and professional lives to help this cookbook come to life. At times, they were testing several recipes per day, all on a volunteer basis. I am forever grateful. All have left their mark on this book, thanks to their baking styles, their intuition, and their useful suggestions. Their culinary expertise was respected to begin with, but their friendship is what I value most. Thanks also to Yvan Huneault, BB's first webmaster.

My thanks to the following companies for their assistance and support: All-Clad Metalcrafters, Big Green Egg, Boyajian of Boston, Breville, Capresso, Chantal Cookware, Fleischmann's Yeast USA and Canada, Emile Henry, Garland Ranges, Harney &

Canada, Emile Henry, Garland Ranges, Harney & Sons, Hodgson Mill, Hulman & Company/Clabber Girl, Le Creuset, KitchenAid, Nielsen-Massey Vanillas, Primo Grill, PT and Company Public Relations, Robin Hood Multifoods, Saco Foods, Scharffen Berger Chocolate Maker, Weber-Stephen Products, and Zojirushi.

To Charles O'Brien, who witnessed, firsthand, my baking career launched in a tiny bookstore bakery café, Terre Etoile, in appreciation for legal expertise generously shared.

My respect, enduring gratitude, and quiet awe for all he does and all he knows to Paul MacKenzie of Elehost Web Design (www.elehost.com) in Toronto, Canada. Your web support goes beyond the call of duty. There is no one more professional, humane, nor as software (and hardware) savvy.

To the team at Whitecap Books: Robert McCullough, a true gentleman of publishing, and in every other sense of the word; editor Taryn Boyd, art director Michelle Mayne, and designer Five Seventeen, for their unerring taste in words and aesthetics, and a love of cookbooks to match their talents; Jan Westendorp, for her courtesies in all ways; and to Ryan Szulc and prop stylist Madeleine Johari, for making the recipes come to life. To all at Whitecap, my thanks is above all reserved for the incredible welcome and for the experience of sheer joy in creating this special book.

Last and by no means least, I'd like to express my appreciation to the many visitors who have found their way to BetterBaking.com. They, too, are my testers at large. I am fortunate to welcome home bakers and cooks who love what they do, and who enjoy sharing information as much as I do. Some found BB early on and have kept in contact. Others happen by, and their notes of praise and interest keep the home fires of my test kitchen burning. To them, and to my readers in whatever the medium, in whatever part of the globe, my warmest thanks for the pleasure of your company in my kitchen.

Introduction

· ·

A MODERN-DAY FAIRY
TALE, OR THE STORY OF HOW
BETTERBAKING.COM BEGAN

· ·

ONCE UPON A TIME, in 1997 to be precise, there was a little bakery that existed in a mythical place called cyberspace in a country called the World Wide Web. It was the dawn of a new age, of a new millennium in fact. This bakery, while it had recipes galore, and a wonderful display case of beguiling treats, and its own test kitchens, was only visible on a computer screen in a place called a website. The bakery was called Baker Boulanger, or as it was soon nicknamed, BetterBaking.com, because very simply, it was all about better baking. This bakery did not *sell* bread and cookies; instead, it *shared* recipes and advice with all who visited. Bread to swoon over? Sumptuous squares? How to make perfect pie dough and a pip of a pecan pie? What is the mystery of sourdough bread? Anything anyone wanted to know, along with the recipes to make the best baked foods: it was *the* place to find out.

In time, visitors from around the world came to the bakery. They came from France, New Zealand, Canada, Australia, Israel, and Russia. Mostly, they came from the United States, where home bakers seemed to know a good thing when they saw it. Literally millions of people heard about this special place and dropped by to visit. The scents and flavors of this bakery were just too good to pass up.

BetterBaking.com was warm and inviting, and open 24 hours a day, seven days a week. One friend would tell another, and letters from all over poured in. Many contained compliments and eloquent words of praise; others had lists of questions; and some were filled with requests for recipes that had been lost or forgotten, or advice or helpful baking tips.

Food editors from the *New York Times* and other papers called on the site for advice; (the late and beloved) Julia Child dropped me a line; Eric Clapton's road manager—apparently he likes rugalach—popped by; other professional bakers wrote; and colleagues and sponsors were regularly at the door. Something good was always in the oven. Something new was always being created. The front-window display had to be changed often!

Places opened nearby, but this little bakery had a special touch. Some say it was the recipes; others contend it was the inviting writing that drew them in. The bakery grew and grew and grew. Yet, as famous as the bakery became, some people felt it was not real enough. Some said *I do not know anything about computers and websites. I just want to bake. Could you not put your finest recipes in a book?*

And so the cookbook came to pass.

Some people recognized the bakery in its new form; others just thought they had stumbled on a most beguiling cookbook.

Websites have come and gone and evolved greatly, but BetterBaking is still about testing, baking, writing, and having a good time. I've kept my site simple over the years. So, whether you're a novice or an experienced yeast hound, you'll find something on the site to whet your appetite.

Speaking of which . . .

Is It Fat-Free?

I receive many messages from people who are looking for low-fat versions of my recipes. I refer them to sites that specialize in this category of food. Early on, I even wrote an editorial to explain my position on this matter. I suggested that unless you have special dietary requirements, a reasoned approach to eating will serve you better than an obsession with fat. For example, some will gasp at the volume of ingredients that some cheesecake recipes call for. However, some of my cheesecakes are designed to make 14 to 18 servings. At my site, I make no apologies for using the best of the best, and I refuse any shortcuts to good taste. Too often, what particular dietary dictates produce is what I call compromised baking. I offer no judgment on replacing butter with applesauce or prune puree, or fiddling with egg replacements and ersatz sweeteners, but those approaches to baking are just not my focus. On the other hand, I'll help you make the best bran muffins (page 195) or the most sumptuous Tiramisu Cheesecake (page 263) or the most buttery Parker House Rolls (page 63). Moderation (as difficult as it may be to exercise at times) tastes best. Besides, you can always join me on the treadmill or in my tango class!

From Online to In Print

In a nutshell, *The New Best of BetterBaking.com* is a collection of stellar recipes, contemporary and classic, traditional and trendy—but each and every one is innately toothsome. I've tried to capture the spirit and the fun of my unique website-cum-baking magazine. If you have never heard of BetterBaking.com, you will still enjoy baking with me. If you're a BB regular, welcome home.

I have to emphasize that this is not a website that has been simply plunked into a book; it is a cookbook rich in my most treasured blue-ribbon recipes from the site—now officially retired into this print collection—as well as new ones created especially for this volume. The book is also jam-packed with helpful baking information, anecdotes, and serendipitous but useful facts from the website. I add to this a distinct palate and a good measure of global influence. I have hosted many international visitors at the site, and I have learned from them as much as they have learned from me.

I see recipe chat and swapping on the site as part of the delightful interchange between home bakers. It's like neighbors talking across their garden fence; only the Internet has made the fence much longer. This book brings with it the voices of many home bakers, distilled to my kitchen via their email. It is through this means that I have begun to fathom, more than ever before, what and how people bake. I have learned how to respond to their varied needs for technical information and basic baking advice; anticipate their appetite for new as well as tried-and-true recipes; and share in both their baking dilemmas and successes. Such a collaborative spirit has often resulted in my creation of recipes by request, or in tweaking classics that everyone needs in their repertoire.

In a way, BetterBaking.com has been a route to teaching baking around the world. Now I am simply taking the best of what I have been doing in one medium and transmitting it to a more traditionally understood one: a cookbook you hold in your hand, take to your kitchen, and get lovingly spattered with vanilla and butter stains. I find it wonderfully ironic that something like a website, a relatively new medium, can inspire something as old-fashioned as a home-baking book. The best things in life never change.

This cookbook follows the website's lead, grouping recipes by styles or occasion-based need. I know for myself, sometimes I want a muffin or scone for a friend or just for a casual snack; on other occasions, only a big cake or monstrous loaf will do. On the site, my collection of bread offerings has had many appellations over the years, "Bread Machinations" being one of the first. In the book, this ever-popular part of BetterBaking.com appears as Chapter 1, "The Bread Board, or Yeasty Tales." In it, you will find all sorts of loaves, including sourdough and even some rustic breads that I bake on the grill. My interest in yeast is carried through to Chapter 2, "Small Loaves and Rolls," as well as into Chapter 3, "Rustic Pizzas and Flatbreads," where I explore zesty pizzas, flatbreads, and more exotic little breads. Subsequent chapters present coffee and tea treats; cookies and biscotti; scones and muffins; fine pastries; and cakes, including glamorous cheesecakes.

You'll also find notes about ingredients and equipment, odd bits of trivia, and more. The Source Guide (page 299) gathers all the contact information for the suppliers of ingredients and equipment. Each and every source I have and share with you is as valuable as the recipes in this book.

So, find some butter, yeast, fresh and pure vanilla, and bags of flour. You are going to be doing a whole lotta baking!

THE BETTERBAKING.COM TEST KITCHEN

MY WELL-EQUIPPED, bustling-with-three-growing-boys home kitchen is the official BetterBaking.com test kitchen, and as such, it is the heartbeat of the website. It is where I create recipes for BetterBaking.com as well as for my newspaper and magazine articles; develop my baking courses; teach the odd private baking lesson; and give equipment and ingredients their test runs. The kitchen, while it is well appointed by professional standards, is as snug as a ship's galley, with each and every thing in its place. I have a large butcher-block counter surface and a six-burner, two-oven Garland gas range, one of the special residential-commercial models some companies launched several years ago. Sometimes both burners and both ovens are pumping away while three bread machines chug and hum. Meanwhile, the KitchenAid is slugging out brioche dough, and a food processor is making short work of some scones. I am somewhere in the middle, hands on, listening to this special symphony. Some days, the kitchen almost explodes with food and flavor. Other days, disaster lurks as melted chocolate seizes, raisins (for a terrific new cinnamon-raisin bread) are nowhere to be found, or a scorched sourdough loaf emerges from the oven. Baking is not a perfect science. No two ovens are alike, no two bags of flour absorb the same amount of moisture,

and most importantly, no two bakers are alike. To ensure success, recipe developers and writers have to design recipes that work with all these variables mixed into the equation. Mediocre, untested recipes are a dime a dozen. Good, tested recipes that work are relatively rare. I am fortunate to have recipe testers at large. These people are friends. As volunteers, they receive no salaries or expense accounts. Some of them live down the street, others live halfway around the world. Some testers are fans who I met via the website. They just want to be helpful, and their advice, encouragement, and skills contribute invaluably to the testing effort. The results are delicious!

When testing begins, email messages to and from my testers begin to fly. Recipes are divvied up according to preferences and specialties. After their initial creation, most recipes generally "work," but a good tester adds his or her taste and expertise and lets you know if a recipe is both truly special and easy enough for a broad baking audience to want to make. You have to know how to bake to be a good tester, but also how to dissect a recipe and assess its culinary logic. It is also helpful to have different sets of chops to do the tasting. Fortunately, this is rarely a problem.

I talk more specifically about tricks and tips in each chapter introduction, where I focus on certain aspects of each genre of baking, but three tricks of the trade are just about inscribed on the walls of my kitchen:

1. Double your baking sheet.

I often suggest, unless otherwise stated in a recipe, that bakers double their baking sheets, that is, insert one baking sheet on top of another. This insulates the top sheet and disperses the heat throughout the baking sheet more evenly. Double sheeting ensures even results: nice edges on cookies that do not have any of those thinned-out, overbaked parts on them; squares that are flat and without raised, dried edges; and cakes that are nicely browned, without unsightly spots of under- or overbrowning. Double sheeting also makes that usual caution of revolving baking sheets to promote even baking unnecessary.

If you are baking in a loaf or cake pan, I suggest that you put the pan on top of a baking sheet, again to ensure that cakes or breads bake through without their bottoms being dry or unduly brown while the top is just fine. I also recommend that you put a sheet of parchment paper on the baking sheet underneath. This is traditional professional pastry chef and bakery practice, and it ensures a neat and clean bakery operation. If you are setting a cake or bread pan on a baking sheet topped with parchment, no grease or scorched bits will adhere if there is leakage or overspills. Lastly, parchment modifies the heat of a metal baking pan, and I prefer to have a metal pan sit on parchment than directly on the hot metal base.

2. Plastic bags make great proofing tents.

My second *truc* of the trade is using large plastic bags as proofing tents. Rising breads adore a nice, humid, draft-free environment. Nothing works better than large, clear plastic bags, usually sold as leaf bags. You simply slip a rising bowl, formed loaf of bread in its pan, or a sheet of rolls into the plastic bag and seal it lightly, by either rolling it closed or loosely tying it with a twist tie or the drawstring many of these bags conveniently feature. This creates a tent for the bread, ensuring proper humidity and protection from drafts. It also helps to prevent rising dough from drying out. If you cover a bowl of dough with a damp tea towel, often you will find that the towel sticks and you still need plastic wrap over the tea towel—all in all,

cumbersome and, compared to the ease of inserting a bowl of dough into a roomy plastic bag, bothersome. Chucking the whole affair into a nice, spacious bag makes perfect sense. To make sure that the plastic bag does not stick to the dough, periodically lift the bag up and away from the dough's surface.

3. Use nonstick spray on rising dough.

My last trick is to spray a little nonstick cooking spray, unless otherwise stated, on rising doughs. Rising doughs can dry out, depending on your kitchen humidity. A swift spray of nonstick cooking spray does wonders to preserve a moist surface, especially during the final rise. You can still glaze the dough just before baking with whatever glaze, if any, is called for (egg wash, for example).

EQUIPMENT

Before I launch into the recipes, I want to offer my test kitchen's best advice and recommendations about hardware (equipment and tools) and software (ingredients). I think of recipes as "art" and these associated accoutrements as the frame. Surely, recipes are the main event, but it's my professional test kitchen's tips that make those recipes (and the baker) shine. Here I give you specifics and opinionated opinions on why I choose and use what I do.

Always use the best ingredients and baking tools you can find. Baking is a series of little things done well. I often tell baking students that whereas you might not be able to have that yearned-for yacht or Italian race car, you can procure the best butter, chocolate, and vanilla, or simply a great baking sheet, professional parchment paper, or a well-crafted cheesecake pan. In the Source Guide (page 299), you will find additional notes and contact information for my recommended ingredient and equipment suppliers.

Angel Food Cake Pans

I prefer angel food cake pans to tube pans because they yield higher cakes, 4½ inches high or more; tube pans, while homey, generally have lower sides and a wider base, resulting in lower-slung cakes. Cakes are always nicer when impressively high, and 9- or 10-inch angel food cake pans ensure that high-rising cakes have room to grow. Avoid the models with removable bottoms; unmolding is rarely a problem in cakes made in angel food cake pans, and the chance of a thin batter leaking out the removable bottom is not worth troubling with.

Cheesecake Pans (Springform Pans)

Look for heavy-duty aluminum models. Clip pans do not wear well, although I have had some luck with American-made Hillside pans. With other brands, however, the clips often break and the outer ring gets bent out of shape. I rely on Wilton professional-weight springform pans, but sometimes you can find unmarked brands that are nice and hefty. Quite often, removable-bottom springform pans are also taller and allow you to make a great big coffee cake or cheesecake without worrying about batter pouring over the sides.

Cookie Cutters and Novelty Cutters

Matfer, from France, as well as Wilton and Ateco, offer nested cookie cutter sets, and I stock both a plain-edge set and a serrated-edge one, each in nine nested sizes. Rochow cookie and biscuit cutters, from Rochow Swirl Mixer Company in Rochester, New York, is my choice for industrial-weight gingerbread man, teddy bear, scone, doughnut, and heart cutters.

Danish Dough Whisk

This flat-wired configuration on the end of a wooden stick looks like an old-fashioned rug beater. I call it my carrot cake–, scone-, and muffin-making tool. It is just the thing for mixing gloppy, heavy batters or for lightly combining a scone batter. I have seen these in kitchen stores (they are imported from the Danesco Company in Denmark), and they are also available from Golda's Kitchen. I also recommend some other basic whisks (see Whisks on page 11).

Deep Quiche Pan

This 9-inch fluted pan can be hard to find, but Beryl's Cake Decorating carries them, as does Golda's Kitchen in Canada (see Source Guide). This pan is

Batterie de Cuisine: Equipment Essentials

Here's a list of baking pans I find the most handy. It is my basic, minimum collection. If you find you use some pans more often, or bake two cakes or pies at once, double up on those items. An equipment glossary follows.

2 to 4 large baking sheets (15 by 21 inches)*
2 to 4 standard baking sheets (12 by 17 inches)
1 rectangular baking pan (9 by 13 inches)
1 square pan (8 by 8 inches)
1 pie pan (9 inches)
1 springform pan (9 inches)
1 springform pan (10 inches)
1 deep quiche or tart pan with removable bottom (9 or 10 inches, 3½ inches high)
1 loaf pan (12 by 5 inches)†
2 loaf pans (9 by 5 inches)
2 loaf pans (8 by 4 inches)
1 tube pan (9 or 10 inches)
1 angel food cake pan (9 or 10 inches)
1 Bundt pan (12-cup volume)
2 round cake pans (9 inches)
1 brownie pan (7 by 11 inches)
2 twelve-cup nonstick muffin tins

OPTIONAL:

- Various dollar-store layer and cheesecake pans, miniature and novelty
- Foil loaf pans
- Other novelty pans

* Measure your oven first to ensure it can accommodate this size. You may need to use 12- by 15-inch baking sheets instead.

† This is a special size pan that I often use; you can find it through bakeware catalogs or stores.

extra deep (3 to 3½ inches) and works for both quiche and the many coffeecakes, cheesecakes, and tarts I make in it. It immediately gussies up the ordinary, and I would be lost without the several I keep in stock.

Dough Scraper (Bench Cutter)

It seems like a simple tool, but once you've used one of these, you'll always have it at hand. It's great for cutting or dividing dough, scraping dough from a work surface, mixing, and kneading. My dough scrapers have wood or urethane handles with stainless-steel blades. I prefer LamsonSharp scrapers for their perfect design: they are just the right heft, dimension, and sharpness. They have a great grip and wear well for years. There are several models, and I rely on a slew of these nifty, helpful tools. I use one to clean my wood work surface, too. Dough scrapers can also be the plastic variety: lightweight, half-moon-shaped flat plastic blades. These are used to scrape batter out of bowls, as their curved edges do that job nicely. I use rubber spatulas just as often for that job.

Food Processors

I prefer the KitchenAid because of its capacity, motor strength, well-designed feed tube, and stability on the counter, but both Viking and Cuisinart also make very fine, heavy-duty stand mixers. My test kitchen puts food processors through the ringer, and I have found that time and time again the KitchenAid is reliable, able to withstand a lot of mixing and blending, and its capacity is just right for my recipes. The company offers 5-cup, 7-cup, 9-cup, and 11-cup models in a range of great colors.

Cuisinart makes superb food processors as well, but the cumbersome feed tube hinders some baking procedures (more-recent models of Cuisinart processors have an improved feed tube). Braun makes a handy processor with a generous work bowl in the larger model, but the machine itself is quite light; I prefer a heavy, more stable food processor.

Knives

One good knife will cost you more than an entire set of cheap knives, but it's worth the investment. A good knife is well balanced, has a certain heft and a full tang, and holds an edge. I like the Wüsthof-Trident and LamsonSharp brands, just to name a couple, but any well-made knife you like and maintain in peak condition is a good choice. LamsonSharp makes an amazing bread knife, and I have a few of their 8-inch chef's knives. If you can find it, a 9-inch chef's knife is handy, and for big jobs (or big hands), a 10-inch knife is recommended. Paring knives are essential (a regular one and a bird's-beak style). LamsonSharp also offers two super little knives, one made just for apple peeling and one wonderfully old-fashioned-looking one, a little askew and offset, called Grandma's New Used Parer. Have your knives sharpened every six months or so by a professional, unless you are adept at sharpening them yourself. In between times, hone them on a butcher's steel.

Loaf Pans

I cannot recommend commercial or other high-quality bakeware enough. Lightweight loaf pans make for burnt bottoms and/or breads that lack color. Of course, you also have the option of baking breads and rolls free-form on parchment-lined baking sheets. The results need not be perfect or uniform—the irregularity is part of the charm of small breads in particular.

I also like nonstick loaf pans. They offer great release, and because of their heavy weight, they tend to bake breads thoroughly without scorching. However, dark pans do brown baked goods a bit faster so I often line the pans with pieces of parchment paper first, and even then, place the loaf pans on a parchment-lined baking sheet as an extra caution against scorched bottoms.

I use Lockwood, Ekco, and Chicago Metallic reinforced steel-and-aluminum pans or reinforced steel-and-tin pans. My favorite loaf pan is a large 12- by 5-inch model that is available via bakery specialty suppliers such as King Arthur Flour, La Cuisine, and Golda's Kitchen, or from restaurant-supply stores. This oversized loaf pan makes big, dramatic breads. If you prefer, use two 9- by 5-inch or 8- by 4-inch loaf pans instead. My commercial 12- by 5-inch pan is made by Lockwood in Canada, but Chicago Metallic, Ekco Glaco, and American Pan Company offer similar models. They are usually glazed with nonstick coating and will serve you well for countless loaves, no matter what style of bread you are baking.

Measuring Cups and Spoons

Look for a solid set of long-handled measuring cups and spoons. They will cost you more than the dime-store variety, but you'll be rewarded with durability and good design. Always have at least two spoon sets—don't be fishing in the dishwasher for a batter-covered measuring spoon set midrecipe. Beehive Kitchenware Company produces a lovely series of heart-shaped pewter spoons and a museum-of-fine-art-worthy copper and silver 1-cup measure. Most houseware companies offer a host of nice cups and spoon sets to choose from.

Mixers

For me, there is but one word for mixers: KitchenAid. If you have no mixer, or if it's time to replace that chrome artifact your great-grandmother bestowed on you, look into buying a KitchenAid stand (heavy-duty) mixer. As mentioned, I also like the Viking and Cuisinart mixers, but options (attachments, colors), design, and repair outlets (in the rare event something goes amiss with your KitchenAid) still favor KitchenAid. There are several models available, ranging from the classic 250-watt model to a 6-quart, 525-watt bruiser. The largest KitchenAid does great work with double batches of cookies and cakes, while the 5-quart model is a wonderful all-purpose machine large enough to make a generous batch of yeast dough or cookies or a large cake. (The line of 5-quart mixers features a tilt-back head, which used to be available only on the smaller models.) The 4½-quart machine is perfect for smaller yeast doughs and cakes; if you have a bread machine as backup for making yeasted doughs, then the 4½-quart size makes a lot of sense. If you are not charmed by bread machines, despite their ability to knead and proof dough superbly, or if you have limited space, invest in the 5-quart model.

No matter which model with whatever wattage you choose, all the power you need is there. A KitchenAid will cost you more than most other brands, but this is an investment that will last a lifetime. Beyond the power and the versatility, there is the beauty: KitchenAid mixers come in a series of neat colors, especially in the 300-watt-model range.

I talk more about mixers and bread machines in Chapter 1, specifically how to prepare yeast doughs

using either. I encourage you to be flexible and do as I do: try different machines with the same recipe, just to see which works best.

Muffin Pans

If you're serious about muffins, nonstick muffin pans, much like their counterparts in loaf pans, are your best option for the durability and release they offer. Commercial glazing ensures that muffins unmold easily and without incident—no more sticky muffin tops or sheared tops and bottoms—and that the pans wash up with barely a wipe of a damp cloth. The heavyweight construction also prevents scorched muffin bottoms and ensures that the pans last a lifetime. The pans can do double duty for other confections, as well as for appetizer quiches, miniature cheesecakes, and nested potatoes. When you bake with these pans, you also have the option of using paper liners. The Lockwood Classic Muffin Tin is a fine piece of equipment, as are muffin frames (as muffin pans are known in the trade) by Ekco and Chicago Metallic. These companies manufacture regular 12-cup muffin frames; mushroom, or "Texas-sized," frames for super muffins; mini-muffin frames for 24 miniatures; and mini loaf pans. Since commercial pans come in many sizes, verify that the pan you choose fits your oven.

Muffin Scoops or Professional Ice-Cream Scoops

For best results, scoop muffins into muffin pans using a professional ice-cream scoop, available at any restaurant supply store or kitchen mail-order house. This simple tool gives a rounded finish to muffins. Note that scoops are calibrated by a number indicating how many portions of ice cream per quart they furnish. For example, a No. 16 scoop produces 16 scoops of ice cream per quart. Scoops can be as large as a No. 10 or 12. Scoops also do double duty for dispensing ice cream, melon and matzo balls, hamburger patties, and, of course, mashed potatoes. The Zyliss Company manufactures a fine assortment of superb restaurant-grade stainless-steel scoops, as do Vollrath and other manufacturers.

Ovens

A properly calibrated home oven is necessary for all your baking needs. Gas ovens tend to preheat far faster than electric. I tested all the recipes in this book in both types of ovens, with negligible differences in results. In my test kitchen, I rely on a Garland range but also highly recommend other brands such as Thermador, Viking, 5 Star, and Wolfe, to name a few. I also use the Green Egg and Primo grills, and a Weber gas grill for many of my rustic breads (see page 49 for more on grill baking). I find my Garland oven and other "commercial-for-residence" ovens, as they are called, exceptionally well designed in that the air flow is even throughout the oven cavity. They are what the industry calls "naturally convective." Convection ovens are those that include a fan that is supposed to create an even air flow, thus shortening baking and cooking times. My own experience is that these ovens do bake faster, but that goods baked in them brown less (while still being baked through) and have hardened top surfaces. If you have such an oven, you can experiment by *not* using the fan if you have the option to turn it off.

You can buy a true commercial oven too, as I once did, but they are not designed for the home. This means that you cannot get a warranty, and an electrician may balk (rightly so) at installing a commercial range in a home kitchen. Check with a contractor and your fire department on what you can use in your home kitchen. One of the reasons the commercial-range manufacturers began making commercial-for-residence ovens was that home cooks were buying commercial ovens, warnings aside, and installing them themselves. Viking is the pioneer in this area and works with chefs and home cooks to regularly innovate their line of stoves.

Unless a recipe specifies otherwise, all baked goods should be baked on the center or lower shelf of the oven.

Paper Goods

Generous bakers like to share the results of their labors with others. If you're going to bake well, present just as appealingly. Leave the aluminum foil and plastic wrap and plastic tubs at home. Visit Google to search for what you need, or visit a local kitchen, bakery, or restaurant supply store, or check your local Yellow Pages or warehouse store. Stock up on commercial cake boxes, bags, decorative waxed paper sheets, and other odds and ends. Your baked goods will look far better. Add a ribbon, a gift card, a business card, and you have a gift like no other. Mail-order companies (see the Source Guide, page 299), are a good source for a lot of these items, as are party supply centers, but again, almost anything and everything you need can be found online by doing a search. Another good source of supplies is eBay. Also try dollar stores and thrift stores. Consider all sorts of interesting boxes, cans, and glassware with which to present your treats.

Parchment Paper

If there is one tool that you should not be without for baking, it's parchment paper, which is also called silicone paper by professional bakers. Professional-grade parchment paper is generally inexpensive, can be reused, will save you time, and will make baking more fun. You will find parchment paper mentioned in most of my recipes. Look for it in better kitchen stores, or contact a local commercial kitchen supply house or a wholesale bakery or restaurant supplier to buy it in bulk. Some bakers like using silicone mats called Silpats. They work well but are somewhat pricey. Parchment is more economical for my needs and can be cut to fit whatever pan you are using. Also, I don't use Silpats in my test kitchen because I just find baking on a sheet of plastic, however state-of-the-art, somewhat unappealing. Still, many bakers swear by them.

Pie Pans or Plates

Pyrex and aluminum pie pans are fine, although with Pyrex, you have to remember to lower the oven temperature by 25°F because of how it bakes. I also like graniteware: kitchenware coated with decorative color enamel. You can find graniteware at flea markets and hardware stores. I adore ceramic and use Emile Henry ceramic pie plates, as well as Chantal Cookware's colorful line. Le Creuset makes great nonstick cast-iron bakeware. I particularly like aluminum pie pans from Doughmakers, with their unique, pebbled-aluminum surface. Robinson Ransbottom and James Sloss Pottery of Oregon both make rustic and glazed ceramic pie plates in mellow hues.

Rolling Pins

A baker can never have too many rolling pins or rolling-pin options. Some pins are better suited for certain jobs than others. Two musts are a 15-inch ball-bearing pin and a French tapered pin, with no moving parts. An 18-inch ball-bearing pin is great for tough, elastic yeast doughs such as cinnamon rolls, and an extra 12-inch pin is handy for small batches of shortbread. I rely on Banton, Thorpe, or Adams pins. As for French tapered pins, I'm so finicky about them that I once designed my own. Alas, my pins (I had two designs: one for pie and pastry and one for pizza and other yeast doughs) are no longer available.

Whisks

Whisks do a lion's share of work in my kitchen, and because of that, I stock a few sizes in both oblong and balloon styles. Unlike the Danish dough whisk (page 7), which looks like a rug beater, these are more traditional in design. I blend dry ingredients with whisks, aerate flour with them, and use them to blend water and yeast. In fact, when you note in my bread instructions, or anywhere else, the phrase "hand whisk" ingredients, this refers simply to whisking by hand with a large, sturdy whisk. Nothing blends better and does short jobs more expediently than a whisk. Save your wooden spoons for stirring; whisks are the original blending utensil. I prefer the commercial grade here as well, and use an assortment made by Best and Vollrath.

INGREDIENTS

As the head baker at BetterBaking.com, I insist on the best ingredients. To begin with, make sure your ingredients are fresh! Sniff and taste before dumping something into a bowl. If it doesn't smell or taste good before you bake, it won't be magically transformed in the baking process. Never assume that, because you open a new package of something, that it is fresh or of top quality. Be discerning about the components you use, and the final results will reflect your choices.

Baker's Caramel

Caramelized sugar, or "caramel," is a classic preparation that is made by slowly heating sugar and a touch of water until the sugar melts and thickens to an amber-colored syrup. Baker's caramel consists of caramelized sugar and, depending on the manufacturing process, a few other things. It is used to add color and a touch of flavor to foods. Recipes for pumpernickel rolls and bread, for example, will often call for baker's caramel. I purchase baker's caramel (nicknamed "blackjack" by some chefs) at Golda's Kitchen, King Arthur Baker's Catalogue, or bakery supply houses.

Baking Powder and Baking Soda

Though they are both chemical leaveners, baking powder and baking soda are different products. Baking powder is a combination of acid elements (such as cream of tartar) with bicarbonate of soda (baking soda), an alkali. When the mixture is added to a liquid (such as in the form of a batter), the acid reacts with the alkali, forming carbon dioxide bubbles that have a leavening effect. Most commercial baking powders are "double-acting," which means that the initial leavening action (called "bench action" by bakers, for the counter the batter bowl is sitting on) is followed by a secondary leavening action that occurs when the batter is exposed to the heat of the oven. I test all my recipes with Clabber Girl baking powder and swear by the brand for its sheer performance power and proven history. You can also use Davis, Calumet, and other brands with good results. In Canada, the choice is usually one name: Magic brand. No matter which product you choose, always check the expiration date, since baking powder begins to lose its potency after six months or so. To test if baking powder is still viable, add ½ teaspoon to a cup of warm water; if it fizzes and bubbles, it's ready to use.

Baking soda is an older leavener than baking powder (which was invented around 1850), and it was first used in conjunction with acidic ingredients like sour milk to create the necessary chemical reaction for leavening. Now, baking soda is typically used—sometimes in tandem with baking powder—to neutralize excess acid components in a batter, leavening it in the process. When a recipe calls for yogurt, buttermilk, sour cream, cocoa powder, or lemon juice, baking soda is usually nearby. Unlike baking powder, baking soda has a long shelf life, but you should replace it periodically to ensure you have a fresh batch for baking (it does absorb odors). Baking soda has a more pronounced flavor than baking powder, and when too much is used, it can give baked goods an "off" taste; so take care to measure baking soda carefully.

Brown Sugar

In general, I use golden, or light brown, sugar, and unless otherwise stated, you should too, although interchanging dark with light will not hurt a recipe. Sometimes, I use both in the same recipe! In any event, regardless of which brown sugar you are using, measure and pack it down firmly, adding more if required, for the correct measure. To keep brown sugar moist in the container, add a sugar bear, one of those little terra-cotta bears that are widely available. Alternatively, you can simply put a cut-up orange or half of an apple in with the brown sugar.

Butter

Butter is the binding flavor of many baked goods, and unsalted (or sweet, as it is sometimes called) butter is the baker's and pastry chef's first choice. Do not substitute salted butter and then omit the salt in a recipe. Avoid whipped butters, butterlike spreads, and margarine of any kind. Margarine, in particular, is often whipped and quite salty. If you are absolutely set on margarine, at least look for unsalted block margarine. It is not always easy to find, but it does exist and is far better than whipped salted margarine.

In general, I find blocks of butter are a better value than separately wrapped sticks. As far as measuring butter goes, I use cup measurements unless the recipe calls for a small quantity, in which case I use tablespoons. I find this easier than advising bakers to measure butter in half sticks or in large numbers of tablespoons when purchasing butter in a solid block.

An easy reference is:

2 cups butter = 1 pound
1 cup butter = 8 ounces (½ pound)
½ cup butter = 4 ounces (¼ pound)
4 tablespoons or ¼ cup butter = 2 ounces (⅛ pound)

Cold butter works best in scones and other pastries. Room-temperature or softened butter is best for blending into cookies, cakes, and yeasted recipes. In pie doughs, you can use a combination of unsalted butter and shortening. When the recipe calls for melted butter, let the butter cool for a few minutes before using it. I use a microwave to melt butter and do so in 1-minute increments. If you put the butter in for much longer than that, depending on its temperature to begin with, it might melt faster and splatter the interior of your microwave. If you absolutely cannot use butter or have concerns about dairy fat, you can replace it, when melted butter is called for, with vegetable oil.

Buttermilk

Buttermilk is low in fat, high in protein, calcium rich, and best for baking—what more could you want? There are two ingredients I've nicknamed "white gold." One is flour and the other is buttermilk. The buttermilk of yesteryear was the fluid remaining after cream was churned into butter, which is the prime reason why many people presume it is butter laden, or at the very least, fat laden. Nothing could be further from the truth. *Buttermilk*, much like *plum pudding*, is pretty much a misnomer. It is almost as low in fat as skim milk, weighing in at approximately 99 calories an 8-ounce glass, with an astonishingly low fat count of 2.2 grams (whole milk has 157 calories and 8.9 grams of fat). Though sometimes dismissed as the poor man's sour cream, buttermilk is far more liquidy than sour cream and has an almost bubbly acidic taste that is as thirst-quenching as cold beer.

Today's buttermilk is made from fresh pasteurized or ultrapasteurized milk, usually low-fat or skim milk with nonfat dry milk solids added. A culture

is incorporated to develop acid and flavor. This product is heated, or incubated, at 68°F to 72°F until the desired acidity of 0.8 to 0.9 percent lactic acid is achieved (pH 4.6). The product is then gently stirred and cooled to stop fermentation or to moderate its acidity. Buttermilk flakes or liquid butter may be added to cold buttermilk to give the product a churned-buttermilk appearance. A tiny touch of salt is added, and sometimes a wee bit of citric acid or sodium citrate, which dairies say enhance flavor. Is this the buttermilk of the good old days? Ah, no. But in baking it does the trick. Or you can do as I prefer and use dry buttermilk powder.

In baking, the acid in buttermilk interacts nicely with baking soda to produce a little more carbon dioxide, resulting in fluffier baked goods. Happily, too, buttermilk, as with all dairy delights, helps with browning (dairy solids have natural sugar, which assists caramelization) and tenderness (the acidic nature tenderizes flour) in a recipe.

Soured Milk: If you don't have any buttermilk on hand, you can use soured milk instead. Simply add 1 to 2 tablespoons fresh lemon juice or white vinegar to 1 cup whole or low-fat milk and let it stand and curdle for about 2 minutes. Spoiled milk is *not* the same as soured milk, so do not consider using spoiled or rancid milk in baking!

Buttermilk Powder

I'm a buttermilk powder fan for many reasons. It is convenient and keeps, refrigerated, for up to 4 months. If I have an impulse to bake with buttermilk, and no fresh buttermilk is around, then I'm covered. But more than that, I can prepare my own dry mixes such as a buttermilk scones mix or my favorite buttermilk pancake mix. Relying on buttermilk powder allows me to have my own always-ready pantry mix that is chemical and additive free. You just have to add liquid and eggs and you have a bed-and-breakfast pancake in minutes.

Saco Buttermilk Blend is my favorite, and you can also get buttermilk powder in bulk at most natural foods stores, though I find it less fragrant. Make sure it is fresh and has been properly stored in the bulk bins where you purchase it. To use dry buttermilk, mix it with the dry ingredients. Do not try to reconstitute it. Use 3 to 4 tablespoons buttermilk blend or powder to replace 1 cup of fresh buttermilk, and add 1 cup liquid to replace the liquid component. For the liquid, you can use water, apple juice or cider, orange juice, coffee, tea, ginger ale, seltzer water, or any liquid that works well with your recipe.

Cheese

Cheese and baking are natural partners, and I go through blocks and blocks of many varieties in my test kitchen. Cheddar is a first choice in many recipes because of its popularity and availability in so many sizes, strengths, and flavors. You can select the sharpness you like, or perhaps make a blend. I am also fond of Havarti and Colby for their melting qualities; Gruyère and raclette for rustic breads; and a combination of Havarti, mozzarella, and goat cheese (*chèvre*) on pizzas. In a spunky cheese bread or my cheese scones, a sharp orange cheddar from Cabot's in Vermont, or Black Diamond or Balderson in Canada, are my preference. Wisconsin Asiago is another pet cheese of mine. You can rarely go wrong, no matter which cheese you choose or substitute. Always buy real cheese, avoiding "processed cheese food" and anything with the word *lite* in the name. It may be fine for eating, but it might not perform as well in baking.

Cinnamon

Cinnamon can be bold, it can be shy, but it is not to be underestimated. Cinnamon is one of the oldest spices. It consists of the inner bark of a tree that can take up to 30 years to mature before harvesting can begin. There are two main types of cinnamon. The most familiar to North Americans is the cassia variety grown in Asia. Vietnamese and Chinese cassia are the sweetest and strongest varieties. Korintje cassia, grown in Indonesia, has a smooth flavor and less bite. Lower-grade Korintje cassia is what you will find in supermarkets. The second type of cinnamon is Ceylon cinnamon. It originated in Sri Lanka (formerly called Ceylon) but is now grown in various places. This top-grade cinnamon is less sweet and has more of a citrus taste. Much like pure vanilla, Ceylon cinnamon will take your baking to a higher plane (see the Source

Guide, page 299). Cinnamon can be great or as acrid and astringent as a chemical, and since it's such a core spice for so much baking, it's worth locating one that is special (sometimes I buy several types from Penzeys and mix them for a complex, bold, spicy-sweet flavor). If all you make are cinnamon buns, seeking out the best will make all the difference. This all said, sometimes I've found great cinnamon, at super prices, at warehouse stores such as Costco.

Chocolate

Chocolate for baking comes in several varieties: milk, white, semisweet, bittersweet, and unsweetened, or baking, the latter having fallen out of vogue with home bakers. Most bakers opt for the middle ground of bittersweet or semisweet chocolate, which, depending on the manufacturer, has varying percentages of sugar to chocolate liquor in the mix. It is a matter of selecting, among the many quality domestic and imported chocolates (Scharffen Berger, Callebaut, Valrhona, Ghirardelli, and Suchard, to name a few), the one that you like best for its taste and baking performance. As you work with chocolate, you also see which varieties handle more easily.

Depending on the company, semisweet and bittersweet might be interchangeable terms, although companies that know their craft well, such as Scharffen Berger, are clear about the distinct differences between these terms and specify the percentage of pure chocolate (cacao) on the label of each of their products. Chefs who specialize in chocolate would be quick to point out that blending chocolate varieties in a recipe is what accounts for a dynamic chocolate taste.

Store your chocolate in a cool, dry environment. Humid, warm, or fluctuating storage conditions will cause bloom, whereby surface moisture dissolves some sugar and leaves crystals behind. The chalky film or whitish discoloration that results is unattractive, but does not affect performance.

Citrus Zests

I use a lot of orange and lemon zest in my test kitchen. You can grate zest, or you can use a zester to remove fine shreds of zest, then a chef's knife to mince them. Wüsthof-Trident and Victorinox make good zesters.

I have never found a domestic or low-end zester that I like, although Good Grips makes a decent one. Microplanes are a recent entry into the zest market. These filelike utensils come in several sizes (larger for grating cheese; finer-slotted blades for zesting) and are made by several companies.

Cocoa Powder

Unsweetened cocoa powder is easily blended with dry ingredients and provides a mellow richness to recipes. I have used Scharffen Berger, Ghirardelli, Hershey's, Fry's (in Canada), Valrhona, and Saco cocoa, and while there are subtle taste differences, each cocoa-based recipe, regardless of the brand, has a pleasing bouquet. For hot cocoa, Scharffen Berger makes a delightfully complex cocoa that is terrific for baking as well. "Dutch-process," or "Dutched," cocoa is a cocoa powder that has been treated with alkali in order to reduce acidity. Smoother, richer, and darker than unprocessed "natural" cocoa, it is the standard cocoa in Europe. The Dutching process is accomplished by soaking the cocoa beans in calcium carbonate, a naturally occurring mineral. You should be aware that Dutched cocoa may not be suitable for many North American recipes, since its low acidity affects how leavening agents behave. Use regular cocoa unless Dutched is specified. One of my favorite cocoas—Saco Premium—is a blend of Dutched and regular cocoas, and it performs well in most any recipe. Store your cocoa in an airtight container to prevent it from absorbing ambient odors.

Eggs

All of my recipes are developed and tested using large eggs. Opting for another size will affect the outcome of the recipe. Let your eggs warm to room temperature (or immerse them in warm water for a couple of minutes) before you use them. Cold eggs do not perform as well, as they make the dough or batter cold, and cold doughs and batters have to work that much harder to rise in the oven.

Flour

My recipes were tested with Hodgson Mill and Robin Hood products from the United States and Canada, respectively. I also use other fine flours, such as King

Arthur, Pillsbury, Giusto, White Lily, and Gold Medal. I encourage you to experiment with different flours, but for consistent results in your kitchen, choose one all-purpose and one bread flour that you prefer and learn how they perform in a variety of recipes. Brand loyalty pays off in consistent baking results. Remember, though, that in different seasons and with different crops of wheat, you might have to add more flour or use a bit less, especially in bread recipes. That said, flour companies do try and keep their product consistent, especially in terms of the flour's protein percentages, by blending flours based on each year's crop results. With your own chosen brand, note these differences and changes and be flexible in your response to them. A great flour will perform differently in your kitchen, in the same recipe, as the seasons change.

Be attentive when you purchase flour in bulk. You might not know what you are getting unless the retailer is reputable and knowledgeable. Often, a bulk foods store can order one sort of bread flour, and if it is not available, find another source for the next stocking. I generally recommend you purchase packaged flour with an identifiable brand on it, or buy good bread flour from a local baker you know and trust (provided he or she is inclined to accommodate you).

Store flour in sealed canisters. You do not need to refrigerate your white flours unless you are unable to ensure a bug-free, humidity-resistant storage area. A bay leaf placed in your flour canister is an old-fashioned deterrent to bugs.

White flour generally does not turn bad or grow rancid. What does happen is that flours with bran and wheat germ in them, such as whole-wheat flours, contain trace oils that over time will spoil. I suggest you purchase small amounts of whole-wheat or multigrain flours to use quickly. Store these flours in the refrigerator or freezer.

For absolute accuracy, professional bakers weigh rather than measure flour. However, I have found that most home bakers do not weigh flour. To make sure that you have the same results as I do in my test kitchen, measure flour as I do: first, hand whisk the flour a bit in the container it is stored in, or move a large wooden spoon around in it to fluff it up; then scoop it with a measuring cup and level it off with a knife or a dough scraper.

All-Purpose Flour: All-purpose flour is the basic flour for most of my nonyeasted recipes. Essentially a mix of hard, red spring wheat flours and softer winter wheat flour, it has a lower protein, or gluten, content than bread flour. The average protein content of all-purpose flour (it ranges from company to company, season to season) is between 11¾ percent and 12½ percent. All-purpose flour, as its name implies, is versatile: good for many purposes and applications, though dedicated to none in particular. To my mind, however, it is an ideal flour for our North American home-baking tradition. In a hotel or pastry shop kitchen, a baker or pastry chef would combine hard and soft flours, that is, bread flour and cake or pastry flour, to replicate our familiar all-purpose flour (which chefs call "baker's flour," or "family flour").

I prefer and always test with unbleached, or naturally aged, all-purpose flour. Unbleached all-purpose flour has a lightly golden tinge to it (instead of starkly white), and I prefer it for its color and flavor. Some bakers swear they can taste the bleaching agents in bleached flour. I also like the fact that unbleached flour is naturally aged, rather than hastened to maturity with chemical agents.

Bread Flour: When I call for bread flour, I insist on bread flour. All-purpose flour will not yield the same results, although for some yeasted recipes, all-purpose flour can be used alone or in combination with bread flour (this is noted in the recipe). Bread flour should be specified on the package of the product you choose to use. It has a higher protein content than all-purpose flour, usually 13 to 14½ percent. It is milled from hard, red spring wheat bred from strains originally brought over by Scottish settlers, who were delighted to find that their beloved grain grew even better in the New World than at home. Bread flour from Canada's prairies and the American Great Plains is prized by bakers worldwide.

The protein component in bread flour comes from its *gluten* content, gluten being the component that gives a bread dough its elasticity and baked bread its chewy texture. Home bakers can get hung up on the numbers game in bread flour, assuming that the higher the protein percentage, the better the bread flour. There is some truth to this, but professional bakers know that it is the *quality* of the protein and how a dough is handled that determine the final results. French bakers produce wonderful breads with flours far less noble than our North American varieties, because they know how to coax the most flavor out of their ingredients.

Pastry or Cake Flour: This variety of flour is made of soft, white wheat and has very low gluten or protein (anywhere from 7½ to 11 percent). I don't use this flour very often in my test kitchen. It is more often used by commercial bakers.

Rye Flour: *Light* and *medium* varieties of rye flour are interchangeable for light and sour rye loaves. *Dark rye* is used for pumpernickel and black breads. Rye flour is combined with bread flour in most recipes. Look for a good stone-ground medium or dark rye for the best flavor.

Whole-Wheat and White Whole-Wheat Flours: Whole-wheat flour is ground with the whole wheat berry. You can buy whole-wheat flour in all-purpose, bread, cake, and pastry varieties. Because it contains the entire wheat berry (bran, endosperm, and germ), it is perceived as more nutritious and offers more fiber. Whole-wheat flour also absorbs more moisture due to the extra fiber content, so you have to take care that whole-wheat doughs are well hydrated. Whole-wheat flour combines nicely in many recipes with white flour, either all-purpose or bread, as required.

Most whole-wheat flour is milled from red spring wheat and can be a trifle bitter. Until the advent of white whole-wheat flour, introduced to consumers by King Arthur Flour, bakers endured this slight fault and focused on the nutritional benefit. However, white whole-wheat flour, milled from winter wheat, offers the benefits of whole wheat with a performance and taste reminiscent of regular unbleached white flours. I use white whole-wheat flour often in my recipes, and if you want the added fiber, feel free to interchange or combine it with unbleached all-purpose flour.

Malt Powder

Malt is sometimes added to bread, especially to bagels, to add color and a subtle but distinctive taste. I use it in breads as well as bagels, and it is particularly helpful in browning the crust of French breads (which, being fat and sugar free, are typically lean and can sometimes benefit from a browning agent). It is also a nice addition to homemade pancake mix if you want your flapjacks to have that diner taste. Malt comes in powder or syrup form, but powder is easier to use. It's available by mail order or in home-brewing supply stores and some natural foods stores. I get mine from bakery suppliers or, on occasion, from local bagel bakeries who will sell a pound or two. If you do not have malt powder on hand, you may substitute the same amount of brown sugar or, as some recipes may state, leave it out entirely. If you cannot obtain malt powder, you can use malt syrup. Choose a regular syrup, not one that is flavored or says, "with hops." Malt syrup is sticky and not as easy to measure in baking, but I do use it in the boiling water bath for my New York–style bagels (though I use dry malt in the dough itself).

Nuts

I like to use walnuts, pecans, and almonds in my baking. I prefer California walnuts, but Chinese walnuts are excellent. Pecans are sweeter, while almonds offer a more subtle nuttiness in some recipes. I am partial to almonds in biscotti. Do taste nuts before baking with them to ensure they are fresh and that their natural oils have not gone rancid.

Toasting Nuts: Toasted nuts always yield more flavor. To toast, spread nuts out on a parchment-lined baking sheet. Bake in an oven preheated to 325°F for 10 to 15 minutes, or until they just begin to color and emit a faint fragrance. Remove from the oven and let cool.

Toasting and Skinning Hazelnuts: Toast hazelnuts as above, then roll them in a clean kitchen towel to remove their skins.

All of my recipes call for either chopped or ground nuts. My measured cup of nuts weighs about 4 ounces. When I say 1 cup chopped walnuts, I mean a cup's worth of chopped (not whole or halved) walnuts. For instance, ½ cup ground nuts means ½ cup nuts, ground before measuring, not ½ cup whole nuts that are then ground.

Oils

When I specify vegetable oil in a recipe, I mean canola, safflower, or corn oil, and I use them interchangeably in my recipes. If required, olive oil is called for by name. Do taste your oil before using to ensure that it is fresh. Don't wait until you take a finished cake out of the oven to find out that your oil is rancid!

Raisins and Other Dried Fruits

Raisins, as well as other dried fruits, such as cranberries, currants, apricots, and sour cherries, add a lovely concentrated flavor to baked goods. I use both golden and dark raisins in my recipes—and just as often a mix of the two.

Plumping Dried Fruits: Make the most of your dried fruit by *plumping* it before use. Cut larger fruit, such as apricots and prunes, in quarters or halves with oiled kitchen scissors before plumping. Put the dried fruit in a small bowl and add boiling or simmering water to cover. Let stand for 5 to 10 minutes. Drain well and then dry the fruit by blotting well with a paper towel before using in a recipe.

Salt

Some contend that salt is salt, but I disagree. The right salt is as important in baking as the finest chocolate, and as a basic ingredient, I far prefer kosher salt. You can purchase it either finely ground or coarse. Kosher salt has no additives, and being iodine free means its pure taste is preserved. It is also a tad less salty than regular table salt. Check the kosher section of your supermarket or a natural foods store. If you cannot find it, substitute regular table salt.

Spices

Seasonings can make or break a dish. Too often, home bakers rely on the spices at their local store, never once considering they might be mediocre or past their shelf life, especially if it is an unusual or less-often-used spice and turnover is not rapid. Find a good spice source. Imported foods stores, specifically Asian, Italian, and Middle Eastern markets, are good bets, as are online spice specialists.

If you use spices rarely, do not assume that your cloves, mace, allspice, and nutmeg are fresh. Replace them if they are not fragrant. Spices last for about 2 months at their optimum level. I purchase small amounts and expect to run out, rather than having a pantry full of aging, lackluster ones.

Sugar

White granulated sugar is the most common sweetener in my recipes. Some of my recipes call for superfine sugar (referred to as *castor sugar* in Britain). You can make your own superfine sugar by simply grinding white sugar in your blender or food processor for 20 to 30 seconds. Superfine sugar is quite similar to regular white sugar and performs much the same without any recipe adjustments needed.

Vanilla and Other Flavorings

Use pure vanilla extract in your baking. Once you've tried the real thing, you will never call anything "plain old vanilla" again. A good vanilla extract will cost more than several bottles of the artificial kind, but the results are well worth it. The same applies to citrus oils and other flavorings. The difference between an artificial extract (how can something artificial be called an *extract*, anyway?) and a pure flavoring is stunning. Like most bakers in North America who have sought out quality vanilla, my choice is Nielsen-Massey. I use several, including their Madagascar Bourbon and Tahitian. They also offer double-strength vanilla, and I often use it (without changing a recipe) for a more rounded, pronounced vanilla taste. You can do this by doubling the amount of regular vanilla (if you do not have double-strength), or just use the amount called for, for a subtle vanilla taste. The Source Guide (page 299) lists some places to obtain quality vanilla, or you can contact Nielsen-Massey directly (page 301).

Boyajian (page 299) makes fine citrus oils, such as orange, lemon, lime, grapefruit, and tangerine. If you cannot find them either via mail order or a local gourmet store, use a pure citrus extract plus 1 teaspoon of minced citrus zest.

Yeast

I use instant yeast in all of my test baking. However, in view of the fact that nothing is more fascinating and for some, intimidating, than baking with yeast, I'll share the lowdown on all varieties of yeast here. The more you know about yeast, the more you will appreciate the joys of working with it. Many bakers are loyal to one variety or brand. In professional circles, consistency is very important and yeast is chosen very carefully. At home, I need yeast that will adapt easily to a variety of baking needs.

What is really neat about yeast is that we're surrounded by it. There are billions of microscopic wild yeast spores floating around in the air. I think of them as wild horses, and the yeast in the packages or tins as a stable of domesticated horses. No two baking environments are alike; some have many more wild yeast spores than others. Packaged yeast is augmented by wild yeast spores, as is a natural sourdough. Any bread you bake in your home will be unique. I've talked a bit about yeast in the introduction, now let's meet the whole (domesticated) family.

Fresh Yeast: Your grandmother and, for sure, your great-grandmother probably used fresh yeast. Purists (myself included) adore it. Dough made with fresh yeast is supple and bouncy, and the fragrance is sweet and subtle. The strains that are used to make fresh yeast are different from those used to make dry yeast. Dry strains are selected for their stability under stress (drying, rehydration, poor handling). Dry yeast contains 5 to 8 percent moisture, compared to 70 to 72 percent moisture in fresh yeast. After being dissolved in water for proofing or being mixed with other ingredients, dry yeast requires a *lag phase* in order to become active again. Fresh yeast has no lag phase.

Despite all the nice attributes of fresh yeast, it does have its drawbacks. Fresh yeast requires precise measuring by weight. It requires refrigeration and is far less stable than dry yeast. It does not like changes in temperature, and its quality diminishes (yeast cells die off) with each passing day or any mishandling. Commercial bakeries have fresh yeast delivered every other day (often by the tanker truckload) in compressed (or cream) form, whereas home bakers must rely on a professional baker to obtain it, or purchase compressed yeast in the dairy case where it's available. Since fresh yeast does not require proofing, it's difficult to tell if it's truly fresh by the usual test of waiting for any foaming or bubbles to appear. You simply have to be certain it was fresh when you bought it and proceed. In its block form (usually 1- or 2-pound blocks), fresh yeast looks like gray clay. It is moist and subtly fragrant when fresh; if old, it might emit a pungent order or be cracked or dry, all indications to avoid using it.

Fresh yeast keeps for 10 to 20 days. If you buy a large block of fresh yeast from a bakery, you can freeze it for up to 1 month. To do this, wrap it well in waxed paper, then in plastic wrap. It is important to keep the yeast from drying or getting freezer burn. Let the yeast defrost gradually in the refrigerator the night before you plan to use it. The longer the yeast is stored, the less potent it will be. When in doubt, discard.

Active Dry Yeast: Some cookbooks specify *active dry yeast*. Active dry is being slowly upstaged and perhaps will eventually be replaced by *instant yeast*. When active dry yeast is called for, you may substitute instant yeast if you like (consult the substitution guide that follows). Alternatively, you can use active dry yeast in the same amount as instant yeast, but allow for a slightly longer rise, up to 25 percent more time. Under most circumstances, active dry yeast must be proofed, or reconstituted with water and a bit of sugar, before use. A container of active dry yeast should be well sealed and refrigerated or frozen and can last a few months after being opened, but always take note of the expiration date.

YEAST SUBSTITUTION GUIDE

2½ teaspoons instant (or bread machine) yeast
= 1 tablespoon active dry yeast
= ¾ ounce fresh yeast

Instant Yeast (Fast-Rising, Rapid Rise, or Bread-Machine Yeast): I test all my recipes with one reliable yeast, and for my money, for home bakers, nothing beats instant yeast. It is also known as *fast-rising, rapid rise,* or *bread machine* yeast, and it is the BetterBaking .com yeast of choice.

Instant yeast is a strong, resilient product that was developed for commercial bakers. It was formulated to function in a wide range of environments, so it offers you a broad margin for error and experimentation. It activates rapidly in warm water, or it can be added to other ingredients in its dry state. It will keep for 3 to 4 months in the refrigerator or freezer. Instant yeast is a good choice for rich yeasted coffee cakes and sweet breads that you may wish to freeze, or for a dough that will rise slowly in the refrigerator.

Instant yeast's fine qualities become liabilities when you use too much of it. A too-quick rise, that is, the dough rises more rapidly than the recipe suggests, and/or an overtly yeasty, "beer" odor, are signs you have used too much. Such overfermented dough will rise and collapse. Sometimes this happens once a loaf reaches the oven. You pop a billowy loaf in there and down she goes! Make sure you do not allow dough to rise beyond double its original size. You can always opt for more fermentation in the final rise. Overfermented dough also reduces the shelf life of the final product. The solution is simple: less is more. Decrease the yeast portion of your recipe by 15 to 25 percent. If you happen to use too little yeast, don't fret—you will just have to be patient as the dough rises more slowly. The final taste and structure of the loaf will be fine. In a rich dough, however, too little yeast can be more of a problem, as the dough needs a healthy proportion of yeast to raise the rich dough.

No two bakers, or kitchens, or ovens, are alike. Don't be afraid to do some tweaking, but for the most part rely on the recipes. They have been carefully formulated, factoring in user error, to still come out shining.

Chapter 1

· ·

THE BREAD BOARD,
OR YEASTY TALES

· ·

ALTHOUGH BETTERBAKING.COM IS A FULL-SERVICE baking website, bread recipes are the foundation of my visitors' interest in home baking. Nothing compares with the scent of homemade bread or the sheer magic of its creation. If you have bread, you have a meal. Add cheese or cold chicken and a glass of wine, and you have a banquet. The expression "Man does not live by bread alone" is true enough. Bakers' bias aside, I tend to think that bread alone is, quite frankly, a fine start.

I feature all kinds of baking at the BB website, and I am as well known for classic breads as I am for more inventive ones. I give a nod to the basics with my beloved Wondrous Bread (page 28), reach for higher ground with New York Bakery Corn Bread (page 56), and I always have some multigrain loaves on hand as well.

I see bread as hospitality food as well as the hallmark of the baker's craft. I also know that bread, and yeast baking in particular, can be intimidating. I have become a specialist at demystifying bread making. How do I do this? I hold my visitors' hands, via email, as they try their skills in their own kitchens. New bakers want perfection from the start; veteran bakers want "definitive" anything. I aim to keep the passion alive and feel the only wrong way to

make bread is not to make it at all. When it comes to baking bread, be a cowboy. Throw caution to the wind, knowing persistence (and faith) will win the day. If you fail (or, rather, "learn" something, as I prefer to think of it), you'll end up with pita bread instead of a French brioche, or soft pretzels, perhaps, instead of bagels. The key is, you will still have something warm, fresh, and wonderful. No, this is not the same as discovering you have baked with rancid milk or sour butter and have to chuck something out, knowing you cannot repair it. This is about seeing a slightly different result as a testimony to the resilience and adaptability of bread.

The more you work with yeast doughs, the more confident you will become. Part of that confidence in baking comes from knowing that a bigger or smaller rise, a slightly lighter or denser crumb, or a softer or more crackly crust are welcome variables rather than indicative of a definitive success or failure. Each bread you produce is yet another delicious, satisfying way to learn about the craft of baking.

How can anything be simple and complex, or ordinary and sacred at the same time? Bread, "the staff of life," is exactly that. For starters, if you'll pardon the pun, four basic elements make up bread: flour, water, yeast, and salt. Flour forms the body and the structure of bread. It is awakened by the water and lifted by the yeast, which, in turn, is regulated to a stately pace by the salt.

How is it possible that four simple ingredients can produce things as varied as focaccia, sourdough, pizza or bagels, baguettes or pita or Wonder Bread? You fiddle with timing and handling, you play with starters and sponges, you alter the flour, change the form of the dough, add another grain here and there, and before you know it, you've invented a whole new loaf. So it goes, and so it grows. Bread, for all its noble symbolism and history, is not as unapproachable as you think. It won't fail if you don't fail it. Never give up in the middle of bread making. It will turn out—maybe not as grand as you planned but usually it will be something pretty special.

When I teach courses on bread making, a lot of "what if?" and "how do you know when?" questions arise. Few recipes can be 100 percent foolproof because variations in climate, flour, water, yeast (both that is added and that floats by), and other factors will affect the outcome. When I am asked how I know this or that about bread, I often reply, "let the bread teach you." If you are tuned-in and begin to connect what you are doing with the weather, the temperature of the water, how much flour you threw in, what brand of flour you used, and how you handled the dough, you will see cause and effect throughout the process. Ah, you might say to yourself one Saturday afternoon, I see that if I let the dough stand a bit, it develops more body on its own, without kneading. Maybe it is too whimsical to say the bread teaches you. Experience is guiding you. Even for veteran bakers, bread never fails to surprise and inspire.

In the BetterBaking.com test kitchen, I never get tired of playing with dough, experimenting with new yeast, flour, and methods. I bake in the oven, on the grill (see page 49), and, on occasion, in a wood-burning Franklin stove. I play around with flours, adding chunky goodness with raisins and nuts, hunks of cheese, and wedges of apple. Sourdough is a favorite pursuit, and artisan bread is the subject of much writing and exchange of email. Starters made with grapes, apples, rye, organic flours, and other ingredients are always frothing away. Some days it's hard to tell if I'm working in a kitchen or in an alchemist's lab! A yeast-scented kitchen offers a perfume no Paris *parfumerie* could rival. Knowing that this fragrance is the promise of fresh-baked bread is a huge bonus.

This collection includes some of my favorite and oft-requested loaves, including *straight dough* breads, sourdoughs, multigrain loaves, and several unique approaches in-between. Straight doughs are bread doughs made by adding yeast and water to flour and other ingredients, then mixing, kneading, rising, and baking. They are in contrast to *prefermented-dough* breads, made with sponges or starters. Straight-dough and rustic sourdough-style breads both have their virtues. In this chapter, you will find loaves that are pure of crumb, and some that are stuffed with character, but each and every one of them is a crusty wonder from the heart of the hearth.

READ BEFORE YOU KNEAD

Kneading bread has stirred many a great debate among bakers. Is there a better way to make and knead the dough? Is it a competitive or philosophical issue? I think it's a matter of matching the method to the baker, the occasion, the recipe, and the personal taste and needs of the moment.

I use a bread machine, a food processor, my trusty mixer with a dough hook, and, of course, my hands, which are the best tools of any baker. Machines do a great job, but you still need to touch the dough to see what stage it is at since visual clues are not always sufficient. Not everyone wants to use their hands for the whole method, however, because of time constraints or other reasons. You might have kneaded your bread before clicking away on a computer gave you carpel tunnel syndrome, or you might like a machine to assist while you hand finish a bread. Perhaps your preference is for handmade pie crust, and you are content to let a bread machine prepare the pizza dough. See? More than one road leads to Rome. What I encourage home bakers to consider is that there are usually several approaches to the same task. Being flexible, while retaining a sense of your own bread values, broadens your abilities. In the end, use the method that will keep you baking. Experiment afresh every once in a while, trying the same recipe a new way, and be willing to experiment with a new flour or another sort of tool.

For the purposes of clarity, I outline all the methods for preparing and kneading yeasted doughs here. In the recipes, however, I focus on the electric stand mixer with dough hook attachment as the basic method of choice. When you want to switch methods or experiment with a combination, refer to this overview.

Electric Stand Mixer with Dough Hook

I test recipes most often with the following method. I prefer that the yeast be dissolved in warm water before any mixing begins. When I say "warm water," I mean between 100°F and 110°F, which is a trifle warmer than lukewarm. A few degrees higher or lower will not make a difference in my recipes. Since I use instant yeast (see page 19), the yeast does not have to foam and bubble, though it will probably swell a bit. In the instructions, I simply say, "hand whisk the water and yeast together in the bowl of an electric mixer." A quick swish or stir of the water and yeast with a hand whisk is adequate.

Once the yeast is dissolved, after 2 to 3 minutes, briskly stir in the salt, oil or butter, or sugar, if included; you want to avoid having the salt, sugar, or fat sit directly on top of yeast, as this inhibits the yeast's performance. Next, add most of the flour and mix by hand with a large, sturdy whisk (my preference), or with the mixer paddle attachment on the lowest speed, to make a soft mass.

At this point, you can stop mixing and let the dough rest for 10 to 15 minutes, even if the recipe does not stipulate to do so (in this book or any bread recipe). This rest, called the *autolyse* by French bakers, is a wonderful technique that allows the flour to absorb moisture, thus transforming it from a somewhat slack or unwieldy dough into a smoother mixture that is easier to knead. It's a nice trick of the trade that helps any bread dough.

After the rest, attach the dough hook and begin to knead the dough on the lowest speed for 5 to 8 minutes, gradually adding more flour as required until the dough is smooth and clears the sides and bottom of the workbowl. Transfer the dough to a lightly floured surface and knead it briefly by hand. Place the dough in a lightly greased bowl and place the bowl in a large, clean plastic bag. I use clear plastic bags, the kind used for gathering leaves in autumn.

The bag acts as a home *proofing tent*, or *proofer* (see page 6). Make sure the dough does not come into contact with the plastic by loosely closing the bag, allowing the dough ample headroom to rise.

Mixing by Hand

In a large bowl, stir the water and yeast together and let it sit a moment until the yeast dissolves. Then whisk in any other ingredients, eggs and oil for instance, and most of the flour, changing to a sturdy wooden spoon when necessary. When the mixture can no longer be stirred by hand, begin kneading on a lightly floured work surface. Dust in a little more flour as required. After 5 minutes, stop and let the dough rest for 10 to 15 minutes. Knead once again for 10 to 15 minutes, or until the dough is smooth, supple, and elastic. You can try slapping it around on the work surface a few times in between bouts of kneading to help the dough get into shape; the dough will hold together more cohesively, be more elastic to the touch, and have a smooth, rather than crinkled or wet-looking, surface. Place the dough in a lightly greased bowl and place the bowl inside a large, clean plastic bag. Close the bag and let the dough rise, following the instructions in the recipe.

Bread Machine

Purists will suggest that the only way to make bread is *la main à la pâte*, or hands on the dough. Your bread machine, however, will garner you a bit of free time in the kitchen if you allow it to assist with part of the process, rather than the whole voyage. My stalwart test-kitchen bread machines are pressed into service almost every day. I use a bread machine for mixing, kneading, and rising only—never for baking. For baking, it does a reasonable, albeit unimpressive job. Breads cannot swell and expand in the narrow bread pan. It makes adequate sandwich loaf bread that is meant to be consumed in one day, but breads baked in a bread machine tend to become stale faster. Besides, I am not fond of the constrictive look of the finished bread. A bread machine is a great time saver, though, as well as a neat and efficient dough kneader. You needn't worry about keeping the dough covered and in a warm area, and the nonstick bread pan ensures you can remove the dough with little fuss.

To use a bread machine to knead dough, combine

the water and yeast and whisk it with a small whisk or spoon. Then put it in the machine and add the remaining ingredients and set the machine to the dough cycle. Once the kneading cycle begins, let the machine do its thing for about 6 minutes. (Often, I help the cycle along at the outset by using a rubber spatula to mix the ingredients.) Then stop the machine for 10 to 15 minutes. Next, turn the machine back on to the dough cycle. As it mixes and kneads, you can make adjustments by adding a bit of flour or water, if needed, to make the dough come together correctly. Usually you can make this assessment 5 to 8 minutes into the dough cycle. Once the kneading stops, simply let the dough rise in the machine. When the machine beeps that the dough is ready, gently remove it or invert the bread pan onto a lightly floured board. Gently deflate the dough and proceed with the recipe.

Be careful when making doughs that contains chunky bits like cheese, fruit, or nuts, as these additions tend to be pulverized by the machine. It's best to add them by hand once the kneading cycle is complete or, if you have such an option on the machine, add them when the machine signals you to do so.

Food Processor

Put the water and yeast in the bowl of a food processor fitted with the metal blade. Pulse briefly to stir them together, about 5 seconds. Stop the machine and add the sugar, salt, and if the recipe calls for them, eggs, oil, or butter. Pulse for about 10 seconds to combine. Add the flour all at once and process for 10 to 20 seconds, or until a soft ball or a sticky, ragged mass forms. Stop the machine and let the dough rest in the machine for 10 to 15 minutes. Process again to form a thick mass of soft dough. Remove the dough from the machine and knead briefly, shaping it into a round by hand, on a lightly floured surface. Put the dough in a lightly greased bowl and place the bowl inside a large, clean plastic bag. Close the bag and let the dough rise according to the instructions in the recipe.

VANILLA-CINNAMON SWIRL BREAD

MAKES 2 SMALL LOAVES

DOUGH

1⅓ cups warm water

2½ teaspoons instant yeast

2 tablespoons unsalted butter, softened

½ cup sugar

2 eggs

2 teaspoons pure vanilla extract

1¼ teaspoons salt

1 teaspoon ground cinnamon

2 tablespoons nonfat dry milk

¼ cup instant potato flakes

3½ to 4½ cups bread flour

FILLING

Milk for brushing

1 cup raisins, plumped and patted dry (see page 18)

2 tablespoons ground cinnamon

¼ cup sugar

Simple but spectacular, this is a great loaf with which to begin baking. Instant potato flakes make this bread extra moist. Slice it nice and thick for toasting and use the leftovers for French toast or bread pudding. One of my testers, a chocoholic, inspired the chocolate variation below.

Spray two 8- by 4-inch loaf pans with nonstick cooking spray. Line a baking sheet with parchment paper. Set aside.

For the dough, hand whisk the water and yeast together in the bowl of an electric mixer and let stand for 2 to 3 minutes to dissolve the yeast. Stir in the butter, sugar, eggs, vanilla, salt, cinnamon, dry milk, potato flakes, and 3½ cups of the flour. Mix to make a soft mass. Knead with the dough hook on the lowest speed of the mixer for 8 to 10 minutes, adding more flour as required to form a soft dough. Turn the dough out onto a lightly floured surface and form the dough into a ball. Place the dough in a lightly greased bowl. Place the bowl in a large plastic bag, close the bag loosely, and let the dough rise for 30 to 45 minutes, or until almost doubled.

Gently deflate the dough. Turn the dough out onto a lightly floured surface. Roll the dough out into a 12- by 10-inch rectangle. For the filling, brush with milk and sprinkle on the raisins, cinnamon, and sugar. With the shorter end facing you, roll up the dough snugly into a log. Cut it in half widthwise and place in the prepared pans.

Spray the dough lightly with nonstick cooking spray and return the pans to the plastic bag. Close the bag loosely and let the dough rise for 30 to 45 minutes, or until it puffs up ¾ to 1 inch above the pan rim.

Preheat the oven to 350°F. Place the pans on the prepared baking sheet and bake for 35 to 45 minutes, or until the loaves are lightly browned. Let cool in the pans on a wire rack for at least 15 minutes before unmolding.

VARIATION: Use chocolate chips instead of raisins, and replace the cinnamon with 2 tablespoons unsweetened cocoa powder.

WONDROUS BREAD

MAKES 1 LARGE LOAF

1⅓ cups warm water

4½ teaspoons instant yeast

2 tablespoons sugar

2 teaspoons salt

5 tablespoons (2½ ounces)
    unsalted butter, melted

2 cups all-purpose flour

1 to 2 cups bread flour

¼ cup semolina or all-purpose or
    bread flour

Spongy, soft, and tall, and great for toast, school lunches, and sandwiches, this bread is one of the most popular recipes at BetterBaking.com. When it was published in the Washington Post, fans of the website were delighted, and a wave of new visitors stopped by as well.

~❦~

Spray a 9- by 5-inch loaf pan with nonstick cooking spray. Line a baking sheet with parchment paper. Set aside.

In the bowl of an electric mixer, hand whisk the water and yeast together and let stand for 2 to 3 minutes to dissolve the yeast. Stir in the sugar, salt, 4 tablespoons of the butter, the all-purpose flour, 1 cup of the bread flour, and the semolina. Mix to make a soft mass. Knead with the dough hook on the lowest speed of the mixer for 8 to 10 minutes, gradually adding more bread flour as required to form a soft dough. Turn the dough out onto a lightly floured surface and form it into a ball. Place the dough in a lightly greased bowl. Place the bowl inside a large plastic bag, close the bag loosely, and let the dough rise for 30 to 45 minutes, or until almost doubled.

Gently deflate the dough. Turn the dough out onto a lightly floured surface and form it into an oblong loaf. Place the dough in the prepared loaf pan. Spray the dough lightly with nonstick cooking spray and return the pan to the plastic bag. Close the bag loosely and let the dough rise for about 45 minutes, or until it puffs up about 1 inch above the pan rim. Brush the loaf with the remaining 1 tablespoon melted butter.

Preheat the oven to 350°F. Place the pan on the prepared baking sheet and bake for 30 to 35 minutes, or until evenly browned. Let cool in the pan on a wire rack for at least 15 minutes before unmolding.

My Famous Homemade Butter Spread

MAKES ABOUT 3½ CUPS

2 cups (1 pound) unsalted butter at
    room temperature

1 teaspoon salt, or to taste

1 cup vegetable oil

1 cup water at room temperature

This buttery blend offers the convenience of soft margarine and the taste and nutrition of butter. Adding water and oil reduces the cholesterol and fat content of the butter. This is really great for kids and toast fans who want a natural butter taste in a soft product. I make tubs and tubs of this and freeze it. It is for spreading only, not for baking. Be certain the butter and water are at room temperature so they will blend well.

~◊~

Process the butter in a food processor for a few moments to soften. With the machine running, gradually add the salt and pour in the oil and then the water in a thin stream to allow the butter to absorb the liquids. Process for 1½ minutes, or until the mixture is very smooth, like a pudding. Pour it into a dish, cover, and refrigerate for at least 2 hours or freeze for 2 to 3 hours to firm it up. The spread will keep, refrigerated, indefinitely.

CLASSIC WHITE BREAD
MAKES FOR A STAND-UP LOAF

Until recently, I was a bread snob. All I could talk about was sourdough and other artisanal breads. I worked on loaves that took 10 days to prepare, 30 minutes to bake, and 5 minutes to devour. I researched baking stones, refractory tiles, and kits that were designed to turn my domestic oven into an artisan bread inferno that would meet with the approval of the finest French baker. I even attempted to design a steam injector for home ovens. (Steam helps promote a good crust, among other things, and I approached several houseware companies with my idea. I was ahead of my time, apparently, as they all were fascinated but declined to collaborate.) To me, *straight loaves* were *déclassé*, made up as they are with the most basic of ingredients that you simply mix, knead, rise, and bake—too bland, quick to spoil, and not

challenging enough, especially in this era of artisanal breads. Still, a straight loaf made well, in the wake of trends, remains the cornerstone of many a good bakery—and a home kitchen, as I was soon to learn.

Not long ago, my youngest son, who thinks toast is his real mother, asked, "Mom, could I have store-bought bread for a change? You know, like Wonder Bread?" I blanched. Could this be my son? Rather than fetch a store-bought loaf, I created my own version of Wonder Bread (opposite), and we had a bread-and-butter picnic. With every bite, I was reminded of the comfort and satisfaction a good straight loaf can bring. It doesn't require much planning, and the results remind me of a culinary world where James Beard can wax poetic about a perfect soft-boiled egg.

THE GOURMET SHOP'S APPLE BREAD

MAKES 1 LARGE LOAF

DOUGH

2 cups warm water

2 tablespoons instant yeast

½ cup (4 ounces) unsalted butter, melted

2 tablespoons apple juice concentrate (optional)

1 teaspoon pure vanilla extract

2 eggs

⅓ cup sugar

1¼ teaspoons salt

¼ teaspoon ground cinnamon

5 to 6 cups bread flour

FILLING

5 to 6 large apples, preferably McIntosh or Courtland, peeled or unpeeled, cored, and diced (4 to 5 cups)

½ cup fresh or dried cranberries, plumped and patted dry (see page 18), optional

¾ cup sugar

1½ teaspoon ground cinnamon

EGG WASH

1 egg

1 egg yolk

Pinch of sugar

1 tablespoon water

White or coarse sugar for sprinkling

Ground cinnamon for dusting

Featuring a slightly sweet dough that cradles chunks of apples (and cranberries, if you wish), this loaf is bursting at the seams. This moist and showy bread is a treat for breakfast, coffee klatch, holidays, or as a special gift.

Stack 2 baking sheets together and line the top one with parchment paper. Set aside.

For the dough, hand whisk the water and yeast together in the bowl of an electric mixer and let stand for 2 to 3 minutes to dissolve the yeast. Stir in the butter, apple juice concentrate, vanilla, eggs, sugar, salt, cinnamon, and 5 cups of the flour. Mix to make a soft mass. Knead with the dough hook on the lowest speed of the mixer for 8 to 10 minutes, gradually adding more flour as required to form a soft and elastic dough. Turn the dough out onto a lightly floured surface and form it into a ball. Place the dough in a lightly greased bowl. Place the bowl inside a large plastic bag, close the bag loosely, and let rise for 30 to 45 minutes, or until almost doubled.

Gently deflate the dough. Spray the top with nonstick cooking spray and return the bowl to the plastic bag. Close the bag loosely and let the dough rest for 20 minutes. Meanwhile, make the filling. In a large bowl, toss the apples and cranberries with the sugar and cinnamon.

On a lightly floured surface, roll the dough out into a 10-inch circle. Press half of the apple mixture into the dough, leaving a ½-inch border around the edges. Fold the dough over to completely cover the apples. Some apples may pop out, which is fine; just press them back in the dough. Flatten the dough with a rolling pin to distribute the apples. Press the remaining filling into the top of the dough. Fold the dough over again and pinch the edges to seal. The dough will be bulky and some apples may puncture it, which again is fine. Shape the dough into a fat oblong 8 inches wide and 10 inches long, tucking in apples if they fall out.

Put the loaf on the prepared baking sheets. Using a sharp knife, make 4 diagonal slits on the top of the loaf. Spray the loaf with nonstick cooking spray and put the pan inside the plastic bag. Let rise for 30 to 50 minutes, or until puffy.

Preheat the oven to 350°F. For the egg wash, hand whisk or blend all the ingredients together in a small bowl. Brush the loaf with the egg wash, then sprinkle with sugar and dust with cinnamon. Bake for 35 to 45 minutes, or until well browned. Let cool in the pan on a wire rack for 15 to 20 minutes before unmolding.

MY BEST TWELVE-GRAIN BREAD

MAKES 2 SMALL LOAVES

SPONGE

3 cups warm water

1 tablespoon instant yeast

1½ cups bread flour

1¼ cups whole-wheat flour

¼ cup spelt, dark rye, or kamut
    flour

DOUGH

1 cup couscous or millet

⅔ cup 12-grain or multigrain cereal

Sponge, above

3 tablespoons nonfat dry milk
    (optional)

3 tablespoons molasses

2 tablespoons firmly packed brown
    sugar

1 teaspoon baker's caramel
    (optional)

2 tablespoons flaxseed oil

2 tablespoons vegetable oil

½ teaspoon sesame oil

2 tablespoons honey

2½ teaspoons salt

Pinch of ground cumin

⅛ teaspoon ground cinnamon

3 to 4 cups bread flour

1 cup sunflower seeds or cracked
    wheat for coating

Any multigrain cereal will work here, whether it's 7-, 10-, or 12-grain. Flours made from ancient grains such as spelt and kamut are available in natural foods stores and offer added nutrition. In this recipe, the trick is to toast and soak the grains. Toasting accentuates the nutty flavor of the grains, while soaking ensures that they add moistness to the loaf. Serve this bread with a sharp cheese or smoked turkey, and green tea. I add milk powder for a boost of calcium, but if you want a dairy-free loaf, leave it out. Baker's caramel darkens this to a rustic hue and can be found via specialty baking sources.

Spray two 8- by 4-inch loaf pans with nonstick cooking spray. Line a large baking sheet with parchment paper and set aside.

For the sponge, hand whisk the water and yeast together in the bowl of an electric mixer and let stand for 2 to 3 minutes to dissolve the yeast. Stir in the flours to make a thick batter. Place the bowl inside a large plastic bag, close the bag loosely, and let the sponge stand for at least 1 hour or up to 3 hours; the mixture should be quite spongy and puffy looking.

For the dough, toast the couscous in a nonstick pan over medium-low heat, stirring with a wooden spoon, for 5 minutes, or until lightly colored. Set aside and let cool.

Bring a small pot of water to a boil. Stir the couscous and cereal together in a small bowl. Add boiling water to cover and let stand for 5 minutes, or until the grains are swollen. Drain well.

Stir down the sponge to deflate it, then mix in the grain mixture. Hand whisk in the dry milk, molasses, brown sugar, baker's caramel, flaxseed oil, vegetable oil, sesame oil, honey, salt, cumin, cinnamon, and 3 cups of the flour. Mix to make a soft mass. Knead with the dough hook on the lowest speed of the mixer for 8 to 10 minutes, gradually adding more flour as required to form a soft dough. Turn the dough out onto a lightly floured surface and form the dough into a ball. Place it in a lightly greased bowl. Place the bowl in a large plastic bag, close the bag loosely, and let rise for 30 to 35 minutes, or until almost doubled.

Gently deflate the dough. Turn the dough out onto a lightly floured surface. Divide the dough in half and roll each half into a ball. Roll each ball in the sunflower seeds to cover generously, or press the seeds into the dough.

Put the balls in the prepared loaf pans, spray the dough with nonstick cooking spray, and return the pans to the large plastic bag. Allow the dough to rise until almost doubled, about 30 minutes.

Preheat the oven to 375°F. Place the pans on the prepared baking sheet and bake for 25 to 35 minutes, or until the loaves are medium brown in color and the seeds are beginning to brown. Unmold onto a wire rack and let cool for at least 15 minutes before slicing and serving.

MICROBREWERY BEER BREAD

MAKES 1 LARGE LOAF

¼ cup warm water

1 tablespoon instant yeast

2 tablespoons sugar

1½ cups warm beer

2 tablespoons vegetable oil

1½ teaspoons salt

2 cups whole-wheat flour

2 to 2½ cups bread flour

1 egg white, beaten until foamy, for glazing

To me, beer is just beer. I bake with it once in a while, and I think I once tried it as a hair rinse a few years ago. To aficionados, beer can be as refined a beverage as any fine wine. Use a dark brew for a robust bread, and a lighter brew for a more subtle loaf. You may also add caraway seeds and raisins, or toss in some cubes of sharp cheddar cheese. Enjoy this bread with some Stilton or cheddar, and a chilled mug of your favorite brew. One visitor to the site wrote, "This bread is outstanding. Lovely color, fabulous subtle taste of malt. Addicted to this bread!"

Spray a 9- by 5-inch loaf pan with nonstick cooking spray. Line a baking sheet with parchment paper. Set aside.

In the bowl of an electric mixer, hand whisk the water, yeast, and sugar together and let stand for 2 to 3 minutes to dissolve the yeast. Stir in the beer, oil, salt, whole-wheat flour, and 1 cup of the bread flour. Mix to make a soft mass. Knead with the dough hook on the lowest speed of the mixer for 8 to 10 minutes, gradually adding more bread flour as required to form a smooth and elastic dough. Turn the dough out onto a lightly floured surface and form it into a ball. Place the dough in a lightly greased bowl. Place the bowl in a large plastic bag, close the bag loosely, and let the dough rise for 30 to 45 minutes, or until almost doubled.

Gently deflate the dough. Turn the dough out onto a lightly floured surface. Shape the dough into an oblong and place it in the prepared loaf pan. Brush the loaf with the beaten egg white and put the pan in a large plastic bag. Allow the dough to rise for 30 to 40 minutes, or until almost doubled.

Preheat the oven to 375°F. Using a sharp knife, slash the bread on the diagonal and sprinkle with flour. Place the loaf pan on the prepared baking sheet and bake for 35 to 40 minutes, or until browned. Let cool on a wire rack in the pan for at least 15 minutes before unmolding.

The Health Food Club's Millet and Soy Bread

MAKES 2 SMALL LOAVES

SPONGE

1½ cups warm water

1 tablespoon instant yeast

2 cups bread flour

DOUGH

1 cup millet

Sponge, above

1 cup warm water

½ cup soy flour

2 tablespoons nonfat dry milk

3 tablespoons honey

2½ teaspoons salt

2 to 3 cups bread flour

This bread is nutty, nutritious, colorful, and delicious toasted. The dough would also make great hamburger buns for meat or vegetarian burgers.

~(◊)~

Stack 2 baking sheets together and line the top one with parchment paper. Set aside.

For the sponge, hand whisk the water and yeast together in the bowl of an electric mixer and let stand for 2 to 3 minutes to dissolve the yeast. Stir in the flour to make a thick batter. Place the bowl in a large plastic bag, close the bag loosely, and let the sponge stand for at least 1 hour or up to 3 hours.

For the dough, toast the millet in a dry cast-iron skillet over medium heat, tossing with a fork or wooden spoon to evenly toast the grains for about 5 minutes, or until the millet browns lightly. Put the millet in a bowl and add water to cover. Let stand for 20 to 30 minutes to absorb the water, then drain.

Stir down the sponge to deflate it and add the millet, warm water, soy flour, dry milk, honey, salt, and 2 cups of the flour. Mix to make a soft mass. Knead with the dough hook on the lowest speed of the mixer for 8 to 10 minutes, gradually adding more flour as required to make a soft dough. Turn the dough out onto a lightly floured surface. Form the dough into a ball and place in a lightly greased bowl. Place the bowl in a large plastic bag, close the bag loosely, and let rise for 30 to 45 minutes, or until almost doubled.

Gently deflate the dough. Spray the top of the dough with nonstick cooking spray and return it to the plastic bag. Close the bag loosely and let the dough rise for another 20 minutes. Deflate again and divide the dough in half. Shape each half into a ball and place the balls on the prepared baking sheets. Spray the top of the loaves with nonstick cooking spray and place the baking sheets in the plastic bag. Close the bag loosely and let the dough rise for 30 to 60 minutes, or until puffy and almost doubled in size.

Preheat the oven to 375°F. Bake for 25 to 30 minutes, or until nicely browned. Let cool on the sheets on a wire rack for at least 15 minutes before serving.

LOGAN'S FAMOUS CHEESE BREAD

MAKES 2 LOAVES

DOUGH

1⅓ cups warm water

2 tablespoons instant yeast

2 eggs

4 tablespoons (2 ounces) unsalted butter, softened

2½ teaspoons salt

2 teaspoons sugar

1 cup shredded sharp cheddar cheese (optional)

5 to 6 cups bread flour

FILLING

Freshly ground black pepper for sprinkling

Paprika for sprinkling

2 to 3 cups (8 to 12 ounces) cheddar cheese, a mixture of chunks and shredded

Years ago, Logan's was a traditional bakery in Montreal that celebrated the best of English baking: scones, pies, berry tarts, giant cookies, and cheese loaves. People would call ahead to reserve their Logan's cheese bread. Cheddar is my standard for this recipe. For a pronounced cheese-flavored dough, add the optional cheddar cheese. This bread is good fresh or lightly toasted. Add a smack of Dijon mustard and some smoked ham, or some end-of-harvest ripe tomatoes with a drop of balsamic vinegar and a fine olive oil, and you have it made.

~◊~

Spray two 8- by 4-inch loaf pans with nonstick cooking spray. Line a baking sheet with parchment paper. Set aside.

For the dough, hand whisk the water and yeast together in the bowl of an electric mixer and let stand for 2 to 3 minutes to dissolve the yeast. Stir in the eggs, butter, salt, sugar, cheese, and 5 cups of the flour. Mix to make a soft mass. Knead with the dough hook on the lowest speed of the mixer for 8 to 10 minutes, gradually adding more flour as required to make a soft dough. Turn the dough out onto a lightly floured surface. Form the dough into a ball and place in a lightly greased bowl. Place the bowl in a large plastic bag, close the bag loosely, and let the dough rise for 30 to 45 minutes, or until almost doubled.

Gently deflate the dough. Turn the dough out onto a lightly floured surface and divide it in half. Using a rolling pin, roll out each half into an oval. For the filling, sprinkle with black pepper and paprika. Dot the surface of each oval with half the cheese chunks (reserve the shredded cheese for topping). Roll up the ovals jellyroll style. Place in the prepared pans. Slash the top of each loaf with a sharp knife. Spray the tops with nonstick cooking spray and dust with flour. Place the pans in a large plastic bag, close the bag loosely, and let the dough rise for about 40 minutes, or until it puffs up 1 inch above the pan rim.

Preheat the oven to 375°F. Place the pans on the prepared baking sheet and bake for about 35 minutes, or until browned. Sprinkle with the reserved shredded cheese. Bake for an additional 5 to 10 minutes, or until the cheese melts. Let cool in the pans on a wire rack for at least 15 minutes before unmolding and cooling on the counter.

RUSTIC DARK PUMPERNICKEL

MAKES 1 LARGE LOAF OR 2 SMALL LOAVES

Cornmeal for dusting

SPONGE

1 cup warm water

1 tablespoon instant yeast

1 cup dark rye or pumpernickel
    flour

¼ cup bread flour

DOUGH

Sponge, above

¾ cup warm water

1½ teaspoons instant yeast

2 tablespoons firmly packed brown
    sugar

2¾ teaspoons salt

½ teaspoon malt powder
    (optional)

4 to 6 teaspoons baker's caramel
    (optional)

2 tablespoons caraway seeds

3½ to 4 cups bread flour

Beaten egg white or Baker's
    Cornstarch Glaze (opposite)

Cracked wheat, caraway seeds,
    black cumin seeds, or cornmeal
    for garnish

This is perhaps the heartiest loaf in my collection, and its intense rye and caraway aroma wafts up from a moist, rustic crumb. The baker's caramel and malt powder are optional, but the caramel will give the dough a nice color, and the malt powder adds flavor. The sponge can be prepared up to 1 day ahead.

Spray a 12- by 5-inch loaf pan or two 8- by 4-inch loaf pans with nonstick cooking spray and sprinkle cornmeal on the bottom. Line a large baking sheet with parchment paper. Set aside.

For the sponge, hand whisk the water and yeast together in the bowl of an electric mixer and let stand for 2 to 3 minutes to dissolve the yeast. Stir in the flours to make a thick batter. Place the bowl in a large plastic bag, close the bag loosely, and allow the sponge to stand for at least 2 hours or as long as overnight.

For the dough, stir down the sponge to deflate it and add the water, yeast, brown sugar, salt, malt powder, baker's caramel, caraway seeds, and 3½ cups of the flour. Mix to make a soft mass. Knead with the dough hook on the lowest speed of the mixer for 8 to 10 minutes, gradually adding more flour as required to form a soft and bouncy dough. Turn the dough out onto a lightly floured surface. Form the dough into a ball and place in a lightly greased bowl. Place the bowl in a large plastic bag, close the bag loosely, and let rise for 30 to 45 minutes, or until almost doubled.

Gently deflate the dough. Turn the dough out onto a lightly floured surface. Divide the dough into thirds (or into 6 pieces if using 2 pans) and shape each portion into a ball. Place the balls next to one another in the prepared loaf pan(s). Spray the top of the dough with nonstick cooking spray and return to the plastic bag. Close the bag loosely and let the dough rise for 40 to 60 minutes, or until puffy.

Preheat the oven to 375°F. Brush the top of the dough with the beaten egg white and sprinkle on your garnish of choice. Place the pan(s) on the prepared baking sheet and bake for 35 to 40 minutes, or until the bread is lightly browned and sounds hollow when tapped on the top surface. Unmold onto a wire rack and let cool for at least 15 minutes before slicing and serving.

BAKER'S CORNSTARCH GLAZE

MAKES ½ CUP

½ cup water

2 tablespoons cornstarch

Ever wonder how professional bakers put that lovely sheen on their loaves? It's simple. Use this glaze to brush the tops of pumpernickel and rye loaves. Brush it on about 10 minutes before baking is complete and then repeat 3 minutes before baking is complete.

In a small saucepan, whisk the water and cornstarch together. Warm the mixture over medium-low heat for 1 to 2 minutes, or until it bubbles slightly, becomes translucent, and begins to thicken. Let cool completely.

B.B.
Test Kitchen
Notes

The Measure of a Good Recipe

A few years ago, when I was researching a feature on bread machines for the website, I had a chance to chat with a designer from a leading appliance manufacturer. We talked about the challenges of designing a bread machine. He told me that slapping together a motor, tub, agitator, timer, and heating element was not nearly as complex as it was to design recipes for a bread machine. He said, "Most people scan the instruction manual once or twice at the beginning, but after that, they wing it." Bread machine recipes (at least those supplied by the manufacturers) are designed with some margin for error, but that margin is very narrow. Too much of this or too little of that will make your loaf pop out of the machine like some mutant jack-in-the-box. This is why the instruction manual implores you to measure very carefully if you plan to bake in the machine. I never bake in the machine (see page 25). Just the same, I suggest you take the time to measure carefully with any recipe.

LIGHT-RYE SANDWICH BREAD

MAKES 3 SMALL LOAVES

SPONGE

¾ cup warm water

½ teaspoon instant yeast

1 cup bread flour

DOUGH

Sponge, above

2 cups warm water

1 teaspoon instant yeast

½ teaspoon malt powder or firmly
    packed brown sugar

1 tablespoon caraway seeds

2 tablespoons cornmeal

2 teaspoons baker's caramel
    (optional)

1 tablespoon salt

1 tablespoon honey

1½ cups dark rye flour

5 to 6 cups bread flour

Cornmeal for dusting

Rye and white flours combined with a simple sponge make this rye rustic but light. Rye recipes that do not call for a sponge or starter produce rather dry, forgettable loaves. A tuna melt with raclette cheese on a slice of this bread makes a wonderful lunch. The sponge can be prepared 1 day ahead.

Stack 2 baking sheets together and line the top one with parchment paper. Set aside.

For the sponge, hand whisk the water and yeast together in the bowl of an electric mixer and let stand for 2 to 3 minutes to dissolve the yeast. Stir in the flour to make a thick batter. Place the bowl in a large plastic bag, close the bag loosely, and allow the sponge to stand at room temperature for at least 4 hours or as long as overnight.

For the dough, stir down the sponge to deflate it. Add the water, yeast, malt powder, caraway seeds, cornmeal, baker's caramel, salt, honey, rye flour, and 5 cups of the bread flour. Mix to make a soft mass. Place the bowl in a large plastic bag, close the bag loosely, and let the dough stand for 1 hour, or until almost doubled.

Knead with the dough hook on the lowest speed of the mixer for 8 to 10 minutes, gradually adding more bread flour as required to form a soft dough. Turn the dough out on a lightly floured surface and form the dough into a ball. Place it in a lightly greased bowl. Place the bowl in the large plastic bag, close the bag loosely, and let the dough rise for 30 to 45 minutes, or until almost doubled.

Gently deflate the dough and let it rest for 30 minutes longer. Turn the dough out onto a lightly floured surface, divide it into thirds, and shape each portion into a ball. Dust the tops with cornmeal. Place the balls on the prepared baking sheets and place the sheets in the large plastic bag. Close the bag loosely and let the dough rise for 45 to 60 minutes, or until nearly doubled.

Preheat the oven to 425°F. Place the loaves in the oven and bake for 15 minutes. Lower the heat to 375°F and bake for an additional 30 minutes, or until well browned. Let cool on a wire rack for at least 15 minutes before serving.

HERBED SALLY LUNN LOAF

MAKES 1 LARGE ROUND LOAF

½ cup warm water

4½ teaspoons instant yeast

½ cup warm milk

¾ cup (6 ounces) unsalted butter,
    softened

2 teaspoons sugar

1¾ teaspoons salt

3 eggs

1 cup loosely packed fresh flat-leaf
    parsley leaves, minced

2 cups all-purpose flour

2 to 3 cups bread flour

2 tablespoons unsalted butter,
    melted, for brushing

History suggests that Sally Lunn was a baker who lived in England in the late 1700s. Her name has been lent to many baking recipes that vary in ingredients but are similar overall. This bread tastes like a cross between buttery biscuits and a light slicing loaf. It's perfect with a fried chicken supper, grilled fish, or cheese, or straight up with butter.

~⟨◊⟩~

Spray a 9- or 10-inch angel food cake pan with nonstick cooking spray. Line a large baking sheet with parchment paper. Set aside.

In the bowl of an electric mixer, hand whisk the water and yeast together and let stand for 2 to 3 minutes to dissolve the yeast. Stir in the milk, softened butter, sugar, salt, eggs, parsley, all-purpose flour, and 2 cups of the bread flour. Mix to make a soft mass. Using the paddle attachment, mix on the lowest speed of the mixer for 8 to 10 minutes, gradually adding more bread flour as required to form a loose batter. Pour the batter into the prepared pan. Using a pastry brush, lightly brush the top with the melted butter. Place the pan in a large plastic bag, close the bag loosely, and let the dough rise for about 1½ hours, or until quite puffy.

Preheat the oven to 350°F. Place the pan on the prepared baking sheet and bake for 35 to 40 minutes, or until lightly browned. Let cool in the pan on a wire rack for at least 15 minutes before unmolding. Pull apart sections of this bread rather than slicing.

PERFECT GRILLED CHEESE BREAD

MAKES 2 MEDIUM LOAVES

1 tablespoon instant yeast

2 cups warm water

4 teaspoons sugar

1 tablespoon salt

3 tablespoons olive oil

1 egg

1 teaspoon distilled white vinegar

6 cups (approximately) bread flour

Everyone needs a stand-up bread for perfect grilled cheese sandwiches, and this is it. This bread is amazing on its own, but also sturdy enough for a homemade grilled cheese sandwich. I suggest Monterey Jack, sharp orange cheddar, and a bit of raclette cheese.

~❦~

Spray two 9- by 5-inch loaf pans with nonstick cooking spray and set aside. Line a large baking sheet with parchment paper.

In the bowl of an electric mixer, hand whisk the yeast and water and let stand for 3 minutes. Whisk in the sugar, salt, oil, egg, and vinegar and blend briefly. Stir in 4 cups of the flour and blend with a wooden spoon. Next, attach the dough hook and knead on the slowest speed of the mixer, adding in the remaining flour as required to make a soft, bouncy dough, about 8 minutes.

Place the mixing bowl in a large plastic bag and let the dough rise until almost doubled in size, 45 to 60 minutes.

Gently deflate the dough and turn out onto a lightly floured work surface. Shape the dough into a ball, cover with the plastic bag, and let rise 20 minutes.

Gently deflate and divide the dough into 2 equal portions. Shape each into a rounded loaf and place them on the prepared baking sheet. Alternatively, shape the dough into oblongs, place them in prepared loaf pans, and place these on the prepared baking sheet. Insert the entire baking sheet into a large plastic bag and let rise until almost doubled in bulk.

Preheat the oven to 375°F. Place the breads on the lower rack of the oven and bake for 20 minutes, then reduce the oven temperature to 350°F and bake another 20 minutes, until well browned. Cool the bread for a few minutes before turning it out onto a wire cooling rack.

CRUSTY ENGLISH MUFFIN BREAD

MAKES 2 LARGE LOAVES

Cornmeal for sprinkling

¾ cup warm water

2 tablespoons instant yeast

1½ cups warm milk

2 tablespoons unsalted butter, softened

1 tablespoon sugar

1 tablespoon honey

1 teaspoon salt

½ teaspoon baking soda dissolved in 1 tablespoon of cold water

2 cups all-purpose flour

1 cup whole-wheat flour

2 cups bread flour

Recipes for English muffin bread have been around for years. There is no kneading required, there are no exotic ingredients, and I like the idea of fiddling with baking soda and yeast in the same recipe. The result is a coarse, grainy loaf with an English muffin texture and taste. I opt for three types of flour to produce chewiness, density, and nutrition. You can use two large coffee cans to make nice round loaves if you wish.

Spray 2 large coffee cans or two 9- by 5-inch loaf pans with nonstick cooking spray and sprinkle with cornmeal. Line a baking sheet with parchment paper. Set aside.

In the bowl of an electric mixer, hand whisk the water and yeast together and let stand for 2 to 3 minutes to dissolve the yeast. Stir in the milk, butter, sugar, honey, salt, baking soda, all-purpose flour, whole-wheat flour, and 1 cup of the bread flour. Mix to make a soft mass. Using the paddle attachment, mix on the lowest speed of the mixer for 3 to 5 minutes, gradually adding more of the bread flour as required to form a thick batter. Divide the batter equally between the prepared pans. Place the pans in a large plastic bag, close the bag loosely, and let the dough rise for 30 to 40 minutes, or until almost doubled.

Preheat the oven to 375°F. Place the pans on the prepared baking sheet and bake for 35 to 40 minutes, or until the loaves are lightly browned and sound hollow when tapped on the surface. Unmold onto a wire rack and let cool for at least 15 minutes before serving.

B.B.
Test Kitchen
Notes

Slick Measuring

Measure the oil in a recipe before you measure sticky ingredients like honey. The oil on your spoon or in your measuring cup will allow the sticky ingredient to slide right out.

CUBAN SANDWICH BREAD

MAKES 4 NARROW LOAVES

SPONGE

⅓ cup warm water

¾ teaspoon instant yeast

⅓ cup bread flour

DOUGH

Sponge, above

1½ cups warm water

4½ teaspoons instant yeast

1 tablespoon sugar

4 tablespoons vegetable shortening

2¾ teaspoons salt

4 to 5 cups bread flour

Renowned Cuban sandwiches—the Cuban connection to panini—start with this bread. Traditionally, palm fronds are draped over the rising dough. Once removed, they leave a decorative imprint on the top of the loaves. If you feel particularly adventurous, you can search out the fronds (or banana leaves) in a Latino market. This sponge can be made the night before using. If you already have some mature sourdough starter (page 53) on hand, let it warm up a bit and use about ½ cup of it in place of the sponge.

Stack 2 baking sheets together and line the top one with parchment paper. Repeat with 2 more baking sheets. Set aside.

For the sponge, hand whisk the water and yeast together in the bowl of an electric mixer and let stand for 2 to 3 minutes to dissolve yeast. Stir in the flour to make a thick paste. Place the bowl in a large plastic bag, close the bag loosely, and allow the sponge to stand for at least 8 hours or up to overnight.

For the dough, stir down the sponge to deflate it. Remove and reserve half for another use (it will keep, refrigerated, for 1 to 2 days before it needs to be fed again). Add the water, yeast, sugar, shortening, salt, and 4 cups of the flour. Mix to make a soft mass. Knead with the dough hook on the lowest speed of the mixer for 8 to 10 minutes, gradually adding more flour as required to form a stiff dough. Turn the dough out onto a lightly floured surface. Form the dough into a ball and place it in a lightly greased bowl. Place the bowl in a large plastic bag, close the bag loosely, and let the dough rise for 30 to 35 minutes, or until almost doubled.

Gently deflate the dough. Turn the dough out onto a lightly floured surface. Divide the dough into 4 portions and shape each into a roll 12 to 14 inches long. Place 2 rolls several inches apart on each of the prepared baking sheets. Spray the tops of the loaves with nonstick cooking spray, and place each set of baking sheets in a large plastic bag. Close the bags loosely and let the dough rise for 30 to 60 minutes, or until almost doubled.

Preheat the oven to 375°F. Place the baking sheets in the oven on the center and lower shelves, lower the heat to 350°F, and bake for 30 to 35 minutes, or until the loaves are lightly browned and sound hollow when tapped. Let cool on a wire rack for at least 15 minutes before slicing for sandwiches.

CUBAN-STYLE SANDWICHES

A *plancha* griddle is traditionally used to grill Cuban sandwiches, which resemble panini. I weigh down my sandwiches in a cast-iron skillet with a couple of heavy plates. If you can't bake fresh bread, any hearty white bread will do in a pinch.

To make sandwiches, cut 1 loaf in half lengthwise. Spread 1 tablespoon mayonnaise and some Dijon mustard on each half of the bread. Add a few slices of cold pork (or smoked chicken) and some sliced cold ham (or smoked turkey). Top with Swiss cheese, tomatoes, lettuce, and pickles. Melt some butter in a large skillet over medium heat. Place the sandwich in the pan, weigh it down with a heavy pot or several plates, and grill for 2 to 3 minutes on each side.

**B.B.
Test Kitchen
Notes**

The Global Baker

The bulk of the recipes at BetterBaking.com are based on North American and European baking traditions, but I, and many of my visitors, have begun to explore the baking on the rest of the planet. I've been happy to provide bakers with recipes for South American *Alfajores* (page 153), Indian nan (page 107), Armenian Lavosh (page 104), and other treats, but sometimes I'm stumped. One visitor asked how to make Japanese *panko* bread crumbs at home. These bread crumbs have the consistency of crushed potato chips, and they give foods a terrific crunchy texture. I was unable to come up with a workable formula for homemade panko crumbs (you can find them in most Asian markets), but that got me looking into Japanese baking. The global baker marches on!

LITTLE ITALY ITALIAN BREAD

MAKES 2 LARGE LOAVES

SPONGE

¾ cup warm water

½ teaspoon instant yeast

1 cup bread flour

DOUGH

Sponge, above

3¼ cups warm water

1½ teaspoons instant yeast

1 tablespoon salt

6 to 7 cups bread flour

I'm a baker who writes and a writer who bakes, depending on the day. I also love movies and the role food plays on-screen. At the site, there are a few recipes "inspired by the reel." This recipe salutes the film Moonstruck, a favorite of mine, in which Nicholas Cage plays Johnny Cammareri, owner of an Italian bakery. The love of food and the respect for how the simplest dish is prepared stand out in the film. The sponge can be made 1 day ahead.

Stack 2 baking sheets together and line the top one with parchment paper. Set aside.

For the sponge, hand whisk the water and yeast together in the bowl of an electric mixer and let stand for 2 to 3 minutes to dissolve the yeast. Stir in the flour to make a thick batter. Place the bowl in a large plastic bag and let stand at room temperature for at least 4 hours or up to overnight.

For the dough, stir down the sponge to deflate it and add the water, yeast, salt, and 6 cups of the flour. Mix to make a soft mass. Knead with the dough hook on the lowest speed of the mixer for 8 to 10 minutes, gradually adding more flour as required to form a soft dough. Turn the dough out onto a lightly floured surface. Form the dough into a ball and place it in a lightly greased bowl. Place the bowl in a large plastic bag, close the bag loosely, and let the dough rise for 30 to 40 minutes, or until almost doubled.

Turn the dough out onto a lightly floured surface and form it into a ball. Return the dough to the bowl, spray it with nonstick cooking spray, and return to the plastic bag to rise for 1 hour. Turn the dough out onto the floured surface and divide the dough in half. Form each half into a ball and place several inches apart on the prepared baking sheets. Spray with cooking spray and place the baking sheets in the plastic bag. Let the dough rise again for 45 to 90 minutes, or until almost doubled in size.

Preheat the oven to 450°F. Place the loaves in the oven. Using a spray bottle filled with water, lightly mist the loaves. Place the loaves in the oven and spray the oven walls, being careful to avoid the light. Lower the oven temperature to 425°F. Bake, misting the loaves and the oven walls every few minutes for the first 15 minutes, for 40 to 55 minutes, or until very well browned. Let cool on a wire rack for at least 15 minutes before serving.

New York City Bagel Bread

MAKES 1 LARGE LOAF

DOUGH

2½ cups warm water

5½ teaspoons instant yeast

1 teaspoon malt powder or firmly
    packed brown sugar

1 tablespoon white sugar

2 tablespoons honey

2½ teaspoons salt

2 tablespoons vegetable oil

6 to 7 cups bread flour

Rye flour or cornmeal for dusting

TOPPING

2 tablespoons vegetable oil

2 tablespoons water

1 onion, finely chopped

6 cloves garlic, minced

3 tablespoons poppy seeds

Coarse salt for sprinkling

There are bagels, bagel boards, bagel sticks, and my New York bagel bread, which is bagel dough fashioned into a twisted loaf. It bakes up with a crusty, bagel-like exterior and a tender, light crumb. Add a hefty coating of minced garlic, onions, and poppy seeds and a touch of coarse salt, and you have a centerpiece for a brunch.

Stack 2 baking sheets together and line the top one with parchment paper. Set aside.

For the dough, hand whisk the water and yeast together in the bowl of an electric mixer and let stand for 2 to 3 minutes to dissolve the yeast. Stir in the malt powder, white sugar, honey, salt, oil, and 6 cups of the bread flour. Mix to make a soft mass. Knead with the dough hook on the lowest speed of the mixer for 8 to 10 minutes, gradually adding more bread flour as required to form a soft, elastic dough. Turn the dough out onto a lightly floured surface and form it into a ball. Place the dough in a lightly greased bowl. Place the bowl in a large plastic bag, close the bag loosely, and let the dough rise for 30 to 45 minutes, or until almost doubled.

Gently deflate the dough. Turn the dough out onto a lightly floured surface. Divide the dough into 6 portions and form each into a rope about 8 inches long. Place 2 sets of 3 ropes side by side and braid each set together. Place one braid on top of the other and pinch the ends together to seal.

Place the loaf on the prepared baking sheets and generously dust the top with rye flour. Place the baking sheets in the plastic bag, close the bag loosely, and let the dough rise for 2 to 4 hours in a cool place (a chilly garage is fine), or until almost doubled in size.

Preheat the oven to 375°F. For the topping, toss all the ingredients together in a bowl. Cover the loaf with the topping and sprinkle with the salt. Place the bread in the oven and bake for 30 minutes. Lower the heat to 350°F and bake 25 to 35 minutes longer, or until the loaf is well browned. Let cool on a wire rack for at least 15 minutes before serving.

FRENCH COUNTRY BREAD

MAKES 1 LARGE ROUND LOAF

SPONGE

1 cup warm water, preferably
  spring water

½ teaspoon instant yeast

1¼ cups bread flour, preferably
  organic

2 tablespoons whole-wheat flour,
  preferably organic

2 tablespoons rye flour, preferably
  organic

DOUGH

Sponge, above

1 cup warm water, preferably
  spring water

¾ teaspoon instant yeast

2½ teaspoons salt

1 tablespoon white sugar

½ teaspoon malt powder or firmly
  packed brown sugar

3 to 4 cups bread flour

This is one of my favorite tried-and-true breads. I point new and old bakers toward this recipe when they request a rustic bread with a crisp crust. The recipe uses a sponge, also referred to as a poolish, which is essentially an immature starter. As with a starter, it is a slurrylike mixture of flour, water, and yeast that develops with time into what bakers call a "pre-ferment" or starter. The sponge can be made the night before the bread is baked.

Stack 2 baking sheets together and line the top one with parchment paper. Set aside.

For the sponge, hand whisk the water and yeast together in a small bowl and let stand for 2 to 3 minutes to dissolve the yeast. Stir in the flours to make a thick mixture. Loosely cover the bowl with plastic wrap and let stand at room temperature for at least 4 hours or up to overnight.

For the dough, stir down the sponge to deflate it. In the bowl of an electric mixer, combine the water and yeast and hand whisk briefly. Add the sponge and hand whisk for a minute or two to combine the ingredients. Stir in the salt, white sugar, malt powder, and 3 cups of the bread flour. Mix to make a soft mass. Let stand for 12 to 15 minutes. Knead with the dough hook on the lowest speed of the mixer for 8 to 10 minutes, gradually adding more bread flour as required to form a soft but resilient dough. The dough will be smooth and elastic but not too stiff. Turn the dough out onto a lightly floured surface, and form into a ball. Place the dough in a lightly greased bowl. Place the bowl in a large plastic bag, close the bag loosely, and let the dough rise for 45 to 90 minutes, or until almost doubled in size.

Gently deflate the dough. Turn it out onto a lightly floured surface and form it into a taut ball, tucking the bottommost parts of dough in and underneath toward the center of the ball to increase surface tension. Place the ball on the prepared baking sheets. Spray it with nonstick cooking spray and place the sheets in the plastic bag. Let the dough rise again for 2 to 4 hours, or until almost doubled in size.

Preheat the oven to 475°F. Slash the top of the loaf across the middle with a sharp knife. (If the dough deflates when you slash it, it rose too much—the heat of the oven should help it spring back.) Using a spray bottle filled with water, mist the top of the loaf, then dust it lightly with flour. Place the loaf on the lower shelf and spray the oven walls with water, taking care to avoid the oven light. Bake for 20 minutes, misting the loaf every 5 minutes for the first 15 minutes. Lower the heat to 425°F. Bake 15 to 20 minutes longer, or until the loaf is well browned. Let cool on a wire rack for at least 15 minutes before slicing. Store, cut side down, on a counter, lightly wrapped in a clean towel.

FRENCH COUNTRY BREAD ON THE GRILL

MAKES 2 ROUND LOAVES

French Country Bread (page 47), prepared through the first rise of the dough

Summers used to pose a problem for the baker girl. As balmy temperatures arrived, my sons would vow, nay, threaten, that if I so much as glanced at, let alone dare preheat the oven to bake bread, our familial ties would be history. Desperate to bake in the summer (and to engage others in the same pursuit), I even sent away for detailed plans to build a scaled-down version of an outdoor wood-fired bread oven. I still have the plans, and lots of aged maple firewood, but no outdoor oven.

One day, after spending a little time in the NIMIK (Necessity-Is-the-Mother-of-Invention Kitchen), I had it: why not use the grill! In a flash, I suddenly realized that my trusty Weber gas grill was, in fact, my summer oven. My foray into grill baking began with an herb and garlic focaccia, and was quickly followed by farmhouse-style potato bread. Then came pita and, best of all, pizza on the grill (see page 89). When I made a batch of nan to go with a dinner of tandoori chicken and basmati rice, my guests swooned. When I baked French country bread on the grill, I became a legend.

~♦~

Stack 2 baking sheets together and line the top one with parchment paper.

On a lightly floured surface, divide the dough in half and shape it into 2 balls. Place the balls several inches apart on the baking sheets. Place the baking sheets in a large plastic bag, close the bag loosely, and let the dough rise for 2 to 4 hours, or until almost doubled.

Preheat a gas grill to high, 450°F to 475°F. Place the baking sheets directly on the grill and close the cover. Immediately lower the heat to medium (400°F). Bake for 25 minutes, or until well browned. Decrease the heat to low and place the bread directly on the grill. Bake for an additional 5 minutes, or until the loaves sound hollow when tapped on the top surface. Let cool on a wire rack for at least 20 minutes before serving.

B.B.
Test Kitchen Notes

A Good Complexion Needs Moisture and Rest

French loaves should have a taut *skin*, or membrane. This produces the thin, crisp crust that is prized by bakers. When you form your loaves, try to keep the surface of the dough as taut as you can, particularly when using the heel of your hand to seal the edges. It's almost as if you are pulling a membrane of the dough over itself. Once the loaves are in the oven, mist them with water every few minutes for the first 10 to 15 minutes of baking to create a shiny crust.

TIPS FOR GRILLING

Though charcoal grills will certainly work for breads, I prefer the controlled heat of gas grills. I tested my grill-bread recipes with several gas models. Weber is my favorite because of its design, consistent performance, pervasive and even heat, and surface capacity. But there are other great choices, and the upscale grill market grows each year.

For all grill baking, you will have to watch your grill closely. You'll soon learn to be flexible as far as methods go, adjusting the heat and your technique according to what you are baking and the ambient conditions. In general, large, round loaves require a medium heat of about 400°F to bake well. On a cool day, a higher setting may be necessary. Thin or flat loaves can be baked at a very high temperature (450°F to 500°F) as long as you watch them closely. Be prepared to move in quickly to turn flat loaves over—they can be ready in as few as 5 minutes. Larger loaves will take 25 to 35 minutes to bake. On a chilly evening, however, you might have to crank up the grill to high.

The best way to bake a large loaf thoroughly and not burn the bottom is to start it on doubled-up baking sheets. I advise placing parchment paper on the top sheet and allowing the loaf to rise on it. Place the baking sheets on a preheated grill and let the loaf bake until it appears to be about three-quarters done, or when it appears set up and firm but only beginning to color. Remove the loaf from the sheets, decrease the heat to low, and finish baking directly on the grill. You may also use a cast-iron skillet to bake a loaf or a pizza (see page 89) for extra-crisp bottom crusts.

Start your pan on medium, then lower the heat after 5 minutes and finish the loaf directly on the grill. No matter your method, make sure you equip yourself with heavy-duty elbow-length oven mitts and a pair of long tongs.

If you are using a charcoal grill for breads, I recommend a combination of three-quarters briquettes and one-quarter hardwood charcoal, such as mesquite. The former burn longer and more evenly, while the latter heats fast and adds a nice flavor to the bread. You can also scatter some presoaked hickory or maple chips on the coals. Prepare a medium-hot fire and allow the grill to preheat for about 15 minutes with the cover closed before adding the bread. Place the bread, set on the doubled baking sheets, directly on the grill and close the grill top. You may open it periodically to check on the baking process. For longer-baking breads or if making multiple pizzas, you may have to replenish the coals, so keep an eye on the heat level.

I have also explored a unique grill called the Big Green Egg (see page 304). This egg-shaped grill resembles a huge hinged Mason jar. The shell is made of a porcelain-glazed ceramic, and the unit burns lump charcoal. It can serve as a grill, smoker, and all-around outdoor bread and pizza oven, and it can even replicate a tandoor for my nan bread (page 107). A Big Green Egg will cost you more than a conventional grill, but if you're looking for something different, I recommend it.

PAIN ORDINAIRE: NOT-SO-ORDINARY FRENCH BREAD

MAKES 3 LOAVES

Cornmeal for dusting

¼ cup warm water

1 tablespoon instant yeast

2 cups cold water

2 teaspoons salt

½ teaspoon malt powder or firmly packed brown sugar

5½ to 6½ cups all-purpose or bread flour

At BetterBaking.com, I receive many requests for French bread recipes. Usually, my visitors are searching for "French-looking" bread. Looks can be deceiving. This recipe produces the kind of bread baked every day in France. It is in the shape of a stubby baguette, sometimes referred to as a bâtard or parisienne. Much like a vin ordinaire, which is everyday table wine, this is pain ordinaire. It is thin of crust and light of crumb and delicious with cheese or fruit, or as the foundation for a cold-cut sandwich.

~❦~

Stack 2 large baking sheets together and line the top one with parchment paper. Sprinkle the parchment paper with cornmeal. Set aside.

In the bowl of an electric mixer, hand whisk the warm water and yeast together and let stand for 2 to 3 minutes to dissolve the yeast. Stir in the cold water, salt, malt powder, and 5½ cups of the flour. Mix to make a soft mass. Knead with the dough hook on the lowest speed of the mixer for 8 to 10 minutes, gradually adding more flour as required to form a soft, springy dough. Turn the dough out onto a lightly floured surface and form into a ball. Place the dough in a lightly greased bowl. Place the bowl in a large plastic bag, close the bag loosely, and let the dough rise for 3 to 4 hours in a cool place (a chilly garage is fine), or until almost doubled.

Gently deflate the dough. Spray the top with nonstick cooking spray, and return it to the plastic bag. Close loosely and let the dough rise for 1½ to 2 hours, or until almost doubled.

Gently deflate the dough. Turn the dough out onto a floured surface and divide into 3 portions. Using a rolling pin, roll out each portion into an oval about 8 by 10 inches. Fold in the left and right sides of the dough, meeting in the center. Fold the top down to meet the bottom edge. Use the heel of one hand to seal the edges. Roll the dough to form a 14-inch cylinder. Repeat with the remaining portions. Place the loaves on the prepared baking sheets, several inches apart. Spray the tops of the loaves with nonstick cooking spray and place the sheets in large plastic bags. Let the loaves rise for 45 to 60 minutes, or until puffy and almost doubled.

Preheat the oven to 450°F. Slash each loaf diagonally with a sharp knife. Using a spray bottle filled with water, lightly mist the loaves. Place the loaves in the oven on the center and lower shelves and spray the oven walls, being careful to avoid the oven light. Immediately lower the oven temperature to 425°F and bake, misting the oven walls every few minutes in the first 10 minutes, for 20 to 25 minutes, or until the loaves are lightly browned and sound hollow when tapped. Let cool on a wire rack for at least 15 minutes before serving.

Mediterranean Stuffed Sun-Dried Tomato Bread

MAKES 1 LOAF

Semolina or cornmeal for dusting

FILLING

4 tablespoons minced fresh flat-leaf parsley

¼ cup finely chopped onion or scallions

¾ cup finely chopped dry-packed sun-dried tomatoes, plumped and patted dry (see page 18)

3 cloves garlic, minced

1 cup black olives, pitted and chopped

3 tablespoons extra virgin olive oil, plus more for topping

½ teaspoon salt

½ teaspoon freshly ground black pepper

½ to 1 teaspoon dried oregano

½ to 1 teaspoon dried basil

1 cup crumbled feta cheese

French Country Bread (page 47), prepared through first rise of the dough

Zesty and chock-full of summery flavor, this is pure picnic and party fare. Room-temperature squares of this bread work well as an appetizer with wine or sangria, and big warm wedges make salad a meal. This recipe was one of the first I designed to be baked on an outdoor grill (see page 49), but I often make it in a traditional oven. It's such an interesting bread that, if you're in a hurry, even store-bought frozen white-bread dough will produce a unique bread.

Stack 2 baking sheets together and line the top one with parchment paper. Sprinkle with semolina. Set aside.

For the filling, toss all the ingredients together in a medium bowl.

After the first rise is complete, place the dough on a lightly floured surface and gently deflate the dough. Form it into an 8- by 10-inch oval shape, ½ to ¾ inch thick. Press half of the topping mixture into the dough. Fold the top of the dough over to meet the bottom and pinch the edges to seal. Let the loaf rest for 5 to 8 minutes. Flatten the loaf with a rolling pin, taking care to keep the filling inside. Press the remaining filling into the top of the dough. Fold the dough over again and pinch the edges to seal. Spread a bit of olive oil on top of the loaf. Place the loaf on the prepared baking sheet and place the sheet in a large plastic bag. Close the bag loosely and let the loaf rise for 45 to 90 minutes, or until puffy.

Preheat the oven to 400°F. Bake for 15 minutes, then lower the heat to 350°F. Continue baking for 20 to 30 minutes, or until lightly browned. Let cool on a wire rack for at least 15 minutes before serving.

A French Butter Dish

If bread and butter are staples in your home, consider acquiring a French butter dish, or butter "keeper." It consists of a lid with a high lip, and a container in which the lid is placed. Fresh butter or My Homemade Butter Spread (page 29) is packed into the lid, which is inverted onto a base filled with water. This creates a seal that keeps air away from the butter, ensuring that the butter stays fresh and soft. The dish works very well in a temperate environment, but refrigeration is required if temperatures rise above 90°F. At room temperature, the dish will retard spoilage, but it will not prevent it. The butter will stay fresh for about 1 week. Pack the butter in tightly to prevent air pockets and clean the dish thoroughly now and then. My favorite French butter dish is made by James Sloss in Oregon (see Source Guide, page 306).

SOURDOUGH BREAD

MAKES 1 LARGE LOAF

Cornmeal for sprinkling

1½ cups mature White Sourdough Starter (opposite), at room temperature and recently refreshed

1½ cups water

2 teaspoons instant yeast

½ teaspoon malt powder or firmly packed brown sugar

2 teaspoons salt

1 teaspoon white sugar

3 tablespoons olive oil

2 tablespoons semolina (optional)

4 to 5 cups bread flour

This is a rustic loaf that bakers in Montreal sometimes call a Canadienne, but it is more generically known as a boule, or a round loaf. It's not as airy as a baguette, and it has a softer crust. This dough makes outstanding pizza, too. I prefer a sourdough that is mildly acidic. If your sourdough tastes more like a sour rye, your starter is probably too acidic. To remedy this, remove and discard several cups of your starter (instead of the usual 1 cup) before each feeding. Eventually, the mixture will mellow.

This recipe calls for added yeast; if you decide to work without it, double or triple your rising times.

Stack 2 baking sheets together and line the top one with parchment paper. Sprinkle with cornmeal. Set aside.

In the bowl of an electric mixer, stir down the starter to deflate it. Stir in the water, yeast, malt powder, salt, white sugar, olive oil, semolina, and 4 cups of the flour. Mix to make a soft mass. Let rest for 10 to 12 minutes. Knead with the dough hook on the lowest speed of the mixer for 8 to 10 minutes, gradually adding more flour as required to form a soft dough. Turn the dough out onto a lightly floured board and form it into a ball. Place the dough in a lightly greased bowl. Place the bowl inside a large plastic bag, close the bag loosely, and let the dough rise for 30 to 45 minutes, or until almost doubled.

Gently deflate the dough. Spray the top with nonstick cooking spray and return the dough to the plastic bag. Let rise for 1 to 2 hours, or until puffy and 75 to 80 percent larger in volume.

Gently deflate the dough. Turn the dough out onto a lightly floured surface and form it into a large ball. Place it on the prepared baking sheets and spray the dough with nonstick cooking spray. Place the baking sheets in the plastic bag, close the bag loosely, and let the dough rise for 2 to 4 hours, or until puffy.

Preheat the oven to 500°F. Using a sharp knife, make 3 or 4 diagonal slashes 1½ inches apart on the top of the loaf. Using a spray bottle filled with water, lightly mist the top of the loaf, then dust it with flour. Place in the oven and immediately lower the heat to 450°F. Lightly mist the oven walls, taking care to avoid the oven light. Mist the oven several times in the first 10 minutes of baking, then lower the heat to 400°F. Bake for an additional 35 to 45 minutes, or until the loaf is well browned. Let cool on a wire rack for at least 30 minutes before serving.

WHITE SOURDOUGH STARTER

MAKES 5 TO 8 CUPS

2 cups plus 5 cups water, preferably
  spring water, at room
  temperature

2 cups plus 5 cups bread flour or
  all-purpose, preferably organic

Hand whisk 2 cups of the water and 2 cups of the flour together in a medium bowl to make a puddinglike mixture. Cover loosely with plastic wrap and let stand at room temperature for at least 2 days or up to 4 days, or until it bubbles and has a slightly sour, fermented aroma.

Whisk in 1 cup of the water and 1 cup of the flour at about the same time every day for 5 days. After the 5 days of feeding have passed, the starter should be bubbly and foamy. It can be used immediately or refrigerated in a sealed glass container. (See page 54 for instructions on maintaining a starter.)

If your starter is sluggish—meaning that it looks flat and lifeless, with no form or bubbles—it may need more time or another day or two of feedings. Alternatively, you can at any point stir in ¼ to ½ teaspoon instant yeast to move it along. This will change its nature slightly, but it will still be very good for baking.

**B.B.
Test Kitchen
Notes**

A Good Bread Knife—the Kindest Cut of All

Cutting a fresh loaf of bread into relatively neat slices is a challenge. If you have a few thousand dollars to spare, you can purchase one of those commercial slicers (they sound like a hardware-store paint-can shaker, and they always cut the heel of a loaf too thinly). You can buy a wooden cutting board equipped with guide demarcations. Or you can simply rely on your basic cutting board. In any event, invest in a good knife. I like a 10-inch serrated blade that is slightly curved so that you can reach the last bit of crust as you saw. LamsonSharp makes a 10-inch offset slicer that I'm very fond of (even though it is not formally sold as a "bread knife"), but their 10-inch, rosewood-handled bread knife is the best one I have ever used. See the Source Guide (page 306), and spend a few dollars to see your bread-baking efforts through to an elegant conclusion.

Sourdough—the word conjures up mystery and the promise of unique flavors. Many believe the creation of a good sourdough is the pinnacle of the baking art. By their very nature, no two sourdough loaves are alike, and no two bakers will agree entirely on ingredients and technique. Essentially, a new starter ingests wild yeast spores in the air, thus starting the fermentation process. A "sour" fragrance develops as the starter matures, which is what lends the finished bread its characteristic tang. When the elements come together well, the pursuit of the perfect sourdough can become a passion. You can make a sourdough with a mature starter, dough from a previous batch of dough, with a sponge, or with commercial dry-starter packets. I'll address each type of starter in turn.

BASIC STARTER

A *basic starter*, such as the one on page 53, is made up of flour and a liquid (usually spring water) combined to form a puddinglike mixture that is fermented at room temperature. Starters can also be made with other liquids, such as milk, yogurt, or potato water. Some bakers are purists and eschew anything but water and flour—the natural elements of bread—in their sourdoughs. Others are more adventurous and see compatibilities among flour, water, and a host of different ingredients.

I recommend using organic flour for your starter or sponge, as starters made with organic flour seem to capture the more interesting yeasts. The resulting crumb, crust, and flavor are wonderful. Since most mainstream flour companies now offer a line of organic flours, tracking them down isn't as hard as it once was. Organic loaves can be more challenging and take more experience (the dough can be sluggish and heavy, or need a more leisurely rise), but the effort is well worth it. You may wish to launch your starter with organic flour and feed it with all-purpose flour thereafter. Otherwise, use the best bread flour you can find. You may wish to add a bit of whole-wheat or rye flour to the mixture for extra flavor (even if you prepare a white loaf with the starter). Spring water is the perfect complement for your fine flours; chlorine and other substances in tap water can interfere with the delicate fermentation process.

In order to grow, a starter must be fed, much like any other living thing. Add flour and water, in equal proportions, every day for 5 days to nourish and strengthen your crop of wild yeast. Your starter should show signs of activity within 3 days or so, depending on the ambient temperature. A good starter will be frothy and bubbly, and it will smell slightly yeasty and sweet. Trust your senses and growing expertise. If you detect any "off" odors, discard the mixture and start again. That said, a good starter smells a touch musty and acidic. A pinkish color is a sign that the starter has been taken over by unwanted bacteria, and you should discard it immediately. With billions of yeast spores floating around, it's the luck of the draw. After 5 days of feeding, a successful starter can be used immediately or refrigerated in a sealed container.

To maintain the vitality of a starter, you should refresh it once a week. Remove it from the refrigerator and allow it to warm to room temperature for about 2 hours. Discard 1 cup of the starter and stir in 1 cup each of flour and water. Let the starter stand at room temperature for 2 to 6 hours, until it is bubbly, foamy, and active. Return the starter to the refrigerator. If you happen to miss a weekly feeding—or several—not to worry; starters are hearty and can stay dormant for months in the refrigerator without attention. Simply feed the starter as described above; if it bubbles and foams after the feeding, warmth, and attention, it's alive and well.

To use a mature starter, remove it from the refrigerator the night before baking and allow it to warm to room temperature for about 1 hour. Discard 1 cup and feed the starter with 1 cup each of flour and water, stirring to incorporate. Let the starter sit out overnight and proceed with the recipe the next day. If the starter isn't bubbly and foamy, you can revive it by adding ½ teaspoon instant yeast and allowing another 2 to 4 hours to rise.

Some loaves are made with natural yeast starter alone, and others (including the one on page 52) call for commercial yeast as well. Purists will tell you that the addition of yeast alters the nature of the starter. The dough will rise faster and more dependably if you use commercial yeast, however, and the result will be almost as good. A touch of commercial yeast can also be added to a sluggish starter to get things rolling.

PÂTE FERMENTÉE

Another way to make a starter is to make a regular batch of dough (sour or otherwise) and set aside about 1 generous cup of it in the refrigerator or freezer. This starter is called *pâte fermentée*, or "old dough." It's an effective and convenient (if less magical) way to make sourdough, and another insight into how versatile (as well as inventive and forgiving) this class of breads is. Many commercial bakeries use this method because it's more convenient than maintaining a conventional starter. For every batch of dough, they hold back about 10 percent to use as a starter for the next batch. To use *pâte fermentée* as your starter, let it warm to room temperature and add it to the other dough ingredients. It will keep in the freezer for up to 2 months.

SPONGE

Because of their many advantages, I use sponges extensively in my test kitchen. A sponge (also known as a *poolish*) is a comparatively quicker, or less mature, starter consisting of equal parts water and flour, and a touch of yeast (¼ to ½ teaspoon per cup of flour). The puddinglike mixture can stand at room temperature from 2 to 16 hours and not lose its potency or need feeding. If you don't have a starter, if your starter is not ready, or if you're new to starter baking, a sponge is a good way to begin. Sponge-based bread is less complex in flavor and texture than a full-fledged sourdough, but has a more interesting crumb than a conventional straight dough. Frankly, I sometimes prefer a sponge starter for a white rustic bread, and I preserve my matured sourdough starters for breads where I'm really after that rustic tang and chewy, hearty crust.

COMMERCIAL STARTER

Commercial sourdough starters are practically an oxymoron. Even if the dry starter packet reads "San Francisco Sourdough," by the time you feed it water and flour from Ohio or Mississippi, its character is transformed. (I'm told that yeast companies are mastering the sourdough gene pool, and you soon may indeed be able to preserve the cultural character of sourdough by using dry starters.) A commercial starter may produce good dough, but the idea behind a traditional starter is that it draws on the diverse elements in your own environment in order to produce unique flavors. Besides, tending your own starter from scratch is much more fun and rewarding.

Many books have been written about sourdough baking. You can get caught up with temperatures, thermometers, and feeding schedules, or you can just dive in and experiment. Nothing terrible will happen. At first you will have sluggish, dense breads. Then they will gradually become higher, better, crustier— but all the while, you will have fresh, hot, real bread of your own making that is light years ahead of the corner store variety and just plain fun and instructive to make.

B.B.
Test Kitchen Notes

The "Holy Crumb" of Sourdough

A wet, loose dough tends to produce loaves with large holes: the "holy crumb" of sourdough. At first, you may find it difficult to resist adding more flour, but in time, you will learn that wet (albeit less manageable) dough makes for great bread. Invest in a dough scraper. Once you have just brought your dough into a mass, let it rest for 10 to 15 minutes. This rest (or autolyse) allows the dough to strengthen, reducing the amount of flour you need to add to make the dough more manageable.

Sourdough takes quite a while to rise (in fact, the longer the better). Forget the damp kitchen towel or plastic wrap over the rising dough—you need a good "proofing tent." Place your bowl or baking sheet in a large plastic bag, close the bag loosely, and park it in a cool area. It should sit undisturbed while the magic happens inside.

New York Bakery Corn Bread

MAKES 2 LARGE LOAVES

RYE STARTER

3½ cups warm water

1 teaspoon instant yeast

3 cups dark rye or pumpernickel
flour

½ cup bread flour

Cornmeal for sprinkling

DOUGH

Rye Starter, above

2 cups warm water

½ cup stone-ground cornmeal

1 tablespoon salt

2 tablespoons caraway seeds

4 cups dark rye flour

3 to 4 cups bread flour

This corn bread is hardly corny at all—it's actually a dense, lightly colored rye loaf and my favorite emissary of sourdough culture. This recipe calls for a rye starter, as opposed to a white starter, and will yield enough dough for 2 good loaves. The starter needs to be made 2 days before baking. For more insights into sourdough, see page 54.

For the starter, hand whisk the water and yeast together in the bowl of an electric mixer and let stand for 2 to 3 minutes to dissolve the yeast. Stir in the rye and bread flours to make a thick batter. Place the bowl in a large plastic bag, close the bag loosely, and let the starter stand for 2 days in a cool place. The starter should be foamy and bubbly.

Stack 2 baking sheets together and line the top one with parchment paper. Sprinkle cornmeal on top. Set aside.

For the dough, stir down the starter to deflate it. Stir in the water, cornmeal, salt, caraway seeds, rye flour, and 3 cups of the bread flour. Mix to make a soft mass. Knead with the dough hook on the lowest speed of the mixer for 8 to 10 minutes, gradually adding more flour as required to form a soft dough. Turn the dough out onto a lightly floured surface and form the dough into a ball. Place it in a lightly greased bowl. Place the bowl in a large plastic bag, close the bag loosely, and let the dough rise for 2 to 4 hours, or until almost doubled.

Gently deflate the dough. Spray the top with nonstick cooking spray, return it to the plastic bag, and let rise for 1 to 2 hours, or until quite puffy. Turn the dough out onto a lightly floured surface. Shape the dough into 2 large, round loaves, and place them on the prepared baking sheets. Allow the loaves to rise for 1 to 2 hours, or until they have grown two-thirds in size.

Preheat the oven to 425°F. Using a sharp knife, make 3 or 4 diagonal slashes 1½ inches apart on top of each loaf. Using a spray bottle filled with water, lightly mist the tops of the loaves, then dust the tops of the loaves lightly with flour. Misting the oven several times in the first 10 minutes of baking, bake the bread for 35 to 45 minutes, or until the loaves are well browned. Let cool on a wire rack for at least 15 minutes before serving.

CARROT-CINNAMON-RAISIN BREAD

MAKES 1 LARGE OR 2 SMALLER LOAVES

3 large carrots, peeled and halved

1½ cups warm water

2 tablespoons instant yeast

⅓ cup sugar, plus more for sprinkling

2 teaspoons salt

¼ cup vegetable oil

1½ teaspoons ground cinnamon, plus more for dusting

Zest of 1 orange, finely minced

¼ teaspoon orange oil or extract (optional)

5 to 6 cups bread flour

1¼ cups raisins, plumped and patted dry (see page 18)

⅓ cup walnuts, toasted and chopped (see page 17), optional

Melted butter or milk for glazing

If you like carrot cake, you'll enjoy this perky loaf. It takes well to cream cheese, and it's delicious toasted and spread with honey and butter.

⁓⟨◇⟩⁓

Spray one 12- by 5-inch or two 8- by 4-inch loaf pans with nonstick cooking spray. Line a large baking sheet with parchment paper. Set aside.

Cook the carrots in a saucepan of boiling water for about 5 minutes, or until fork-tender but not mushy. Drain and rinse the carrots with cold water to halt cooking. Using the large holes of a box grater, shred the carrots and measure out 2 cups.

In the bowl of an electric mixer, hand whisk the warm water and yeast together and let stand for 2 to 3 minutes to dissolve the yeast. Stir in the carrots, sugar, salt, oil, cinnamon, orange zest, orange oil, and 5 cups of the flour. Mix to make a soft mass. Knead with the dough hook on the lowest speed of the mixer for 8 to 10 minutes, gradually adding more flour as required to form a soft dough. Turn the dough out onto a lightly floured surface and form the dough into a ball. Place the dough in a lightly greased bowl. Place the bowl in a large plastic bag, close the bag loosely, and let the dough rest for about 30 to 40 minutes.

Gently deflate the dough. Turn the dough out onto a lightly floured surface and press the raisins and nuts into it. Form the dough into a large ball, return to the bowl, and spray the top lightly with nonstick cooking spray. Return the bowl to the plastic bag, close the bag loosely, and let the dough rise for 30 to 45 minutes, or until almost doubled.

Turn the dough out onto a lightly floured surface and divide the dough into 5 portions if using 1 large pan, 6 portions if using 2 pans. Form the pieces into small balls and place the balls in the large pan, or divide between the 2 pans. Brush the tops with melted butter, then sprinkle with sugar and dust lightly with cinnamon. Return the pan(s) to the plastic bag, close loosely, and let the dough rise for 30 to 45 minutes, or until almost doubled.

Preheat the oven to 350°F. Place the pan(s) on the prepared baking sheets and bake for 35 to 40 minutes, or until the bread is lightly browned. Let cool on a wire rack for 10 minutes before unmolding to cool completely.

VIDALIA ONION BREAD

MAKES 1 LARGE LOAF

DOUGH

1½ cups warm water

2 tablespoons instant yeast

2 tablespoons sugar

2½ teaspoons salt

1 egg

¼ cup vegetable oil

5 to 6 cups bread flour

FILLING

2 tablespoons vegetable oil

1½ pounds Vidalia or other sweet
    white onions, diced (4 cups)

¼ teaspoon salt

1 tablespoon poppy seeds

1 egg, lightly beaten, or butter-
    flavored nonstick cooking spray

Bread and onions are a favorite combination at BB. This onion bread, baked in a round pan, is chock-full of onions, fragrance, and good looks. A wedge of this loaf with Swiss cheese, Dijon mustard, and pastrami or smoked turkey is heavenly.

Spray a 9- or 10-inch round springform pan with nonstick cooking spray. Line a baking sheet with parchment paper. Set aside.

For the dough, hand whisk the water and yeast together in the bowl of an electric mixer and let stand for 2 to 3 minutes to dissolve the yeast. Stir in the sugar, salt, egg, oil, and 5 cups of the flour. Mix to make a soft mass. Knead with the dough hook on the lowest speed of the mixer for 8 to 10 minutes, gradually adding more flour as required to form an elastic dough. Turn the dough out onto a lightly floured surface and form it into a ball. Place the dough in a lightly greased bowl. Place the bowl in a large plastic bag, close the bag loosely, and let the dough rise for 30 to 45 minutes, or until almost doubled.

Meanwhile, make the filling. In a small saucepan, heat the oil over low heat and sauté the onions for 3 to 5 minutes, or until soft. Transfer the onions to a bowl and toss with the salt and poppy seeds. Set aside.

Gently deflate the dough. Turn the dough out onto a lightly floured surface and roll out into a round about 12 inches in diameter. Let the dough rest for 1 to 3 minutes or so if it retracts as you are doing this. Press the onions into the dough. Fold the dough in half to cover the onions. Cut it with a sharp knife into 16 equal hunks. Arrange the dough pieces in the prepared pan. Brush the tops with the beaten egg. Return the pan to the large plastic bag, close the bag loosely, and let rise for 30 to 45 minutes, or until almost doubled in bulk.

Preheat the oven to 350°F. Place the pan on the prepared baking sheet and bake for 40 to 45 minutes, or until well browned. Let cool in the pan on a wire rack for 10 minutes before removing the sides of the pan.

ANOTHA' CHALLAH

MAKES 1 LARGE LOAF

DOUGH

1½ cups warm water

2 tablespoons instant yeast

½ cup vegetable oil

½ cup sugar

2 eggs

1 egg yolk

1 tablespoon salt

6 to 7 cups bread flour

EGG WASH

1 egg

1 egg yolk

1 tablespoon water

Sesame seeds for sprinkling

I like to tweak recipes to create unusual variations. There are several recipes for challah on the website and many more in my first book. This particular challah is a velvety, golden loaf that is a touch sweeter and richer than many. It offers tender strands and an addictive crumb, and is especially delicious in my Bread Pudding Muffins (page 188).

~⟨◊⟩~

Spray a 12- by 5-inch loaf pan or two 9- by 5-inch loaf pans with nonstick cooking spray. Line a large baking sheet with parchment paper. Set aside.

In the bowl of an electric mixer, hand whisk the water and yeast together and let stand for 2 to 3 minutes to dissolve the yeast. Stir in the oil, sugar, eggs, egg yolk, salt, and 5 cups of the flour. Mix to make a soft mass. Let the dough rest in the bowl for 10 minutes. Then knead with the dough hook on the lowest speed of the mixer for 8 to 10 minutes, gradually adding more flour as required to form a soft dough. Turn the dough out onto a lightly floured surface and form the dough into a ball. Place it in a lightly greased bowl. Place the bowl inside a large plastic bag, close the bag loosely, and let the dough rise until almost doubled, 45 to 60 minutes.

Turn the dough out onto a lightly floured surface. Gently deflate the dough. Divide it into 3 equal portions (or 6 if using 2 pans) and form each into a ball. Arrange them side by side in the prepared loaf pan. Spray the tops lightly with nonstick cooking spray, place the pan inside the plastic bag, and close loosely. Let the dough rise for 30 to 60 minutes, or until it is very puffy and has risen 1 inch above the pan rim.

Preheat the oven to 375°F. For the egg wash, whisk the egg, egg yolk, and water together in a small bowl. Using a pastry brush, generously glaze the bread. Sprinkle the sesame seeds over the bread. With the pan(s) set on the prepared baking sheet, place in the oven and immediately lower the temperature to 350°F. Bake for 35 to 40 minutes, or until the bread is golden brown. Let cool on a wire rack for 10 minutes before unmolding to cool completely.

Chapter 2

· ·

SMALL LOAVES AND ROLLS

· ·

ARE YOU AMONG THOSE who judge a restaurant by the quality of the bread it serves? An entrée and a main course can be wonderful, but if the contents of the bread basket are dry and undistinguished, it detracts from the enjoyment of the meal. A restaurateur who takes as much care in baking or selecting bread as he or she does in selecting meat, fish, and produce is the only one worthy of the name. Harrumph. Can you tell that I like good bread?

In this chapter, I bring you some of my more popular recipes for bread to accompany a meal, or to make a meal. My suggestions range from simple and delicious rolls and biscuits to bagels and soft pretzels (I even throw in a ballpark mustard recipe). Good small breads have a personality all their own; they aren't just spin-offs of larger loaves. Because they are "little-er" breads, rising times are shorter and handling is easier than for larger doughs. So there's even more reason to try one of these recipes to spruce up a simple supper or Sunday-night repast.

This is still bread territory, and that means most recipes call for bread flour. I strongly suggest that you make the effort to track down unbleached bread flour if you want the best results from these recipes. The product should be clearly labeled "bread flour." All-purpose or "suitable for bread" varieties will do in a pinch, but are not the same. A good high-gluten bread flour will make these recipes sing. Sometimes you will see one of my recipes call for a combination of bread flour and all-purpose flour, but this is stated specifically by recipe. For more tips on bread and baking with yeast, refer to Chapter 1.

SESAME-BUTTERMILK PAN ROLLS

MAKES 1 DOZEN ROLLS

¼ cup warm water

2 tablespoons instant yeast

1 cup buttermilk, warm

⅓ cup (3 ounces) unsalted butter, melted

1 teaspoon sesame oil

⅓ cup sugar

2¼ teaspoons salt

2 eggs

1 egg yolk

4 to 5 cups bread flour

Sesame seeds for sprinkling or flour for dusting

These rolls are incredibly moist and feathery light. They tend to disappear quickly, so count on making extra batches. For even more sesame flavor and an extra bit of texture, add sesame seeds to the dough, too.

Line a 12-inch cast-iron skillet with 3 rounds of parchment paper. Set aside.

In the bowl of an electric mixer, hand whisk the water and yeast together and let stand for 2 to 3 minutes to dissolve the yeast. Stir in the buttermilk, butter, sesame oil, sugar, salt, eggs, egg yolk, and 4 cups of the flour. Mix to make a soft mass. Knead with the dough hook on the lowest speed of the mixer for 8 to 10 minutes, gradually adding more flour as required to form a soft, springy dough. Turn the dough out onto a lightly floured surface and form it into a ball. Put the dough in a lightly greased large bowl. Place the bowl in a large plastic bag, close the bag loosely, and let the dough rise for 30 to 45 minutes, or until almost doubled.

Gently deflate the dough. Turn the dough out onto a lightly floured surface and divide into 12 portions. Shape each portion into a ball and place the balls close together in the prepared cast-iron skillet. Spray the rolls with nonstick cooking spray. Sprinkle generously with sesame seeds or dust with flour. Place the pan inside the plastic bag, close the bag loosely, and let the rolls rise for 20 to 30 minutes, or until puffy.

Preheat the oven to 375°F. Bake the rolls for 25 to 35 minutes, or until golden. Transfer to a wire rack and let cool slightly or completely.

B.B.
Test Kitchen Notes

Don't Milk Your Yeast

Yeast recipes that call for milk will yield better results if the yeast is first dissolved in water and the milk is added afterward. Milk and other dairy products slow the action of yeast.

RESTAURANT-STYLE PARKER HOUSE ROLLS

MAKES 1 DOZEN ROLLS

¼ cup warm water

2 tablespoons instant yeast

1¼ cups warm buttermilk or milk

4 tablespoons (2 ounces) unsalted butter, slightly softened and cut into small chunks

¼ cup sugar

2½ teaspoons salt

2 cups all-purpose flour

3 to 4 cups bread flour

½ cup (4 ounces) unsalted butter, melted, for dipping

Tender, buttery bundles of dough tucked into muffin cups bake up into a roll reminiscent of a French croissant in taste, but with the velvety crumb of a traditional white bread roll. Perfect for Thanksgiving, these rolls also figure into the weekly repertoire of my test kitchen as a coffee-break snack.

~⟨◊⟩~

Generously grease a 12-cup muffin pan with nonstick cooking spray. Place the muffin pan on a baking sheet lined with parchment paper. Set aside.

In the bowl of an electric mixer, hand whisk the water and yeast together and let stand for 2 to 3 minutes to dissolve the yeast. Stir in the buttermilk, butter, sugar, salt, all-purpose flour, and 3 cups of the bread flour. Mix to make a soft mass. Knead with the dough hook on the lowest speed of the mixer for 8 to 10 minutes, gradually adding more bread flour as required to form a soft dough. Turn the dough out onto a lightly floured surface and form the dough into a ball. Place the dough in a lightly greased bowl. Place the bowl in a large plastic bag, close the bag loosely, and let the dough rise for 45 to 60 minutes, or until almost doubled in bulk. You may also refrigerate the dough overnight. If you refrigerate it, let the dough warm to room temperature before proceeding. It will rise as it warms, and should be doubled in 1½ to 3 hours.

Gently deflate the dough. Turn the dough out onto a lightly floured surface and divide it into 12 portions. Cut each portion into 3 chunks and dip each in the melted butter. Place 3 chunks in each muffin cup. Drizzle any leftover melted butter over the rolls. Place the entire baking sheet inside a large plastic bag, close the bag loosely, and let the rolls rise for 20 to 30 minutes, or until almost doubled.

Preheat the oven to 375°F. Bake the rolls for 10 minutes. Lower the temperature to 350°F and bake for 15 to 20 minutes, or until lightly browned. Transfer to a wire rack to let cool slightly or completely.

DELI-STYLE RYE, CRANBERRY, AND RAISIN ROLLS

MAKES 12 TO 16 ROLLS

SPONGE

1 cup warm water

1 tablespoon instant yeast

2 tablespoons caraway seeds

2 teaspoons malt powder or firmly
    packed brown sugar

1 cup coarse or dark rye flour

¼ cup bread flour

DOUGH

Sponge, above

½ cup warm water

2 teaspoons baker's caramel
    (optional)

2¼ teaspoons salt

⅓ cup firmly packed brown sugar

¼ teaspoon ground cinnamon

2½ to 3 cups bread flour

½ cup dried cranberries, plumped
    and patted dry (see page 18)

½ cup dark raisins, plumped and
    patted dry (see page 18)

1 egg white, beaten, for glaze

Caraway seeds for sprinkling

These rolls are zesty and full of character, with a dense, moist, chewy crumb studded with dried fruits and tangy caraway seeds. Dark stone-ground rye flour is the key ingredient. Dried currants can be substituted for the raisins.

Stack 2 baking sheets together and line the top one with parchment paper. Repeat with 2 more baking sheets. Set aside.

For the sponge, hand whisk the water and yeast together in the bowl of an electric mixer and let stand for 2 to 3 minutes to dissolve the yeast. Add the caraway seeds, malt powder, rye flour, and bread flour. Stir to make a thick mixture. Place the bowl in a large plastic bag, close the bag loosely, and let stand for 1 hour, or until foamy and the volume has increased 40 to 80 percent.

For the dough, stir down the sponge to deflate it and add the water, baker's caramel, salt, sugar, cinnamon, and 2½ cups of the bread flour. Mix to make a soft mass. Knead with the dough hook on the lowest speed of the mixer for 10 to 12 minutes, gradually adding more bread flour as required to make a soft, springy dough. Turn the dough out onto a lightly floured surface. Let the dough rest for 2 minutes, then press the cranberries and raisins into it. Shape the dough into a ball and place it in a well-greased large bowl. Place the bowl in a large plastic bag, close the bag loosely, and let the dough rise for about 45 minutes, or until almost doubled.

Turn the dough out onto a lightly floured surface and divide it into 12 or 16 portions. Form each into a ball or oval. Place the pieces 3 inches apart on the prepared baking sheets. Brush each roll with egg white and sprinkle on some caraway seeds. Place the baking sheets inside plastic bags, close loosely, and let the rolls rise for 30 to 45 minutes, or until quite puffy.

Preheat the oven to 400°F. Bake for 15 to 18 minutes, or until the rolls are light brown and slightly firm when pressed with fingertips. Transfer to wire racks to let cool slightly or completely.

TRIPLE BUTTER CREAM BUNS

MAKES 16 TO 24 BUNS, DEPENDING ON SIZE

DOUGH

4½ teaspoons instant yeast

1½ cups warm water

2 cups bread flour

5 teaspoons sugar

1 egg

½ cup (4 ounces) unsalted butter, softened

¾ cup whipping cream at room temperature

¼ cup milk at room temperature

4 cups all-purpose flour

2½ teaspoons baking powder

½ teaspoon baking soda

1¾ teaspoons salt

BUTTER ROLL-IN

2 cups (1 pound) unsalted butter

½ cup (4 ounces) salted butter, melted, for brushing

EGG WASH

2 eggs, whisked

What tastes like croissants, is as easy as pie, and bakes up as fast as Pillsbury crescent rolls? Triple Butter Cream Buns. I won't kid you—these are rich and fabulous. I tested them with milk, water, and cream, but the cream version is so unbelievably better it is worth each extra calorie. If I told you they will beg for this recipe over chocolate chip cookies, cheesecake, and brownies, it would not be a fib.

Line 2 baking sheets with parchment paper and stack each one inside another baking sheet (you will have 4 sheets altogether, each double-stacked).

In a large mixing bowl fitted with a dough hook (or use a bread machine), whisk together the yeast and water and let stand for 1 minute. Whisk in the bread flour, and then the sugar, egg, and softened butter. Stir in the cream, milk, most of the all-purpose flour, the baking powder, baking soda, and salt. Stir to make a soft dough. Attach the dough hook and knead for 8 to 10 minutes to make a soft, supple dough, adding more flour as required. Remove the dough hook, spray the dough with nonstick cooking spray, and cover the entire mixer, dough and all, with a large plastic bag. Let rise for 45 to 60 minutes, until almost doubled in size (or refrigerate overnight).

Gently deflate the dough and divide it in 2. On a lightly floured work surface, roll out one section at a time into a 16-inch circle. Using a cheese slicer or potato peeler, scatter 1 cup of unsalted butter slivers over the surface of the dough. Using a pastry wheel, cut the dough into 8 to 12 wedges (depending on how big you want the rolls; larger is better, but smaller is better for dinner rolls). Roll each wedge into a croissant shape. Place on the baking sheet. Repeat with the second section of dough.

Place the crescents on the prepared stacked baking sheets. Brush each one very generously with the Egg Wash. Lightly cover with a large plastic sheet or bag and let rise until almost doubled in size, 45 to 60 minutes.

Preheat the oven to 375°F. Place the buns in the oven. After 30 minutes, lower the oven temperature to 350°F and continue baking until the rolls are deeply browned. Remove from the oven and brush each roll several times with the melted, salted butter.

Big 'n' Buttery Bake Sale Buns

MAKES 12 TO 14 BUNS

1½ cups warm water

2 tablespoons instant yeast

⅓ cup sugar

2¼ teaspoons salt

2 eggs

½ cup (4 ounces) unsalted butter, softened

5 to 6 cups bread flour, plus more for dusting

½ cup (4 ounces) unsalted butter, melted, for glazing

These little buns, brushed with butter and dusted with flour, have a nice old-fashioned look. They are easy to make, as most straight doughs are, but feature a croissantlike taste. Pull them apart and serve warm. A tester simply wrote "Excellent" on a butter-stained recipe sheet for this one. I make these several times a month for family suppers.

Spray a 10-inch round springform pan or a 9- by 13-inch baking pan with nonstick cooking spray. Line a baking sheet with parchment paper. Set aside.

In the bowl of an electric mixer, hand whisk the water and yeast together and let stand for 2 to 3 minutes to dissolve the yeast. Stir in the sugar, salt, eggs, the ½ cup softened butter, and 5 cups of the flour. Mix to make a soft mass. Knead with the dough hook on the lowest speed of the mixer for 8 to 10 minutes, gradually adding more flour as required to form a soft dough.

Turn the dough out onto a lightly floured board and shape the dough into a ball. Place in a lightly greased large bowl. Place the bowl in a large plastic bag, close loosely, and let the dough rise for about 45 minutes, or until almost doubled in size.

Gently deflate the dough. Let it rest for 20 minutes. Turn the dough out onto a lightly floured surface. Gently deflate the dough if it has risen again somewhat, and divide into 12 or 14 portions. Shape each portion into a ball or leave as is. Arrange the portions in the prepared baking pan. Brush generously with the melted butter and dust with flour. Place the pan in the plastic bag, close the bag loosely, and let the rolls rise for 20 to 30 minutes, or until very puffy.

Preheat the oven to 350°F. Place the pan on the prepared baking sheet and bake for 30 to 35 minutes, or until golden brown. Transfer to a wire rack to let cool slightly or completely.

FLAVORED BUTTERS

My flavored butters transform informal meals into special occasions. My standby is My Homemade Butter Spread (page 29), but the following butters are perfect for a variety of occasions. Blend all the ingredients together in a bowl and then pack the butter into a small serving crock, or use a pastry bag fitted with a star tip to pipe the butter into rosettes on a baking sheet lined with parchment paper. Top with crushed ice. Butter curlers and melon ballers can also be used for a decorative touch.

Sweet Butters

HONEY-PECAN BUTTER: To ½ cup (4 ounces) softened unsalted butter, add ½ cup churned honey and ⅓ cup chopped, toasted pecans (see page 17). Makes about 1¼ cups.

ORANGE-CRANBERRY BUTTER: To ½ cup (4 ounces) softened unsalted butter, add the minced zest of 1 orange; ½ cup plumped dried cranberries (see page 18), minced; ½ cup fresh cranberries, minced; and ¼ cup confectioners' sugar. Makes about 1 cup.

CINNAMON BUTTER: To ½ cup (4 ounces) softened unsalted butter, add 2 tablespoons cream cheese, ¼ cup confectioners' sugar, and 1 to 2 teaspoons ground cinnamon. Makes about ½ cup.

Savory Butters

ROASTED GARLIC AND CILANTRO BUTTER: To ½ cup (4 ounces) softened unsalted butter, add 2 tablespoons olive oil, 2 tablespoons minced fresh cilantro, ¼ cup roasted garlic pulp, and ⅓ cup finely chopped roasted red bell pepper. Makes about ¾ cup.

HORSERADISH AND DIJON BUTTER: To ½ cup (4 ounces) softened unsalted butter, add 2 tablespoons Dijon mustard and 2 teaspoons prepared white horseradish. Makes about ½ cup.

LEMON AND HERB BUTTER: To ½ cup (4 ounces) softened unsalted butter, add 1 tablespoon minced lemon zest, ¼ cup minced fresh flat-leaf parsley, and 1 teaspoon *each* dried basil and oregano. Makes about ½ cup.

OLD-FASHIONED ENGLISH MUFFINS

MAKES 18 TO 22 MUFFINS

SPONGE

2 cups warm water

½ teaspoon instant yeast

2 cups all-purpose flour

½ cup whole-wheat or all-purpose flour

DOUGH

Sponge, above

¾ cup warm water

2 teaspoons instant yeast

¾ cup warm milk

¼ cup buttermilk powder (see page 14) or nonfat dry milk

2 tablespoons honey

2 tablespoons white sugar

2 tablespoons corn flour or cornmeal

2½ teaspoons salt

½ teaspoon malt powder or firmly packed brown sugar

¼ teaspoon ground cinnamon

4 to 5 cups bread flour

Cornmeal for sprinkling

A combination of bread flour and whole-wheat flour give these muffins a nice texture, and butter and honey round out the taste. Don't overlook this recipe because it uses a sponge. A 2-hour sponge greatly improves the flavor, and overnight is even better. A 12-inch cast-iron pan is a perfect baking surface.

Line 2 large baking sheets with parchment paper. Set aside.

For the sponge, hand whisk the water and yeast together in the bowl of an electric mixer and let stand for 2 to 3 minutes to dissolve the yeast. Stir in the flours to make a thick batter. Place the bowl in a large plastic bag, close the bag loosely, and let stand for 2 hours or up to overnight, or until puffy and almost doubled.

For the dough, stir down the sponge to deflate it. Stir the sponge, water, and yeast together and let stand for 2 to 3 minutes. Stir in the milk, buttermilk powder, honey, white sugar, corn flour, salt, malt powder, cinnamon, and 4 cups of the bread flour. Mix for about 5 minutes, to make a thick batter. The consistency should be between a batter and a dough. Add the remaining 1 cup flour if needed to thicken the batter. Place the bowl in the plastic bag, close the bag loosely, and let the dough rise for about 45 minutes, or until almost doubled.

Gently deflate the dough. Turn the dough out onto a work surface sprinkled with cornmeal. Roll or pat out to ¾ inch thick. Using a cookie cutter, cut into 3½-inch rounds. Place 2 to 3 inches apart on the prepared baking sheets and spray lightly with nonstick cooking spray. Place the baking sheets inside the plastic bag, close the bag loosely, and let the muffins rise for about 45 minutes, or until almost doubled.

Heat a 12-inch cast-iron skillet or a griddle over medium heat. Sprinkle with cornmeal. Gently arrange the rounds in the pan (about 3 or 4 at a time) and bake on the stovetop for 5 to 8 minutes, or until browned on the bottom. Turn over and bake the other side for 1 to 3 minutes, or until the muffins have risen on the other side and are well browned. Lower the heat if the muffins are browning too quickly. Let cool completely on a wire rack. Split in half with a fork to serve.

SOFT PRETZELS

MAKES 1 DOZEN LARGE PRETZELS

DOUGH

1 cup warm water

2 tablespoons white sugar

2 teaspoons instant yeast

2 tablespoons vegetable oil

1 teaspoon salt

½ teaspoon malt powder or finely packed brown sugar

4 to 5 cups bread flour

1 egg white, beaten until foamy, for glazing

Coarse salt for sprinkling

All-Star Ballpark Mustard (opposite) for serving

Soft pretzels, a beer or lemonade, tied in the ninth, two outs, home team up, heart-of-the-order at the plate, maybe even an interleague duel—as the boys of summer say, "It's all good." Just add mustard.

~{◊}~

Stack 2 large baking sheets together and line the top one with parchment paper. Set aside.

In the bowl of an electric mixer, hand whisk the water, white sugar, and yeast together, then quickly whisk in the oil, salt, malt powder, and 4 cups of the flour. Knead with the dough hook on the lowest speed of the mixer for 5 to 10 minutes, gradually adding more flour as required to form a soft dough. Place the bowl in a large plastic bag, close the bag loosely, and let the dough rise for 30 to 45 minutes, or until almost doubled in size.

Gently deflate the dough. Turn the dough out onto a lightly floured surface. Divide the dough into 12 portions and let them rest for a few minutes. To form the pretzels, roll each portion into a 15-inch-long rope. Form one rope into an upside-down U. Cross the ends about a third of the way from the rounded part of the U, fold the ends up at an angle, and press them together to seal (as for a commercial pretzel shape). Place on the prepared baking sheets, spray with nonstick cooking spray, and place the baking sheets inside a large plastic bag. Close the bag loosely and let the pretzels rise for 30 to 45 minutes, or until very puffy.

Preheat the oven to 400°F. Brush the pretzels with the beaten egg white and sprinkle with coarse salt. Bake the pretzels for 18 to 20 minutes, or until nicely browned. Transfer to wire racks and let cool completely. Serve with the mustard.

VARIATION: For a more authentic version, boil the pretzels before baking them. Cook them in simmering water with 3 tablespoons baking soda and 1 tablespoon white sugar added. Cook for 1 to 2 minutes, or until puffy. Transfer to a parchment-lined baking sheet, and sprinkle with coarse salt. Bake in a preheated 425°F oven for 15 to 20 minutes, or until browned. Transfer to a wire rack to let cool slightly or completely.

ALL-STAR BALLPARK MUSTARD

MAKES ABOUT 1 CUP

1 cup dry mustard

4 tablespoons ground turmeric

1¼ teaspoons salt, or to taste

2 teaspoons sugar, or to taste

1½ cups water

Tiny pinch of citric acid (see page 128)

Tiny pinch of ground allspice

2 tablespoons distilled white vinegar

Old-fashioned yellow mustard is a commercial classic, but it's getting harder and harder to find recipes for the do-it-yourselfer. Old-fashioned yellow mustard is required for many things like pretzels and hot dogs. This version is Tweety Bird yellow and downright perky. Turmeric is used as a coloring, as it is in most commercial yellow mustards.

In a medium bowl, stir all the ingredients except the vinegar together. Cover and let stand overnight at room temperature. The heat of the mustard powder will dissipate considerably. The next day, put the mixture in the top of a double boiler and heat over simmering water for 5 to 10 minutes. Remove from the heat, let cool completely, then stir in the vinegar. Adjust the salt and sugar to taste. Cover and refrigerate for up to 2 months.

BIG ARCHES BISCUITS

MAKES ABOUT 30 BISCUITS

5 cups all-purpose flour

8 teaspoons baking powder

2 teaspoons salt

½ teaspoon baking soda

3 tablespoons sugar

4 tablespoons (2 ounces) cold unsalted butter, plus melted butter for brushing

½ cup cold vegetable shortening

5 teaspoons instant yeast

½ cup warm water

1¾ to 2 cups warm buttermilk

If you want to imitate "Mc-you-know-who" biscuits, this is where you start. A trio of leavening agents—yeast, baking powder, and baking soda—makes these biscuits extra light. An overnight rise has them ready when you are. Traditionally, a big batch is made and kept refrigerated; portions are then cut off as required and baked. If you prefer fried biscuits, this dough will also work nicely.

In a large bowl, stir the flour, baking powder, salt, baking soda, and sugar together. Using a pastry cutter, cut the 4 tablespoons cold butter and the shortening into the dry ingredients until the mixture is crumbly.

In a small bowl, sprinkle the yeast over the warm water, stir briefly, and let stand for 2 to 3 minutes to dissolve the yeast. Add the yeast mixture and 1¾ cups buttermilk to the dry ingredients and toss with a fork to blend and moisten, creating a soft dough. Add the additional ¼ cup buttermilk if the dough is too firm.

Place the bowl in a large plastic bag, close the bag loosely, and refrigerate for at least overnight or up to 2 days.

Stack 2 baking sheets together and line the top one with parchment paper. Set aside.

To bake, remove a half portion of the dough. On a lightly floured surface, roll the dough out approximately 1 inch thick. Cut into rounds, wedges, or squares with a knife or biscuit cutter. Brush generously with melted butter. Repeat with the remaining half portion of dough. Place the biscuits on the prepared baking sheet and brush a second time with melted butter or sprinkle lightly with flour.

Preheat the oven to 400°F. Bake the biscuits for 12 to 18 minutes, or until lightly browned. Transfer to a wire rack to let cool slightly or completely.

HOMEMADE HAMBURGER BUNS

MAKES 8 LARGE BUNS

DOUGH

1½ cups warm water

5 teaspoons instant yeast

⅓ cup vegetable oil

½ cup white sugar

2½ teaspoons salt

¼ teaspoon malt powder or firmly packed brown sugar

¼ cup nonfat dry milk

5 to 6 cups bread flour

Milk for brushing

Sesame seeds for sprinkling

Additions such as malt powder, sugar, and oil make these buns resemble commercial products, but with a superior taste.

Stack 2 baking sheets together and line the top one with parchment paper. Set aside.

In the bowl of an electric mixer, hand whisk the water and yeast together and let stand for 2 to 3 minutes to dissolve the yeast. Stir in the oil, white sugar, salt, malt powder, milk powder, and 5 cups of the flour. Mix to make a soft mass. Knead with the dough hook on the lowest speed of the mixer for 8 to 10 minutes, gradually adding more flour as required to form a soft, bouncy dough. Turn the dough out onto a lightly floured surface and form the dough into a ball. Place the dough in a lightly greased bowl. Place the bowl in a large plastic bag, close the bag loosely, and let the dough rise for 45 to 60 minutes, or until almost doubled.

Turn the dough out onto a lightly floured surface and let rest for 10 minutes. Divide the dough into 8 portions and let rest for 5 minutes. Shape each portion into a ball and place the balls, evenly spaced, on the prepared baking sheets. Spray with nonstick cooking spray. Place the baking sheet in the plastic bag and let the dough rise for 20 to 30 minutes, or until quite puffy.

Preheat the oven to 375°F. Remove the baking sheet from the bag. Flatten each roll gently with the palm of your hand. Brush with milk and sprinkle with sesame seeds. Bake the rolls for 18 to 20 minutes, or until nicely browned. Let cool on a wire rack for 15 to 20 minutes before serving.

B.B. Test Kitchen Notes

Sugar, Yikes!

Some of my bread recipes, such as my Homemade Hamburger Buns, call for sugar as well as salt. Occasionally, I receive an email from a baker who suggests that the sugar is unnecessary.

If you like, you can reduce the sugar in these buns to ¼ cup, but you must also reduce the salt to 2 teaspoons.

MONTREAL BAGELS REVISITED

MAKES 12 TO 14 BAGELS

DOUGH

1½ cups warm water

2¼ teaspoons instant yeast

4 tablespoons white sugar

1¼ teaspoons salt

1 tablespoon honey

2 tablespoons beaten egg

3 tablespoons vegetable oil

1 teaspoon malt powder or firmly
    packed brown sugar

6 to 7 cups bread flour

¼ cup honey

1½ cups sesame seeds or poppy
    seeds (or half of each) for
    sprinkling

Bagels and pizza generate the most email at BB. Bagel wars never end. Most websites that feature a Montreal bagel recipe refer to BB, I'm proud to say. Traditionally made in a wood-fired oven, Montreal bagels are enriched with honey, eggs, and oil. Usually, there is no salt in the dough, but here it has been added to create a hybrid taste. For me, Montreal bagels are always a work in progress!

Line 1 baking sheet with parchment paper. Stack 2 baking sheets together and line the top one with parchment paper. Set aside.

For the dough, hand whisk the water and yeast together in the bowl of an electric mixer and let stand for 2 to 3 minutes to dissolve the yeast. Stir in the white sugar, salt, honey, egg, oil, malt powder, and 6 cups of the flour. Mix to make a soft mass. Knead with the dough hook on the lowest speed of the mixer for 10 to 12 minutes, gradually adding more flour as required to form a very stiff, smooth dough. Cover the dough with plastic wrap and let it rest for 10 minutes.

Turn the dough out onto a lightly floured surface and divide it into 12 to 14 portions. Roll each into a 10-inch rope. Make each rope into a ring and gently rock back and forth on the counter to seal the ends. Place on the single baking sheet. Let the bagels rest for 12 to 15 minutes, or until slightly puffy.

Preheat the oven to 450°F. Fill a soup pot or Dutch oven three-fourths full with water. Add the honey and bring to a boil. Lower the heat to a simmer and add the bagels a few at a time. Boil them for about 1½ minutes, turning them over once at the midpoint. Using a perforated skimmer, transfer the bagels to the single parchment-lined baking sheet to drain.

Put the sesame seeds in a shallow bowl. Dip each bagel in the bowl to coat with seeds and then transfer to the parchment-lined doubled baking sheets. Place them in the oven. Immediately lower the temperature to 425°F and bake for 15 to 20 minutes, or until lightly browned. Turn the bagels over and bake for 3 to 5 minutes longer, or until well browned on both sides. Transfer to a wire rack and let cool for at least 15 minutes before serving.

A BAGEL BY ANY OTHER NAME

Austria and Poland are tied to the birth of the bagel. In the 17th century, as the story goes, a baker in Vienna made a roll in the shape of a stirrup to honor the king of Poland for saving the Austrian city from invading hordes. The word bagel was derived from *bugel*, the German word for "stirrup." The Viennese baker was Jewish, and the popularity of the bagel quickly spread throughout first Jewish, then other, communities in Europe. In Poland, bagels were officially sanctioned as gifts for women who had recently given birth as a symbol of the circle of life. Bagels made handy teething rings for kids. Early in the 20th century, bagels were introduced to the New World by Jewish immigrants.

As far as I'm concerned, there are only two types of authentic bagels produced in North America: the Montreal style and the New York style. (Sorry, but those puffy bread doughnuts with mumps that some people call bagels aren't bagels.) Montreal bagels use malt, a touch of egg, and no salt, and they are boiled in a honey-sweetened bath, then baked in a wood (not gas) bagel oven. New York bagels may or may not use malt and they contain salt. These bagels are much larger than the Montreal variety and are neither bathed in honey-sweetened water nor baked in a wood oven. While New York bagels can be found in a variety of flavors, Montreal bagels are typically flavored with poppy or sesame seeds. The Montreal variety has been in production (at the venerable Fairmount Bagel Bakery) since 1919. Production in New York began a few years earlier. The taste and texture may be different, but both varieties are the real bugels.

Incidentally, my first ever food feature was an article on Montreal Bagels—for the *New York Times*, no less. (My brother took the bagel shots to help me sell the feature.)

Big Apple Bagels

MAKES 1 DOZEN BAGELS

Cornmeal for sprinkling

DOUGH

1½ cups warm water

2 teaspoons instant yeast

1 tablespoon vegetable oil

1 tablespoon white sugar

2 teaspoons malt powder or firmly
packed brown sugar

2 teaspoons salt

4 to 5 cups bread flour

2 tablespoons malt syrup, firmly
packed brown sugar, or honey
(optional)

1 teaspoon kosher salt

1½ cups sesame seeds or poppy
seeds (or half of each) for
sprinkling (optional)

Outside New York City, these are known as "water bagels." Add as much flour to the mixture as you can in order to produce a slick dough. Bagels should be simmered—not boiled. Malt syrup is available at home-brewing and health-foods stores and via mail order. It sweetens the bagels a touch and gives them shine. You can also leave it out—the bagels are as good without it.

Line 1 baking sheet with parchment paper. Stack 2 baking sheets together, line the top one with parchment paper, and sprinkle generously with cornmeal. Set aside.

For the dough, hand whisk the water and yeast together in the bowl of an electric mixer, and let stand for 2 to 3 minutes to dissolve the yeast. Stir in the oil, white sugar, malt powder, salt, and 4 cups of flour. Mix to make a soft mass. Knead with the dough hook on the lowest speed of the mixer for 10 to 12 minutes, gradually adding more flour as required to form a very stiff dough. Place the bowl inside a large plastic bag, close the bag loosely, and let stand for about 20 minutes.

Turn the dough out onto a lightly floured surface and divide it into 12 portions. Roll each portion into a 10-inch-long rope. Make each rope into a ring and gently rock back and forth on the counter to seal the ends. Place on a lightly floured surface near your stove. Let the bagels rest for 15 to 20 minutes, or until half-risen and puffy.

Preheat the oven to 450°F. Fill a soup pot or Dutch oven three-fourths full with water. Add the malt syrup and salt to the water and bring to a boil. Lower the heat to a simmer and add the bagels to the water a few at a time. After they rise to the surface, simmer for 45 seconds. Turn each bagel over and simmer about 45 seconds longer (1½ minutes total). Using a perforated skimmer, transfer the bagels to the single parchment-lined baking sheet to drain. Sprinkle with the seeds.

Transfer the bagels to the parchment-lined doubled baking sheets. Immediately lower the temperature to 425°F and bake for 17 to 22 minutes, or until very lightly browned. Turn the bagels over and bake for 3 to 5 minutes longer, or until well browned on both sides. Transfer to a wire rack and let cool 15 minutes before serving.

ONION PLETZELS

¼ cup cornmeal for sprinkling

DOUGH

1½ cups warm water

2 tablespoons instant yeast

5 teaspoons sugar

2½ teaspoons salt

5 to 5½ cups bread flour

TOPPING

½ cup dehydrated minced onion
(see note)

2 tablespoons vegetable oil

2 tablespoons poppy seeds

1 egg beaten with 2 tablespoons
water

1 tablespoon coarse salt for
sprinkling (optional)

Where I grew up, a disk of dough with a slight depression in the center, topped with diced onions and poppy seeds, was called an onion pletzel. In New York, it might be called a bialy. Call it what you will, it's an enticing flatbread that takes well to cream cheese. These freeze nicely, especially if you enjoy them split, toasted, and slathered with cream cheese.

~◊~

Stack 2 baking sheets together and line the top one with parchment paper. Sprinkle with the cornmeal. Repeat with 2 more baking sheets. Set aside.

For the dough, hand whisk the water and yeast together in the bowl of an electric mixer to dissolve the yeast. Stir in the sugar, salt, and 3½ cups of the flour and mix to make a soft mass. Knead with the dough hook on the lowest speed of the mixer for 8 to 10 minutes, gradually adding more flour as required to form a soft dough. Place the bowl inside a large plastic bag, close the bag loosely, and let the dough rest for about 45 minutes, or until almost doubled in size.

For the topping, soak the onion in hot water to cover for 15 minutes. Drain and toss with the oil and poppy seeds. Set aside.

Gently deflate the dough. Turn the dough out onto a lightly floured surface and divide into 8 portions. Let the dough portions rest for 10 minutes. Roll or stretch each portion into a 4- to 5-inch oval or circle. Be careful not to overwork the dough. Place the pletzels on the prepared baking sheets. Lightly glaze with the egg wash. Spoon about 2 tablespoons of the topping all over each pletzel and sprinkle with coarse salt. Spray with nonstick cooking spray. Place the baking sheets inside large plastic bags, close loosely, and let the pletzels rise for 30 to 40 minutes, or until puffy.

Preheat the oven to 450°F. Bake the pletzels for 25 to 30 minutes, or until golden brown. If they brown too quickly, lower the oven temperature to 425°F. Transfer to wire racks and let cool for at least 15 minutes before serving.

VARIATION: You may substitute 1 cup finely chopped onion for the dehydrated onion. However, the dehydrated onion is easier to work with and sticks to the dough well.

VIENNA (OR KAISER) ROLLS

MAKES 16 ROLLS

1½ cups warm water

5½ teaspoons instant yeast

2 eggs

1 egg white

2 teaspoons salt

⅓ cup white sugar

1 tablespoon malt powder or firmly
     packed brown sugar

⅓ cup vegetable oil

4½ to 5½ cups bread flour

Poppy seeds for sprinkling

Vienna rolls, also called kaiser rolls, are round rolls with a thin, hard crust and a light interior. Commercial versions tend to be uninspiring, while a handcrafted kaiser roll looks like an overblown rosette. This is the result of what some call "klopping," a Yiddish word that describes the sound and motion delivered as a baker molds the dough into shape. If you want an authentic look, kaiser roll stamps are available (see Source Guide, page 299); otherwise, add the marks with the back of a chef's knife.

~⟨◇⟩~

Stack 2 baking sheets together and line the top one with parchment paper. Repeat with 2 more baking sheets. Set aside.

In the bowl of an electric mixer, hand whisk the water and yeast together and let stand for 2 to 3 minutes to dissolve the yeast. Stir in the eggs, egg white, salt, white sugar, malt powder, and oil. Stir in 4½ cups of the flour and mix to make a soft mass. Knead with the dough hook on the lowest speed of the mixer for 5 to 8 minutes, gradually adding more flour as required to form a soft, elastic dough.

Turn the dough out onto a lightly floured surface and form it into a ball. Place the dough in a lightly greased bowl. Place the bowl in a large plastic bag, close the bag loosely, and let the dough rise for 30 to 40 minutes, or until almost doubled.

Gently deflate the dough. Turn the dough out onto a floured surface and divide it into 16 portions and let rest for 3 to 5 minutes. Shape each portion into a ball. Using the back of a knife, make 8 wedge indentations in each ball, pressing in lightly.

Place the rolls, indented side down, on the prepared baking sheets. Place each set of baking sheets inside a large plastic bag, close the bags loosely, and let the dough rise for 30 to 40 minutes, or until almost doubled.

Preheat the oven to 400°F. Gently turn the rolls indented side up, spray them generously with nonstick cooking spray, and sprinkle with poppy seeds. Place the rolls in the oven on the middle and upper shelves. Immediately lower the oven temperature to 350°F. Bake for 15 to 20 minutes, or until evenly browned. Let cool on a wire rack for at least 15 minutes before serving.

FRENCH-STYLE HEARTH ROLLS

MAKES 1 DOZEN ROLLS

SPONGE

1 cup warm water

2½ teaspoons instant yeast

1½ cups bread flour

DOUGH

Sponge, above

1 cup water

1 tablespoon honey

2¾ teaspoons salt

½ teaspoon malt powder or firmly
    packed brown sugar

2 tablespoons olive oil

3 to 4 cups bread flour

Flour for dusting

Crusty outside, tender and airy inside, these rolls with just a tossed salad will make a meal. Bake them in miniature loaf pans or as free-form rolls. Malt powder helps to color the rolls and adds a lovely extra bit of flavor.

Spray 12 miniature loaf pans with nonstick cooking spray. Place the pans on a large baking sheet lined with parchment paper. Set aside.

For the sponge, hand whisk the water and yeast together in the bowl of an electric mixer and let stand for 2 to 3 minutes to dissolve the yeast. Whisk in the flour to make a puddinglike paste. Place the bowl inside a large plastic bag, close the bag loosely, and let the sponge stand for about 1 hour, or until bubbly.

For the dough, stir down the sponge. Stir in the water, honey, salt, malt powder, oil, and 3 cups of the flour together. Mix to make a soft mass. Knead with the dough hook on the lowest speed of the mixer for 8 to 10 minutes, gradually adding more flour as required to form a soft, elastic dough. Turn the dough out onto a lightly floured surface and form the dough into a ball. Place the dough in a lightly greased bowl. Place the bowl in the plastic bag, close the bag loosely, and let the dough rise for 30 to 45 minutes, or until doubled.

Gently deflate the dough. Turn the dough out onto a lightly floured surface and divide into 12 portions. Make 2 balls from each portion and place them side by side in each prepared loaf pan. Spray the rolls lightly with nonstick cooking spray. Place the pans on the baking sheet inside the plastic bag, close the bag loosely, and let rise for about 30 minutes, or until puffy and almost doubled in size.

Preheat the oven to 400°F. Using a spray bottle filled with water, lightly mist the rolls. Dust the rolls with flour and place in the oven. Spray the oven walls, being careful to avoid the oven light. Misting the inside of the oven several times during the first 10 minutes of baking, bake for 15 to 20 minutes, or until medium brown. Let cool for 15 to 20 minutes on a wire rack before serving.

ROUND ROLLS: After the first rise, divide the dough into 12 portions. Form them into ovals or rounds and place on parchment-lined doubled baking sheets. Spray the rolls lightly with nonstick cooking spray. Let rise and bake as above.

SLAB ROLLS: After the first rise, use a sharp knife to cut the dough into small slabs. Place them on parchment-lined doubled baking sheets. Spray lightly with nonstick cooking spray. Let rise and bake as above.

Chapter 3

· ·

RUSTIC PIZZAS AND FLATBREADS

· ·

FLATBREADS—HOW DO I LOVE YOU?

Let me count the ways. Pita, focaccia, nan, panini—all lovely, delightful flatbreads from the world kitchen. Flatbreads never cease to amaze me in their variety. Their rustic tastes, ethnic roots, and odd shapes suit all sorts of occasions. They are great for wrapping and scooping, and they make terrific sides for salad and soup. My Bomba Hot Dipping Sauce (page 99) is just the thing to have on hand when you have some fresh, hot flatbread coming out of the oven.

Then there's pizza. I bake it in the oven and I bake in on the outdoor grill, a specialty of mine in the summer (see page 89). The commercial pizza trade is the most secretive and competitive in the professional baking world. It's easy to see why. Great pizza dough can form the foundation of an entire business. The recipes in this collection are among the most requested on the website.

Exotic though they may be, flatbreads are easy to make. Don't worry about crusts or rising times too much. Look at it as an adventure in dough. And if you master just one of these recipes, you'll be a star at home.

STICKS AND STONES MAKE BETTER PIZZAS AND FLATBREADS

· ·

There are many great products out there to help you make pizzas that also work well for flatbreads, such as focaccia or pita. I find most of my tools in kitchen shops or restaurant supply stores.

PIZZA WHEELS

Track down a hefty restaurant-grade cutter to make cutting a fresh pizza a breeze.

PIZZA STONES

Make sure the stone you buy is as large as will comfortably fit in your oven and is a thick, not thin, variety (forget chintzy department-store stones). You can use a stone to bake rustic loaves as well. I've also had fantastic results with the HearthKit, an oven insert that replicates the performance of a real hearth oven (see page 87).

CAST-IRON SKILLETS AND PIZZA PANS

Cast-iron skillets make great pizza. Seasoned cast iron, the original nonstick material, offers great release, gives the crust a nice crisp finish, and makes perfectly round pies. To prepare a seasoned cast-iron skillet for pizza, cover the bottom with a film of olive oil, or oil and seasoned bread crumbs. Place the pizza dough on top and ease the edges of the dough to the sides of the pan.

Anodized aluminum pans are an excellent choice if you want a deep-golden crust, since the dark finish attracts heat. Black steel makes for exceptional browning, but it's a little harder to maintain since it must be both seasoned and well dried, or rust sets in. Commercial lightweight untreated aluminum pans are great for thin, crisp pizzas. They're cheap and they come in a wide range of sizes.

PIZZA COMBO SUGGESTIONS

All of my pizza doughs can be dressed with any of these combinations or your own preferences. I recommend my Classic Pizza and Ready-When-You-Are Pizza for good traditional pizza crusts, but any recipe for dough will be fine.

No one says pizza has to be hot and dressed in tomato sauce and mozzarella cheese. You can serve pizza cold, in small squares, in miniature rounds as an appetizer, as an individual first course, or in the traditional rectangular Italian shape. Sauce is optional. You may lightly brush the surface with olive oil, then garnish with your preferred toppings. Here are some favorite combinations.

PIZZA BLANCA

Crushed garlic and olive oil
Béchamel sauce
Mixed shredded Colby and Swiss cheeses
Dusting of grated Parmesan or Asiago cheese

SPINACH PIZZA

Crushed garlic and olive oil
Marinara sauce (such as Bottle-It-and-Sell-It Pizza
    Sauce, page 87)
Chopped, drained cooked spinach
Crumbled feta cheese

SWISS CHEESE AND ONION

Crushed garlic and olive oil
Touch of Dijon mustard
Sautéed onions (lots)
Mixed shredded Gruyère and raclette cheeses
Freshly ground black pepper
Sprinkle of caraway seeds

CANADIAN SMOKED SALMON BRUNCH PIZZA

Cream cheese
Lox strips
Minced fresh dill
Capers
Freshly ground black pepper

THE CALIFORNIAN

Crushed garlic and olive oil
Goat cheese
Strips of roasted red pepper
Chopped oil-packed sun-dried tomatoes
Minced fresh herbs
Sliced kalamata olives

The baking times and temperatures given in the recipes are estimates. You may have to experiment with these depending on the thickness of the crust, the number and heaviness of the toppings, and the efficiency of your oven. For example, you may want to raise the temperature a bit to give a good blast of heat to "set up" the pizza and brown but not scorch the crust.

CLASSIC PIZZA

MAKES THREE 9-INCH PIZZAS

DOUGH

1½ cups warm water

2½ teaspoons instant yeast

2 teaspoons sugar

1½ teaspoons salt

2 tablespoons olive oil

1 tablespoon semolina or cornmeal

1 cup all-purpose flour

2 to 3 cups bread flour

Olive oil for drizzling

1½ cups Bottle-It-and-Sell-It Pizza Sauce (page 87) or your favorite jarred sauce (optional)

Toppings of your choice (opposite)

The title says it all—this pure and simple dough is a wonderful foundation for any topping combination.

Coat three 9-inch pizza pans generously with olive oil. Set aside.

For the dough, hand whisk the water and yeast together in the bowl of an electric mixer and let stand for 2 to 3 minutes to dissolve the yeast. Stir in the sugar, salt, oil, semolina, all-purpose flour, and 2 cups of the bread flour. Mix to make a soft mass. Knead with the dough hook on the lowest speed of the mixer for 5 to 8 minutes, gradually adding more flour as required to form a soft, elastic dough. Turn the dough out onto a lightly floured surface and form it into a ball. Place the dough in a lightly greased bowl. Place the bowl in a large plastic bag, close the bag loosely, and let rise for 30 to 45 minutes, or until almost doubled.

Preheat the oven to 425°F.

Turn the dough out on a lightly floured surface and divide it into 3 portions. Let the dough rest for 10 minutes. Press or roll the dough out to fit the prepared pizza pans. If the dough resists or otherwise retracts, let it rest for a few minutes, then gently coax it to fit the pan. Drizzle a bit of olive oil on top of the dough. Spread on the sauce and add the toppings of your choice.

Bake the pizzas for 15 minutes, then lower the temperature to 375°F. Bake for 10 to 15 minutes longer, or until the cheese is melted and lightly browned.

B.B. Test Kitchen Notes

Pizza on the Go

If you are in a hurry, purchase pizzeria dough (many local pizzerias sell dough in 1-pound bags) or use frozen commercial bread dough for your pizza crusts.

SUN-DRIED TOMATO PESTO

MAKES ABOUT 2 CUPS

1 (28-ounce) jar oil-packed sun-
    dried tomatoes, drained

10 cloves garlic

½ to 1 cup olive oil

Salt and freshly ground black
    pepper

Pureed sun-dried tomatoes make a flavorful paste or pesto that enhances many preparations. Small jars of puree cost a fortune, and pureeing small amounts yourself is not practical. Instead, purchase a large jar of sun-dried tomatoes and make a big batch. I add a tablespoon or two of this to purchased spaghetti or pizza sauce, or smear it as is on pizza crusts. It's also great on sandwiches, chicken, and eggs.

~⟨◊⟩~

Put the tomatoes in a medium bowl and add very hot water to cover. Stir for a few minutes, then drain. (This softens the tomatoes and gets rid of some of the packing oil.) In a food processor, combine the tomatoes, garlic, olive oil, and salt and pepper to taste. Puree until smooth. Cover and refrigerate for up to 2 weeks.

BOTTLE-IT-AND-SELL-IT PIZZA SAUCE

MAKES ABOUT 4 CUPS (ENOUGH SAUCE FOR THREE 15-INCH PIZZAS OR SEVERAL SMALLER ONES)

4 oil-packed sun-dried tomato halves

1 (28-ounce) can ground plum tomatoes

1 (12-ounce) jar roasted red bell peppers, drained

3 tablespoons extra virgin olive oil

4 cloves garlic, crushed

¼ teaspoon citric acid (see page 128)

⅛ teaspoon red pepper flakes

¼ teaspoon onion powder

¾ teaspoon salt

½ teaspoon sugar

¼ teaspoon freshly ground black pepper

2 tablespoons minced fresh basil or oregano, or a combination, or 2 teaspoons dried

1 tablespoon minced fresh flat-leaf parsley

You can always use canned sauce, but this homemade pizza sauce is spicy and fragrant. It freezes well, and you can easily double or quadruple the recipe.

In a small bowl, cover the sun-dried tomatoes with boiling water. Let stand for 5 minutes and drain. In a food processor, combine the sun-dried tomatoes, canned tomatoes, and roasted red bell peppers. Process until smooth (a couple of minutes).

In a medium saucepan, heat the olive oil over low heat, and sauté the garlic for 1 to 2 minutes. Stir in the tomato mixture and cook for about 5 minutes. Add all the remaining ingredients and cook for another 5 minutes, or until thick and saucy. Remove from the heat. Taste and adjust the seasoning.

Let cool completely. Cover and refrigerate for up to 2 weeks.

B.B.
Test Kitchen
Notes

Hearth Cooking in the Home

My test kitchen recently got acquainted with the Hearth Kitchen Company's HearthKit, a ceramic oven insert (see the Source Guide, page 306). In 60 seconds, this full-fashioned hearth baking stone kit literally turned my test kitchen oven into an artisanal bread oven. What do I love about it? Everything.

Put simply, the HearthKit is the indoor-oven home chef's answer to the outdoor bread oven. The easy-to-install kit comes in different sizes to fit your oven, making the most of your oven's capacity. It will convert your home oven into a boulangerie and pizzeria, making you the envy of any European village baker (almost).

A typical oven stone is a small, thin rectangle or circle of stoneware that heats un-evenly and often burns crusts. The HearthKit's criblike design lets heat radiate around your baked goods, providing the all-over baking that breads need. The result is evenly browned breads with incredible blistered crusts and moist, hole-laden interiors—per-fect for pizza, focaccia, and other rustic doughs.

ITALIAN BAKERY PIZZA

MAKES 1 LARGE RECTANGULAR PIZZA

Olive oil for drizzling

Semolina or cornmeal for dusting

DOUGH

1¾ cups warm water

2 tablespoons instant yeast

⅓ cup olive oil

2½ teaspoons salt

2 tablespoons sugar

3 cups all-purpose flour

1 to 2 cups bread flour

TOPPING

1 (28-ounce) can plum tomatoes, drained

⅔ cup Bottle-It-and-Sell-It Pizza Sauce (page 87) or your favorite jarred sauce

Freshly ground black pepper

1 teaspoon salt, or to taste

½ teaspoon sugar

¼ cup olive oil

1 clove garlic, crushed

2 tablespoons minced fresh basil, oregano, or flat-leaf parsley, or a combination, or 1 tablespoon dried herbs

4 to 5 cups shredded mozzarella cheese

Thinly sliced pepperoni to taste

This is one of my top 10 favorite recipes of all time, and my youngest son, Benjamin, is partial to it, too. It's is about as basic as pizza gets, and purists will suggest that it is about as complex as pizza should get. The crust is thick and the toppings are very simple: crushed plum tomatoes, herbs, olive oil, cheese, and pepperoni (even the pepperoni is optional).

~◊~

Stack 2 large baking sheets together and line the top one with parchment paper. Generously drizzle the paper with olive oil and dust with semolina. Set aside.

For the dough, hand whisk the water and yeast together in the bowl of an electric mixer and let stand for 2 to 3 minutes for the yeast to dissolve. Stir in the oil, salt, sugar, all-purpose flour, and 1 cup of the bread flour. Mix to make a soft mass. Knead with the dough hook on the lowest speed of the mixer for 5 to 8 minutes, gradually adding more bread flour as required to form a soft, elastic dough. Turn the dough out onto a lightly floured surface. Form the dough into a ball and place in a lightly greased bowl. Place the bowl in a large plastic bag, close the bag loosely, and let the dough rise for 30 to 45 minutes, or until almost doubled.

For the topping, put the tomatoes in a large bowl. Crush with a fork to break them up. Add the sauce, pepper, salt, sugar, oil, garlic, and herbs and stir well.

Turn the dough out onto a lightly floured surface and let it rest for a few minutes. Press or roll the dough out to fit the prepared baking sheets. If the dough resists or otherwise retracts, let it rest for a few more minutes, then gently coax it to fit the pan. Drizzle a bit of olive oil on top of the dough. Spread on the tomato topping and top with the cheese and pepperoni. Place the baking sheets inside the plastic bag, close the bag loosely, and let the dough rise for 30 to 45 minutes, or until quite puffy.

Preheat the oven to 425°F. Bake the pizza for 15 minutes, then lower the heat to 375°F. Bake for 15 to 20 minutes longer, or until the cheese is melted and lightly browned.

100 ACRES OF PIZZA

. . . .

Pizzalike herbed flatbreads go back to the time of the ancient Egyptians. After that period, it is said that the Greeks taught the Italians how to cook, and this is how Italy adopted and adapted the pizza. (The Latin word *picea* describes the blackening of a crust placed over a fire.) The Neapolitans (in pre-Renaissance Naples) apparently created the venerable pie as we know it today. The first pizzas were simple affairs: flour, olive oil, lard, cheese, and herbs. No tomatoes—for years, they were thought to be poisonous. Eventually, tomatoes, basil, and cheese (red, green, and white, the colors of the Italian flag) were combined to make a pizza in honor of Italian Queen Margherita, and the tomato-based pie was born. These days, North Americans are said to eat some 100 acres of pizza every day.

B.B.
Test Kitchen
Notes

Pizza on the Grill: Get Fired Up About It

. . . .

The BB test kitchens got involved in baking outdoors one crazy, hot summer when my first Weber grill arrived. The grill did terrific things for bread, and it truly excelled with pizza. The high heat of a grill is perfect for giving pizza dough a good, quick bake. The style of pizza a grill produces will depend on the grill design (I have tested pizza on the Weber gas grill, the Big Green Egg charcoal grill, and Prino Grill) and on the recipe.

More often than not, I prepare pizza dough in the bread machine and have a few batches reserved in the refrigerator (packed in lightly oiled self-sealing plastic bags). If you have the dough and the toppings prepared, pizza can be made in less than 30 minutes.

Preheat your grill to medium-high (400°F to 450°F). You can put pizzas in cast-iron skillets and place these directly on the grill. If you use conventional pizza pans, place the pan on the grill, and once the pizza has baked for a few minutes, slide it off and finish it directly on the grill on low heat. If you're using a pizza stone, put your pizza on a piece of parchment paper and start baking it on the paper (the edges of the paper may scorch, but that's okay). Once the pizza is set, remove the paper and finish baking directly on the stone.

With practice, you will identify your grill's "sweet spot" for baking. Your initial efforts will require a lot of lifting and checking. You may scorch a pizza here and there, but once you learn the ropes, you'll be hooked. For more on baking breads on the outdoor grill, see page 49.

RUSTIC WHOLE-WHEAT AND HONEY PIZZA

MAKES THREE 9-INCH THIN-CRUST PIZZAS

SPONGE

1 cup warm water

2 teaspoons instant yeast

1¼ cups all-purpose flour

DOUGH

Sponge, above

½ cup warm water

2 tablespoons mild-flavored honey

1½ teaspoons salt

2 tablespoons olive oil

1 teaspoon baking powder

1 cup whole-wheat flour

½ cup all-purpose flour

½ to 1 cup bread flour

Olive oil for drizzling

1½ cups Bottle-It-and-Sell-It Pizza Sauce (page 87) or your favorite jarred sauce

Toppings of your choice (page 84)

Honey helps with browning and flavor in this lean dough. I receive many requests for whole-grain recipes, and this is one of my favorites. I like it with a vegetarian topping or just olive oil and fresh basil.

Coat three 9-inch pizza pans generously with olive oil. Set aside.

For the sponge, stir the water and yeast together in the bowl of an electric mixer. Let stand for 2 to 3 minutes to dissolve the yeast. Stir in the flour to make a thick batter. Place the bowl inside a large plastic bag, close the bag loosely, and let stand at room temperature for at least 30 minutes or up to 2 hours, or until the sponge is foamy.

For the dough, stir down the sponge mixture. Stir in the water, honey, salt, oil, baking powder, whole-wheat flour, all-purpose flour, and ½ cup of the bread flour. Mix to make a soft mass. Knead with the dough hook on the lowest speed of the mixer for 8 to 10 minutes, gradually adding more bread flour as required to form a soft, elastic dough. Turn the dough out onto a lightly floured surface. Form the dough into a ball and place in a lightly greased bowl. Place the bowl in a large plastic bag, close the bag loosely, and let the dough rise for 30 to 45 minutes, or until almost doubled.

Preheat the oven to 425°F.

Turn the dough out onto a lightly floured surface and divide it into 3 portions. Let the dough rest for 10 minutes. Press or roll the dough out to fit the prepared pizza pans. If the dough resists or otherwise retracts, let it rest for a few minutes, then gently coax it to fit the pan. Drizzle a bit of olive oil on top of the dough. Spread on the sauce and toppings.

Bake the pizzas for 8 minutes, then lower the oven temperature to 375°F. Bake 3 to 5 minutes longer, or until the crust is lightly browned.

B.B.
Test Kitchen Notes

Through Thick or Thin, Chewy or Crisp

Adjusting pizza crust to your liking can be as simple as adjusting the amount of yeast you use. For a thick, chewy crust, increase the amount of yeast called for by ½ teaspoon. For a crisp, thin crust, decrease the amount of instant yeast by ½ teaspoon, and allow for little or no rising.

My love affair with sponges continues with pizzas doughs. Sponges are shortcuts to flavor. Even an extra hour or two of slow rise can make all the difference.

READY-WHEN-YOU-ARE PIZZA

MAKES THREE 9-INCH PIZZAS

SPONGE

1 cup warm water

¾ teaspoon instant yeast

1¼ cups all-purpose flour

DOUGH

Sponge, above

½ cup warm water

1¼ teaspoons salt

1 tablespoon sugar

2 tablespoons olive oil

1 tablespoon stone-ground
    cornmeal

1½ to 2½ cups bread flour

Olive oil for drizzling

1½ cups Bottle-It-and-Sell-It Pizza
    Sauce (page 87) or your favorite
    jarred sauce

Toppings of your choice (page 84)

Wouldn't it be nice to have pizza dough ready when you come home from work or a busy shopping run? This dough, which makes use of an overnight sponge, develops at a leisurely pace while you're away. The slow rise yields better flavor. This is a favorite at the BB test kitchen, and judging by the deluge of email over the years, a favorite of my visitors. If you forget to make the sponge the night before, then make my Classic Pizza dough (page 85) using half the yeast, and let the dough rise all day.

For the sponge, stir the water and yeast together in the bowl of an electric mixer. Let stand for 2 to 3 minutes to dissolve the yeast. Stir in the flour to make a thick batter.

Place the bowl in a large plastic bag, close the bag loosely, and let stand at room temperature overnight.

For the dough, stir down the sponge and add the water, salt, sugar, oil, cornmeal, and 1½ cups of the bread flour. Mix to make a soft mass. Knead with the dough hook on the lowest speed of the mixer for 8 to 10 minutes, gradually adding more flour as required to form a soft, elastic dough. Turn the dough out on a lightly floured surface. Form the dough into a ball and place in a lightly greased bowl. Spray the dough with nonstick cooking spray and place the bowl in the plastic bag. Let rise at room temperature for 6 to 8 hours, or until doubled in size.

Preheat the oven to 450°F. Coat three 9-inch pizza pans with olive oil. Set aside.

Turn the dough out onto a lightly floured surface and divide it into 3 portions. Let the dough rest for 10 minutes. Press or roll the dough out to fit the prepared pizza pans. If the dough resists or otherwise retracts, let it rest for a few minutes, then gently coax it to fit the pans. Drizzle a bit of olive oil on top of the dough. Spread on the sauce and add the toppings of your choice.

Bake the pizzas for 8 minutes, then lower the oven temperature to 425°F. Bake 3 to 5 minutes longer, or until the crust is lightly browned.

CHICAGO DEEP-DISH STUFFED PIZZA

MAKES ONE 12-INCH DEEP-DISH PIZZA

Seasoned bread crumbs or
    cornmeal for sprinkling

DOUGH

2 cups warm water

5 teaspoons instant yeast

1 tablespoon sugar

⅓ cup olive oil

2½ teaspoons salt

3 tablespoons semolina or
    cornmeal

1 cup all-purpose flour

5 to 6 cups bread flour

SAUCE

2 cloves garlic, minced

2 tablespoons olive oil

1 (28-ounce) can Italian plum
    tomatoes

1 small onion, finely chopped

1 small green bell pepper, seeded,
    deribbed, and finely chopped

1½ teaspoons dried oregano

1 teaspoon dried basil

½ teaspoon fennel seeds

½ teaspoon salt

¼ teaspoon freshly ground black
    pepper

1 tablespoon fresh lemon juice

2 tablespoons dry red wine

Once I attended a food writers' conference in Chicago. I was wined and dined in some of the better restaurants in the city, but every chance I had, I snuck out to eat "street" pizza. It was simply the best.

No two Chicagoans will tell you exactly the same thing about making deep-dish pizza, but these are the basics: Chicago deep-dish pizza takes its name from being baked in a deeper pan, with sides about 1 inch high. It is made with a relatively thin crust dressed more or less in the opposite fashion of regular pizza. That is, mozzarella cheese is placed directly on the dough, and additional ingredients like sausage and mushrooms follow. Then you add tomato sauce, and a little sprinkling of cheese and spices. Can this kind of pizza be reproduced authentically outside Chicago? It depends how close you are to Lake Michigan, according to one pizza maven. Apparently, the water makes all the difference in the dough. I'll take his word for it.

This recipe looks long and complicated, but it's not. My version has two layers of dough and takes liberties in assembling the filling (for example, I do not put cheese directly on the dough). Layer cake pans work as deep-dish pizza pans. Sizes vary, but the sides are usually ¾ to 1 inch high.

Coat a 12-inch deep-dish pizza pan with olive oil and sprinkle with seasoned bread crumbs.

For the dough, hand whisk the water and yeast together in the bowl of an electric mixer and let stand for 2 to 3 minutes to dissolve the yeast. Stir in the sugar, oil, salt, semolina, all-purpose flour, and 5 cups of the bread flour. Mix to make a soft mass. Knead with the dough hook on the lowest speed of the mixer for 5 to 8 minutes, gradually adding more flour as required to form a soft, elastic dough. Turn the dough out onto a lightly floured surface and form it into a ball. Place the dough in a lightly greased bowl. Place the bowl in a large plastic bag, close the bag loosely, and let the dough rise for 30 to 45 minutes, or until almost doubled.

For the sauce, sauté the garlic in the oil over low heat for 1 to 2 minutes. Add all the remaining ingredients. Lower the heat to low and simmer for

FILLING

3 bunches spinach, cooked, drained, and coarsely chopped

¼ teaspoon salt

¼ teaspoon freshly ground black pepper

1 teaspoon dried basil

¼ teaspoon dried oregano

2 cloves garlic, minced

2 tablespoons olive oil

10 ounces white mushrooms, thinly sliced

3 large Italian sausages, removed from casings and cooked (1½ cups), or 1 cup thinly sliced pepperoni (optional)

3 cups (12 ounces) shredded mozzarella cheese

½ cup grated Parmesan cheese

20 to 30 minutes, or until the sauce thickens. Remove from the heat and let cool thoroughly.

Preheat the oven to 450°F.

For the filling, toss the spinach, salt, pepper, basil, oregano, garlic, and oil together in a large bowl.

Turn the dough out onto a lightly floured board. (You may also refrigerate the dough in a well-greased plastic bag for up to 2 days. Before using, let the dough come to room temperature for about 30 minutes.) Divide into 2 pieces, one about two-thirds of the whole and the other one-third. Let the dough rest for 10 minutes. Press or roll out the larger piece into a 16-inch round. If the dough resists or otherwise retracts, let it rest for a few more minutes. Line the prepared pan with the dough, leaving a 2-inch overhang.

Spoon in a touch of sauce, then all of the filling. Top with the mushrooms and sausage. Roll the remaining dough out into a 12-inch round. Place on top of the pizza pan and crimp the edges. Top with the remaining sauce, then the mozzarella and Parmesan.

Bake for 30 to 40 minutes, or until sizzling and golden. Remove from the oven and let cool for 10 minutes before cutting.

THE WINDOWPANE TEST FOR PIZZA DOUGH

At home, good bread flour is required in order to develop the gluten required for elasticity, and the dough should be kneaded sufficiently. To test the readiness of the dough, perform a windowpane test. Take up a bit of well-kneaded dough and gently stretch it to see if you can create a thin membrane that is translucent when held up to light. Keep kneading, checking, and stretching until you succeed. The trick here is not to overwork the dough, as that will cause it to tear. There's a sweet spot in there, and a little practice is required.

NEAR-PERFECT
HUT-STYLE PAN PIZZA

MAKES THREE 9-INCH PIZZAS

3 tablespoons olive oil

DOUGH

1⅓ cups warm water

1 tablespoon instant yeast

1 tablespoon sugar

1½ teaspoons salt

¼ cup nonfat dry milk

2 tablespoons vegetable oil

2 teaspoons baking powder

1 cup all-purpose flour

2 to 3 cups bread flour

1 cup Bottle-It-and-Sell-It Pizza
   Sauce (page 87) or your favorite
   jarred sauce

Garlic powder and Italian herb
   seasoning for sprinkling

3 cups (12 ounces) shredded
   mozzarella cheese

3 cups thinly sliced pepperoni for
   topping (optional)

The generous amount of oil in the pan helps produce that crisp bottom crust that pizza chains offer. Moreover, the use of milk powder, baking powder as well as yeast, and a small proportion of all-purpose flour make this similar to the crusts found in chain restaurants. I especially recommend this for kids who enjoy a tender-crisp pizza in a deep pan.

~◊~

Generously coat three 9-inch round cake pans with 1 tablespoon olive oil each. Set aside.

For the dough, hand whisk the water and yeast together in the bowl of an electric mixer and let stand for 2 to 3 minutes to dissolve the yeast. Stir in the sugar, salt, dry milk, oil, baking powder, all-purpose flour, and 2 cups of the bread flour. Mix to make a soft mass. Knead with the dough hook on the lowest speed of the mixer for 5 to 8 minutes, gradually adding more flour as required to form a soft, elastic dough. Turn the dough out onto a lightly floured surface. Form the dough into a ball and place in a lightly greased bowl. Place the bowl in a large plastic bag, close the bag loosely, and let the dough rise for 30 to 45 minutes, or until almost doubled.

Turn the dough out onto a lightly floured surface. Divide the dough into 3 portions. Let the dough rest for 10 minutes. Roll out each dough to a 9-inch round, about ⅜ inch thick, and place in the prepared pans. If the dough resists or otherwise retracts, let it rest for a few more minutes. Spray the dough with nonstick cooking spray, and place the pans inside plastic bags. Let the dough rise for 45 to 90 minutes, or until almost doubled.

Preheat the oven to 450°F. Spread about ⅓ cup sauce on each pizza, then sprinkle with garlic and herbs. Top with the cheese and the pepperoni.

Bake the pizzas for 12 to 17 minutes, or until the cheese is bubbling and the edges are lightly browned.

FRIED PARMESAN PIZZA WEDGES

MAKES 12 WEDGES

DOUGH

1¼ cups warm water

1½ teaspoons instant yeast

2 teaspoons honey

1¼ teaspoons salt

2 tablespoons olive oil

2 tablespoons cornmeal

1 cup all-purpose flour

1 to 2 cups bread flour

⅓ cup vegetable oil

Grated Parmesan cheese or
    cornmeal for dusting

Garlic powder for dusting

Bomba Hot Dipping Sauce
    (page 99)

Some of my recipes are inspired by what I eat in restaurants and some are created for the restaurateurs themselves. I have worked as a restaurant consultant for several years. A client once asked me to create easy-to-prepare bites for patrons to munch on at the bar while they waited for their tables. Since there was plenty of pizza dough and several hot fryers on standby in this place, these fried pizza wedges were born. I'm not sure if that restaurant still serves them, but they've become a snack staple in my home. Having refrigerated dough on hand makes these a cinch. Even store-bought frozen bread dough will do.

For the dough, hand whisk the water and yeast together in the bowl of an electric mixer and let stand for 2 to 3 minutes to dissolve the yeast. Stir in the honey, salt, oil, cornmeal, all-purpose flour, and 1 cup of the bread flour. Mix to make a soft mass. Knead with the dough hook on the lowest speed of the mixer for 5 to 8 minutes, gradually adding more bread flour as required to form a soft, elastic dough. Turn the dough out onto a lightly floured surface and form it into a ball. Place the dough in a lightly greased bowl. Place the bowl in a large plastic bag, close the bag loosely, and let the dough rise for 30 to 45 minutes, or until almost doubled.

Turn the dough out onto a lightly floured surface and divide into 12 portions. Let the pieces rest for 10 minutes. Roll or stretch each portion into a slab ¹⁄₁₆ to ⅛ inch thick.

In a cast-iron skillet, heat the vegetable oil over medium heat. Fry the wedges a few at a time, turning to brown each side. As soon as the wedges puff and brown, remove with a slotted spoon and drain on paper towels.

Toss quickly with some Parmesan cheese and dust with garlic powder. Serve hot, wrapped in a towel in a basket, along with the dipping sauce.

FAMOUS BB PIZZA CROISSANTS

MAKES 12 PIZZA CROISSANTS

Semolina or cornmeal for
    sprinkling

Classic Pizza dough, prepared up
    through first rise (page 85)

¼ cup olive oil

3 cloves garlic, crushed

½ teaspoon Italian herb seasoning

¼ teaspoon salt

⅛ teaspoon freshly ground black
    pepper

1¼ cups Bottle-It-and-Sell-It Pizza
    Sauce (page 87) or your favorite
    jarred sauce

3 cups (12 ounces) shredded
    mozzarella cheese, plus more
    for sprinkling

¾ cup grated Parmesan cheese,
    plus more for sprinkling

6 to 8 ounces pepperoni, finely
    chopped

Melted unsalted butter or olive oil
    for brushing

Sesame seeds for garnish

This is one of the easier ways to make yourself a legend in your own lunchtime. Rolled wedges of dough and savory ingredients come out of the oven as cheesy, golden "croissants" that taste even better than they look. These can rise a bit (for a chewier snack) or not (for a crispier texture). Make them up, freeze, and bake as needed. Variations include smoked turkey and Swiss cheese, feta and spinach, and smoked ham and sharp cheddar. Make larger wedges and increase the filling ingredients slightly to make oversized versions to serve as a meal. This recipe has been downloaded 5,718 times!

~❖~

Preheat the oven to 425°F. Stack 2 baking sheets together and line the top one with parchment paper. Lightly coat with olive oil and sprinkle with semolina.

Turn the dough out onto a lightly floured surface. Roll the dough into a 14- to 16-inch-long oval. If the dough resists let it rest for a few minutes before proceeding. Brush with the olive oil. Mix the garlic with the herbs, salt, pepper, and pizza sauce. Spread over the dough. Sprinkle on the mozzarella, Parmesan, and pepperoni. Using a large pizza wheel, cut the dough into 12 wedges. Starting from the wide end, roll up each wedge to the point and bring the ends together slightly to form a crescent.

Brush with the butter, sprinkle with the cheeses and sesame seeds, and place on the prepared baking sheets. Let rise for 20 to 30 minutes, or bake right away for crispier croissants.

Place in the oven, lower the temperature to 400°F, and bake for 25 to 30 minutes, or until medium brown. Serve hot.

FOOD COURT BREAD STICKS

MAKES 24 BREAD STICKS

Cornmeal for sprinkling

DOUGH

1½ cups warm water

2 teaspoons instant yeast

2 teaspoons sugar

1¼ teaspoons salt

2 tablespoons olive oil

2 tablespoons cornmeal

1 teaspoon baking powder

¼ teaspoon garlic powder

¼ teaspoon onion powder

1 cup all-purpose flour

1 to 2 cups bread flour

GARNISH

⅓ cup melted unsalted butter and
    olive oil, in equal amounts

¼ cup seasoned bread crumbs or
    semolina

Olive oil for brushing

Parmesan cheese

Garlic powder or minced fresh or
    dried herbs

Bottle-It-and-Sell-It Pizza Sauce
    (page 87) or Bomba Hot
    Dipping Sauce (opposite)

This recipe is a crowd pleaser and reminiscent of the bread sticks some pizzerias offer. You can use leftover pizza dough (about half a batch) or follow the recipe below. These are tender and chewy—dare I say "commercial tasting"? For thicker, breadlike pizza dough, add an additional ½ teaspoon yeast.

Lightly coat a 7- by 11-inch brownie pan or similar shallow pan with olive oil. Sprinkle lightly with cornmeal. Set aside.

For the dough, hand whisk the water and yeast together in the bowl of an electric mixer and let stand for 2 to 3 minutes to dissolve the yeast. Stir in the sugar, salt, oil, cornmeal, baking powder, garlic powder, onion powder, all-purpose flour, and 1 cup of the bread flour. Mix to make a soft mass. Knead with the dough hook on the lowest speed of the mixer for 5 to 8 minutes, gradually adding more bread flour as required to form a soft, elastic dough. Turn the dough out onto a lightly floured surface and form the dough into a ball. Place in a lightly greased bowl. Place the bowl in a large plastic bag, close the bag loosely, and let the dough rise for 30 to 45 minutes, or until almost doubled.

Turn the dough out into the prepared pan and gently pat out to fill the pan, about ½ inch thick. Lightly paint with the butter mixture. Sprinkle with the bread crumbs. Let the dough rise for 15 minutes.

Preheat the oven to 425°F. Bake the dough for 15 to 18 minutes, or until golden brown. Remove from the oven, brush with olive oil, and sprinkle with Parmesan cheese and a touch of garlic powder. Using tongs, lift the baked dough onto a cutting board. Using a pizza wheel or sharp knife, cut the bread into ½-inch-wide strips.

Serve as is, or with pizza sauce for dipping.

BOMBA HOT DIPPING SAUCE

MAKES ABOUT 4 CUPS

2 small carrots, chopped

½ cup small dried red chiles

½ cup dry-packed sun-dried tomatoes

1 small onion, cut up

½ cup canned mushroom pieces

½ cup stuffed or pitted green olives

½ cup drained, canned artichoke hearts

2½ cups vegetable oil

2 tablespoons minced garlic

1 tablespoon chile powder

1 teaspoon cayenne powder

½ teaspoon paprika

1 tablespoon salt

1 teaspoon fresh lemon juice

2 teaspoons white vinegar

1 teaspoon red wine vinegar

2 teaspoons hot sauce

I serve this sauce with Fried Pizza Parmesan Wedges (page 95), a plate of balsamic vinegar and olive oil, and black olives. It is also good for pizza and pasta (try it tossed with angel hair pasta and capers), and excellent with bread sticks.

Cook the carrots in salted simmering water for 6 to 8 minutes, or until just barely tender. Drain and let cool.

Soak the chiles and tomatoes in hot water to cover for 10 minutes. Drain well. In a food processor, combine the carrots, chiles, tomatoes, onion, mushroom pieces, olives, and artichokes. Process for 30 to 45 seconds to make a coarse paste.

Heat the oil in a medium saucepan over medium heat. Lower the heat and stir in the vegetable mixture. Stir in the garlic, spices, salt, lemon juice, vinegars, and hot sauce. Simmer for 3 to 5 minutes. Remove from the heat and let cool. Use immediately, or cover and refrigerate for up to 2 weeks.

Some Like It Hot

. . . .

I like my flatbreads served up with a nice hot sauce for dipping, such as this Bomba Hot Dipping Sauce. You may like your sauce hot, or you may like it hotter. In any event, a little heat is good for you. Before the days of refrigeration, chile peppers were used to "improve the flavor" (mask the taste) of foods that were past their "best before" dates. Scientists have since discovered that hot spices also help to preserve food—especially in warmer climates where bacteria multiply quickly. There are also indications that chiles can reduce levels of so-called bad cholesterol, and some claim they can cure the common cold. With all these benefits, eat up, and feel the burn.

Garlic Bubble Bread

MAKES 1 LARGE LOAF

White bread dough such as
Wondrous Bread (page 28),
prepared up through first rise

⅓ cup garlic olive oil, or extra virgin
olive oil with lots of minced
fresh garlic

⅓ cup (3 ounces) unsalted butter,
melted

Salt or seasoned salt and freshly
ground black pepper

2 tablespoons minced fresh flat-leaf
parsley

2 tablespoons minced garlic

½ cup crumbled fresh white goat
cheese or grated Parmesan
cheese (optional)

Sesame seeds for sprinkling
(optional)

Store-bought garlic oil makes this one easy. Do not slice the bread. Serve it warm and simply pull apart sections to serve.

Spray a 9- by 5-inch loaf pan with nonstick cooking spray. Line a large baking sheet with parchment paper. Set aside.

Turn the dough out onto a lightly floured surface. Divide the dough into 2-inch pieces and form each into a ball. Whisk the garlic oil and butter together. Dip the dough balls in the oil mixture. Layer the balls on top of one another in the prepared loaf pan, sprinkling each layer with salt, pepper, parsley, garlic, and cheese. Sprinkle the top with sesame seeds. Place the pan in a large plastic bag, close the bag loosely, and let the dough rise for about 45 minutes, or until doubled.

Preheat the oven to 350°F. Place the loaf pan on the prepared baking sheet and bake for 30 to 40 minutes, or until golden and crusty. Let cool on a wire rack for 15 minutes before serving.

B.B.
Test Kitchen
Notes

Go for the Gold

The world of gourmet olive oils is as rarefied as that of fine wines, or so some people would like us to believe. In the end, it's all a matter of taste—your taste. Most fine olive oils come from the Mediterranean region. Olive growers in California and elsewhere also produce excellent products. "Extra virgin" oil (how can something be "extra virgin"?) comes from the first pressing of the olives. You will pay more for this variety. Many oils are blends, and while an extra virgin oil will be relatively dark, the intensity of the color has little to do with the taste. Experts say, however, that a very bright green color may indicate that leaves were crushed with the fruit. Purchase pure or virgin olive oil for high-temperature cooking and general use, and follow your taste buds to an extra virgin brand you like for use in salads, for dipping, and so on.

FOCACCIA

Semolina or cornmeal for dusting

DOUGH

1 cup warm water

2 teaspoons instant yeast

1 tablespoon honey

1¼ teaspoons salt

2 tablespoons extra virgin olive oil

2 tablespoons semolina

1 cup all-purpose flour

1 to 2 cups bread flour

Olive oil for drizzling

Salt and freshly ground black
     pepper to taste

6 to 8 large cloves garlic, minced

I like to bake this Italian flatbread on the grill (see variation below). Check out "Pizza on the Grill" (page 89) for some tips. This bread is terrific with fresh, warm roasted garlic on the side.

Coat a baking sheet or a 16-inch pizza pan with olive oil. Dust with semolina. Set aside.

In the bowl of an electric mixer, hand whisk the water and yeast together and let stand for 2 to 3 minutes to dissolve the yeast. Stir in the honey, salt, oil, the 2 tablespoons semolina, the all-purpose flour, and l cup of the bread flour. Mix to make a soft mass. Knead with the dough hook on the lowest speed of the mixer for 5 to 8 minutes, gradually adding more bread flour as required to form a soft, elastic dough. Turn the dough out onto a lightly floured surface and form it into a ball. Place the dough in a lightly greased bowl. Place the bowl in a large plastic bag, close the bag loosely, and let rise for 30 to 45 minutes, or until almost doubled.

Deflate the dough and let rest 15 minutes longer. (You can also refrigerate the dough in an oiled plastic bag for up to 2 days. Before using, let the dough come to room temperature for about 30 minutes.)

Preheat the oven to 425°F.

Turn the dough out onto the prepared pan and flatten gently into a 15-inch round. If the dough resists or otherwise retracts, let it rest for a few more minutes. Dimple the top of the dough with your fingertips. Drizzle with the olive oil and sprinkle with salt, pepper, and garlic.

Bake for 12 to 14 minutes, or until lightly browned on top. Transfer to a wire rack to cool.

VARIATION (FOCACCIA ON THE GRILL): Preheat a gas grill to medium. Place the baking sheet or pan on the grill and close the cover. After 2 minutes, lower the temperature to low. Uncover and, with a metal spatula, ease the bread directly onto the grill. Bake for 5 to 8 minutes, or until lightly browned. If at any time the bread seems to be cooking too quickly, lower the heat.

ITALIAN BISTRO PANINI

MAKES 5 PANINI

Semolina or cornmeal for dusting

SPONGE

1 cup warm water

1 tablespoon instant yeast

1 cup bread flour

DOUGH

Sponge, above

½ cup warm water

1 teaspoon instant yeast

2 tablespoons olive oil

2 teaspoons sugar

1½ teaspoons salt

3 tablespoons semolina or
   cornmeal

3 to 4 cups bread flour

A sponge is used in this recipe to lend a little extra flavor and crumb development, and a touch of semolina makes these rolls a bit more interesting. Leftover rolls freeze beautifully or make terrific garlic bread.

Stack 2 baking sheets together and line the top one with parchment paper. Dust with semolina. Set aside.

For the sponge, combine all the ingredients in a small bowl and stir to make a puddinglike mixture. Cover loosely and let stand for 1 to 3 hours, or until bubbly and foamy.

For the dough, hand whisk the water and yeast together in the bowl of an electric mixer and let stand for 2 to 3 minutes to dissolve the yeast. Stir in the sponge, oil, sugar, salt, semolina, and 3 cups of the flour. Mix to make a soft mass. Knead with the dough hook on the lowest speed of the mixer for 5 to 8 minutes, gradually adding more flour as required to form a soft, elastic dough. Turn the dough out onto a lightly floured surface. Form the dough into a ball and place in a lightly greased bowl. Place the bowl inside a large plastic bag, close the bag loosely, and let the dough rise for 30 to 45 minutes, or until almost doubled.

Turn the dough out onto a lightly floured surface and divide into 5 portions. Let the dough rest for 10 minutes. Shape each portion into an oval like a plump hot dog bun. If the dough is too slack, just cut out slabs. The irregular shape is fine. Place on the prepared baking sheets.

Spray the tops of the rolls with nonstick cooking spray. Place the baking sheet inside the plastic bag, close the bag loosely, and let the dough rise for about 30 minutes, or until quite puffy.

Preheat the oven to 375°F. Score the tops of the rolls with a knife and dust generously with flour. Bake the loaves for 20 to 25 minutes, or until lightly golden. Let cool completely on wire racks before making into sandwiches.

PANINI SANDWICHES

· ·

To make a sandwich, split the roll in half lengthwise. Drizzle on a little olive oil. Add the filling and replace the top half. Wrap the sandwich in aluminum foil for moister bread, or leave unwrapped for crisp bread.

Heat a lightly oiled cast-iron skillet over medium heat. Add the sandwich to the skillet. Using a couple of plates or a heavy pot as a press, weigh down the sandwich. Cook for 3 to 4 minutes, then turn and cook for 3 to 4 minutes on the other side.

PANINI FILLING SUGGESTIONS:

- Goat cheese, sun-dried tomatoes, roasted garlic, and sautéed broccoli raab

- Feta cheese, black olive tapenade, slivered onions, fresh tomato slices, and sprouts

- Swiss cheese, slivered ham or roast beef, prepared horseradish, Dijon mustard, and caramelized onions

- Tuna salad or vegetable pâté, sprouts, shredded carrots and lettuce or cabbage, and pickled peppers

- Sliced grilled steak, roasted garlic, goat cheese or aged cheddar or blue cheese

- Grilled chicken, roasted red peppers, grilled eggplant, slivered red onion, and Italian vinaigrette

- Grilled peppers, sliced black olives, and goat cheese

ARMENIAN LAVOSH

MAKES 4 FLATBREADS

DOUGH

½ cup warm water

1 teaspoon instant yeast

2 teaspoons sugar

1 teaspoon salt

2 tablespoons vegetable oil or
   melted unsalted butter

4 egg whites

2½ to 3 cups all-purpose flour

TOPPING

1 egg white, beaten until foamy

Poppy, sesame, or caraway seeds
   for sprinkling (optional)

Unlike some flatbreads, this is crisp and great for dipping. If you bake it for only 10 to 12 minutes, until lightly colored, it will be soft enough to use as a wrap. Serve it with dips, pâté, or cheese.

Stack 2 baking sheets together and line the top one with parchment paper. Coat with olive oil. Set aside.

For the dough, hand whisk the water and yeast together in the bowl of an electric mixer and let stand for 2 to 3 minutes to dissolve the yeast. Stir in the sugar, salt, oil, egg whites, and 2½ cups of the flour. Mix to make a soft mass. Knead with the dough hook on the lowest speed of the mixer for 5 to 8 minutes, gradually adding more flour as required to form a soft, elastic dough. Let the dough rest in the bowl for 10 minutes.

Turn the dough out onto a lightly floured surface and form it into a ball. Place the dough in a lightly greased bowl. Place the bowl in a large plastic bag, close the bag loosely, and let the dough rise for about 1½ hours, or until almost doubled.

Preheat the oven to 400°F. Turn the dough out on a lightly floured surface and divide into 4 portions. Let the dough rest for 10 minutes. Roll each dough into a round about ⅛ inch thick. Place them on the prepared baking sheet. Brush the tops with the egg white and sprinkle with the seeds. Prick the dough all over with a fork. Bake for about 15 minutes, or until golden brown.

B.B. Test Kitchen Notes

A New Equation—the Bread Machine Sous Chef

Bread machine dough cycle + half the yeast = ready-when-you-are dough: if you want pizza dough, focaccia dough, or practically any dough, for that matter, ready for supper when you have been out all day, use only ½ teaspoon yeast for the dough. Let the "dough" cycle of your bread machine do its thing, and by the time you return home (in 6 to 8 hours), the dough is ready to go. Proofing the dough inside a plastic bag works the same way.

PITA BREAD

MAKES 16 PITAS

2½ cups warm water

4 teaspoons instant yeast

2 teaspoons sugar

2½ teaspoons salt

1 teaspoon honey

2 tablespoons olive oil

4½ to 5½ cups bread flour

Pita is a typical bread of the Middle Eastern table. Roll it, wrap it, dunk it. White whole-wheat flour can be substituted in this recipe.

Stack 2 baking sheets together and line the top one with parchment paper. Set aside.

For the dough, hand whisk the water and yeast together in the bowl of an electric mixer and let stand for 2 to 3 minutes to dissolve the yeast. Stir in the sugar, salt, honey, oil, and 4½ cups of the flour. Mix to make a soft mass. Knead with the dough hook on the lowest speed of the mixer for 5 to 8 minutes, gradually adding more flour as required to form a soft, elastic dough. Turn the dough out onto a lightly floured surface. Form the dough into a ball and place in a lightly greased bowl. Place the bowl in a large plastic bag, close the bag loosely, and let the dough rise for 30 to 45 minutes, or until almost doubled.

Turn the dough out onto a lightly floured surface and divide the dough into 16 portions. Let the dough rest for 10 minutes. Form each portion into a ball. Cover with a damp kitchen towel and let the pieces rest for 2 minutes. Flatten each ball with a rolling pin into a disk 6 to 8 inches in diameter and ¼ inch thick. If the dough is resistant and springy, let it rest for a couple of minutes.

Cover the disks with a damp tea towel and let them rise for 15 to 25 minutes, or until slightly puffy.

Preheat the oven to 475°F. Place as many pitas as will comfortably fit, about 6, on the prepared baking sheet. Bake for 2 to 3 minutes, or until they puff. Turn and briefly bake on the other side. Lower the oven temperature to 425°F if the pitas are browning too fast. Let cool completely on the baking sheet, and wrap the baked pitas in clean tea towels to keep them soft. Repeat with the remaining pitas.

CUMIN GARLIC HUMMUS

MAKES ABOUT 2 CUPS

1 (19-ounce) can chickpeas (garbanzo beans), drained, liquid reserved

2 to 4 tablespoons tahini (sesame paste)

2 to 4 cloves garlic, minced

½ to ¾ teaspoon salt

⅛ teaspoon freshly ground black pepper

¼ cup olive oil, plus olive oil for drizzling

2 to 4 drops hot sauce

2 to 3 teaspoons ground cumin (optional)

¼ teaspoon ground coriander

¼ cup fresh lemon juice

Minced fresh flat-leaf parsley and cilantro for garnish

Pita without hummus? Don't be silly. Hummus is a staple of the Middle Eastern kitchen. Recipes vary. I like cumin in hummus, but often it is made without it in restaurants. Presentation is important for this dish, so follow the directions carefully. Tahini is available in natural foods stores and Middle Eastern markets.

In a food processor, process the chickpeas for 30 to 60 seconds. Add all the remaining ingredients except the reserved chickpea liquid, the olive oil for drizzling, and the garnish and pulse to make a paste. With the machine running, add enough chickpea liquid to make a thick, smooth paste. Taste and adjust the seasoning. Chill, then spoon into a shallow dish or platter. Using the back of a teaspoon, make a trough in the puree and drizzle with olive oil. Sprinkle with parsley and cilantro.

BOMBAY PALACE–STYLE NAN BREAD

MAKES 10 TO 15 BREADS

1½ cups warm water

5 teaspoons sugar

1¾ teaspoons salt

1 egg

2 tablespoons melted unsalted
    butter or vegetable oil

1 cup half-and-half or light cream

2½ teaspoons baking powder

½ teaspoon baking soda

4 cups all-purpose flour

1 to 2 cups bread flour

Most recipes for nan call for yogurt and milk, but this version is adapted from one provided by the famed Bombay Palace Restaurant of Montreal, with a sister restaurant in Washington, DC. Rustic, chewy, addictive—this is perfect for a mountain of tandoori chicken or just about any main dish.

Stack 2 baking sheets together and line the top one with parchment paper. Set aside.

In the bowl of an electric mixer, hand whisk the water, sugar, and salt together. Whisk in the egg and butter. Stir in the cream, baking powder, baking soda, all-purpose flour, and 1 cup of the bread flour. Mix to make a soft mass. Knead with the dough hook on the lowest speed of the mixer for 10 to 15 minutes, adding more bread flour as required to form a soft, supple dough. Turn the dough out onto a lightly floured surface and form it into a ball. Place the dough in a lightly greased bowl. Place the bowl in a large plastic bag, close the bag loosely, and let rise for 2 to 4 hours.

Turn the dough out onto a lightly floured surface and divide into 10 to 15 portions, each the size of a large orange. Let them rest for 10 minutes, then roll them into rounds the size of your hand. Stretch gently lengthwise and sidewise to make a teardrop shape. Place the pieces on the prepared baking sheets and cover with a damp tea towel. Let rest for 10 to 15 minutes.

Preheat the oven to 475°F. Place a cast-iron skillet in the oven to preheat for 20 minutes. Place a nan in the pan. Bake for 1 to 2 minutes, or until browned and blistered on the bottom, then turn and bake for 1 to 2 minutes longer. Repeat with the remaining pieces.

VARIATION (NAN ON THE GRILL): Light a fire in a charcoal grill or preheat a gas grill to high (450°F to 500°F). Place the nan directly on the grill and close the cover. Bake for 3 to 5 minutes, or until the dough puffs. Using tongs, turn and bake on the other side for 3 to 5 minutes. The nan may look scorched in areas but this is okay. Serve immediately, or cover with aluminum foil to keep warm.

Chapter 4

· ·

THE CORNER CAFÉ

· ·

FEW THINGS IN LIFE ARE MORE SATISFYING than a hot cup of coffee or tea and a nice bite to accompany it. This has not been lost on the entrepreneurs responsible for the proliferation of coffee shops in North America. They are more than happy to offer you a baked treat to go along with your Kenyan decaf extra-skim double latte with Indian cinnamon and an unbleached, recycled-paper napkin. Unfortunately, many of the food items that coffee shops serve up to accompany your "cuppa" of coffee or tea taste like an unbleached, recycled-paper napkin.

The reason is simple: many shops, even the large chains, purchase their goods from local outfits that mass-produce baked goods. Homemade doesn't always mean pretty, but it does mean better taste. That said, with a little help from the BB test kitchen, you can turn your homey sweets into pretty, tasty treats.

When it comes to coffee- and teatime desserts, I admit to having been inspired by some of the baked goods discovered in coffee shops. Of course, I can't leave well enough alone, and I have to tweak even the most basic classics to suit my tastes. Bigger is better in this genre of baking, and with that in mind, I urge you to stay away from modest slices and servings and cut big, bold portions. These baked goods may not be fancy, but they are special treats for family and friends as well as for company.

As for baking tips, you should note that my recipes call for brown sugar. I most often use golden or light brown sugar in my coffeehouse baking, but dark brown sugar can be substituted in any recipe. Be sure to use unsalted butter and pure vanilla extract in all your baking.

FRIED FLAPS OF DOUGH THAT RESEMBLE THE TAIL OF THE CASTOR CANADENSIS

MAKES ABOUT 2½ DOZEN FLAPS

DOUGH

½ cup warm water

5 teaspoons instant yeast

1 cup warm milk

⅓ cup sugar

1½ teaspoons salt

1 teaspoon pure vanilla extract

2 eggs

⅓ cup vegetable oil

4 to 5 cups bread flour, or half all-purpose and half bread flour

Vegetable oil for deep-frying

Sugar for dusting

Ground cinnamon for dusting (optional)

Jam for serving (optional)

This is the longest recipe title of any. The "flaps" are a BB hall-of-famer, one of my most popular recipes. These "flaps" or "tails" of dough are made from doughnut dough, not too sweet nor too rich, that is formed into ovals before being stretched and briefly fried. Forget a deep fryer. In the test kitchen, I prefer a wok and long stainless-steel tongs. After frying, the flaps are tossed in sugar, with a touch of cinnamon if you like. Fresh from the fryer or even at room temperature, these are the next best thing to being at a country fair.

~(◊)~

For the dough, hand whisk the water and yeast together in the bowl of an electric mixer and let stand for 2 to 3 minutes to dissolve the yeast. Stir in the milk, sugar, salt, vanilla, eggs, oil, and 4 cups of the flour. Mix to make a soft dough. Knead with the dough hook on the lowest speed of the mixer for 5 to 8 minutes, gradually adding more flour as required to make a firm, smooth, elastic dough.

Gather the dough into a ball shape in the bowl. Place the bowl inside a large plastic bag, close the bag loosely, and let rise for 30 to 40 minutes, or until almost doubled.

Gently deflate the dough. Turn the dough out onto a lightly floured surface and let rest for 10 minutes.

Pinch off a golf-ball-sized piece of dough. Roll or gently stretch it out into an oval about 4 inches long. Repeat with the remaining dough. Let the pieces rest, covered lightly with a tea towel, for about 15 minutes.

In a wok or a Dutch oven, heat 3 inches oil to 385°F, or until a tiny bit of dough added to the oil sizzles and swells immediately.

Stretch the ovals into a tail by pulling them out twice as long as they were. Gently place 1 or 2 pieces in the hot oil. Fry for 8 to 15 seconds on each side, or until a deep brown, using tongs to turn. Using a slotted spoon, transfer to paper towels to drain. Dredge in a shallow bowl of sugar mixed with cinnamon to taste, and shake to remove the excess. Serve immediately, with jam.

BEAVER TALES AND PIE IN THE SKY: OUR LIFE IN THE FOOD COURT

. . . .

A couple of years ago, when I had just launched the site, two legal firms contacted me and threatened me with prosecution if I did not cease using these registered trademarks: Derby Pie and Beaver Tails. In both instances, I was not aware that the names were registered, and I complied with the request to stop using them. The fact that the names appear in countless cookbooks, church-group collections, and elsewhere made no difference to the lawyers, nor did the fact that I was not deriving any profit from their use. Nonetheless, I respect the notion of intellectual property.

This story even became the subject of an article in the *Washington Post* entitled "Pie Fight!"

OVEN-FRIED DOUGH

MAKES 2½ TO 3 DOZEN SQUARES

DOUGH

1½ cups warm water

2 tablespoons instant yeast

½ cup (4 ounces) melted unsalted
    butter or ½ cup vegetable oil

½ cup sugar

2 eggs

1 egg yolk

1 teaspoon pure vanilla extract

1 tablespoon salt

2 cups all-purpose flour

4 to 5 cups bread flour

TOPPING

⅓ cup (3 ounces) unsalted butter,
    melted

1 cup sugar

3 to 4 teaspoons ground cinnamon

Confectioners' sugar (optional)

This is essentially a variation on Fried Flaps of Dough (page 110). Sometimes I'm in no mood to fry, or simply want to make a lot of something fast. Here, sweetened dough is smeared with butter and sugar, then baked. Served fresh, this oven version will earn you rave reviews. If you like doughnuts, you'll love these.

Stack 2 large baking sheets, or 2 sets of smaller sheets, together and line the top one with parchment paper. Set aside.

For the dough, hand whisk the water and yeast together in the bowl of an electric mixer and let stand for 2 to 3 minutes to dissolve the yeast. Stir in the butter, sugar, eggs, egg yolk, vanilla, salt, all-purpose flour, and 3 cups of the bread flour. Mix to make a soft dough. Knead with the dough hook on the lowest speed of the mixer for 8 to 10 minutes, gradually adding more bread flour as required to make a smooth, elastic dough. Place the bowl inside a large plastic bag, close the bag loosely, and let rise for 45 minutes, or until almost doubled in bulk.

Turn the dough out onto a lightly floured surface and roll it out to fit the prepared baking sheets. If the dough retracts, let it rest for 3 to 5 minutes. You can also stretch the dough by hand. Transfer the dough to the baking sheets, let it rest for 1 minute, then pull it to fit the sheet. Place the baking sheets in a large plastic bag, close the bag loosely, and let the dough rise 30 to 40 minutes, or until puffy.

Preheat the oven to 350°F. Brush the dough liberally with the melted butter several times. Combine the sugar and cinnamon in a bowl. Dust with the cinnamon sugar. Bake for 30 to 40 minutes, or until browned. Remove from the oven and let cool to the touch. Transfer to a cutting board and cut into 4 by 2½-inch portions with a pizza wheel or a sharp knife. Dust with confectioners' sugar. Serve warm or at room temperature.

TRUCK-STOP ORANGE CAKE DOUGHNUTS

MAKES 2½ DOZEN DOUGHNUTS

DOUGH

2 tablespoons melted vegetable
shortening or vegetable oil

1 cup sugar

2 eggs

1 cup milk

Grated zest of 1 orange

1 teaspoon orange extract, or
½ teaspoon orange oil

½ teaspoon salt

3 cups all-purpose flour

1 tablespoon baking powder

Vegetable oil for deep-frying

ORANGE GLAZE (OPTIONAL)

1 cup confectioners' sugar

½ cup fresh orange juice

Confectioners' sugar for dusting
(optional)

Here is a rich cake doughnut, fragrant with orange zest and dusted with confectioners' sugar or dipped in orange glaze.

~(0)~

For the dough, combine the shortening, sugar, eggs, milk, orange zest, and orange extract in a large bowl. Stir to blend well. Stir in the salt, flour, and baking powder to make a stiff dough. Cover and refrigerate for 1 hour.

On a lightly floured surface, roll the dough out ½ inch thick. With a doughnut cutter, cut out rings. Reserve the centers to fry separately.

In a wok or a Dutch oven, heat 3 to 4 inches oil to 375°F, or until a tiny bit of dough added to the oil sizzles and swells immediately. A Dutch oven or other pot should be about half full of oil, while a wok needs to be only one-third full.

Gently lower a few doughnut rings at a time into the hot oil. Fry for about 1 minute, or until golden brown, then turn and fry for 30 to 40 seconds, or until brown on the second side. Using a slotted spoon, transfer to paper towels to drain. Let cool 8 to 10 minutes.

For the glaze, stir all the ingredients together in a medium bowl. Dip the doughnuts in the glaze to cover the top surface lightly. Let the glaze set for 5 to 8 minutes. Or dust the doughnuts with confectioners' sugar.

SPICE DOUGHNUTS: Replace the orange extract with vanilla extract and omit the orange zest. Add ½ teaspoon ground nutmeg and ¼ teaspoon *each* ground cinnamon, mace, allspice, and ginger.

BOSTON CREAM PIE DOUGHNUTS

MAKES 18 TO 20 DOUGHNUTS

DOUGH

¼ cup warm water

2 tablespoons instant yeast

1 cup warm milk

¼ cup vegetable shortening

2 eggs

¼ cup sugar

1 teaspoon salt

3½ to 4 cups bread flour

CUSTARD FILLING

¼ cup sugar

3 tablespoons all-purpose flour

3 egg yolks

1 cup plus 2 tablespoons milk

1 tablespoon unsalted butter

½ teaspoon pure vanilla extract

Vegetable oil for deep-frying

CHOCOLATE GLAZE

1 tablespoon unsalted butter

2 ounces semisweet chocolate, chopped

1½ cups confectioners' sugar

½ teaspoon pure vanilla extract

About ⅓ cup hot water

The commercial version of these doughnuts is always a highlight of the local doughnut shop. In a pinch, you could use instant pudding as the filling.

For the dough, hand whisk the water and yeast together in the bowl of an electric mixer and let stand for 2 to 3 minutes to dissolve the yeast. Whisk in the milk and shortening. Stir in the eggs, sugar, salt, and 3 cups of the flour. Mix to make a soft dough. Knead with the dough hook on the lowest speed of the mixer for 8 to 10 minutes, gradually adding more flour as required to form a soft but elastic dough. Place the dough in a lightly greased bowl, cover the bowl with a damp cloth, and place the bowl in a large plastic bag. Close the bag loosely and let the dough rise for 30 to 45 minutes, or until almost doubled.

For the filling, whisk the sugar, flour, and egg yolks together in a bowl. In a small saucepan, bring the milk to a boil. Stir 2 tablespoons of the milk into the egg mixture to temper the yolks and prevent curdling. Whisk the egg mixture into the milk and stir constantly until the mixture thickens and begins to boil gently, then immediately remove from heat. Stir in the butter and vanilla and let cool. Place in a bowl and cover with plastic wrap, pressing it directly on the surface to keep a skin from forming. Refrigerate.

Turn the dough out onto a lightly floured surface. Pinch off pieces of dough and form into small balls about the size of golf balls. Cover with plastic wrap and let rise for 25 minutes.

In a wok or a Dutch oven, heat 4 inches of oil to 375°F. Add the doughnuts a few at a time and fry for 30 to 40 seconds, until deep brown on the first side. Turn and fry on the second side for 15 to 30 seconds. Using a slotted spoon, transfer to paper towels to drain, and let cool.

Whisk the custard to smooth and fluff it. Put the custard in a pastry bag fitted with a large plain tip. Split each doughnut in half and pipe or spoon in some custard.

For the glaze, melt the butter and chocolate in a double boiler over barely simmering water. Add the confectioners' sugar and vanilla and stir until smooth. Add enough water to make a thin glaze. Let cool for 1 minute, then drizzle over the doughnuts. If the glaze gets too stiff, add more hot water to make it workable again.

YIN-YANG
CREAM CHEESE BROWNIES

MAKES ABOUT 20 BROWNIES

CREAM CHEESE LAYER

8 ounces cream cheese at room
   temperature

¼ cup sugar

1 egg

½ teaspoon pure vanilla extract

1 tablespoon all-purpose flour

BROWNIE LAYER

⅓ cup (3 ounces) unsalted butter

4 ounces semisweet chocolate,
   chopped

2 eggs

1 cup sugar

1 teaspoon pure vanilla extract

¼ teaspoon salt

½ cup all-purpose flour

½ cup miniature semisweet
   chocolate chips (optional)

A two-toned treat that is as neat to look at as it is to eat. These moist, fudgelike brownies are tunneled with swirls of cheesecake. Yes, they are rich, but isn't that the whole point of a good brownie? These are good cut into miniature squares and wrapped as gifts. They are best slightly chilled, which creates a denser texture and makes the brownies easier to cut.

~✧~

Preheat the oven to 350°F. Spray a 7- by 11-inch pan with nonstick cooking spray and set aside. Line a baking sheet with parchment paper. Set aside.

For the cream cheese layer, combine the cream cheese and sugar in a medium bowl. Blend well. Stir in the egg, vanilla, and flour until smooth. Set aside.

For the brownie layer, melt the butter and chocolate in a double boiler over barely simmering water or in a microwave. Stir until smooth. Let cool to room temperature.

Put the chocolate mixture in a large bowl. Stir in the eggs, sugar, vanilla, and salt. Gradually stir in the flour until smooth.

Spread three-fourths of the brownie batter in the prepared pan. Use a small spatula dipped in water to smooth the batter. Drop on dollops of the cream cheese batter. Sprinkle with the chocolate chips, then top with the remaining brownie batter by placing small dollops on top of the cream cheese batter. Using a knife, cut through the batters to marbleize. Smooth the top with a wet knife or metal spatula.

Place the pan on the prepared baking sheet and bake for 30 to 35 minutes, or until the cream cheese swirl is set. It is hard to tell when these are done, so follow the time closely and make sure the cheesecake layer seems set. Let cool on a wire rack, then refrigerate for at least 1 hour before cutting.

AWARD-WINNING NOTTING HILL BROWNIES

MAKES 12 TO 16 LARGE BROWNIES

2 cups (1 pound) unsalted butter, melted and cooled

2 cups white sugar

1½ cups firmly packed brown sugar

1½ teaspoons pure vanilla extract

6 eggs

1⅓ cups unsweetened cocoa powder

2 cups all-purpose flour

⅜ teaspoon baking soda

½ teaspoon salt

2 cups (8 ounces) chopped walnuts or pecans (optional)

Confectioners' sugar for dusting (optional)

Another recipe that needs its own Hall of Fame, or at least a culinary Oscar. This recipe is inspired by the scene in the movie Notting Hill in which the characters compete for the last brownie left on the dessert plate after dinner. These megabrownies are superstars in their own right. Chewy, but not mucky or sludgy, these are my test kitchen's favorite. They are great served with a scoop of ice cream, or rolled in sugar as in the Brownies under the Snow variation.

~⟨◊⟩~

Preheat the oven to 350°F. Spray a 9- by 13-inch baking pan lightly with nonstick cooking spray. Line the bottom with parchment paper. Line a baking sheet with parchment paper. Set aside.

In the bowl of an electric mixer fitted with the paddle attachment, combine the melted butter, both sugars, vanilla, and eggs. Beat well on the lowest speed. In a medium bowl, hand whisk the cocoa, flour, baking soda, and salt together. Fold into the batter and blend well with the mixer, stopping once or twice to scrape the bottom and sides of the bowl. Fold in the nuts (if using). Pour into the prepared pan. Smooth the top with a wet knife or metal spatula.

Place the pan on the prepared baking sheet and bake for 35 to 45 minutes, or until set and slightly firm but not dry. Let cool completely on a wire rack, then freeze for 1 hour. Unmold and peel off the parchment paper. Cut into squares roughly 2½ by 2½ inches. Wrap each in waxed paper and keep frozen or refrigerated. To serve for a party, pile the brownies on a platter and dust with confectioners' sugar.

BROWNIES UNDER THE SNOW: I once saw brownies similar to these in a café. No one would let me in on the recipe, so I worked it out for myself. The "snow" is simply a crisp finish of superfine sugar. It makes a nice contrast for the dense, fudgelike brownies: simply cut a batch of Notting Hill Brownies into small squares and toss them in superfine sugar or regular white sugar that has been pulverized in a food processor.

VARIATION: Skip the "snow" above and drizzle the brownies with melted bars of Belgian milk and white chocolates.

MASTER BROWNIE FROSTING

MAKES 3 TO 4 CUPS, ENOUGH FOR TWO 9- BY 13-INCH
OR FOUR 7- BY 11-INCH BROWNIE PANS

4 ounces semisweet chocolate,
      melted and cooled

3½ cups confectioners' sugar

½ cup unsweetened cocoa powder

½ cup (4 ounces) unsalted butter,
      softened

1 teaspoon pure vanilla extract

2 to 4 tablespoons water

When it comes to icing brownies, house tradition rules. I prefer a brownie without frosting. If you like your brownies dressed, here's a cornerstone frosting for you. I also use this to frost chocolate cakes or cupcakes. This frosting can be frozen or refrigerated and used as needed. Make sure to rewhip it after it thaws or warms.

In the bowl of an electric mixer fitted with the paddle attachment, combine the melted chocolate, confectioners' sugar, cocoa, and butter. Blend on the lowest speed of the mixer until smooth. Stir in the vanilla and add water as required to achieve spreading consistency. You may rewhip the frosting on a higher speed if it has been refrigerated.

YOU'VE GOT CAKE

Not long after BetterBaking.com was launched (1997), visitors got wind of the fact that I was pretty good at replicating baked goods. Soon I began to receive chunks of baked goods by courier from people all over North America. One woman wanted a recipe for a cake she had enjoyed in a favorite diner (the diner owner refused to part with the recipe). A man sent along a store-bought sweet that he wanted to make at home "so it tastes just as good as it does coming out of the store." I came through, for the most part, but I quickly realized that I couldn't spare all the ingredients and time it took to come up with these recipes. Not to mention that I found myself eating strange food, sent by perfect strangers, from places unknown. I balked when a custard-filled pastry arrived, knowing that good taste and salmonella don't go together. Dyspepsia outranks curiosity every time. Finally, I imposed a fee on my recipe replication services, and the gooey shipments stopped coming. One great recipe that came of all this is the Buttery Orange Soda Bread Cake (page 136). Honolulu Health Scones (page 210) is a close second.

BROWNIE POINTERS

· · · · · · · · · · · · · · · · · · · ·

Brownies seem to have been around forever, and no one really knows their origin. Legend has it that one day a harried baker forgot the leavening agent in her chocolate cake batter, and the dense, fudgelike squares were born. Another tale suggests that a cake was dropped, thus changing its airy nature. A vintage Southern cookbook has a recipe for brownie prototypes called chocolate chew bread. In any event, eating a good brownie is like coming home. It is familiar and comforting, simple but satisfying. Here are a few tips for making better bars.

CHOCOLATE AND COCOA

Use semisweet or bittersweet chocolate and cocoa of the best quality. I like Scharffen Berger chocolate and Saco Chunks (see the Source Guide, page 299) for their melting ability and taste. For cocoa, I like Saco Premium (a blend of Dutch and natural cocoa) and Scharffen Berger, which is not Dutch processed and so gives a milder color to the finished brownies (for more on cocoa, see page 15). I also have tested and like Ghirardelli, Droste, and Callebaut chocolates.

When using cocoa, scoop it with a metal measuring spoon or cup, then sift it or whisk it gently with the flour to make sure it is free of lumps.

PANS

Pan size and shape are important in any recipe but especially with brownies, as the depth of the batter affects their taste and texture. Shallower batter makes chewy, more candylike brownies, while deeper batter makes denser, chewy but cakelike brownies. I suggest using a brownie pan, which is a 7- by 11-inch rectangle.

A 9- by 13-inch pan works for larger recipes. I prefer aluminum, nonstick aluminum, or tin pans. Pyrex does not yield neat, square-edged brownies (and you have to remember to lower your oven temperature by 25°F if you're using glass bakeware). If yours is a big brownie household, purchase several inexpensive brownie pans for baking and freezing batches in the pan so you will always have brownies on hand.

SPATULAS

Small metal spatulas are as an essential utensil for spreading brownie batter and icing. Dip the spatula in hot water before using.

BAKING

Place brownie pans on a parchment-lined baking sheet to bake. This prevents the brownie bottoms from browning too much or scorching before the tops of the brownies are set or done.

It is hard to ascertain when brownies are done, so it is generally best to go by baking times given in recipes. You can touch the brownies slightly and see if they are just set, but not jiggly or soft and battery. Brownies tend to firm up as they cool, and in doing so, change their look and texture (and inner crumb). Because they are rich and chocolaty, it takes experience with the same recipe and your own oven to reach perfection.

It is easy to overbake brownies, and that makes them dry when cooled. If you do err, it is best to err by underbaking as brownies can then be chilled for dense, fudgy squares that are equally good.

Baileys Irish Cream Brownies

MAKES 16 TO 20 BROWNIES

BROWNIES

1 cup (8 ounces) unsalted butter

14 ounces semisweet chocolate, coarsely chopped

4 tablespoons unsweetened cocoa powder

2⅓ cups sugar

2 teaspoons pure vanilla extract

1 tablespoon Irish whiskey

6 eggs

2 cups all-purpose flour

Pinch of salt

½ cup walnuts (optional)

IRISH CREAM GANACHE FROSTING

½ cup Baileys Irish Cream

½ cup whipping cream

1½ cups semisweet chocolate, finely chopped

STICKY IRISH WHISKEY TOFFEE SAUCE

2 cups sugar

¼ cup water

⅓ cup whipping cream

¼ cup Baileys Irish Cream

3 tablespoons unsalted butter

These brownies are so good you'll hear about it from Kilkenny to Kildare to Kansas. The brownies are dolled up with a unique Irish Cream ganache, which looks like icing, but tastes like a molten chocolate truffle. Then, if you want to be extra nice to those around you, serve these with a puddle of warm sticky toffee sauce. Irish cream liqueur is a blend of Irish whiskey with pure Irish cream and touches of vanilla.

Preheat the oven to 350°F. Generously spray a 9- by 13-inch pan with nonstick cooking spray and place it on a parchment paper–lined baking sheet.

For the brownies, in a heavy-bottomed 2-quart saucepan over low heat, melt the butter and chocolate together, and stir until smooth. Stir in the cocoa. Remove from the heat, spoon into a large bowl, and let cool to room temperature. Stir in the sugar and vanilla, then add the whiskey and eggs and stir until smooth. Fold in the flour and salt, then fold in the walnuts and stir to make a smooth batter. Pour or spoon into the prepared pan.

Bake for 35 to 40 minutes, or until the brownies seem just set.

Cool the brownies completely.

For the Irish Cream Ganache Frosting, in a small saucepan, heat the Baileys and whipping cream until just simmering. Stir in the chocolate and whisk to melt, then remove from the heat, stirring to a smooth consistency. Chill until firm, about 1 hour.

While the brownies are baking, prepare the Sticky Irish Whiskey Toffee Sauce. In a heavy-bottomed, 2½-quart saucepan over low heat, combine the sugar and water. Cook, stirring occasionally, for 15 to 20 minutes, until it has turned a dark amber color. Throughout the cooking, brush the inner sides down with a pastry brush dipped in cold water (this prevents crystals from forming on the sides and going into the syrup). Remove from the stove and place the saucepan in a sink. Taking great care to avoid spattering, stir in the whipping cream, Baileys, and butter. This will cool the mixture, but it will also foam and bubble up quite significantly, so take care. You should have a thick caramel.

Soften the Irish Cream Ganache Frosting (warm it up a bit or stir it with a wooden spoon). Spread it on the brownies and refrigerate until 1 hour before serving.

To serve, place a brownie on each plate and drizzle with the warm sauce.

WHITE CHOCOLATE CHUNK BLONDIES

MAKES ABOUT 3 DOZEN SMALL OR 20 LARGE BLONDIES

1½ cups (12 ounces) unsalted butter

3⅓ cups firmly packed brown sugar

3 eggs

3 cups all-purpose flour

½ teaspoon baking powder

⅜ teaspoon salt

1 cup coarsely chopped or whole pecans or walnuts

5 ounces white chocolate, coarsely chopped, or 1 cup semisweet chocolate chips

Big, dense, golden, and buttery, these vanilla and brown sugar versions of chocolate brownies are a real treat.

Preheat the oven to 350°F. Spray the sides and bottom of a jellyroll (11- by 15-inch) pan (for extra-chewy squares) or a 9- by 13-inch pan with nonstick cooking spray. Line a baking sheet with parchment paper and set aside.

In a large saucepan, combine the butter and brown sugar. Cook over very low heat for 3 to 5 minutes, or until the butter melts and the sugar partially dissolves. Remove from the heat and let cool for 15 minutes. Pour into a bowl or mixer bowl.

Hand whisk the eggs into the butter mixture until well blended. In a medium bowl, combine the flour, baking powder, and salt. Whisk to blend. Stir into the wet mixture. Stir in the nuts and chocolate. Pour the batter into the prepared pan. Smooth the top with a wet knife or metal spatula.

Place the pan on the prepared baking sheet and bake for 20 to 25 minutes, or until set and not jiggly. Be careful not to overbake, as this will result in hard, rather than chewy, squares. Remove from the oven and cut into squares. Let cool in the pan on a wire rack.

B.B.
Test Kitchen
Notes

Fair Trade in the Coffee Klatch

The Fair Trade Certified label on coffee guarantees that the farmers who produced the coffee received a fair price for their harvest. Fair prices mean small family farmers can improve their standard of living. You will find fair-trade products for sale in coffee shops, supermarkets, and online.

Molten Caramel Cheesecake Brownies

MAKES 16 TO 20 BROWNIES

BROWNIES

1 cup (8 ounces) unsalted butter

1 cup semisweet chocolate chips

1¾ cups sugar

1¾ cups plus 2 tablespoons all-
purpose flour

4 eggs

¼ teaspoon salt

¼ teaspoon baking soda

1½ teaspoons pure vanilla extract

½ cup semisweet chocolate chips

½ cup white chocolate chips

½ cup caramel bits (mini caramels)

CREAM CHEESE FILLING

¼ cup sugar

6 ounces cream cheese, softened

1 egg

1 tablespoon all-purpose flour

½ teaspoon pure vanilla extract

FINISHING TOUCHES

½ cup semisweet chocolate,
melted

3 to 5 tablespoons melted caramel
sundae topping, warmed dulce
de leche, or melted caramels
for drizzling

These are over-the-top, kitchen sink–exploding fudgy brownies swirled with cheesecake filling and fused with caramel chunks and caramel sauce. Kraft now sells miniature caramels, which look like butterscotch chips but are actually chewy caramels, without the wrappers to deal with. They are a wonderful addition to this extravagant ode to a trio of my favorite flavors: chocolate, caramel, and vanilla cheesecake. Definitely worth 15 extra minutes in spinning class!

Preheat the oven to 350°F. Line a large baking sheet with parchment paper. Line a 9- or 10-inch springform pan with a circle of parchment paper and spray the interior with nonstick cooking spray. (Or use a 9-inch square baking pan lined with parchment paper.) Place the pan on the baking sheet.

For the brownies, in a 2-quart saucepan, combine the butter and chocolate chips. Cook over low heat, stirring occasionally, until melted, 4 to 6 minutes. Remove to a medium bowl and stir in all the remaining brownie ingredients. Spoon the batter into the prepared pan.

For the filling, in a small bowl or food processor, blend all the ingredients together until smooth. Spread the filling over the brownie mixture and swirl with a knife. Bake for 30 to 35 minutes, or until the brownies are just set.

Remove the brownies from the oven and chill them for 1 to 2 hours. Keep them chilled until ready to serve. Remove the brownies from the pan and drizzle on the melted chocolate and caramel. Cut into wedges or squares to serve.

S'MORES BROWNIES

MAKES ABOUT 16 BROWNIES

BOTTOM LAYER

1 cup finely crushed graham, Oreo, or chocolate wafer cookies

3 tablespoons firmly packed brown sugar

4 tablespoons (2 ounces) unsalted butter, melted

BROWNIE LAYER

4 tablespoons (2 ounces) unsalted butter

2 ounces semisweet chocolate, chopped

1 cup sugar

2 eggs

1 teaspoon pure vanilla extract

½ cup all-purpose flour

Pinch of salt

GRAHAM CRACKER LAYER

1 cup graham cracker crumbs

4 tablespoons (2 ounces) unsalted butter, melted

TOPPING

2 cups miniature marshmallows

1 cup coarsely chopped milk chocolate bars (two to three 10- to 12-ounce bars)

Here is another classic combination of tastes: a cookie bottom, a brownie middle, a graham cracker layer, and a marshmallow top, which equals confectionary bliss, kid style. They are visually riveting, with their textured surface of cookie and marshmallow set in chocolate, and they have a taste to match. Kids of all ages go wacky over these.

Preheat the oven to 350°F. Grease an 8-inch square pan or a 7- by 11-inch pan and line it with parchment paper, leaving an overhang with which to lift the brownies. Line a baking sheet with parchment paper and set aside.

For the bottom layer, combine all the ingredients in a small bowl and stir to blend. Press the bottom layer mixture into the prepared pan. Refrigerate for 10 minutes.

For the brownie layer, melt the butter in a small saucepan. Remove from heat and stir in the chocolate to melt. Stir in the sugar. Let cool just to warm, then whisk in the eggs, vanilla, flour, and salt. Spread the mixture over the bottom layer in the pan.

For the graham cracker layer, toss the graham cracker crumbs with the melted butter in a small bowl and distribute over the batter. Place the pan on the prepared baking sheet and bake for 22 to 24 minutes, or until set. Remove from the oven and preheat the broiler.

For the topping, sprinkle the top of the brownies with the marshmallows. Place under the broiler for 20 to 60 seconds, or until the marshmallows start to brown. Remove from the oven and sprinkle with the chopped milk chocolate. If desired, smear the chocolate with a knife as it melts. Let cool on wire racks to room temperature, then refrigerate for 20 to 30 minutes before cutting.

B.B.
Test Kitchen
Notes

Not-So-Plain Vanilla

The native Totonaco people of Mexico were the first to use vanilla. The secrets of the bean were then acquired by the Aztecs, the conquering Spaniards, and Europe. Today, Madagascar is the largest producer of vanilla. The beans are also grown in Indonesia, Mexico, and Tahiti, but the Madagascar Bourbon variety is said to be the best. Regardless of which type of pure vanilla you choose, it will open a new world of flavor for you. Nielsen-Massey Vanillas is the BB test kitchen supplier of record, and I tend to prefer their double-strength varieties. I often combine their Madagascar with their Tahitian for a nuanced vanilla blend.

BAKE SALE DATE SQUARES

MAKES 16 TO 20 SQUARES

FILLING

2½ cups pitted dates (about 1¼ pounds)

¾ cup firmly packed brown sugar

1 cup water

1 teaspoon pure vanilla extract

1 tablespoon fresh lemon juice

¼ teaspoon orange oil or orange extract

CRUST

1½ cups all-purpose flour

1½ cups old-fashioned rolled oats

¾ cup firmly packed brown sugar

½ teaspoon baking powder

¼ teaspoon salt

⅛ teaspoon ground cinnamon

1 cup (8 ounces) cold unsalted butter, cut into small pieces

The first recipe I made in food-service college was date squares. It took me six hours. At the end, the teacher held them up and inquired "Are these suitable to serve to doctors and nurses at a hospital social?" I was unable to make a convincing case for my squares. I left food-service college shortly thereafter, and went on to study to become a pastry chef at hotel school. In the meantime, my date squares have been revisited and refined. I think these would win fans anywhere.

Preheat the oven to 350°F. Lightly coat a 9-inch square or 7- by 11-inch baking pan with nonstick cooking spray. Line a baking sheet with parchment paper and set aside.

For the filling, combine all the ingredients in an 2 quart saucepan. Bring to a simmer over medium heat. Cook for 2 to 3 minutes to soften the dates. Remove from the heat and let cool completely. Puree in a food processor until smooth. Wash and dry the food processor.

For the crust, combine the flour, oats, brown sugar, baking powder, salt, and cinnamon in the food processor. Pulse to combine. Add the butter and pulse until crumbly. Pat two-thirds of the crumb mixture into the pan. Spread the date filling on top and then top with the remaining crumb mixture. Press down lightly.

Place the pan on the prepared baking sheet. Bake for 30 to 40 minutes, or until the topping is golden brown. Let cool in the pan for 15 minutes. Refrigerate for 1 hour and then cut into squares.

BB'S BAKE SALE PRIMER

Each fall I get emails asking for new bake-sale recipes. It's comforting to know that, as fast-paced and technologically inclined as our society has become, baking and bake sales still exist. On my website each autumn, I often offer tips for successful bake sales, along with my latest bake-sale treats.

MILLIONAIRE BARS

MAKES 24 TO 30 BARS

BUTTERY COOKIE BASE

½ cup white sugar

2 tablespoons light brown sugar

Tiny pinch of salt

2¼ cups all-purpose flour

1 cup (8 ounces) unsalted butter

MILLIONAIRE FILLING

½ cup (4 ounces) unsalted butter, in small chunks

½ cup light brown sugar

1 (14-ounce) can sweetened condensed milk

1 teaspoon pure vanilla extract

MILLIONAIRE TOPPING

1 cup semisweet chocolate chips or coarsely chopped imported chocolate

1 cup coarsely chopped milk chocolate

½ cup white chocolate chips or coarsely chopped white chocolate

A buttery shortbread base is the throne for a special caramel filling, topped off with a unique chocolate crown. No wonder these are called Millionaire Bars—they are a veritable treasure. Forget about the Dow Jones; breathe in, breathe out, and munch on one of these.

~❀~

Preheat the oven to 325°F. Line a baking sheet with parchment paper. Spray a 9- by 13-inch pan with nonstick cooking spray and place it on the baking sheet. For chunkier bars (which I prefer), use an 8- by 11-inch pan.

For the Buttery Cookie Base, in a food processor, process both sugars and the salt together to make a fine mixture. Add the flour and blend briefly. Then add the butter and pulse to make a coarse or sandy mixture; continue to blend until the mixture just starts to hold together into a dough.

Press the dough into the prepared pan and cover it with a square of parchment paper, which you can use to lightly smooth or press the dough neatly into the pan. Remove the paper. Prick the dough with a fork all over and bake for 25 minutes, until lightly brown. Cool until needed.

Meanwhile, for the Millionaire Filling, in a 3-quart saucepan (use the heaviest saucepan you have), heat the butter, brown sugar, and condensed milk over medium-low or low heat (you do not want the mixture to burn or stick). Allow the mixture to barely simmer, stirring constantly, until it is thickened and has turned a medium caramel color. Remove from the heat and stir in the vanilla. Pour the filling over the Buttery Base and spread. Allow it to cool completely (it can go in the refrigerator for up to an hour).

To make the Millionaire Topping, heat the 3 types of chocolate separately (in small bowls in the microwave is fine). Drop spoonfuls of each sort of chocolate on the caramel topping and, using a sharp knife or wood skewer, wiggle lines and threads of melted chocolate all over the top to marbleize. Let it set in the refrigerator. Cut into bars.

EUROPEAN APPLE-BLUEBERRY SQUARES

MAKES 16 TO 20 SQUARES OR WEDGES

DOUGH

2 cups (1 pound) unsalted butter

1½ cups sugar

4 egg yolks

½ teaspoon pure vanilla extract

4 cups all-purpose flour

2 teaspoons baking powder

½ teaspoon salt

¼ cup half-and-half cream

FILLING

2½ pounds apples, preferably McIntosh, Cortland, or Golden Delicious, peeled

1 cup frozen blueberries

¾ cup sugar

½ teaspoon ground cinnamon

1 tablespoon fresh lemon juice

2 tablespoons all-purpose flour

⅔ cup apricot or raspberry preserves (optional)

Confectioners' sugar for dusting

These squares feature a tart-dough base spread with lightly sweetened grated apples and blueberries, and topped with shredded dough. Once you have the components ready, this dessert comes together in just a few minutes. The recipe can be halved, and the squares freeze well.

Lightly spray a 9- by 13-inch baking pan or a 10-inch springform pan with nonstick cooking spray. Line a baking sheet with parchment paper. Set aside.

For the dough, cream the butter in a mixer or food processor until light and fluffy, 30 to 60 seconds. Add the sugar, egg yolks, and vanilla and process until smooth. Add the flour, baking powder, and salt and process until well combined. Gradually add the cream through the feed tube to make a soft dough.

Turn the dough out onto a lightly floured surface and knead to make a cohesive mass. Divide in half. Wrap each half in plastic wrap and refrigerate one portion for 30 to 45 minutes. Freeze the other half.

Meanwhile, make the filling. Using the large holes of a box grater, shred each apple over a large bowl until you come to the core of the apple. Discard the cores. Add the blueberries, sugar, cinnamon, lemon juice, and flour. Toss to mix.

Preheat the oven to 375°F.

Press the refrigerated dough into the prepared pan, patching as needed. Spread on the preserves. Top with the apple-blueberry mixture.

Remove the reserved frozen dough from the freezer. Using the large holes of a box grater, shred the dough over the apples. Place the pan on the prepared baking sheet. Bake on the lower shelf of the oven for 35 to 45 minutes, or until the apples begin to ooze juice and the top pastry is browned. Remove from the oven and let cool on a wire rack until warm. Dust with confectioners' sugar and cut into squares, or remove the pan sides and cut into wedges if using a springform pan.

PUCKER-UP
LEMON-RASPBERRY BARS

MAKES 16 TO 20 BARS

CRUST

1 cup (8 ounces) unsalted butter, softened

2 cups all-purpose flour

½ cup confectioners' sugar

½ teaspoon baking powder

¼ teaspoon salt

1 teaspoon grated lemon zest

LEMON TOPPING

6 eggs

2 cups sugar

½ cup fresh lemon juice

¼ teaspoon lemon oil (optional)

½ teaspoon citric acid, or ¼ teaspoon for less bite (see below)

¾ teaspoon baking powder

4 teaspoons all-purpose flour

½ cup raspberry preserves (optional)

When I think about making a great new cookie, square, or cake, I always try to imagine what will make it sing and dance with flavor. In this recipe, as in many others, you will note that lemon zest, lemon juice, and lemon oil are used. Each contributes its own dynamic to the overall flavor of the bars. I feel that if you want to make something lemony, you should make it good and lemony. If you're a purist, omit the raspberry layer. These are hefty, lofty squares (low-slung squares have no oomph to them) with an in-your-face lemon zap.

Preheat the oven to 350°F. Spray an 8- by 11-inch baking pan or 9-inch square pan with nonstick cooking spray. Line a baking sheet with parchment paper. Set aside.

For the crust, combine all the ingredients in a medium bowl and stir with a wooden spoon until a soft dough forms. Press evenly into the prepared pan. Refrigerate for 10 minutes. Bake the crust for 15 minutes, then let cool in the baking pan for 15 minutes.

For the lemon topping, combine all the ingredients in a medium bowl. Whisk until blended.

Spread the raspberry preserves evenly over the baked crust. Pour the lemon topping over the raspberry layer.

Place the pan on the prepared baking sheet. Bake for 20 to 25 minutes. Lower the oven temperature to 325°F and bake for 20 to 25 minutes longer, or until the topping is set. Transfer the baking pan to a wire rack and let cool completely. Refrigerate for at least 1½ hours before cutting. Store at room temperature or in the refrigerator if you prefer chilled squares.

Citric Acid

A modest amount of citric acid (also known as "sour salt") will increase flavor in many savory and sweet recipes, adding tartness without an identifiable flavor. I use it in baking and to perk up a minestrone soup or pizza sauce. Citric acid is a natural product, and it's available in drugstores, in the kosher section of large supermarkets, or via mail order. See the Source Guide on page 299.

FUDGE GRANOLA BARS REDUX

MAKES 12 TO 16 BARS

½ cup (4 ounces) unsalted butter, melted and cooled

⅓ cup honey

⅓ cup firmly packed brown sugar

2 eggs

½ teaspoon pure vanilla extract

2 cups granola

5 ounces semisweet or milk chocolate, chopped

½ cup sweetened shredded coconut

¾ cup chopped dates

⅓ cup chocolate-covered raisins

¼ teaspoon ground cinnamon

¼ teaspoon salt

2 tablespoons unsweetened cocoa powder

¼ cup all-purpose flour

2 tablespoons sesame seeds

⅔ cup whole pecans

2½ ounces semisweet chocolate, chopped, melted, and cooled, for drizzling

Who says granola has to be boring? Once you've tried these, the packaged commercial versions will seem lame indeed. These bars are big, boldly flavored, and filled with chewy, sweet additions and a deep chocolate taste.

Preheat the oven to 350°F. Line the bottom of a 7- by 11-inch brownie pan or a 9-inch square pan (for thinner bars) with parchment paper and spray the paper with nonstick cooking spray. Line a baking sheet with parchment paper and set aside.

In a large bowl, stir the butter, honey, brown sugar, eggs, and vanilla together. Stir in the granola, chopped chocolate, coconut, dates, raisins, cinnamon, salt, cocoa, flour, sesame seeds, and pecans until blended. Pat the mixture into the prepared pan. Place the pan on the prepared baking sheet.

Bake on the lower shelf of the oven for 20 to 24 minutes, or until the top seems set, the edges seem dry, and the center is just a bit jiggly. Let cool completely on a wire rack, then freeze or refrigerate for 1 hour. Cut into squares. Drizzle with melted chocolate and let the chocolate set (or refrigerate to set the chocolate). To store, wrap each square in waxed paper and freeze for up to 2 months.

VARIATION: Substitute dried cranberries for the dates. Add ½ teaspoon orange oil and 2 teaspoons minced orange zest. You may also add 1 cup semisweet chocolate chips.

PURE MAPLE–GRANOLA BARS

MAKES 12 TO 16 BARS

½ cup (4 ounces) unsalted butter, melted and cooled

¼ cup honey

¼ cup pure maple syrup

3 tablespoons firmly packed brown sugar

1 teaspoon pure vanilla extract

½ teaspoon maple extract (optional)

1 egg

2 cups granola

½ cup sweetened shredded coconut

¾ cup chopped pitted dates

⅓ cup raisins

¼ teaspoon ground cinnamon

¼ teaspoon salt

¼ cup all-purpose flour

2 tablespoons sesame seeds

⅔ cup whole pecans

These bars are extremely satisfying and resoundingly maple-y. They must be refrigerated or frozen before cutting. Maple extract intensifies the maple flavor, but it can be omitted if you have a hard time finding it. Pure maple syrup is a must.

Preheat the oven to 350°F. Line the bottom of a 7- by 11-inch brownie pan with parchment paper and spray with nonstick cooking spray. Line a baking sheet with parchment paper and set aside.

In a large bowl, combine the butter, honey, maple syrup, brown sugar, vanilla and maple extracts. Stir to blend. Stir in the egg, then stir in all the remaining ingredients. Pat the mixture into the prepared pan.

Place the pan on the prepared baking sheet and bake for 20 to 25 minutes, or until the top seems set and dry. Let cool completely on a wire rack. Freeze or refrigerate for 1 hour before cutting into squares.

VARIATION: Substitute dried cranberries for dates. Add ½ teaspoon orange oil and 2 teaspoons minced orange zest. You may also add 1 cup chocolate chips.

MAPLE SYRUP
. . . .

Maple syrup is often identified with Canada, since it produces most of the world's supply (more than 70 percent). The largest importer of maple products is the United States, followed by Germany and Japan (in Tokyo, a small can of maple syrup is practically worth its weight in gold). Canadian maple syrups are classified according to color: extra light, light, amber, medium, and dark. Darker syrups have a more pronounced taste and are less expensive. By law, containers must clearly indicate the category of their contents. The most popular grade is Canada No. 1 Medium. This is a subtle-tasting, amber maple syrup. Table syrup usually means a maple-flavored syrup. Sometimes, you will find a maple-flavored syrup that includes a small percentage of real or pure maple syrup. This is referred to as maple blend or a blended syrup. It is less flavorful but also less expensive. I prefer pure maple syrup, of course, whether it hails from Quebec or Vermont.

Nanaimo Bars

MAKES 12 TO 16 BARS

FIRST LAYER

½ cup (4 ounces) unsalted butter

¼ cup sugar

1 egg

1 teaspoon pure vanilla extract

3 tablespoons unsweetened cocoa powder

2 cups graham cracker crumbs

1 cup sweetened shredded coconut

½ cup chopped walnuts or pecans

SECOND LAYER

4 tablespoons (2 ounces) unsalted butter

3 tablespoons half-and-half or light cream

2 cups confectioners' sugar

2 tablespoons Bird's Custard Powder or instant vanilla pudding

TOP LAYER

5 ounces semisweet chocolate, chopped

2 tablespoons unsalted butter

Nanaimo is the name of a picturesque port town on Vancouver Island in British Columbia, Canada. That's about all I know. Food writers and recipe traders in North America and elsewhere have always identified Nanaimo bars as a Canadian treat, but the origins of the formula are nebulous. Some claim the recipe (or a variation thereof) first appeared in the Vancouver Sun newspaper in the mid-1950s. Others suggest the recipe was brought over by English or Dutch immigrants. None of the claims stands up to close scrutiny, making this cookie one of the sweet mysteries of life.

Lightly spray a 9-inch square pan with nonstick cooking spray. Line a baking sheet with parchment paper. Set aside.

For the first layer, combine the butter, sugar, egg, vanilla, and cocoa in a medium bowl. Set the bowl over a pan of simmering water and stir until the mixture is slightly thickened. Stir in the graham cracker crumbs, coconut, and chopped nuts. Turn out and press evenly into pan.

For the second layer, combine all the ingredients in a medium bowl and stir together well. Spread over the first layer. Place the pan in the freezer for 10 minutes.

For the top layer, melt the chocolate in the double boiler over barely simmering water. Stir in the butter until melted. Spread over the second layer. Refrigerate for at least 1 hour. Cut into bars.

B.B.
Test Kitchen
Notes

Melting Chocolate

The traditional method to melt chocolate is to use a double boiler. Set a saucepan, filled halfway with water, over low heat. Place the chopped chocolate in a bowl that you can snugly set over the simmering water. As the chocolate melts, stir with a wooden spoon to smooth out. Let the chocolate cool before using in a recipe. Microwave ovens also do a great job, and there is less danger of the chocolate seizing up. Place chopped chocolate in a large Pyrex cup or a ceramic bowl. Microwave on medium or high until the chocolate is melted, stirring periodically.

SPICE HOUSE CAKE

MAKES 1 CAKE; SERVES 12 TO 16

CAKE

3 or 4 tea bags or 4 teaspoons loose chai, or spiced orange-flavored tea

1 cup boiling water

1 cup (8 ounces) unsalted butter, softened

1½ cups white sugar

½ cup firmly packed brown sugar

4 eggs

2 teaspoons pure vanilla extract

3 cups all-purpose flour

1 tablespoon baking powder

⅜ teaspoon salt

½ teaspoon baking soda

1 tablespoon ground cinnamon

½ teaspoon ground cloves

¼ teaspoon ground ginger

¼ teaspoon ground allspice

⅛ teaspoon ground nutmeg

⅛ teaspoon ground mace

GLAZE

1 cup confectioners' sugar

About 2 tablespoons brewed chai tea or orange juice

¼ teaspoon tangerine oil, orange oil, or orange extract

Finely shredded orange zest for garnish

There's nothing like the punch of a nice spice cake. In place of the brewed chai tea, you may use any spiced orange-flavored tea (Bigelow's Constant Comment is a favorite). In addition to tea, try Boyajian orange oil and a mixture of Penzeys Indian and Ceylon cinnamons to brighten up the spicy notes (see the Source Guide, page 302). For yet another flavor dimension, try steeping the tea—chai or otherwise—in hot ginger ale.

~❖~

Preheat the oven to 350°F. Generously coat a 9-inch round springform pan or angel food cake pan with nonstick cooking spray. Line a baking sheet with parchment paper. Set aside.

Steep the tea bags or tea in the water for 8 to 10 minutes. Remove the tea bag or strain the tea, and let cool to warm.

For the cake, combine the butter and both sugars in the bowl of an electric mixer fitted with the paddle attachment. Cream until light and fluffy. Stir in the eggs and vanilla. In a medium bowl, whisk the flour, baking powder, salt, baking soda, and spices together. Gradually add the dry ingredients to the wet ingredients, mixing until blended. Slowly add the tea while mixing on the lowest speed of the mixer, stopping several times to scrape down the sides and bottom of the bowl.

Spoon the batter into the prepared pan. Place the pan on the prepared baking sheet and bake for 45 to 55 minutes, or until firm to the touch. Let cool completely in the pan on a wire rack.

For the glaze, stir all the ingredients together in a small bowl. Unmold the cake and place it on a wire rack set over a large platter or baking sheet. Drizzle the glaze over the cake. Gather the excess glaze and glaze the cake with a second coat. Garnish with orange zest.

Eat-at-Mom's Banana–Sour Cream Crumb Cake

MAKES 1 LOAF CAKE; SERVES 12 TO 14

CAKE

2 cups sugar

1 cup (8 ounces) unsalted butter, softened

½ cup vegetable shortening

4 eggs

2 teaspoons pure vanilla extract

3¼ cups all-purpose flour

2½ teaspoons baking powder

½ teaspoon baking soda

½ teaspoon salt

1 cup sour cream

¾ cup banana puree (about 2 very ripe bananas)

1½ cups fresh or frozen blueberries (optional)

TOPPING

¼ cup confectioners' sugar

¼ cup all-purpose flour

½ teaspoon ground cinnamon

2 to 4 tablespoons cold unsalted butter, cut into bits

This cake is exceptionally tender and flavorful. The sour cream has a nice tenderizing effect. For more zing, add ¼ to ½ teaspoon ground cinnamon to the crumb topping mixture or to the batter. Frozen raspberries can replace the blueberries, or you may go without berries altogether. I make this in a loaf pan but a 9- by 13-inch pan also works well. This cake freezes very well.

Preheat the oven to 350°F. Lightly coat a 9- by 13-inch rectangular pan with nonstick cooking spray. Line a baking sheet with parchment paper and set aside.

For the cake, combine the sugar, butter, and shortening in the bowl of an electric mixer fitted with the paddle attachment. Cream until light and fluffy, scraping the bottom of the bowl often. Stir in the eggs and vanilla. In a medium bowl, whisk the flour, baking powder, baking soda, and salt together. Gradually add the dry ingredients to the wet ingredients, mixing until blended. Stir in the sour cream, then the banana puree and blueberries. Spoon into the prepared pan.

For the crumb topping, combine all the ingredients in a small bowl. Use your fingers to mix until crumbly. Sprinkle evenly over the batter.

Place the pan on the prepared baking sheet and bake for about 55 to 65 minutes, or until firm to the touch. Let cool completely on a wire rack before unmolding and cutting to serve.

STICKY, CHEWY CHOCOLATE BABKA

MAKES 1 TUBE CAKE; SERVES 12 TO 14

FILLING

1 cup sweetened shredded coconut

1 cup chocolate chips, or 5 ounces semisweet chocolate, coarsely chopped

¼ cup chopped pecans

⅓ cup firmly packed brown sugar

¼ teaspoon ground cinnamon

16 marshmallows

CAKE

1 cup (8 ounces) unsalted butter, softened

1 cup white sugar

½ cup firmly packed brown sugar

1½ teaspoons pure vanilla extract

3 eggs

1½ cups buttermilk

2 cups all-purpose flour

¾ cup unsweetened cocoa powder

2 teaspoons baking powder

½ teaspoon baking soda

¼ teaspoon salt

This is a nonyeasted version of the classic eastern European coffee cake. Chocolate laden and chewy with marshmallows and coconut, the freshly baked cake looks full of crevices, but it sets up nicely as it cools. Do not cut it while it is warm, as the topping needs time to set.

Preheat the oven to 350°F. Generously spray a 9- or 10-inch angel food cake pan (or tube pan) with nonstick cooking spray. Line the bottom with a circle of parchment paper. Line a baking sheet with parchment paper. Set aside.

For the filling, combine all the filling ingredients except the marshmallows in a food processor. Pulse for 20 to 30 seconds to combine coarsely. Add the marshmallows and pulse for 15 to 20 seconds or until they are coarsely chopped.

For the cake, combine the butter and both sugars in the bowl of an electric mixer fitted with the paddle attachment. Cream until light and fluffy. Stir in the vanilla and eggs, then the buttermilk. In a medium bowl, whisk the flour, cocoa, baking powder, baking soda, and salt together. Gradually add the dry ingredients to the wet ingredients, mixing until blended. Spoon half of the batter into the prepared pan and top with one-third of the filling. Top with the remaining batter and sprinkle the remaining filling evenly on top.

Place the pan on the prepared baking sheet and bake for 50 to 60 minutes, or until bubbly and a cake tester inserted in the center of the cake comes out clean (except for the sticky topping). Let the cake cool for 1 hour before unmolding. Unmold onto a parchment-lined plate and then invert onto a serving plate.

B.B.
Test Kitchen Notes

"Curdled" Batter and Other Calamities

Rich batters often look curdled. In fact, some recipes will say that the "batter may look curdled, but that's okay." Well, yes and no. Batter that contains a lot of sugar, butter, and eggs and nothing to bind these ingredients will look curdled. It's not really curdled, of course, but if you add a bit of the flour called for in the recipe and blend it in, the resulting smooth batter will welcome the remaining ingredients more easily.

LE WEEKEND CAKE

MAKES 1 LOAF CAKE; SERVES 8 TO 10

FRUIT

½ cup candied cherries, half whole, half chopped

1 cup candied orange peel

1 tablespoon candied citron or lemon peel

¼ cup dried currants

¼ cup raisins

3 tablespoons rum, fresh orange juice, or strong brewed tea

BATTER

½ cup (4 ounces) unsalted butter, softened

¾ cup confectioners' sugar

1 teaspoon pure vanilla extract

¼ teaspoon lemon oil or extract (optional)

1 tablespoon minced lemon zest

3 eggs

1 teaspoon baking powder

1½ cups all-purpose flour

¼ teaspoon salt

White or coarse sugar for dusting

This French treat is a casual cake that is great for weekend snacking, and also makes a nice coffee cake, tea cake, or gift cake. It can stand in for holiday fruitcake, although it is not dense like a traditional fruitcake. Instead, it is an elegant pound cake with some fruit in it.

For the fruit, toss all the fruits and the rum together in a small bowl and let soak for at least 1 hour or up to overnight.

Preheat the oven to 350°F. Spray a 9- by 5-inch loaf pan with nonstick cooking spray. Line the bottom with parchment paper. Line a baking sheet with parchment paper. Set aside.

For the batter, combine the butter and confectioners' sugar in the bowl of an electric mixer fitted with the paddle attachment. Cream until light and fluffy. Beat in the vanilla, lemon oil, lemon zest, and the eggs, one at a time. If the batter "curdles," add a bit of the flour to bind. Add the baking powder, flour, and salt and blend well. Stir in the fruit mixture. Spoon the batter into the prepared pan. Dust with white sugar.

Place the pan on the prepared baking sheet and bake for 45 to 60 minutes, or until the cake is firm to the touch. Let cool for 20 minutes before unmolding, then cool on a wire rack for at least 40 minutes longer.

B.B. Test Kitchen Notes

Sugar, of Coarse

I glitz up a lot of my pound and coffee cakes in the test kitchens by dusting them with coarse or regular sugar before baking. Coarse sugar can be purchased from a bakery supply store or by mail order. A dash of glittering coarse sugar crystals gives many baked goods an appetizing look and professional touch. Strangely enough, coarse sugar is "purer" than finer granulated sugar. Large crystal sugar is processed from the purest "sugar liquor," or liquid, extracted from the cane. These big crystals resist melting or changing color at high temperatures. Coarse sugar is considered a specialty item in many stores. The King Arthur catalog carries varieties like brown Demerara and Swedish pearl (see the Source Guide, page 301).

BUTTERY ORANGE SODA BREAD CAKE

MAKES 1 SMALL ROUND CAKE; SERVES 6 TO 8

1½ cups all-purpose flour

2 teaspoons baking powder

⅓ cup sugar

½ teaspoon salt

4 tablespoons (2 ounces) cold
    unsalted butter, plus melted
    unsalted butter for glazing

1 egg, lightly beaten

⅓ cup fresh orange juice

1 teaspoon pure vanilla extract

1 cup golden raisins, plumped and
    patted dry (see page 18)

Confectioners' sugar for dusting

This little loaf is part rustic soda bread, part scone, part tea cake. The recipe came about when one of my website visitors requested a recipe replication, inspired by a favorite bakery in New Jersey called King's Bakery. After a couple of test runs based on a sample the visitor sent along, I came up with this recipe. The cake will keep for a couple of days and toasts well in thin slices. It makes a charming and unique gift, if you can manage to part with it.

~❀~

Preheat the oven to 425°F. Lightly coat a 6-inch round cake pan (cake decorating or kitchen supply stores sell these) with nonstick cooking spray. Line a baking sheet with parchment paper and set aside. If you do not have a 6-inch pan, the cake can be shaped by hand (you may have to add a little more flour) and placed on a parchment-lined baking sheet.

In a medium bowl, stir the flour, baking powder, sugar, and salt together. Using a pastry cutter, cut the butter into the dry ingredients until the mixture is crumbly. Make a well in the center of the mixture and add the egg, orange juice, and vanilla. Stir to make a soft dough, then turn out onto a lightly floured surface. Knead the dough a few times until it holds together, pressing in the raisins at the same time. It should be firm, but not heavy or stiff.

Shape the dough into a round. Using a dough cutter or a knife, cut the round into 4 wedges. Reassemble the round in the prepared pan. Place the pan on the prepared baking sheet. To bake on a lined baking sheet without the pan, just cut an X about ½ inch deep in the top of the round.

Brush the round with melted butter and bake for 15 to 20 minutes, or until well browned. Let cool for 10 minutes, then unmold onto a wire rack. Dust with confectioners' sugar.

JOLT OF LEMON TEA LOAF

MAKES 1 LARGE OR 2 SMALL LOAVES; SERVES 10 TO 14

CAKE

1½ cups sugar

Grated zest of 1 lemon

½ cup (4 ounces) unsalted butter, softened

3 eggs

½ teaspoon pure vanilla extract

½ teaspoon lemon oil or lemon extract

2 tablespoons fresh lemon juice

½ cup milk

3 cups all-purpose flour

2½ teaspoons baking powder

½ teaspoon baking soda

½ teaspoon salt

½ teaspoon citric acid (see page 128), optional

GLAZE

⅓ cup fresh lemon juice

⅓ cup sugar

¼ teaspoon citric acid (see page 128)

Grated zest of 1 lemon

Lemon loaves, with their crusty, sugary lemon glaze, are a coffee-klatch and tea-break staple. This one is moist and pungent. Citric acid boosts the lemon flavor. Add ¼ to ⅓ cup poppy seeds to the batter for a nutty variation. There are lemon loaf recipes galore—this one is a 100% blue-ribbon winner.

Preheat the oven to 350°F. Line the bottom of a 9- by 5-inch loaf pan or two 8- by 4-inch loaf pans with parchment paper and butter the paper. Line a baking sheet with parchment paper and set aside.

In the bowl of an electric mixer fitted with the paddle attachment, combine the sugar, lemon zest, and butter. Cream until light and fluffy. Beat in the eggs, one at a time, then beat in the vanilla, lemon oil, lemon juice, and milk. In a medium bowl, whisk the flour, baking powder, baking soda, salt, and citric acid together. Gradually add the dry ingredients to the wet ingredients, mixing until blended.

Pour into the prepared pan(s) and place on the prepared baking sheet. Bake for 45 to 60 minutes, or until the cake springs back when lightly touched. Let cool in the pan(s) for 10 to 15 minutes, then unmold onto a wire rack set over a baking sheet or platter.

Meanwhile, for the glaze, heat the lemon juice in a small saucepan over low heat. Stir in the sugar to dissolve. Add the citric acid and lemon zest. Let cool for 45 to 60 minutes.

Poke holes in the cake(s) with a cake tester or make small slits with a paring knife. Drizzle the glaze over the top. Gather the excess glaze and glaze the cake(s) with a second coat.

Chapter 5

. . . .

THE COOKIE AND BISCOTTI JAR

. . . .

IT'S ESTIMATED THAT THE AVERAGE AMERICAN will eat 35,000 cookies in his or her lifetime. The cookies North Americans are most familiar with are a melting pot of tastes and styles. Yesteryear's cookbooks contained countless recipes for traditional delights like hermits, sand tarts, jumbles, butter cookies, tea cakes, and a myriad of sweets inspired by the Pennsylvania Dutch, the Amish, and other communities.

In 1930, the cookie world was rocked by a new arrival, the Toll House cookie. The original chocolate chip cookies, they were first baked in the kitchen of Massachusetts Toll House innkeeper Ruth Wakefield. One day, instead of the handful or so of raisins she usually used, Mrs. Wakefield threw some chocolate pieces into her Butter Do Drop batter and baked up the legendary prototypes. The Toll House success story awakened a cookie appetite that has never really abated.

Baking trends come and go, but cookies retain their throne, from bake sales to Christmas cookie exchanges to lunch-box bartering. More than any other sort of baked good, cookies embody the warmth of home.

THE BB COOKIE CLINIC

. . . .

I prefer unbleached flour for all my baking, especially for cookies since the bleaching process tightens the flour somewhat, reducing spread.

Chocolate chips are designed to retain their shape during baking, whereas chopped chocolate tends to melt and ooze during baking (often a desired effect). For a variety of textures, mix chunks, hunks, and chips. For my own Toll House–style cookies, I use coarsely chopped Scharffen Berger, Nestlé, Saco, or Van Houten semisweet chocolate.

Most cookie recipes benefit from an extra teaspoon of vanilla, though I hold back when I want subtle flavor, as for sugar cookies. Always use pure vanilla extract (see page 18). I recommend double-strength vanilla.

Many cookie recipes begin by creaming butter and sugar together. You can accomplish this by either using a mixer with the paddle attachment on low speed, or blending by hand, using a wooden spoon or stiff wire whisk. Start with softened butter to make the job easier.

Have your ingredients at room temperature for the batter to blend most easily. Cookie batter behaves best when you let it stand for at least 20 minutes after mixing. In general, softer doughs, such as for Toll House–style and other drop cookies, should be chilled for easier handling and to avoid excess spreading. (Soft dough can spread too quickly or thinly, because the fat in it is warm.) Use a baking sheet lined with ungreased parchment paper to inhibit spreading. However, if you want a thin cookie (in other words, a lot of spread), use dough at room temperature. A greased baking sheet or greased parchment paper liner encourages spreading, as does pressing down on the dough before baking.

You can easily double or even quadruple cookie recipes and freeze the dough for up to 6 months. Freeze the dough in large disks or, if you're ambitious, in individual drops, using a miniature ice-cream scoop. Wrap disks in waxed paper or parchment paper, then place in a freezer bag. For individual drops, freeze them on a baking sheet first and then package them in a freezer bag.

For some reason, oversized cookies seem to taste better. They have a density that their more modest counterparts do not have, and they are generally chewier and have crispier edges. Moreover, they look great. In the BB test kitchen, the chocolate chip and oatmeal cookies are enormous. No one who has had one ever forgets it. If you're concerned about eating too much, split a cookie in half, pour the milk, and invite a friend.

When baking anything, I usually double my baking sheets by stacking one on top of the other. Double sheeting is especially wise council for cookies. Due to their small size and high butter and sugar content, cookies are particularly heat sensitive. The extra insulation ensures even heat distribution and prevents cookie bottoms from burning or browning too quickly. Insulated baking sheets, which are made with two layers of metal, are designed with the same principle in mind, but I prefer stacking two regular sheets. If you have enough room in your oven to bake on two shelves at the same time, then the sheet on the middle shelf does not need to be doubled. But it still should be lined with parchment paper, which ensures that the cookies have an even, rolled edge. A lightly greased baking sheet results in cookies with thinner, more ragged edges.

A cookie's texture can be drastically changed simply by tinkering with ingredient proportions and baking methods. My recipes are formulated with the ideal texture in mind, but by all means, experiment. To make soft or chewy cookies, try changing some of the sugar in your recipe to a liquid sweetener such as honey, corn syrup, or molasses. Experiment by substituting 1 to 3 tablespoons liquid sweetener for sugar. (Too much liquid sweetener will alter the proportions of the ingredients in the recipe.) If you want a crispier cookie, make sure your dough is high in butter and sugar and is not icy cold when it goes in the oven. For a flatter cookie, reduce the soda or baking powder slightly. Baking powder, in particular, makes for puffier cookies. A recipe rich in eggs and baking powder will make more cakelike cookies.

HOW DOES ITALY SPELL "COOKIES"? BISCOTTI!

Some years ago, as coffee shops began springing up all over North America, the delightful cookie-like sticks known as biscotti became an instant morning classic. Biscotti are similar to their European cousin *mandelbrot*, or "almond bread." Mandelbrot, which is usually filled with walnuts or almonds and flavored with a bit of cinnamon, is most often made with oil, a concession to Jewish dietary laws. Biscotti can be made with either butter or oil, and are usually crispier than mandelbrot due to a longer second baking.

Biscotti get a lot of attention in the BB test kitchen. Good pasta is cooked al dente, firm to the tooth. I think of biscotti as an al dente cookie, crunchy and perfect for dunking. Unless you frequent a good bakery that makes decent biscotti, you will find that mass-produced versions are indifferent at best, and a pair of chocolate-dipped sticks drawn from a jar in a coffee shop will cost you almost as much as the Sunday *New York Times*. In any event, the flavors I propose are much too good to pass up. You will have no choice but to make your own.

Biscotti Tips

Many traditional Italian biscotti recipes do not use any oil or butter; biscotti are one of the few baked goods for which you can forgo fat without throwing off the overall balance of the recipe. But know that oil- or butter-free biscotti, while delightful, are very crisp and intended only for dunking in coffee or tea.

Oil or butter for biscotti? I like both, but tend to use melted unsalted butter. I like the buttery taste, and melted butter creams easily with the sugar. If you want to avoid dairy fats, you can substitute corn, canola, or safflower oil in the recipes.

Do not overbake your biscotti. This can be tricky, as biscotti will continue to bake a bit after they are removed from the oven the first time, and will crisp as they cool. Then, they are sliced and baked again. Sometimes, unless you are experienced or know the recipe and your oven very well, it is difficult to ascertain what is enough baking. Let the times in the recipes be your guide, but take biscotti out of the oven during their second bake as soon as they appear lightly colored and dry to the touch. You can also sneak one out of the oven just before you think the whole batch is done. Let it cool for a minute or two and taste. If it is crisp, the batch is ready to be removed and cooled.

For perfect slices of biscotti, cool the baked log of dough, wrap it in aluminum foil, and freeze it overnight. The next day, use a long, sharp serrated knife to cut neat, crumble-free slices. This technique is especially useful when the biscotti contain whole nuts or chunks of other foods.

To glaze biscotti in chocolate, melt 4 to 8 ounces of chopped semisweet or white chocolate. With a small icing knife, spread melted chocolate on one side of each cookie. Let cool on a wire rack for 2 to 4 hours, or until completely set. Or simply dip one end of a cookie in melted chocolate. For two-toned biscotti, dip one end in dark chocolate, the other in white. You can freeze glazed biscotti, but the gloss of the chocolate will dull.

When I have a lot of gift giving to do, the BB test kitchen wraps and freezes logs of many varieties of baked biscotti, as described above. I do the second bake a day before or the same day that I will be wrapping and giving the biscotti as gifts. For gift wrapping, wrap each cookie in waxed paper, and then again in colorful cellophane from a bakery supply store or your local florist.

The Long Tale of Shortbread

A big confession from a pastry chef: I am not terribly fond of sweets. Crème brûlée, cheesecake, and creamy whipped concoctions with names like Chocolate Death, Death by Sugar, and Decadence Torte just do not entice me much, even though I adore creating them for others. Shortbread, on the other hand, is, as my French pastry chef colleagues would say, my *faiblesse*, my weakness. I like its unadulterated taste of butter, its sandy texture, and its simplicity.

Shortbread, richer than sugar cookies, is a cousin to butter cookies. The best shortbread contains but a few premium ingredients and takes just minutes to make. Eggs are not part of shortbread, and neither is vanilla, for that matter. Longstanding feuds about ingredients and procedures come into play when discussing shortbread. Confectioners' sugar, superfine sugar, or regular white sugar? Cornstarch, rice flour, or all-purpose flour? Salted or sweet butter? Cream the butter or break it in? Chill the dough or not? Cut into rectangles, bake in a pan and cut into wedges, press into a shortbread mold, or stamp with a ceramic thistle stamp? Choices, choices.

BIG LEAGUE CHOCOLATE CHIP COOKIES

MAKES ABOUT 1½ DOZEN LARGE COOKIES

1 cup (8 ounces) unsalted butter, melted and slightly cooled

1¾ cups firmly packed brown sugar

¼ cup white sugar

2 eggs

1½ teaspoons pure vanilla extract

2 cups plus 2 tablespoons all-purpose flour

2 teaspoons baking soda

¼ teaspoon salt

3 cups semisweet chocolate chips

I coached boys' baseball for years; despite my winning record, I was more renowned for my baking, and especially this recipe. Even the umps remember me—just for these cookies! This is also the most-visited chocolate chip cookie recipe on the BB website. It was originally featured, alongside Fried Flaps of Dough (page 110), in a collection of baseball-stadium eats for summer sports teams. Make these large if you want crisp sides and chewy centers.

~❀~

Stack 2 baking sheets together and line the top one with parchment paper. Line a third baking sheet with parchment paper. Set aside.

In a large bowl or the bowl of an electric mixer fitted with the paddle attachment, cream the butter and both sugars until fluffy. Stir in the eggs and vanilla. In a medium bowl, combine the flour, baking soda, and salt. Whisk to blend. Stir into the wet ingredients. Stir in the chocolate chips. Refrigerate for 1 hour or overnight.

Preheat the oven to 375°F. For each cookie, spoon out about 4 tablespoons of dough and, using wet hands, round the dough into a ball a tad larger than a golf ball. Place on the prepared baking sheet, spacing the balls 2½ inches apart.

Place the doubled sheet on the bottom shelf of the oven and the single sheet on the middle shelf. Bake for 12 to 14 minutes, or until puffed and just set. Remove from the oven and let cool on the baking sheet for 10 minutes, then transfer to a wire rack and let cool completely.

FOR PUFFY AND WRINKLED COOKIES: Preheat the oven to 375°F. Use slightly cold or chilled balls of dough. Bake only a single sheet, not double-stacked sheets, on the upper shelf of the oven. Bake for 9 to 12 minutes, or until just set. After removing the cookies from the oven, briskly slam the sheet on the counter to deflate the cookies and encourage more wrinkling.

FOR SMALLER COOKIES: Use only 2 tablespoons dough to form each cookie, and space the balls about 2 inches apart. Bake as directed.

TOLL HOUSE–STYLE TARTLETS

MAKES ABOUT 2 DOZEN COOKIES

1 cup (8 ounces) unsalted butter, melted

1⅓ cups firmly packed brown sugar

¼ cup white sugar

1 egg

1 egg yolk

1 teaspoon pure vanilla extract

1 teaspoon baking soda mixed with 1 tablespoon hot water

2 cups all-purpose flour

¼ teaspoon salt

2½ cups miniature semisweet chocolate chips

Imagine—Toll House–style batter pressed into mini-muffin tins. This method produces chewy, caramelized chunks of heaven. I pack these up in waxed paper or cellophane for gift giving. I have also used miniature French tartlet pans, which I found in, of all places, an IKEA store, but you can also find them online.

Line a baking sheet with parchment paper. Spray a 24-cup miniature-muffin pan with nonstick cooking spray. Set aside.

In a large bowl or the bowl of an electric mixer fitted with the paddle attachment, cream the butter and both sugars together until fluffy. Blend in the egg, egg yolk, and vanilla. Stir in the baking soda mixture, then the flour and salt. Stir in the chocolate chips.

Cover and refrigerate for 30 minutes.

Preheat the oven to 350°F. Pack the batter into the miniature muffin cups. Place the muffin pan on the prepared baking sheet.

Bake for 15 to 17 minutes, or until just set. Let cool completely on wire racks. Freeze, in the pan, for 45 minutes to 1 hour.

Remove the cookies from the cups. To store, wrap each cookie in waxed paper or cellophane and refrigerate for up to 1 month. Serve cold.

B.B.
Test Kitchen
Notes

Brainstorm Baking

Change the form of a familiar baked good, and something intriguing and fun emerges. Such is the case with my Toll House–Style Tartlets. I also do a lot of baking in recycled (clean) tuna cans. Tuna-can baking makes for jaunty muffins (see Deli-Style Bran Muffins in Tuna Cans, page 195), baby cakes, and good-looking scones. But almost anything heatproof in tin or some metal, can make for an interesting result in texture and looks.

CHERRY-CHOCOLATE DECADENCE COOKIES

MAKES 2½ TO 3 DOZEN COOKIES

1 cup dried sour cherries, plumped and patted dry (page 18)

⅓ cup cherry liqueur (such as Cherry Heering, Cerisette, or Kirsch)

½ cup (4 ounces) unsalted butter, softened

½ cup white sugar

½ cup firmly packed brown sugar

1 egg

1½ teaspoons pure vanilla extract

¼ teaspoon almond extract

1½ cups flour

½ teaspoon baking soda

¼ teaspoon salt

4 to 6 ounces white chocolate, chopped

4 to 6 ounces semisweet chocolate, chopped

½ cup macadamia nuts (optional)

Inspired by Ben & Jerry's wonderful Cherry Garcia ice cream, this buttery cookie offers the tang of chewy dried sour cherries, along with chunks of white and dark chocolate. Macadamia nuts are optional, but terrific. Use the best white chocolate you can find.

~❦~

Stack 2 baking sheets together and line the top one with parchment paper. Line a third baking sheet with parchment paper. Set aside.

Preheat the oven to 350°F. Toss the plumped cherries with the cherry liqueur. Set aside.

In a large bowl or the bowl of an electric mixer fitted with the paddle attachment, cream the butter and both sugars together until fluffy. Blend in the egg, vanilla, and almond extract.

In a medium bowl, whisk the flour, baking soda, and salt together. Stir into the wet ingredients until blended. Drain the cherries, and stir them, both chocolates, and the nuts into the dough.

Drop heaping tablespoonfuls of dough 2½ inches apart on the prepared baking sheets. Place the doubled baking sheets on the bottom shelf of the oven and the single sheet on the middle shelf. Bake for 12 to 14 minutes, or until the cookies are lightly browned around the edges. Cool on the sheets for 10 minutes before transferring to a wire rack to cool completely.

SUGAR HEARTS

MAKES 3 TO 4 DOZEN COOKIES

1 cup (8 ounces) unsalted butter, softened

1 cup sugar

1 egg

1 egg yolk

1 teaspoon pure vanilla extract

¼ teaspoon almond extract

¼ cup half-and-half cream

3 cups all-purpose flour

½ teaspoon baking powder

½ teaspoon salt

6 ounces semisweet chocolate, melted, for glazing

This is a simple butter-and-sugar cookie dough, baked into hearts. Dip them in melted chocolate or dust them with confectioners' sugar.

Stack 2 baking sheets together and line the top one with parchment paper. Line a third baking sheet with parchment paper. Set aside.

In a large bowl or the bowl of an electric mixer fitted with the paddle attachment, cream the butter and sugar together until light and fluffy. Blend in the egg, egg yolk, vanilla, almond extract, and cream. In a medium bowl, whisk the flour, baking powder, and salt together. Stir into the wet ingredients to make a soft dough. On a lightly floured surface, form the dough into 2 disks. Wrap each in plastic wrap and refrigerate for at least 1 hour or up to 2 days.

Preheat the oven to 350°F. On a lightly floured surface, roll out 1 dough disk ¼ inch thick. Using a 2½-inch heart-shaped cutter, cut out and arrange on the prepared sheet, placing the cookies about 2 inches apart. Gather up the scraps once and reroll. Repeat with the second dough disk. Place the doubled baking sheets on the bottom shelf of the oven and the single sheet on the middle shelf. Bake for 12 to 15 minutes, or until lightly golden. Transfer to wire racks and let cool completely. Dip into cooled melted chocolate or spread the chocolate on with a small metal spatula or dinner knife.

COOKIE COLLECTIBLES

Cookie-jar collecting is a popular hobby, and there are thousands of styles, ranging from advertising promos to cartoon-character models to animal shapes. If you're into antiques, be on the lookout for counterfeit cookie jars. The American Cookie Jar Association says there are tons of bogus biscuit bins out there. The ACJA advises you to let your sense of smell guide you. A genuine antique cookie jar has, usually, been used to store cookies. Even if they've been washed, many jars still retain a faint odor. Check out flea markets, yard sales, and restaurant supply houses for great cookie jars. I have a lot of restaurant-supply glass cookie jars, reminiscent of general-store glass canisters, in my test kitchen. Anchor Hocking is a good source for these big-mouthed, classic glass cookie jars. Robinson Ransbottom of Ohio makes old-fashioned ceramic cookie jars that have a nice retro look to them.

TRIPLE CHOCOLATE CHUNK COOKIES

MAKES 7 TO 10 LARGE COOKIES OR 3 DOZEN SMALLER ONES

1 cup (8 ounces) unsalted butter, softened

½ cup firmly packed light brown sugar

½ cup white sugar

2 eggs

2 teaspoons pure vanilla extract

2½ cups all-purpose flour

3 tablespoons unsweetened cocoa powder

1 teaspoon baking soda

½ teaspoon instant coffee

⅜ teaspoon salt

1 cup semisweet chocolate chips

1 cup chopped semisweet Lindt or other good-quality Swiss chocolate

1 cup chopped white chocolate

This is a triple-chocolate symphony of pure cocoa, melted chocolate, and a ton of both semisweet chocolate chunks and chips and white chocolate chunks. The dough is ready to go once you mix it up, but it makes even more darkly delicious, decadent-tasting cookies if you refrigerate it for a few hours or overnight. If you're after a gorgeous, deeply flavored chocolate cookie, this is the one.

~⟨◊⟩~

Preheat the oven to 375°F. Stack 2 baking sheets together and line the top one with parchment paper. Position the oven rack in the upper third of the oven.

In the bowl of an electric mixer, cream the butter with both sugars until very well blended. Blend in the eggs and vanilla. Fold in the flour, cocoa, baking soda, coffee, and salt and blend well to make a thick batter. Fold in the chocolate chips, chocolate chunks, and white chocolate chunks. Mix well. The dough should be soft but not too loose or greasy; it should hold together.

Cover the dough lightly and let it stand for 15 minutes. If not baking immediately, shape the dough into a flattened disk and wrap it in wax or parchment paper, then store it in a Ziploc bag and refrigerate overnight. When you are ready to bake, remove the dough from the refrigerator and let it sit at room temperature for 1 to 2 hours.

Scoop or form balls of 7 to 8 ounces of dough (it's best to weigh it to make sure you have the right amount). Place the balls of dough on the baking sheet about 2 to 3 inches apart. For small cookies, use walnut-sized chunks of dough. Press the dough very slightly on the baking sheet.

Bake for 15 to 17 minutes (for large cookies) or until cookies look just barely set; for smaller cookies, bake for 12 to 15 minutes. Remove from the oven and let cool on the baking sheet for 15 to 20 minutes.

ADIRONDACK COOKIES

MAKES 12 TO 20 COOKIES

COOKIES

½ cup (4 ounces) unsalted butter

2 tablespoons white sugar

¾ cup firmly packed light brown sugar

1 egg

4 teaspoons molasses

2 teaspoons honey

1½ teaspoons pure vanilla extract

1½ cups rolled oats (any type)

⅓ cup all-purpose flour

¼ teaspoon baking soda

¼ teaspoon baking powder

⅛ teaspoon salt

⅛ teaspoon ground cinnamon

½ cup raisins, plumped and patted dry (see page 18)

½ cup dried cranberries, coarsely chopped

½ cup dried sour cherries, coarsely chopped

½ cup pecans, coarsely chopped

½ cup salted peanuts

¾ cup chopped white chocolate

GLAZE

1 cup confectioners' sugar

½ teaspoon pure vanilla extract

¼ teaspoon pure maple extract

Cream or water as required

Pecans, sour cherries, raisins, and dried cranberries make these crisp-chewy cookies into trailblazers. The slick and sumptuous maple vanilla glaze doesn't hurt, either. If your cranberries and cherries are pretty wizened or dry, plump them first in hot water, drain, dry, and then add them to the recipe.

Preheat the oven to 350°F. Line 1 large or 2 smaller baking sheets with parchment paper. Spray the parchment paper with nonstick cooking spray.

In the bowl of an electric mixer, cream the butter and both sugars until well blended. Blend in the egg, molasses, honey, and vanilla. Add the oats, flour, baking soda, baking powder, salt, and cinnamon and blend well. Fold in the raisins, cranberries, cherries, pecans, peanuts, and white chocolate by hand. This is a soft dough; you can chill it for 10 minutes for easier handling, but it should still be rather soft.

Using wet hands, mold 2 to 3 tablespoons of cookie dough into a ball (just a little smaller than a golf ball) in your palms and round the mounds gently. Place the cookies on the baking sheet, spacing them 3 inches apart, and press down on them slightly. Bake for 15 to 20 minutes, until the cookies are set. They will flatten slightly as they bake.

For the glaze, in a small bowl, blend the confectioners' sugar, vanilla and maple extracts, and cream or water to make a soft glaze. Smear it on the cookies with a flat icing spatula, or dip the cookies into the glaze and take off the excess. Let the glaze set. It's best to wrap these individually in wax paper and keep them chilled.

GRANDMA'S POPPY SEED SUGAR COOKIES

MAKES 7 TO 8 DOZEN COOKIES

6 eggs

1 cup vegetable oil, plus more for brushing

½ cup fresh orange juice

1½ cups sugar, plus more for sprinkling

7 cups (approximately) all-purpose flour

⅔ cup poppy seeds

2 teaspoons baking powder

½ teaspoon salt

When you need some nurturing, reach for one of these. No creaming necessary, just mix and go. These cookies are ideal with ice cream or afternoon tea.

Stack 2 baking sheets together and line the top one with parchment paper. Line a single baking sheet with parchment paper. Set aside.

In a large bowl, combine the eggs, the 1 cup oil, the orange juice, and the 1½ cups sugar. Stir to blend well. In a medium bowl, whisk the flour, poppy seeds, baking powder, and salt together. Stir into the wet ingredients to make a soft dough adding in a bit more flour as required if dough seems too soft. Turn the dough out onto a lightly floured surface. Divide the dough into 6 portions and form each portion into a disk. The dough can be wrapped in plastic and frozen at this point for up to 2 weeks. Each disk makes 12 to 18 cookies.

Preheat the oven to 350°F. On a lightly floured surface, roll out the dough ⅛ inch or ¼ inch thick. Cut out with a 3-inch cookie cutter, gathering the scraps once to reroll. Brush the tops lightly with oil and sprinkle liberally with sugar. Place on the prepared sheets, spacing them about 2 inches apart. Place the doubled baking sheets on the bottom shelf of the oven and the single sheet on the middle shelf. Bake for 12 to 14 minutes, or until the edges of the cookies are golden brown. Transfer the cookies to a wire rack and let cool completely.

FAMOUS TERRE ETOILE OATMEAL COOKIES

MAKES 8 TO 12 VERY LARGE COOKIES

1 cup (8 ounces) unsalted butter

1 cup firmly packed light brown sugar

¾ cup white sugar

2 eggs

1 tablespoon water or light cream

2 teaspoons pure vanilla extract

4 cups rolled oats (I use a mixture of quick-cooking and old-fashioned oats for best results)

1⅓ cups all-purpose flour

1½ teaspoons baking soda

Pinch of ground cinnamon

¼ teaspoon salt

½ cup coconut

½ cup dark raisins (optional)

½ cup light raisins (optional)

I often refer to one of my first jobs, as a creative baker and manager at a wonderful café called Terre Etoile, which existed briefly in Montreal in the mid '80s. There was a bookstore, a stunning skylit café, a health-food store, and the little nook that was my bakery. Left there, free to invent whatever I wanted, I unleashed my creativity with flour, and it never seems to have left me. Terre Etoile drew everyone from New Age types to city groupies who realized early on that it was the place to be. There were work romances aplenty, and other escapades that need their own book. But my TE oatmeal cookies? Ah, those were also special.

Everyone agrees that these are quintessentially perfect oatmeal cookies: not dense or soggy; not too crisp or hard; just perfect. Just follow the recipe to the letter. It has a golden caramel taste with a wee kiss of cinnamon and vanilla. I usually double this recipe and then freeze the extra dough for another day when I need a quick batch of cookies.

~❦~

Preheat the oven to 350°F. Stack 2 baking sheets together and line the top one with parchment paper.

In the bowl of an electric mixer, cream the butter with both sugars. Blend in the eggs, water or cream, and vanilla. Fold in the oats, flour, baking soda, cinnamon, salt, and coconut and blend well. Fold in the raisins (if using).

Form the cookie dough into large balls (about the size of 2 golf balls or 6 to 7 oz of dough). Press the cookies lightly onto the doubled baking sheets. Bake for 14 to 17 minutes, or until the edges are golden brown and the cookies seem set to the touch. Cool on the baking sheet for 3 minutes, then remove to a rack to finish cooling.

Marcy's Lassie Mog Cookies

MAKES 12 TO 20 COOKIES

1 cup (8 ounces) unsalted butter

1½ cups firmly packed light brown sugar

2 eggs

¼ cup molasses

1 tablespoon honey

1½ teaspoons pure vanilla extract

3 cups rolled oats (any type)

1 cup all-purpose flour

½ teaspoon baking soda

½ teaspoon baking powder

¼ teaspoon salt

½ teaspoon ground cinnamon

Pinch each of ground mace, cloves, and allspice

1 cup raisins, plumped and patted dry (see page 18)

¾ cup dates, finely chopped

1 cup pecans, coarsely chopped

What a name! What a cookie! The history of these delightfully named treats can be traced to Newfoundland, where "lassy" is a commonly used term for molasses, and a "mog" is a type of small cake. Laced with butter, caramel, and spices, and stuffed with chunks of dates, pecans, and raisins, this sleeper is the best cookie in the world.

Preheat the oven to 350°F. Line 1 large or 2 smaller baking sheets with parchment paper. Spray the parchment paper with nonstick cooking spray.

In a mixing bowl, cream the butter and sugar until well blended. Blend in the eggs, molasses, honey, and vanilla, then add the oats, flour, baking soda, baking powder, salt, cinnamon, mace, cloves, and allspice and blend well. Fold in the raisins, dates, and pecans. This is a soft dough; you can chill it for 10 minutes for easier handling, but it should still be rather soft.

Using wet hands, mold 2 to 3 tablespoons of cookie dough into a ball (just a little smaller than a golf ball) in your palms and round the mounds gently. Place the cookies on the baking sheet, spacing them 3 inches apart. Bake for 15 to 20 minutes until set. The cookies will flatten slightly while baking.

Tango Cookies (Alfajores)

MAKES ABOUT 40 COOKIES

DULCE DE LECHE

1 (14-ounce) can sweetened condensed milk or 1¼ cups prepared dulce de leche

DOUGH

1½ cups (12 ounces) unsalted butter, softened

1 cup confectioners' sugar, plus more for dusting

¼ teaspoon almond extract

½ teaspoon pure vanilla extract

3 cups all-purpose flour

⅓ cup ground almonds

2 tablespoons sugar

¼ teaspoon salt

These are national treasures of both Latin America and BetterBaking.com. Two almond shortbread cookies cradle a filling of dulce de leche, which can be homemade or purchased. Use any leftover filling in my luscious Dulce de Leche Cheesecake (page 258) or Dulce de Leche Pecan Pie (page 228). It is also sublime over ice cream or swirled into plain yogurt. Prepare the filling several hours or up to the day before. You can also make this cookie dough in a food processor.

For the dulce de leche, pour the condensed milk into the top of a double boiler over simmering water. Cook, stirring occasionally, for 3 to 5 hours, or until the milk thickens and turns a deep butterscotch color. Remove from the heat and let cool completely. It will thicken further as it cools. Use immediately, or cover and refrigerate for up to 1 month. This recipe makes about 1¼ cups.

Stack 2 baking sheets together and line the top with parchment paper. Line a third baking sheet with parchment paper. Set aside.

For the dough, cream the butter and the 1 cup confectioners' sugar in the bowl of an electric mixer fitted with the paddle attachment until light and fluffy. Stir in the almond and vanilla extracts. In a medium bowl, whisk the flour, almonds, sugar, and salt together. Stir into the wet ingredients until blended, periodically scraping the bottom of the mixer bowl. Turn the dough out onto a lightly floured surface and form it into 2 disks. Wrap each disk in plastic wrap and refrigerate for 30 minutes.

Preheat the oven to 350°F. On a lightly floured surface, roll out 1 dough disk ¼ inch thick. Using a 2½- to 3-inch fluted cookie cutter, cut into rounds. Gather the scraps once and reroll. Place the rounds on the prepared sheets, spacing them 2 inches apart. Repeat with the second dough disk. Place the doubled pans on the bottom shelf and the single pan on the middle shelf of the oven.

Bake for 12 to 14 minutes, or until lightly browned around the edges. Transfer the cookies to wire racks and let cool completely. Spread dulce de leche on the bottom of each cookie. Top with another cookie, bottom side down, and press together carefully. Dust tops with confectioners' sugar.

TANGO COOKIE ADVENTURE

I receive many requests at BetterBaking.com, and once in a while one stumps me. Such was the case for cookies called *alfajores* (pronounced *al-fa-hoh-res*). I checked all my sources and found nothing. Finally, a fellow tango dancer who hails from Chile told me that they were Latin American caramel sandwich cookies, but she had no recipe to share. I did find an alfajores recipe in one cookbook, but it made no mention of the caramel filling. Then a visitor to the site said she believed the cookies were from Peru, though she also had no recipe.

I called the Peruvian consulate in Montreal. No immediate reply. I found the sole Peruvian restaurant in the city. After fumbling with various permutations of English, French, and Spanish, the baker, Ingala, who prepared alfajores for the restaurant, informed me that she had no intention of parting with her recipe. Fair enough. I decided to purchase some cookies from the restaurant and perform my own analysis. I was instructed to call ahead. Apparently, the cookies sell very quickly at a dollar apiece.

I arrived at the restaurant at lunchtime. I saw plates of seafood, bowls of fresh soup, and strange side dishes of spices and condiments. Scents of lime and scallion permeated the air. This was no time to grab my alfajores and scurry away. I sat and examined my cookies as if they were pieces of moon rock. I wound up with a giant bowl of *sopa de casa,* "house soup," a chickenlike broth with scallions, lime, and noodles. It was delicious. I could hardly wait to try the cookies. They tasted like shortbread, but with ground almonds, confectioners' sugar on top, and an incredibly pure caramel filling, almost like crème caramel or Quebec sugar pie.

Another chat with the Chilean friend in my tango class further enlightened me (step, one, two, three . . . whatisthefillingforthecookies . . . one, two, three, and turn!). It was dulce de leche, national treat of Latin America and now quite trendy in parts of North America. To make dulce de leche, condensed milk is simmered in a double boiler for several hours until the milk becomes thickened and caramelized. Store-bought or prepared dulce de leche can be easy and convenient, but the flavor is usually not as good as homemade.

Several test batches and six pounds of butter later, I think I may have broken the alfajores code. These are great cookies. Elegant. Unique. Yes, these are alfajores, but to me, they will always be Tango Cookies, named for a passion that is rivaled only by my passion for baking.

CHOCOLATE-CHUNK, OATMEAL, AND RASPBERRY COOKIES

MAKES ABOUT 2½ DOZEN LARGE COOKIES

4 ounces plus 6 ounces semisweet chocolate, chopped

1 cup (8 ounces) unsalted butter, softened

1¼ cups firmly packed brown sugar

¾ cup white sugar

1 teaspoon honey

2 teaspoons pure vanilla extract

1 teaspoon raspberry extract (optional)

2 tablespoons milk

2 eggs

1¾ cups all-purpose flour

½ teaspoon salt

1 teaspoon baking powder

1 teaspoon baking soda

½ teaspoon ground cinnamon

1½ cups old-fashioned rolled oats

1 cup quick-cooking rolled oats

1 cup raisins

½ cup chocolate-covered raisins (optional)

1½ cups unsweetened frozen raspberries

1 cup whole pecans or walnuts

Semisweet chocolate and raspberries make my original oatmeal cookies a whole new deal. Chocolate-covered raisins are a nice touch, but regular raisins will do. Make sure your raspberries are frozen. One of my testers made these with raspberry syrup instead of the extract with excellent results. I use a combination of oats, but using all of one or the other is fine.

Stack 2 baking sheets together and line the top one with parchment paper. Line a third baking sheet with parchment paper. Spray both lined sheets very generously with nonstick cooking spray.

Preheat the oven to 350°F. In the top of a double boiler over barely simmering water, melt the 4 ounces chocolate; set aside to cool. In a large bowl or the bowl of an electric mixer fitted with the paddle attachment, cream the butter, both sugars, and honey together until fluffy. Stir in the vanilla, raspberry extract, milk, and eggs and blend well. Stir in the cooled chocolate. In a medium bowl, whisk the flour, salt, baking powder, baking soda, cinnamon, and both types of oats together. Stir in both types of raisins, the raspberries, nuts, and the remaining 6 ounces of chopped chocolate. Stir this mixture into the wet ingredients until well blended.

Using wet hands, form the dough into balls the size of a golf ball and place on the prepared baking sheets, spacing them 2 inches apart. Press down lightly on each ball. Place the doubled sheets on the bottom and the single sheet on the middle shelf of the oven. Bake for 14 to 17 minutes, or until just set. Let cool on the pans for 10 minutes, then transfer to a wire rack and let cool completely.

RASPBERRY SANDWICH COOKIES

MAKES 30 TO 35 COOKIES

1 cup (8 ounces) unsalted butter, softened

1 cup sugar

1 egg

1 egg yolk

1 teaspoon pure vanilla extract

¼ teaspoon almond extract

¼ cup half-and-half cream

3 cups all-purpose flour

½ teaspoon baking powder

½ teaspoon salt

FILLING AND TOPPING

1 cup raspberry jam

Confectioners' sugar for dusting, or 4 ounces semisweet chocolate, chopped and melted

In one scene in the movie Sleepless in Seattle, *two youngsters plot to arrange the love life of a single dad while they make sugar cookies. Their juxtaposition of cookies and subterfuge works well. On the website one year, I featured these cookies in my Oscar Salute. You may dip them in melted chocolate, and then decorate them before the chocolate sets. If heart shapes don't work for you, a simple round cutter will do.*

Stack 2 large baking sheets together and line the top one with parchment paper. Line a third baking sheet with parchment paper. Set aside.

In a large bowl or bowl of an electric mixer fitted with the paddle attachment, cream the butter and sugar together until light and fluffy. Blend in the egg, egg yolk, vanilla and almond extracts, and cream. In a medium bowl, whisk the flour, baking powder, and salt together. Stir into the wet ingredients until well blended. Turn the dough out onto a lightly floured surface. Divide the dough into 2 disks. Wrap in plastic wrap and refrigerate for at least 1 hour or up to 2 days.

Preheat the oven to 350°F. On a lightly floured surface, roll out 1 dough disk ¼ inch thick. Using a 2½- to 3-inch round or heart-shaped cookie cutter, cut out shapes. Place the cookies on the prepared baking sheets spacing them about 2 inches apart. Place the doubled baking sheets on the bottom shelf of the oven and the single sheet on the middle shelf. Bake for 12 to 15 minutes, or until lightly golden. Transfer the cookies to wire racks and let cool completely.

Spread about 1 tablespoon jam on 1 cookie, and top with another. Dust with confectioners' sugar, dip into melted chocolate, or spread chocolate on with a small metal spatula or butter knife. If using chocolate, leave on wire racks until set.

VARIATION: Brush the cookies with lightly beaten egg white and sprinkle with colored sugar before baking.

HOLIDAY SPRITZ COOKIES

MAKES 3 TO 4 DOZEN COOKIES

¾ cup (6 ounces) plus
    2 tablespoons unsalted butter,
    softened

2 tablespoons vegetable shortening
    or unsalted butter

1 cup white sugar

2 tablespoons firmly packed brown
    sugar

2 egg yolks, blended with
    3 tablespoons half-and-half
    cream

1½ teaspoons pure vanilla extract

2½ cups all-purpose flour

2 tablespoons cup cornstarch

2 teaspoons baking powder

¼ teaspoon salt

These are tender and easy to make, the consummate holiday cookies. They're fine plain or iced, or you can add embellishments, like candied fruit, currants, dried cranberries, minced dried cherries, miniature chocolate or butterscotch chips, oatmeal, or other flavor extracts and colorings. Purists may insist on all butter, but a small amount of shortening makes for a crispier cookie.

Stack 2 baking sheets together and line the top one with parchment paper. Line a third baking sheet with parchment paper. Set aside.

Preheat the oven to 350°F. In a large bowl or the bowl of an electric mixer fitted with the paddle attachment, cream the butter, shortening, and both sugars together until light and fluffy. Blend in the egg yolk mixture and the vanilla. In a medium bowl, whisk the flour, cornstarch, baking powder, and salt together. Stir into the wet ingredients until well blended.

Pack the dough into a spritz cookie gun and extrude the cookies 2 inches apart on the prepared baking sheets. Place the doubled sheets on the bottom shelf of the oven and the single sheet on the middle shelf. Bake for 12 to 16 minutes, or until lightly browned. Transfer the cookies to wire racks to cool completely.

B.B.
Test Kitchen
Notes

Chef Reveals Secret Recipe

We all hear stories about how some chefs refuse to part with their original recipes. But recipes are not always static things; they evolve as we learn and tinker along the way. Chocolate chip cookies are like that for me. They're a work in progress. I melt the butter or just soften it, use pastry or all-purpose flour, add a touch of honey, use oil instead of butter, and so on. One day's chocolate chip cookie recipe might not taste like another day's. A tester once chided me about having a "secret" recipe because I could not reproduce the formula precisely. Chefs often jam, much the way musicians do, and they don't always record what they're doing. Occasionally, a variation on a technique or an ingredient will produce great and unique results. I'm always happy to share those moments—as long as I remember to write them down!

Q&A: A BETTERBAKING.COM MANDATE

I receive many questions at the BetterBaking.com site, and I pride myself on teaching and trouble-shooting as much as I do on sharing recipes and entertaining tips. Questions keep me on my toes. Here are some examples:

FREEZING COOKIE DOUGH VS. FREEZING COOKIES. WHICH IS BEST? CAN ANY COOKIE DOUGH BE FROZEN?

I prefer freezing dough and baking as required. The richer the dough, the better it freezes. For example, I freeze cream cheese rugalach dough for up to 3 months and Toll House–style cookie dough for 3 to 4 months.

IS THERE ANY PRACTICAL WAY OF CONVERTING A MUFFIN RECIPE INTO A CAKE?

Most of my muffin recipes are easily converted into cakes. The pan size required depends on the volume of batter in the muffin recipe. For 2½ cups of batter, use a 7- by 11-inch pan. For 3 cups or more of batter, use a 9- by 13-inch pan or a 10-inch springform pan. Bake in a preheated 350°F oven for 35 to 55 minutes (depending on the quality of batter), or until the cake is springy to the touch. Check the cake after the first 30 minutes. The total baking time will vary with the batter volume.

HOW DO I MAKE VANILLA SUGAR?

Combine 2 cups sugar and 1 vanilla bean split lengthwise in a jar with a cover and shake. Shake occasionally for a few days. The bean may be reused to flavor more sugar. Otherwise, cut up the vanilla bean and process it with the sugar in a food processor to produce a sugar with flecks of vanilla in it. Both kinds are great in coffee and tea, as well as for baking.

TO MAKE CHOCOLATE-COVERED CHERRIES THAT HAVE BEEN COVERED IN FONDANT, WHAT KIND OF CHOCOLATE SHOULD I USE?

Whenever you cover or dip something in chocolate, you must use tempered chocolate. This is chocolate that has been stabilized and remains shiny when it hardens, instead of producing white spots called "bloom." You may purchase tempered chocolate wafers, or you may temper chocolate yourself for better flavor. Invest in a book about cooking with chocolate for full instructions. Beware of "chocolate compound" or "chocolate-flavored" wafers, both of which look like chocolate and melt well, but lack real, intense chocolate flavor.

Oatmeal Cookies the Size of Plates

MAKES ABOUT 8 TO 12 LARGE COOKIES

1 cup (8 ounces) unsalted butter, softened

½ cup firmly packed light brown sugar

½ cup firmly packed dark brown sugar

¾ cup white sugar

1⅓ cups all-purpose flour

½ teaspoon baking powder

1½ teaspoons baking soda

¼ teaspoon ground cinnamon

¼ teaspoon salt

2 cups quick-cooking rolled oats

2 cups old-fashioned rolled oats

½ cup sweetened shredded coconut (optional)

½ cup dark raisins

½ cup golden raisins

2 eggs

2 teaspoons pure vanilla extract

2 tablespoons water or half-and-half cream

Crisp outside, dense and chewy inside, this cookie is wonderfully wholesome but still delivers great cookieness. Even though these would be awesome at any size, do not even consider making these smaller.

Stack 2 baking sheets together and line the top one with parchment paper. Line a third baking sheet with parchment paper. Set aside.

Preheat the oven to 350°F. In a large bowl or the bowl of an electric mixer fitted with the paddle attachment, cream the butter and all three sugars together until fluffy. In a medium bowl, whisk the flour, baking powder, baking soda, cinnamon, and salt together. Stir in both types of rolled oats, the coconut, and both types of raisins. Stir the dry ingredients into the wet ingredients until well blended. Blend in the eggs, vanilla, and water.

Form the dough into large balls about 3 inches in diameter. Place 3 inches apart on the prepared baking sheets. Press each ball to flatten slightly. Place the doubled sheets on the bottom shelf and the single sheet on the middle shelf of the oven. Bake for 12 to 14 minutes, or until the edges are golden and the tops look barely dry. Let cool on the baking sheets for 3 minutes, then transfer to wire racks and let cool completely.

B.B.
Test Kitchen
Notes

Hostess with the Mostest

I have learned something as a professional pastry chef: pros rarely mix dough and bake on the same day. Cookie doughs, and even some cake batters, are often prepared, refrigerated or frozen, then baked as required. The same applies in my test kitchen. Several batches of cookie dough are frozen, and batches are moved to the refrigerator to thaw. A dozen or so fresh cookies are baked each morning or after school. People are often amazed that fresh cookies are readily available in my home, but we're a cookie household, and that's that. Just think ahead, and you too can be the hostess, or host, with the mostest. Note: I freeze cookie dough in 1-pound logs, then defrost them in a microwave on high for a minute or two, or overnight in the refrigerator.

CHINESE RESTAURANT ALMOND COOKIES

MAKES 3 TO 4 DOZEN COOKIES

1 cup vegetable shortening

1½ cups sugar

½ cup ground almonds

1 egg

1 to 2 tablespoons almond extract (to taste)

3 cups all-purpose flour

½ teaspoon baking soda

¼ teaspoon salt

Yellow food coloring (optional)

1 egg yolk beaten with 1 teaspoon water

Almond halves for garnish

These are just like the restaurant cookies: big and dramatic, with crackly tops. Lard would make these more authentic, I suppose, but most restaurants (or their suppliers) now opt for shortening. These are intensely almondy.

Stack 2 baking sheets together and line the top one with parchment paper. Line a third baking sheet with parchment paper. Set aside.

Preheat the oven to 325°F. In a large bowl or the bowl of an electric mixer fitted with the paddle attachment, cream the shortening and sugar together until light and fluffy. Stir in the ground almonds. Blend in the egg and almond extract. In a medium bowl, whisk the flour, baking soda, and salt together. Stir into the wet ingredients until blended. Stir in the food coloring.

Form the dough into balls about 2½ inches in diameter. Place 2 inches apart on the prepared baking sheets. Using the bottom of a drinking glass, press lightly to flatten.

Brush the tops with the egg yolk mixture. Place an almond half on the center of each cookie and press slightly into the dough. Place the doubled baking sheets on the bottom shelf of the oven and the single sheet on the middle shelf. Bake for 15 to 20 minutes, or until the cookies are set and dry to the touch. Cool on the sheets for 10 minutes before transferring to a wire rack to cool completely.

SHAMELESS CHOCOLATE GOBS

MAKES 1½ TO 2 DOZEN COOKIES

½ cup (4 ounces) unsalted butter, softened

1 cup firmly packed brown sugar

¾ cup white sugar

4 eggs

1 teaspoon pure vanilla extract

10 ounces semisweet chocolate, melted

1 tablespoon very strong brewed coffee

2¼ cups all-purpose flour

1½ teaspoons baking powder

½ teaspoon baking soda

¼ teaspoon salt

10 ounces semisweet chocolate (or half milk chocolate, half semisweet), chopped

1 cup chopped pecans (optional)

1 cup dried sour cherries (optional)

As the name suggests, these are oversized, chock-full of chocolate, and almost as dense as a brownie. I am not one to go overboard with chocolate, but these are my undoing, worth every calorie. They are also great with espresso. The dried sour cherries are optional, but I like the contrast. One tester simply wrote: "Wonderful."

Stack 2 large baking sheets together and line the top one with parchment paper. Line a third baking sheet with parchment paper. Set aside.

In a large bowl or the bowl of an electric mixer fitted with the paddle attachment, cream the butter and both sugars together until fluffy. Blend in the eggs and vanilla. Stir in the melted chocolate and coffee until blended. In a medium bowl, whisk the flour, baking powder, baking soda, and salt together. Stir into the wet ingredients until blended. Stir in the chopped chocolate, nuts, and cherries. Cover the bowl with plastic wrap and refrigerate for at least 1 hour or overnight.

Preheat the oven to 350°F. Form the dough into balls about 2 inches in diameter. Place about 3 inches apart on the prepared baking sheets. Place the doubled sheets on the bottom shelf and the single sheet on the middle shelf. Bake for 13 to 17 minutes, or until just set. Let cool completely on the baking sheets.

A BAKING LESSON FOR MRS. GREENBERG'S CLASS, OR BETTERBAKING.COM GOES BACK TO SCHOOL

Children like to tinker with computers, and they like to bake. I once combined these two interests for a visit I made to my son's first-grade class. It was a simple matter of posting on the website a personal message from me, a recipe and baking instructions, some humorous graphics, and, most important, the names of the students who were to attend the class. For a child, seeing your name on a computer screen is practically equivalent to seeing it on TV, and a photograph is even better. I then followed up with an in-class demo. It was all impressive, but nothing was more captivating then the baked results.

NEW YORK BLACK-AND-WHITE COOKIES

MAKES 1½ TO 2 DOZEN LARGE COOKIES

DOUGH

1 cup (8 ounces) unsalted butter, softened

1½ cups sugar

2 eggs

¼ cup half-and-half cream

2 teaspoons pure vanilla extract

4 cups all-purpose flour

1 tablespoon baking powder

½ teaspoon salt

GLAZE

4 cups confectioners' sugar

⅓ to ½ cup boiling water

1 ounce semisweet chocolate, melted

An episode of Seinfeld introduced me to New York City's black-and-white cookies. There are many recipes for this Big Apple treat. My version produces a crisp, dense cookie instead of the more traditional cakey one. For Valentine's or Mother's Day, make these pink and white, for St. Patrick's Day, green and white.

~❁~

Stack 2 baking sheets together and line the top one with parchment paper. Line a third baking sheet with parchment paper. Set aside.

For the dough, cream the butter and sugar in a large bowl or bowl of an electric mixer fitted with the paddle attachment, until light and fluffy. Stir in the eggs, cream, and vanilla. In a medium bowl, whisk the flour, baking powder, and salt together. Stir into the wet ingredients to make a firm dough. On a lightly floured surface, form the dough into 2 disks. Wrap each in plastic wrap and refrigerate for 10 to 15 minutes.

Preheat the oven to 350°F. On a lightly floured surface, roll out 1 dough disk ¼ inch thick. Using a 4-inch cookie cutter, cut into rounds and place 2 inches apart on the prepared baking sheets. Gather up the scraps once and reroll. Place the doubled baking sheets on the bottom shelf of the oven and the single sheet on the middle shelf. Bake for 13 to 15 minutes, or until deeply golden and slightly browned. Transfer to a wire rack and let cool completely. Repeat with the remaining dough disk. The scraps can be gathered together, wrapped, and chilled, then rerolled.

For the glaze, put the confectioners' sugar in a bowl. Gradually stir in the boiling water until smooth. Remove half of the frosting to another bowl and stir in the melted chocolate. With a frosting spatula, decorate one cookie half with white frosting, the other half with chocolate frosting. Let set on the wire racks until thoroughly set.

TIRAMISU BISCOTTI

MAKES ABOUT 2 DOZEN BISCOTTI

1 cup chopped pecans

3 tablespoons plus 1½ cups sugar

1 cup (8 ounces) unsalted butter, melted

2 teaspoons pure vanilla extract

2 tablespoons coffee liqueur (such as Tía Maria)

3 eggs

2 teaspoons baking powder

⅜ teaspoon salt

3 cups all-purpose flour

3 tablespoons freeze-dried coffee or instant espresso powder

2 tablespoons hot water

1 cup semisweet chocolate chips, melted

The BB test kitchen has a lot of fun taking one concept (in this case, the flavors of trendy tiramisu) and making it in another form (in this case, biscotti). This cookie features a vanilla layer, followed by candied pecans, a sludgy layer of chocolate biscotti batter, and a topping of crisp coffee flavor.

Preheat the oven to 350°F. Stack 2 baking sheets together and line the top one with parchment paper. Set aside.

Line another baking sheet with parchment paper. Sprinkle the pecans and dust with the 3 tablespoons sugar. Bake the nuts for 10 to 15 minutes, or until slightly browned. Remove the baking sheet from the oven and let the nuts cool on the sheet for about 15 minutes. Leave the oven at 350°F.

In a large bowl or the bowl of an electric mixer fitted with the paddle attachment, cream the butter and the remaining 1½ cups sugar together until fluffy. Blend in the vanilla, coffee liqueur, and eggs. Stir in the baking powder, salt, flour, and 1 tablespoon of the coffee.

In a small bowl, mix the remaining 2 tablespoons dried coffee with the hot water.

Turn out one-third of the dough onto the doubled baking sheets and shape into a 9- by 5-inch oblong. Pat the pecans into the dough. Place half of the remaining dough in a medium bowl and stir half of the chocolate into it. Pat this chocolate dough on top of the vanilla-pecan dough. For the remaining dough, stir in the brewed coffee with a wooden spoon or rubber spatula. Pat this dough onto the chocolate dough.

Place in the oven and bake for 30 to 40 minutes, or until set. Remove the biscotti from the oven and lower heat to 325°F. Let the biscotti cool on a rack for 20 minutes, then cut on the diagonal into slices about ½ inch thick. Distribute on the prepared baking sheets. Place the doubled sheets on the bottom shelf of the oven and the single sheet on the middle shelf. Bake, turning once, for 12 to 15 minutes, or until dry.

Remove and let cool on a rack for 30 minutes, or until completely cooled. Dip the end of each biscotti in the remaining chocolate and let cool until the chocolate is set.

THE SECRET CARAMEL CHOCOLATE CHIP BISCOTTI

MAKES 2 TO 2½ DOZEN BISCOTTI

1 cup (8 ounces) unsalted butter, melted

2 cups sugar

1 tablespoon pure vanilla extract

1½ teaspoons caramel or butterscotch extract (optional)

5 eggs

½ cup finely chopped toasted almonds

4 cups (approximately) all-purpose flour

1 large package dry caramel or butterscotch pudding mix*

2½ teaspoons baking powder

¼ teaspoon salt

¾ cup semisweet chocolate chips

½ cup caramel or butterscotch chips, or finely chopped Heath bar

⅓ cup chocolate sundae topping or chocolate syrup

4 to 6 tablespoons caramel sauce or dulce de leche (see page 153)

* Different brands of pudding come in slightly different sizes, so don't worry if it's a few ounces more or less. Either instant or noninstant pudding mix is fine.

Want to manifest better biscotti? Well, you need to know The Secret. I baked biscotti for years until I figured out the magic formula that changed everything I knew about this crunchy cookie. The secret is in how you bake it: in a pan, not free-form. That way you get wonderfully uniform café-style biscotti. But the true secret of these amazing biscotti may be the recipe itself: a symphony of double-caramel batter with chunks of chocolate, toasted almonds and ripples of chocolate syrup running through a crisp, crumbly cookie. It is over-the-top divine. And now it's not a secret anymore.

Preheat the oven to 350°F. Line a 9- by 13-inch pan with parchment paper. Spray the sides and bottom with nonstick cooking spray.

In the bowl of an electric mixer, blend together the butter and sugar, then blend in the vanilla and caramel extracts, eggs, and almonds. Fold in the flour, pudding mix, baking powder, and salt. Last, mix in the chocolate and caramel chips.

Spoon the batter into the prepared pan, using wet fingers to spread it evenly. Drizzle the chocolate syrup and caramel sauce on top and swish around with a butter knife to marbleize.

Bake until the biscotti are solid to the touch and set, about 55 to 65 minutes. Cool for 15 minutes and then invert onto a cutting surface. Line 2 baking sheets with parchment paper. Cut the biscotti into ½-inch slices and place them on the prepared baking sheets.

Reduce the oven temperature to 325°F. Rebake the biscotti until they are crisp, 25 to 30 minutes. Remove from the oven and cool well.

The finished biscotti can also be glazed with melted dark or white chocolate—just let it set and dry completely before wrapping.

MY BISCOTTI "SECRET" REVEALED

· · · · · · · · ·

Here is the secret to these fantastic biscotti, or any other biscotti recipe: baking the biscotti in a mold, like a regular 9- by 13-inch pan, instead of baking them free-form on a baking sheet. This particular recipe yields tall, uniform, easy-to-cut biscotti that look just like the ones you see at cafés in those beautiful glass jars. You can wrap the long sticks of biscotti in cellophane and give them as gifts, or start your own biscotti-baking business.

WEDDING FOR BELLA BISCOTTI

MAKES 2 TO 3 DOZEN BISCOTTI

BISCOTTI DOUGH

2 cups blanched almonds

1 cup (8 ounces) unsalted butter

1¾ cups sugar

1 tablespoon pure vanilla extract

Zest of one large orange, finely
	minced (optional)

6 eggs

6 cups all-purpose flour, divided

2 teaspoons baking powder

½ teaspoon salt

FINISHING TOUCHES

1 to 2 egg yolks, beaten with a
	touch of water

White or coarse sugar for dusting

There is an indie film you can still rent on DVD called A Wedding for Bella, starring Scott Baio (yes—from Happy Days*). The film features a beloved landmark biscotti bakery in Pittsburgh called Enrico's Biscotti. This recipe makes huge, sweet, crunchy sticks just like the biscotti in the film. You take one, break it half, and share. The size is a real draw, but it is the taste that calls for "bis." This is a very simple biscotti, allowing you to taste the pure elements of butter, sugar, flour, and eggs. There are recipes on the Internet purporting to be Enrico's, but I prefer my own version, inspired by watching the "biscotti scenes" over and over again.*

~❧~

Preheat the oven to 350°F. Stack 2 baking sheets together, lining the top one with parchment paper.

Spread the almonds on the baking sheets and lightly toast them in the oven for about 10 to 15 minutes. Cool and coarsely chop the almonds and set them aside.

In a large mixing bowl, cream together the butter, sugar, vanilla, and orange zest. Blend in the eggs, adding in 1 cup of the flour with them to help them blend. Add the remaining flour with the baking powder and salt, and, when nearly blended, fold in the almonds. This will make a stiff dough.

Knead the dough briefly on a floured board and shape it into a thick, slightly square mound, 8 by 10 inches. Place it on the doubled baking sheets. Brush the top with the egg yolk and dust with a bit of sugar.

Bake until done, 40 to 55 minutes. Line a third baking sheet with parchment paper. Cool well, then cut the biscotti into lengths ½ inch wide and place them on the prepared baking sheets. Preheat the oven to 350°F. Place the doubled sheets on the bottom shelf of the oven and the single sheet on the middle shelf. Bake again for 15 minutes per side, turning once to dry out (or crisp) the biscotti.

Maple Butter Walnut Biscotti

MAKES ABOUT 1½ DOZEN BISCOTTI

BISCOTTI

1 cup (8 ounces) unsalted butter, melted

1 cup white sugar

¾ cup firmly packed brown sugar

¼ cup pure maple syrup

1 teaspoon pure maple extract*

1½ teaspoons pure vanilla extract

3 eggs

4 cups all-purpose flour

⅓ cup toasted walnuts, finely ground

2 teaspoons baking powder

½ teaspoon salt

½ cup chopped toasted walnuts

MAPLE FONDANT GLAZE†

2 cups confectioners' sugar

½ teaspoon pure maple extract

Cream as required

* Maple extract is available in the baking ingredient aisle of most supermarkets or from baking suppliers online.

† These biscotti are luscious without any finishing touches, but a coating of maple fondant or melted white chocolate makes them special enough for company.

What could be more welcome in spring than a taste of maple, newly drawn from Canadian maple trees? For centuries, maple syrup has had its place in the kitchens of the Northeast—especially in Quebec, also known as Maple Country, where I live. You'll typically find it on pancakes and in homey puddings and pies, but in this recipe, maple syrup is recast in a trendier way. This biscotti combines the heritage of pure maple syrup with creamy butter, toasted walnuts, and a touch of vanilla to round it all out. If you have some real maple sugar on hand, crumble it up to replace some of the brown sugar.

Preheat the oven to 350°F. Stack 2 baking sheets together and line the top one with parchment paper. Line a 9- by 13-inch rectangular pan with parchment paper. Spray the pan and parchment lining with nonstick cooking spray. Have the ground and chopped walnuts prepared and nearby.

In a large bowl, hand whisk the butter with both sugars. Blend in the maple syrup, maple and vanilla extracts, and eggs. Fold in most of the flour, reserving ¼ cup, then fold in the ground walnuts, baking powder, salt, and chopped walnuts. The batter should be stiff. If it is very gloppy, add the reserved ¼ cup of flour. Spread or pat the dough into the prepared pan. Place the pan on the stacked baking sheets.

Bake for 40–50 minutes, until set and firm to the touch. If the biscotti doesn't seem quite baked through (i.e., the sides are done but the middle seems tender), lower the oven temperature to 325°F and bake another 15 to 20 minutes.

Remove from the oven, cool for 30 minutes, then invert the biscotti on another baking sheet. Freeze it for 1 hour (this will facilitate cutting).

Preheat the oven to 325°F. Line a third baking sheet with parchment paper. Cut the biscotti into sticks ½ inch in diameter and place on the prepared baking sheets. Place the doubled sheets on the bottom shelf of the oven and the single sheet on the middle shelf, and bake the biscotti for 15 minutes per side (turning once) to crisp them.

Prepare the Maple Fondant by whisking all ingredients together to make a stiff fondant (soft icing). Alternatively, melt white chocolate (about 1 cup, chopped; Baker's works nicely) in a microwave for 1 minute. If you want a plain white chocolate coating, use it as is. For maple-flavored coating, drizzle in a few drops of maple extract. Smear the fondant or white chocolate on the biscotti (it's nice to have some with white chocolate and some without).

You can leave some of the biscotti in long sticks (café style) and cut some in half for more modest-sized treats. These make a great gift.

SOFT CHERRY BISCOTTI

MAKES ABOUT 18 LARGE BISCOTTI

BISCOTTI

1 (19-ounce) jar or can sour pitted cherries

½ cup cherry liqueur (such as Cherry Heering, Cerisette, or Kirsch)

1 cup dried sour cherries, plumped and patted dry (see page 18), then finely chopped

¾ cup (6 ounces) unsalted butter, softened

1½ cups sugar

4 eggs

2 egg yolks

1 teaspoon pure vanilla extract

1 teaspoon pure almond extract

¼ cup milk

3½ to 4 cups all-purpose flour

1 tablespoon baking powder

⅜ teaspoon salt

TOPPING (OPTIONAL)

1 cup reserved cherry juice

2 tablespoons cornstarch

Oh, heavens. These are heavenly. Ever get tired of crisp, hard biscotti but still love the wonderful cookie sticks? This is a cakey, golden-yellow biscotti with extra egg yolks, studded with both Kirsch-soaked sour cherries and shredded, dried sour cherries. After baking and slicing, the biscotti are slathered with cherry glaze to give them a sticky finish. You can also leave the biscotti plain and just dust them with a wee bit of confectioners' sugar. These are sublime and different, but destined to become a classic in your baking repetoire.

~⟨◊⟩~

The night (or a few hours) before, drain the sour cherries, reserving the juice separately, and put them back in the jar they came in. Pour the cherry liqueur over them and let them stand overnight. Plump the dried cherries, chop finely, and add them to the marinating cherries.

Preheat the oven to 350°F. Stack 2 baking sheets together and line the top one with parchment paper.

Drain the cherries, reserving both cherries and liqueur.

In the bowl of an electric mixer fitted with the paddle attachment, cream the butter and sugar together until fluffy and smooth. Blend in the eggs, egg yolks, vanilla and almond extracts, and milk, and blend well, scraping the bottom of the bowl occasionally to make sure all the ingredients are incorporated. Fold in the dry ingredients and blend well, adding more flour if necessary, to make a soft batter. Fold in the reserved cherries by hand.

Spread out the dough (it will be sticky, so use a wet metal spatula or wet hands) on the prepared baking sheets. It should be about 12 inches long and 4 or 5 inches wide. Bake until lightly golden on top and browned around the edges, 42 to 45 minutes. Remove from the oven and reduce the oven temperature to 325°F. Line a third baking sheet with parchment paper. Cut the biscotti into lengths 1 inch wide and divide them between the prepared baking sheets, separating them slightly. Place the doubled sheets on the bottom shelf of the oven and the single sheet on the middle shelf, and bake for 12 minutes. Remove from the oven.

While the biscotti are cooling, bring ¾ cup of the reserved cherry juice to a boil. Meanwhile, in a separate measuring cup, stir the cornstarch and ¼ cup cherry juice together. Add the cornstarch mixture to the hot cherry juice and whisk to blend. Reduce the heat to low and cook until the topping thickens, about 2 to 3 minutes. Remove from the stove and cool for 5 minutes. Drizzle on the cookies. Or, if preferred, simply dust the biscotti with confectioners' sugar and use the sauce as a dip for the biscotti.

Chocolate Chip Cinnamon-Sugar Biscotti

MAKES 15 TO 20 BISCOTTI

1 cup (8 ounces) unsalted butter, melted

1½ cups sugar

4 eggs

2 teaspoons pure vanilla extract

¼ teaspoon orange oil or extract

4 cups all-purpose flour

1 tablespoon baking powder

½ teaspoon salt

½ cup walnuts

4 ounces semisweet chocolate

¼ cup sugar mixed with
    2 teaspoons ground cinnamon
    for sprinkling

Take a typical biscotti dough, press it into a loaf pan, and bake. Chill, slice, and rebake. Voilà! A new cookie: thick slabs of crisp biscotti, with an interesting layer of chocolate and a pretty topping of cinnamon sugar. These are serious cookies. Espresso anyone?

~❦~

Generously coat a 9- by 5-inch loaf pan with nonstick cooking spray and line the bottom with parchment paper. Line a baking sheet with parchment paper. Set aside.

Preheat the oven to 350°F. In a large bowl or the bowl of an electric mixer fitted with the paddle attachment, cream the butter and sugar together until fluffy. Blend in the eggs, vanilla, and orange oil. In a medium bowl, whisk the flour, baking powder, and salt together. Stir into the wet ingredients to make a stiff dough.

Spoon half the dough into the prepared loaf pan. In a food processor, finely chop the walnuts and chocolate together. Distribute the mixture evenly over the dough and sprinkle half of the cinnamon sugar on top. Top with the remaining dough. Pat into place with wet hands. Sprinkle with the remaining cinnamon sugar.

Place the pan on the prepared baking sheet and bake for 45 to 55 minutes, or until firm to the touch. Let cool completely in the pan on a wire rack. Wrap the pan in foil and place in the freezer for 1 hour.

Preheat the oven to 325°F. Stack 2 additional baking sheets together and line the top one with parchment paper. Turn the loaf out onto a cutting board. Cut crosswise into ½-inch-thick slices with a large serrated knife. Lay the slices on the prepared baking sheets. Place the doubled baking sheets on the bottom oven shelf and the single baking sheet on the middle shelf. Bake for 10 to 15 minutes, or until crisp and slightly browned. Transfer to wire racks to cool completely.

Upright Rippled Shortbread Biscotti

MAKES 15 TO 20 BISCOTTI

1 cup (8 ounces) unsalted butter, melted

1½ cups sugar, plus more for sprinkling

4 eggs

2 teaspoons pure vanilla extract

4 cups all-purpose flour

2½ teaspoons baking powder

½ teaspoon salt

½ cup apricot jam

½ cup raspberry jam

Here, sugar cookie dough is baked in a loaf pan and layered with apricot and raspberry jams. Bake the loaf, slice, rebake, and you have slabs of sugar cookies with dramatic ripples of preserves shooting through each slice. It's a collision of shortbread and biscotti, and a visual treat.

Generously coat a 9- by 5-inch loaf pan with nonstick cooking spray. Line the bottom with parchment paper. Line a baking sheet with parchment paper. Set aside.

Preheat the oven to 350°F. In a large bowl or the bowl of an electric mixer fitted with the paddle attachment, cream the butter and the 1½ cups sugar together until fluffy. Blend in the eggs and vanilla. In a medium bowl, whisk the flour, baking powder, and salt together. Stir into the wet ingredients to make a stiff dough.

Spoon one-third of the dough into the prepared loaf pan. Smooth the dough and top with a layer of apricot jam. Cover with another third of the dough and top with raspberry jam. Top with the remaining dough and smooth it. Sprinkle lightly with sugar.

Place the pan on the prepared baking sheet. Lower the oven temperature to 325°F and bake for about 1 hour, or until firm to the touch. Let cool completely in the pan on a wire rack. Wrap the pan in aluminum foil and freeze for 1 hour.

Preheat the oven to 325°F. Stack 2 additional baking sheets together and line the top one with parchment paper. Turn the loaf out onto a cutting board. Cut crosswise into ½-inch-thick slices with a large serrated knife. Lay the slices on the prepared baking sheets. Place the doubled sheets on the bottom shelf of the oven and the single sheet on the middle shelf. Bake for 12 to 16 minutes, or until crisp. Transfer to wire racks to cool completely.

TRIPLE-ALMOND BISCOTTI

MAKES 24 TO 36 BISCOTTI

7-ounce package almond paste

1¾ cups sugar

½ cup (4 ounces) unsalted butter, softened

½ cup finely chopped almonds

½ cup ground hazelnuts

¼ cup ground walnuts

4 eggs

1 tablespoon pure vanilla extract

2 teaspoons almond extract

3 cups all-purpose flour

1 teaspoon baking powder

½ teaspoon baking soda

¼ teaspoon salt

⅛ teaspoon ground cinnamon

1 cup whole blanched almonds

This recipe uses almond paste and whole almonds to make elegant biscotti with a unique candylike surface. I don't think I ever create a sweet table without these featured somewhere. One of my personal best-ever almond-infused biscotti.

Stack 2 baking sheets together and line the top one with parchment paper. Line a third baking sheet with parchment paper. Set aside.

Preheat the oven to 350°F. Using the large holes of a box grater, shred the almond paste into a large bowl or the bowl of an electric mixer fitted with the paddle attachment. Add the sugar and stir until smooth (the sugar will help break up the almond paste). Add the butter and cream until fluffy. Stir in the chopped almonds, and the ground hazelnuts and walnuts. Blend in the eggs, vanilla and almond extracts.

In a medium bowl, whisk the flour, baking powder, baking soda, salt, and cinnamon together. Stir into the wet ingredients until blended. Stir in the whole almonds.

Spoon half of the dough onto the doubled baking sheets and form into a rectangle about 9 by 4 inches. Repeat with the remaining dough on the single prepared sheet. The dough will spread somewhat.

Place the doubled baking sheets on the bottom shelf and the single sheet on the middle shelf of the oven. Bake for 40 minutes, or until the dough is golden and dry to the touch. If the dough browns too quickly, lower the oven temperature to 325°F and bake a little longer if necessary. Remove from the oven and let cool on the pans on wire racks for 15 minutes.

Transfer the whole biscuits to a cutting board. Using a serrated knife, cut crosswise on the diagonal into slices ½ to ¾ inch thick. (If the whole almonds make cutting the biscotti difficult, freeze the whole biscuits on the pan for 1 hour, then slice.) Lower the oven temperature to 300°F. Lay the cookies on the baking sheets. Bake, turning once, for 35 to 45 minutes, or until brown and crisp. Let cool completely on wire racks.

MARBLEIZED CHOCOLATE CREAM CHEESE AND CHOCOLATE-STREAKED BISCOTTI

MAKES 18 TO 24 BISCOTTI

CHOCOLATE CREAM CHEESE LAYER

4 ounces semisweet chocolate, coarsely chopped

8 ounces cream cheese at room temperature

¼ cup sugar

1 egg

DOUGH

1 cup (8 ounces) unsalted butter, softened

1¼ cups sugar

3 eggs

2 teaspoons pure vanilla extract

2¼ cups all-purpose flour

2 teaspoons baking powder

½ teaspoon salt

4 ounces semisweet chocolate, coarsely chopped

A swirl of chocolate cream cheese snakes its way through these buttery vanilla biscotti dotted with chunks of chocolate. The swirl stays slightly soft and creates a fudgelike surprise. If the visual doesn't draw you in, the taste sure will.

Stack 2 baking sheets together and line the top one with parchment paper. Set aside.

Preheat the oven to 350°F. For the chocolate cream cheese layer, melt the chocolate in the top of a double boiler over barely simmering water. Let cool. In a medium bowl, blend the cream cheese and sugar together. Beat in the egg. Stir in the cooled chocolate until blended.

For the dough, cream the butter and sugar together in a large bowl or the bowl of an electric mixer fitted with the paddle attachment until light and fluffy. Blend in the eggs and vanilla. In a medium bowl, whisk the flour, baking powder, and salt together. Stir into the wet ingredients until blended. Stir in the chopped chocolate.

On a lightly floured surface, gently knead the dough briefly and shape into a log. Make a trough in the log. Spoon the cream cheese mixture into the trough, then fold the dough over and knead it gently to marbleize the dough. Reshape the dough into a log 8 to 10 inches long and 4 or 5 inches wide.

Place the dough on the prepared baking sheets. Bake on the top shelf of the oven for 30 to 38 minutes, or until set and just beginning to brown. Remove from the oven and let cool in the pans on a wire rack for 15 minutes. Wrap the log in foil and refrigerate for 1 hour.

Preheat the oven to 325°F. Remove the log from the refrigerator, unwrap, and cut on the diagonal into slices about ¾ inch thick. Lay the slices on the prepared baking sheets and bake for 8 to 10 minutes, turning once. These are not meant to be too crisp and dry. Let cool completely on a wire rack.

BLACKBERRY WINE CRUNCH BISCOTTI

MAKES 2 TO 3 DOZEN BISCOTTI

½ cup (4 ounces) unsalted butter, melted

1 cup sugar

3 eggs

½ teaspoon pure vanilla extract

½ cup red wine

3¼ cups all-purpose flour

1 teaspoon baking powder

½ teaspoon baking soda

¼ teaspoon salt

¾ cup frozen whole blackberries or raspberries

½ cup fresh or frozen cranberries, coarsely chopped

1 cup walnuts, toasted and coarsely chopped (see page 17)

DIPPING MIXTURE

½ cup medium-dry red wine

¾ cup sugar

This is biscotti art taken up a notch. Blackberries and cranberries dot the dough. After the first bake, the slices are dipped in wine, then pressed in sugar and rebaked to make crusty cookies destined for sangria or espresso. One of my brothers, Mark, often brings wine for dinner with a warning not to use it for baking. I never listen. This test batch was all the sweeter thanks to a lovely Jacob's Creek 1998 Shiraz Mark brought by. Thanks, bro.

~❦~

Stack 2 baking sheets together and line the top one with parchment paper. Line a third baking sheet with parchment paper. Set aside.

Preheat the oven to 350°F. In a large bowl or the bowl of an electric mixer fitted with the paddle attachment, cream the butter and sugar together until fluffy. Beat in the eggs and vanilla, then the wine. In a medium bowl, whisk the flour, baking powder, baking soda, and salt together. Stir into the wet ingredients to make a smooth dough. Stir in the blackberries, cranberries, and nuts.

Spoon half of the dough onto the doubled baking sheets and form into a rectangle about 9 by 4 inches across. The dough will spread slightly. Repeat with the remaining dough on the single prepared sheet. Place the doubled sheets on the bottom shelf and the single sheet on the middle shelf of the oven. Bake for 28 to 35 minutes, or until set. Let cool on the sheets on wire racks for 15 minutes. Leave the oven set at 350°F.

For the dipping mixture, set out shallow bowls. Fill one with the wine and the other with the sugar. Transfer the biscuits to a cutting board. Cut on the diagonal into slices about ½ inch thick. Dip both sides of each slice into the wine, then dip each side into the sugar, pressing lightly. Place on the prepared baking sheets.

Bake the slices for 20 minutes, then turn them over. Bake for 10 to 15 minutes longer on the second side, or until crisp and lightly caramelized. Let cool on wire racks completely.

BISCOTTI BITES: Cut the biscuits into 1½-inch squares. Dip in the wine and roll well in sugar. Bake in a preheated 375°F oven for about 20 minutes, or until crunchy.

CLASSIC SHORTBREAD

MAKES 12 TO 18 COOKIES

1 cup (8 ounces) unsalted butter, softened

⅔ cup sugar

¼ teaspoon salt

2½ cups all-purpose flour

This is my favorite recipe for classic shortbread. It is also one of the simplest. Variations are always an option. I've tested these with cornstarch, rice flour, and confectioners' sugar, but all-purpose flour and white sugar are my preference. Legions of shortbread experts agree.

Stack 2 baking sheets together and line the top one with parchment paper. Set aside.

In a medium bowl or the bowl of an electric mixer fitted with the paddle attachment, cream the butter, sugar, and salt together until fluffy. Stir in the flour to make a stiff dough. On a lightly floured surface, knead to make a smooth dough. Or combine the flour, salt, and sugar in a food processor. Add the butter in chunks and pulse to make a crumbly, mealy mixture. Knead as above.

Wrap the dough in plastic wrap and refrigerate for 15 minutes.

Preheat the oven to 350°F. On a lightly floured surface, roll the dough out to about ½ inch thick. With a 2- to 3-inch biscuit cutter, cut into rectangles or circles. Prick gently with the tines of a fork.

Place the cookies about 2 inches apart on the prepared baking sheets and place in the oven. Immediately lower the heat to 325°F and bake for 25 to 35 minutes, or until lightly colored at the edges. Lower the heat if the cookies are browning too quickly. Let cool on a wire rack.

CAPPUCCINO SHORTBREAD: Flecks of coffee are fabulous in shortbread. Knead about 1 tablespoon freeze-dried instant coffee granules into the dough.

BROWN SUGAR SHORTBREAD: Replace the white sugar with ¾ cup firmly packed light or dark brown sugar.

CASHEW SHORTBREAD: Add ⅓ cup ground toasted cashews to the flour.

SPICE SHORTBREAD: Add ½ teaspoon ground cinnamon, ⅛ teaspoon ground cloves, and a pinch of ground ginger and ground allspice to the dry ingredients. Or use 1 teaspoon apple pie spice.

LINZERTORTE SHORTBREAD: Add spices as for Spice Shortbread, above, and ⅓ cup ground hazelnuts. Add 1 teaspoon pure vanilla extract when creaming the butter and sugar together. Roll the dough out to ¾ inch thick. Cut into rounds using a 2½- to 3-inch cookie cutter. Using a ½-inch cookie cutter, cut a hole in the center of half of the rounds. Bake for 15 to 20 minutes, or until the edges are browned, then let cool completely. Spread a little raspberry jam on the whole rounds, and top each with a cutout cookie. Dust with confectioners' sugar.

Chapter 6

. . . .

SCONE AND MUFFIN MANIA

. . . .

IN THE BB TEST KITCHEN, I tend to group muffins and scones because they appeal to similar appetites and occasions, call for similar ingredients, and both offer broad variations on basic recipes. Do I ever run out of ideas for scones or muffins? No way. To my mind, nothing is as versatile or adaptable to inspirations and personal flavor preferences. I'm not the only one who appreciates muffins and scones. Hardly a day goes by without a visitor requesting a new recipe. Yet despite the similarities, muffins and scones each have their own distinct heritage.

M IS FOR MUFFIN MANIA

. . . .

Muffins were born in Britain, where they peaked in popularity in the mid- to late 1800s. These early muffins were somewhat spongy, yeast-risen affairs (see my recipe for Old-Fashioned English Muffins on page 69). Eventually, the British preference for scones, crumpets, and traditional English muffins won out, and the muffin torch was passed to us feisty colonial cooks who have made a big fuss over them.

Yesterday's muffin, albeit lower in fat and sugar, had a short shelf life and bordered on homely looking. Tastewise they were fine but hardly exciting. How do you bake muffins that are as good to look at as they are to eat? Here are some tricks to making professional-looking muffins in your home oven.

The Ingredients

All-purpose flour is best for muffins. Finer flours like cake or pastry flour (which are lower in gluten) do not provide the grain structure a muffin needs, especially if it is chock-full of fruit and nuts. You may, if you want a very tender muffin, substitute 20 to 25 percent cake or pastry flour for the all-purpose flour called for in a recipe. Similarly, for added nutrition or benefits of added fiber, you may substitute half whole-wheat or white whole-wheat flour. When choosing your all-purpose flour, choose one that is unbleached and bromate free (bromate is a chemical that is sometimes used to strengthen flour).

Although I talk about measuring flour in general on page 17, in muffins it is really important to follow the *stir-and-measure method*. Differences in flour weight can leave your muffins too soft and moist or too dry and tough. Stirring is a reasonable compromise between scooping hard-packed flour and sifting, then measuring. To measure flour, first stir it in its container to fluff it up, then scoop it with the measuring cup and level it off with a knife or dough scraper.

When using bran, cornmeal, oat bran, and wheat germ, I often presoak the grains to allow them to absorb the maximum volume of moisture. The reward is a muffin with a higher cap and a lovely, moist grain.

Muffins can be made with almost any liquid. Citrus juice in particular adds both flavor and tang, whereas milk, half-and-half cream, sour cream, and buttermilk assist with browning and moistness. Many bakers are especially partial to buttermilk in baking (see page 12). I love it for the flavor it imparts, its reaction with leavening agents such as baking soda, and especially for the little extra lift it adds to muffins, ensuring that they are moist and tender.

"Dissolve baking soda in buttermilk and let stand." What? Interestingly, many older cookbooks instruct you to mix the baking soda with the buttermilk. This is from the days when baking soda was coarse and lumpy and dissolving it first in the buttermilk was a way to ensure even distribution in the batter. Unfortunately, many an unknowing baker still follows this procedure, and the result is prematurely activated baking soda. If you have ever done this, you will remember how the baking soda fizzed when added to the buttermilk, which meant that a great deal of the leavening action was dancing away before your eyes. Today's baking soda is lovely and consistent, so no flirting around with buttermilk is required. You can simply add it to the dry ingredients.

If you are using dry buttermilk powder, add it to the dry ingredients. Water or juice (usually 1 cup) replaces the liquid and is added at the point at which the recipe calls for buttermilk (see page 12).

Mixing, Baking, and Storing

You must blend your fats and eggs properly with a wire whisk or food processor. Eggs and fats should be at room temperature, as chilled ingredients do not incorporate as well, and a cold batter has to work harder to rise in the oven. Thoroughly cream the fat with sugar, and then add the eggs. Occasionally, you may find that the blended sugar, fat, and eggs look curdled. If this occurs, add a small portion of the recipe's flour to help bind the batter. (This also will help the remainder of the dry ingredients incorporate more readily.) Blend the dry ingredients together in a separate bowl, then add to the wet ingredients. As the batter becomes thick and sticky, switch to a large

rubber spatula or a wide wooden spoon to mix (if mixing by hand). You may also wish to try a Danish dough whisk (page 7), a nifty item I often use for muffins, scones, and some of my favorite cakes.

"Why don't my muffins look and taste like mall muffins?" you ask. Home bakers are fond of saying baking is really chemistry. This is especially true with breads, but also in something as simple as a muffin. A muffin is measured not only by its taste, but also by its cap or top—proving again that looks (and size) do matter. Commercial muffins, with their large mushroom caps, often resemble small cakes. These impressive specimens are the result of intense product development. Some varieties depend on special leavening agents and disproportionate amounts of fat and sugar. The pros also have access to commercial ovens with precision heating that can be precisely tuned to give baked goods a jump start.

To get a good cap on a muffin in your home kitchen, you must be attentive to a few things. A weak foundation in the form of a very soft batter cannot soar to great heights and stay there, so if you do want high, rounded caps, make sure your batter is not too slack or soft. The best flavor, texture, and looks happen when the oven is properly preheated to a high temperature initially, then lowered after baking begins. Fill muffin cups to the brim and bake in the upper third of the oven if you want higher caps. And make sure you scoop with a large ice-cream scoop, not a spoon.

Baked goods that contain oil keep longer, but solid fats produce a lighter muffin, since the batter takes in more air when you cream in the fat. Butter adds its own wonderful flavor and encourages a muffin to brown well. Shortening is neutral in flavor and has a higher burning point, but it yields a distinct lightness of crumb. These recipes were tested with oil, shortening, butter, and a combination of shortening and butter. Oil works well for some muffins, whereas for others, a combination is more appropriate. Stay with what the recipe specifies for the most part, but if you prefer, 1 cup unsalted butter can always be replaced with 1 cup vegetable oil, and vice versa.

Let baked muffins cool in the pan, set on a wire rack, for about 5 minutes before unmolding them onto the rack and letting them cool for at least 10 minutes before serving. (Muffins that are allowed to cool completely in a hot pan will sweat and will stale prematurely.) Completely cooled muffins can be stored in a brown paper bag at room temperature, or they can be frozen for another occasion.

SLEUTHING THE SCONE

Scones are the quintessential tea and coffee treat. Traditional English scones contain very little butter and sugar. Scone devotees make up for this by reaching for thick cream or preserves. The coffeehouse explosion in North America has led many to rediscover and reinvent the scone, and I like to think the BB test kitchen is at the forefront of such fun. Scone baking is about as forgiving as it comes. You can adjust the amount of fat, add or omit eggs, opt for buttermilk or heavy cream, or use buttermilk powder. As for chunks and flavors, the sky's the limit. You can toss in raisins, dried cranberries, a shower of coarsely chopped chocolate, chunks of banana, a lashing of sharp cheddar, poppy seeds, cinnamon, ground hazelnuts, and so on, and transform a recipe.

All of my scone recipes generally start the same way: cut the butter into the flour by pulsing in a food processor until the mixture is the texture of coarse meal. (Make sure your butter for scones is always as cold as it can be unless otherwise stated.) Next, turn the mixture out into a large bowl and make a well in the center. Add the liquid, extracts, and egg (if called for) and mix with a Danish dough whisk or fork to create a soft dough. If there are remaining ingredients to add, such as raisins or chocolate, fold them in at this point and continue to mix everything together gently. When the dough just begins to come together, turn the mixture out onto a generously floured work surface. Knead by hand or with a dough cutter until smooth. At this point, as you will see in the recipes themselves, you can add more flour as required to achieve the right consistency: a soft but firm dough that can hold its shape to be cut.

To make scones entirely by hand, use a large bowl. Place the dry ingredients, including the sugar, in the bowl, and whisk to blend ingredients well. Add the butter and, using a pastry cutter or fork, cut the butter into the dry ingredients until it is crumbly and mealy looking. Then proceed, as above, adding the remaining ingredients and finishing the mixing process.

A dough scraper or bench cutter comes in handy, and I suggest you keep one on hand for scone work. You can use it during kneading and to cut the wedges once the dough is ready for baking.

I make scones free-form, using an ice-cream scoop, or, more often, in simple rounds or wedges cut with a cookie cutter, knife, or bench cutter. I have also used clean tuna cans, well sprayed with nonstick cooking spray, or tart shells, with or without removable bottoms, to create a new look in scones. All my scones are baked on doubled baking sheets, with the top sheet lined with parchment paper, to protect the bottoms from getting too brown.

Scones are ready to eat when barely cooled from the oven or at room temperature. They will last a day or two stored in a sealed paper bag, or they can be frozen and reheated in a preheated 300°F oven.

LAWSUIT BUTTERMILK MUFFINS

MAKES 1 DOZEN MUFFINS

STREUSEL TOPPING

1 tablespoon cold unsalted butter

⅓ cup firmly packed brown sugar

½ teaspoon ground cinnamon

½ cup finely chopped walnuts

BATTER

½ cup vegetable oil

1⅓ cups firmly packed light brown sugar

1 tablespoon grated citrus zest

1 egg

2 teaspoons pure vanilla extract

1 cup buttermilk

2½ cups to 2¾ cups all-purpose flour

¼ teaspoon salt

2½ teaspoons baking powder

½ teaspoon baking soda

½ teaspoon ground cinnamon

1¾ cups coarsely chopped fruit (see page 182)

This is the "secret formula" (see the story on page 183). Strawberry, cranberry-orange, and blueberry-lemon, all based on this same recipe, are still my three favorite flavor combinations. As good as these are, I might even like my second version (page 184) a wee bit better. Nah! They're both awesome!

Preheat the oven to 400°F. Line 12 muffin cups with paper liners or spray generously with nonstick cooking spray. Grease the top of the muffin pan. Line a large baking sheet with parchment paper. Set aside.

For the streusel, mix all the ingredients together with a fork or your fingertips in a small bowl to make a crumbly mixture. Set aside.

For the batter, whisk the oil, brown sugar, citrus zest, and egg together in a large bowl. The mixture should be pasty. Stir in the vanilla and buttermilk.

In a large bowl, stir together 2½ cups of the flour, the salt, baking powder, baking soda, and cinnamon. Add to the wet ingredients and blend. Fold in the fruit. The use of frozen fruit may help firm up the batter. If not, and the batter seems too loose, add ¼ cup more flour to make the batter a bit stiffer.

Using a large ice-cream scoop, fill the muffins cups to the top. Sprinkle streusel topping evenly over each muffin. Place the muffin pan on the prepared baking sheet.

Bake for 15 minutes, then lower the oven temperature to 350°F and bake for another 12 to 15 minutes, or until the muffins spring back when pressed lightly. Let cool in the pan for 5 minutes before unmolding onto wire racks.

FRUIT VARIATIONS FOR LAWSUIT MUFFINS

Here is a list of what you can use in this recipe:

- Rhubarb, fresh or frozen, diced
- Cranberries, frozen, coarsely chopped
- Blueberries, frozen or semifrozen
- Apples, diced, peeled or not
- Bananas, chopped (add a pinch of nutmeg)
- Frozen raspberries
- Frozen strawberries, chopped
- Dried sour cherries, cranberries, or raisins, plumped and patted dry (see page 18)
- Strawberry and rhubarb combination
- Apple and cranberry combination
- Rhubarb and apple combination

For delicate, highly colored fruit like raspberries, cranberries, strawberries, or blueberries, use semifrozen fruit to preserve the berries and prevent batter discoloration.

The Overmixing Clause

Many muffin recipes include what I call the "overmixing clause," a stern warning that suggests that an overmixed batter will yield rubbery, stunted muffins. Home bakers are urged to stir the batter just to combine, with some lumps remaining. This caution is not necessary with today's richer muffin formulations, which, with their ample fat and sugar, tend to prevent the muffins from getting too tough or chewy.

Nonstick Spray

Some muffin pans are indeed as nonstick as they claim, but some muffins just naturally release from the pan better than others. To ensure that all of your muffins release easily, spray your muffin pan's top surface with nonstick spray.

LAWSUIT BUTTERMILK MUFFINS: THE STORY

I trained as a French pastry chef, but I began my baking career by preparing such everyday fare as Toll House cookies, cheesecake, and muffins. The latter led me to some notoriety when I happened on an exceptional recipe.

One of my first commercial gigs was as a muffin creator and baker for a New Age restaurant and bakery called Terre Etoile. I answered an ad that said "Baker wanted: experience with American-style chocolate chunk cookies helpful." I went to a Sears store the day before and bought a red metal tool chest. I stocked it full of baking tools, as I had seen a chef do in a restaurant where I had interned. Props are everything, and they helped in this case. I auditioned with one of my carrot cakes and some chocolate chunk cookies and was hired on the spot. The next day, I started my new job—at 4 a.m. Time to make the muffins.

Inexperienced as I was, I was named head bakery manager and found myself immediately overwhelmed by my responsibilities. I had a staff of five bakers, and a battery of three brand-new commercial mixers and ovens for our use. I would sit for hours with a calculator and a small scale, meticulously calculating and adapting recipes for commercial production. After stumbling along for a few days, I got things up and running, and my little bakery operation was pumping out many muffins and earning a great reputation in the process.

I couldn't help but notice that, at day's end, one variety of muffins was outselling the others: a buttermilk apple cinnamon streusel number based on a popular domestic formula. I had clipped the original recipe out of *Bon Appétit*'s "RSVP" column. Sunrise Apple Muffins were a specialty of the Sunrise Restaurant at the Orlando (Florida) Airport. I made a number of changes to the recipe, but I must give credit where credit is due.

Something was working right. We were selling some 75 dozen muffins a day. In comparison, muffin booths in malls were selling an average of 15 to 18 dozen a day. We were also selling pies, cheesecakes, carrot cakes, fudge tortes, and brownies the size of paperweights. Customers would show up before we opened and knock on the windows. Some would slide notes under the door, begging to be admitted before we opened.

In short order, I converted my muffin line into The Famous Buttermilk Muffin Collection, using the same base formula with several varieties of fruit: apple, raspberry, strawberry, rhubarb, peach, apricot, blueberry, and a zesty cranberry-orange. Even the base recipe sold well as a cinnamon-vanilla version. Buttermilk was a key ingredient. It contributed taste and height to the muffins (its acidic nature interacts very well with baking soda, among other things).

One day, I arrived to find a whole crew of new bakers working in "my kitchen." My recipes were locked up in the office, and I was asked to hand in my apron. New owners had stepped in, and my services were no longer required. Alas, my finely tuned recipes stayed behind. Were they the property of the bakery or were they mine? In my opinion, they were hijacked, something that is all too common in the entrepreneurial baking world.

I moved on to other things. One day, while I was on a carrot cake run for a local restaurant, a young man stopped me and inquired, "Are you Marcy Goldman, the Muffin Lady?" Once again, I found myself working for a New Age bakery. Later, once again, I found myself out on my butt—recipes left behind. This time, I decided to seek legal counsel and the case was settled out of court for a nominal sum. The rights of an author (yes, bakers, cooks, and chefs are authors) are very difficult to enforce in the food business.

After years of experience, my favorite muffin recipe is still my adapted buttermilk formula, now fondly nicknamed Lawsuit Muffins. There is no secret anymore; these are as delicious as they are foolproof. Just one thing: if you go on to build a business with these, please don't tell me!

LAWSUIT MUFFINS #2

MAKES 9 MUFFINS

VANILLA CINNAMON STREUSEL TOPPING

¼ cup (2 ounces) unsalted butter

3 tablespoons all-purpose flour

½ cup firmly packed brown sugar

2 tablespoons white sugar

½ teaspoon ground cinnamon

2 teaspoons vanilla powder (I use Nielsen-Massey)

½ cup finely chopped walnuts

BATTER

1½ cups firmly packed light brown sugar

½ cup (4 ounces) unsalted butter, melted

¼ cup canola oil

2 eggs

1 cup buttermilk

2 teaspoons pure vanilla extract

3 cups all-purpose flour

2½ teaspoons baking powder

½ teaspoon baking soda

⅜ teaspoon salt

3 cups combination of semi-frozen rhubarb, cranberry, and apple

The original Lawsuit Muffins (see page 181) launched my baking career two decades ago, when I was a very green young baker at a health food café called Terre Etoile, which featured the most decadent baking. My muffin recipe was so successful that it kick-started my journey in cookbooks and food journalism—although it proved to be as difficult to protect as it was inspiring, hence the name. How successful were Lawsuit Muffins? The Terre Etoile bakery sold 60 to 80 dozen a day—about six times as many as the average mall muffin kiosk, and all they sell is muffins!

It's been two decades since I created Lawsuit Muffins, originally known as Rhubarb Buttermilk Muffins, then as Any-Fruit-Will-Do Buttermilk Streusel Muffins. Lawsuit Muffins #2 are bigger, bolder, and filled with 20 years of baker's savvy—and all the sweetness and wisdom that comes with many batches of muffins baked, and much life lived.

Preheat the oven to 400°F. Line a large baking sheet with parchment paper. Position the oven rack in the upper third of the oven.

Spray a muffin tin very generously with nonstick cooking spray or line 9 of the muffin cups with paper liners. Place the tin on the baking sheet.

Prepare the streusel by pulsing all ingredients together in a food processor to get a crumbly mixture. Set aside.

For the muffins, in a large bowl, hand whisk the brown sugar with the butter and oil. Add the eggs, buttermilk, and vanilla and whisk well. Fold in the flour, baking powder, baking soda, and salt to make a smooth batter. Fold in the fruit and blend well. If batter is very soft, add a bit more flour. Let stand 5–8 minutes.

Using an extra-large ice-cream scoop, scoop huge gobs of batter into the muffin cups. Top each with a crown of streusel. Bake for 20 minutes; lower the oven temperature to 375°F, turn the muffin tin, and bake for another 15 to 22 minutes. Remove from the oven and let the muffins stand for 15 minutes to set before attempting to remove them from the pan. You can dust these with confectioners' sugar, but why? They are good as they are.

ALMOND POPPY SEED MUFFINS

MAKES 12 MUFFINS

1 cup sugar

4 ounces almond paste, minced

½ cup finely ground almonds

½ cup (4 ounces) unsalted butter

¼ cup canola oil

2 eggs

1 cup sour cream

⅓ cup milk

1 teaspoon almond extract

1 teaspoon pure vanilla extract

2¾ cups all-purpose flour

2½ teaspoons baking powder

¼ teaspoon baking soda

¼ teaspoon salt

2 tablespoons poppy seeds

FINISHING TOUCHES

Slivered almonds

White or coarse sugar for
    sprinkling

A fan on my website implored me to create a muffin for her son, who is a fan of a particular lemon, almond, and poppy seed muffin sold at some Costco stores. I was intrigued by the flavors and impressed with said son's baking taste, so I had to create this muffin. My team tested this recipe many times until it was perfect, creating many new fans of these almond and poppy seed extravaganzas. When I make these muffins, I sometimes add a teaspoon of lemon extract and a touch of lemon juice for a bouquet of flavor.

Preheat the oven to 375°F. Position the oven rack position in the upper third of the oven. Line 12 muffin cups with paper liners. Line a baking sheet with parchment paper.

In the bowl of an electric mixer, blend the sugar and almond paste together well, about 2 to 4 minutes. Add the ground almonds, butter, and oil and blend well. Fold in the eggs, sour cream, milk, and almond and vanilla extracts, and blend well. Fold in the flour, baking powder, baking soda, salt, and poppy seeds and blend, scraping the bottom of the bowl occasionally to ensure nothing gets stuck in the well of the mixing bowl. If the mixture seems too loose, add a touch more flour. It should be the consistency of thick cake batter.

Scoop the batter into the prepared muffin cups. Top each muffin with some slivered almonds and sugar. Place the muffin cups on the prepared baking sheet.

Bake about 30 to 35 minutes, until the muffins are nicely browned and spring back when lightly touched. Let them cool in the pan for 15 minutes before turning them out onto a rack to cool completely.

SUNRISE CRANBERRY, APPLE, AND ORANGE BUTTERMILK MUFFINS

MAKES 1½ DOZEN MUFFINS

TOPPING

3 graham cracker sheets

½ cup (4 ounces) unsalted butter

¼ cup all-purpose flour

¼ teaspoon ground cinnamon

½ teaspoon pure vanilla extract

½ cup firmly packed dark brown sugar

Pinch of salt

1 cup old-fashioned rolled oats

¼ teaspoon orange oil or extract

1 tablespoon grated orange zest

BATTER

1 cup (8 ounces) unsalted butter, melted

1 cup white sugar

1 cup firmly packed dark brown sugar

4 eggs

1 teaspoon pure vanilla extract

4 cups all-purpose flour

¼ cup wheat bran or wheat germ

½ teaspoon salt

¼ teaspoon ground cinnamon

½ teaspoon baking soda

4 teaspoons baking powder

1 cup fresh orange juice or buttermilk

1½ cups diced tart apples, peeled or not

1½ cups whole or coarsely chopped frozen cranberries

Like many contemporary muffins, these are really mini coffee cakes in muffin cups. This recipe combines a trio of favorite fruity flavors—apples, cranberries, and oranges—that yield sunrise hues and a great start to the day.

~❀~

Preheat the oven to 425°F. Line 18 muffin cups with paper liners or spray generously with nonstick cooking spray. Grease the top of the muffin pans. Line 2 baking sheets with parchment paper. Set aside.

For the topping, break the graham crackers into large pieces. Put them and all the remaining topping ingredients in a food processor and pulse for 15 to 20 seconds to form a crumbly mixture. Empty into a bowl.

For the batter, combine the butter and sugars in a food processor. Pulse to cream, then add the eggs and vanilla, and blend until smooth.

In a medium bowl, combine the flour, wheat bran, salt, cinnamon, baking soda, and baking powder. Stir to blend. Add to the wet ingredients and process for 20 to 30 seconds. Add the orange juice and process to make a smooth batter. Scraping down the sides of the bowl, pour into a large bowl and stir in the fruit.

Using a large ice-cream scoop, fill each muffin cup almost full. Top each with 2 to 3 tablespoons topping. Place the muffin pans on the prepared baking sheets.

Place in the oven and lower the temperature to 400°F. Bake for 20 to 22 minutes, or until the muffins are nicely browned and spring back when gently pressed. Let cool in the pans for 5 minutes before unmolding onto wire racks.

CHOCOLATE-BANANA MUFFINS

MAKES 16 MUFFINS

TOPPING

1½ cups sweetened shredded coconut

½ cup finely ground pecans or macadamia nuts

4 tablespoons (2 ounces) unsalted butter

2 tablespoons firmly packed brown sugar

BATTER

½ cup (4 ounces) unsalted butter, softened

½ cup vegetable oil

1 cup firmly packed light brown sugar

¾ cup white sugar

4 eggs

1 teaspoon pure vanilla extract

1 tablespoon brewed strong coffee

½ cup sour cream

1 cup banana puree (about 2 ripe bananas)

3¾ cups all-purpose flour

4 teaspoons baking powder

¾ teaspoon baking soda

½ teaspoon salt

4 ounces white chocolate, coarsely chopped

½ cup miniature semisweet chocolate chips

½ cup chopped pecans or macadamia nuts

Here, two favorite flavors, chocolate and banana, are combined in a moist muffin. Instead of chocolate chips, you may use finely chopped semisweet or bittersweet chocolate. A hot oven ensures these muffins rise high, but don't overbake them.

Preheat the oven to 425°F. Line 16 muffin cups with paper liners or spray generously with nonstick cooking spray. Grease the top of the muffin pans. Line 2 large baking sheets with parchment paper. Set aside.

For the topping, combine all the ingredients in a food processor and pulse for 10 to 20 seconds to make a crumbly mixture. Transfer to a small bowl.

For the batter, combine the butter, oil, and both sugars in the food processor and pulse to cream. Add the eggs, vanilla, and coffee, and process for about 10 seconds, or until smooth. Add the sour cream and banana puree and process to blend. In a medium bowl, combine the flour, baking powder, baking soda, and salt. Stir to blend. Add to the wet ingredients and process for about 10 seconds, or until smooth. Add the white and semisweet chocolates and the nuts and pulse briefly to mix.

Using a large ice-cream scoop, fill each muffin cup to just over the rim. Top each with 2 to 3 tablespoons of the topping. Place the muffin pans on the prepared baking sheets.

Place on the top and middle shelves of the oven and lower the oven temperature to 400°F. Bake for 20 to 22 minutes, or until the muffins are nicely browned and spring back when gently pressed. Let cool in the pans for 5 minutes before unmolding onto wire racks.

BREAD PUDDING MUFFINS

MAKES 1 DOZEN MUFFINS

7 cups cubed challah, brioche, or croissants

½ cup milk

1½ cups warm half-and-half or light cream

4 eggs

⅔ cup sugar

2 teaspoons pure vanilla extract

1 tablespoon brandy (optional)

½ cup (4 ounces) unsalted butter, melted

⅓ cup all-purpose flour

1 tablespoon baking powder

⅜ teaspoon salt

¼ teaspoon ground cinnamon

½ cup golden raisins, plumped and patted dry (see page 18)

Confectioners' sugar mixed with a touch of cocoa or cinnamon for dusting

A café I frequent offers something just like this, and they sell out of them faster than they can brew their first pot of coffee. I just had to replicate it!

Bread chunks in a buttery, cream-laced custard—are they dessert or breakfast? These mini bread puddings whip up as fast as Jell-O; make use of leftover challah, brioche, or even croissants; and taste and look like a rustic French pastry. You can add pieces of fresh apple to these, or dried cranberries, but I chose golden raisins in my first test.

Preheat the oven to 350°F. Line 12 muffin cups with paper liners or spray generously with nonstick cooking spray. Grease the top of the muffin pan. Line a baking sheet with parchment paper. Set aside.

Pour all but 2 cups of the bread cubes in a large bowl. Add the milk and cream and let stand for 3 minutes, then stir to mush up some of the cubes and let the liquid soak in. Stir in the eggs, sugar, vanilla, brandy, and butter. In a small bowl, stir the flour, baking powder, salt, and cinnamon together, then stir into the wet ingredients. Add the raisins and stir well to make a chunky batter. Stir in the reserved bread cubes just to mix.

Using a large ice-cream scoop, fill each muffin cup to just over the rim. Place the muffin pan on the prepared baking sheet.

Bake for about 30 minutes, or until the muffins are golden, with the tips of the firmer bread cubes golden brown. Let cool in pan for 5 minutes. Unmold onto a serving platter on a wire rack, then dust with the confectioners' sugar.

Baby Carrot Cake Reversals

MAKES 15 MUFFINS

TOPPING

12 ounces cream cheese at room
temperature

1 egg

⅓ cup sugar

½ teaspoon pure vanilla extract

3 tablespoons all-purpose flour

BATTER

2 cups sugar

1¼ cups oil

4 eggs

2 tablespoons fresh lemon juice

2 teaspoons pure vanilla extract

3 cups all-purpose flour

2½ teaspoons ground cinnamon

2 teaspoons baking powder

½ teaspoon salt

½ teaspoon baking soda

3 cups lightly packed shredded
carrots (about 3 large carrots or
12 to 14 ounces)

1 cup golden raisins

½ cup chopped pecans (optional)

Confectioners' sugar mixed with
a little ground cinnamon for
dusting

These are miniature cakes with the cream cheese topping baked on them, instead of being used as an icing (hence, the name "reversals"). Don't leave this recipe lying around. Someone could get rich. It is that good and easy. Look for interesting muffin molds in your favorite kitchen supply store. Wilton, for example, has a myriad of mini Bundt shapes, "baby" cheesecake molds, heart-shaped molds—all designed to produce a generous, single-portion cake or pastry. Tuna cans make another unique mold. Just be sure to fill any mold you are using three-fourths full. These are as sumptuous as they are gorgeous.

Preheat the oven to 350°F. Place muffin liners in fifteen 4-inch tart molds, splaying them out to fit. Spray the exposed parts of the molds with nonstick cooking spray. You may also use 15 clean tuna cans, or 24 regular muffin cups prepared the same way. Line 2 baking sheets with parchment paper. Set aside.

For the topping, combine the cream cheese and egg in a medium bowl and whisk to blend. Stir in the sugar, vanilla, and flour. Whisk to make a smooth, thick mixture.

For the batter, combine the sugar, oil, eggs, lemon juice, and vanilla in a large bowl. Whisk until well blended. In a medium bowl, combine the flour, cinnamon, baking powder, salt, and baking soda. Stir to blend. Stir into the wet ingredients and fold in the carrots, raisins, and pecans.

Spoon the batter into the prepared tart molds, filling each three-fourths to seven-eighths full. Or spoon into the muffin cups, filling each three-fourths full. Using a spoon, distribute the topping evenly over each cake. Place the tart molds or muffin pans on the prepared baking sheets. Dust each cake with the cinnamon sugar.

Bake for 22 to 27 minutes, or until the topping is dry to the touch. Let cool completely on wire racks, unmold, and dust again with cinnamon sugar.

Sour Cream and Cinnamon Coffee Cake Muffins

MAKES 16 MUFFINS

TOPPING

1½ cups sweetened shredded coconut

½ cup finely ground pecans

4 tablespoons (2 ounces) cold unsalted butter

2 tablespoons firmly packed brown sugar

1 teaspoon ground cinnamon

BATTER

½ cup (4 ounces) unsalted butter, softened

½ cup vegetable oil

1¾ cups sugar

4 eggs

1½ teaspoons pure vanilla extract

1 cup sour cream

¼ cup milk

3¾ cups all-purpose flour

4 teaspoons baking powder

½ teaspoon baking soda

½ teaspoon salt

1 cup finely chopped chocolate toffee or Heath Bar chips

A classic sour cream coffee cake tucked into muffin form. You may substitute yogurt for the sour cream. These muffins freeze very well.

~⟨◊⟩~

Preheat the oven to 400°F. Line 16 muffin cups with paper liners or spray them generously with nonstick cooking spray. Grease the top of the muffin pans. Line 2 baking sheets with parchment paper. Set aside.

For the topping, combine all the ingredients in a food processor and pulse for 10 to 20 seconds to make a crumbly mixture. Set aside.

For the batter, combine the butter, oil, and sugar in a bowl. Whisk to blend. Add the eggs, vanilla, sour cream, and milk and beat until smooth. In a medium bowl, combine the flour, baking powder, baking soda, and salt. Stir to blend. Stir into the wet ingredients until smooth. Fold in the chopped toffee.

Using a large ice-cream scoop, fill each muffin cup to just over the rim. Divide the topping among the muffins. Place the muffin pans on the prepared baking sheets.

Place on the top shelf of the oven and lower the temperature to 350°F. Bake for 25 to 30 minutes, or until the muffins are nicely browned and spring back when gently pressed. Let cool in the pans for 5 minutes before unmolding onto wire racks.

LEMON, SOUR CREAM, AND BLUEBERRY MUFFINS

MAKES 1 DOZEN MUFFINS

TOPPING

2 tablespoons cold unsalted butter

2 tablespoons all-purpose flour

¾ cup finely ground toasted walnuts

½ cup sugar

1 teaspoon ground cinnamon

½ teaspoon ground nutmeg

BATTER

4 tablespoons (2 ounces) unsalted butter, softened

¼ cup vegetable shortening

1¼ cups sugar

1 egg

1 teaspoon pure vanilla extract

Grated zest and juice of 1 lemon

2 tablespoons warm water

1 cup sour cream

2¼ cups all-purpose flour

2 teaspoons baking powder

½ teaspoon baking soda

¼ teaspoon salt

1¼ cups fresh or frozen blueberries

A coffee and teatime treat that features two classic flavors, blueberry and lemon. Sour cream makes anything extra tender, but low-fat yogurt will do the same trick. These are pretty and elegant. If you prefer plain (but equally delicious) blueberry muffins, simply omit the lemon zest and juice.

Preheat the oven to 350°F. Line 12 muffin cups with paper liners or spray generously with nonstick cooking spray. Grease the top of the muffin pan. Line a large baking sheet with parchment paper. Set aside.

For the topping, combine all the ingredients in a small bowl. Toss with a fork to make a crumbly mixture. Set aside.

For the batter, combine the butter and shortening in a bowl. Beat until smooth and thick. Add the sugar, egg, vanilla, lemon zest and juice, and water. Beat until smooth. Stir in the sour cream. In a medium bowl, combine the flour, baking powder, baking soda, and salt. Stir to blend. Stir into the wet ingredients until blended. Stir in the berries until evenly distributed.

Using a large ice-cream scoop, fill the prepared muffin cups seven-eighths full. Divide the topping evenly among the molds. Place the muffin pan on the prepared baking sheet.

Bake for 28 to 32 minutes, or until the muffins spring back when lightly pressed. Let cool in the muffin pan for about 15 minutes before unmolding onto wire racks.

RASPBERRY-CORN MUFFINS

MAKES 10 TO 12 MUFFINS

¾ cup vegetable oil

1½ cups sugar

3 eggs

1 cup warm water

1 teaspoon pure vanilla extract

¼ teaspoon lemon oil or extract

1 cup cornmeal

1½ cups all-purpose flour

2½ teaspoons baking powder

1 teaspoon salt

½ teaspoon baking soda

1 cup frozen raspberries

A crunchy exterior and an airy, moist cornmeal interior, along with tart raspberries, make these baby loaves a winner. Frozen sour cherries also work well, as do blueberries.

~(◊)~

Preheat the oven to 400°F. Generously spray 10 miniature loaf molds (1½ by 3 inches), 12 muffin cups, or 10 clean tuna cans with nonstick cooking spray. Line with paper liners, splaying them out to fit. Line a baking sheet with parchment paper. Set aside.

In a large bowl, stir the oil and sugar together. Blend in the eggs, then the water, vanilla, and lemon oil. Add the cornmeal and let stand for 15 minutes. In a medium bowl, combine the flour, baking powder, salt, and baking soda. Stir to blend. Stir into the wet ingredients until blended. Fold in the raspberries.

Using a large ice-cream scoop, fill the prepared molds three-fourths full. Place the molds on the prepared baking sheet.

Bake the muffins for 10 minutes, then lower the temperature to 350°F and bake for 15 to 20 minutes longer, or until the edges are lightly browned and tops are just firm (they may crack) and spring back when touched. Let cool in the pans for 10 minutes before unmolding onto wire racks.

MUFFIN-TOP PANS

. . . .

Many manufacturers sell muffin-top pans, which are simply muffin pans with shallow cups. You could just as easily spoon your muffin batter into mounds on a parchment-lined baking sheet. But if you opt for a muffin-top pan, choose one from a reputable supplier (see the Source Guide, page 299).

FUDGE BROWNIE MUFFINS

MAKES 8 MUFFINS

TOPPING

¼ cup walnuts, toasted and finely
   chopped

3 tablespoons sweetened shredded
   coconut

2 teaspoons unsweetened cocoa
   powder

¼ teaspoon ground cinnamon

2 tablespoons firmly packed brown
   sugar

2 tablespoons all-purpose flour

1 tablespoon cold unsalted butter

BATTER

1 cup all-purpose flour

¾ cup sugar

¼ cup unsweetened cocoa powder

1 teaspoon baking powder

¼ teaspoon baking soda

¼ teaspoon salt

½ cup buttermilk

4 tablespoons (2 ounces) unsalted
   butter, melted

1 egg

1 teaspoon pure vanilla extract

If muffins are comfort food, brownie muffins are luxury comfort. If you want to go all out, plant one of these on a dessert plate, drop a mound of ice cream on top, and drizzle on some hot fudge sauce. Their flat tops make them a perfect "throne" to gussy up.

Preheat the oven to 350°F. Line 8 small muffin molds (2½ to 3 inches) with paper liners that fit (or use mini tart molds, about 1¾ inches), or spray with nonstick cooking spray and dust with flour. Line a baking sheet with parchment paper. Set aside.

For the topping, combine all the ingredients in a small bowl. Toss with a fork to make a crumbly mixture. Set aside.

For the batter, combine the flour, sugar, cocoa, baking powder, baking soda, and salt in a large bowl. Whisk to blend. Make a well in the center and pour in the buttermilk, butter, egg, and vanilla. Stir until smooth.

Using a large ice-cream scoop, fill the prepared molds seven-eighths full. Divide the topping evenly among the molds. Place the molds on the prepared baking sheet.

Bake for 18 to 20 minutes, or until the muffin tops spring back when lightly touched. Let cool in the pan for 10 minutes, before unmolding onto a wire rack. Let cool for at least 10 minutes longer. Serve warm or at room temperature.

Deli-Style Bran Muffins in Tuna Cans

MAKES 8 LARGE MUFFINS

2 cups All-Bran cereal

2 cups soured milk (see page 14) or buttermilk, warm

2 eggs

1 cup oil

1 cup raisins, plumped and patted dry (see page 18)

2 cups all-purpose flour

1 tablespoon baking powder

¼ teaspoon baking soda

¼ teaspoon salt

1½ cups firmly packed brown sugar

1 teaspoon ground cinnamon

⅛ teaspoon ground nutmeg

I saw a muffin like this one in a delicatessen once, and I was immediately smitten. To make these deli-authentic, bake them in clean 7-ounce tuna cans. They will emerge delightfully flat-topped in appearance.

Preheat the oven to 375°F. Grease eight 7-ounce tuna cans. Line a baking sheet with parchment paper and set aside.

In a large bowl, combine the cereal and warm soured milk. Let stand for about 20 minutes, or until most of the liquid is absorbed.

Add the eggs and oil and blend until smooth. Stir in the raisins. In a medium bowl, combine all the remaining ingredients and whisk to blend. Add to the batter and stir until smooth.

Using a large ice-cream scoop, fill the prepared cans three-fourths full. Place the cans on the prepared baking sheet.

Bake for 20 to 25 minutes, or until the muffins spring back when lightly touched. Let cool in the cans for 10 minutes before unmolding onto wire racks.

B.B.
Test Kitchen
Notes

The Brown Sugar Debate: Light vs. Dark

Dark brown sugar contains more molasses than light brown sugar, so its taste is a little more pronounced. I sometimes specify one or the other in my recipes, but generally, light brown sugar, also known as golden, is what I use for testing. The substitution of white sugar for brown sugar will not produce the same results, since brown sugar affects texture as much as it affects taste.

POM BAKERY TOASTER CORN CAKES

MAKES 8 TO 12 CAKES

CORN CAKE BATTER

½ cup shortening or butter, melted

1 cup sugar

2 eggs

2 cups stone-ground cornmeal

2 cups all-purpose flour

2 teaspoons baking powder

¼ teaspoon baking soda

½ teaspoon salt

1 to 1¼ cups buttermilk

HONEY BUTTER GLAZE

⅓ cup honey

¼ cup (2 ounces) unsalted butter

2 tablespoons water

Pom Bakery in Montreal used to make these marvelous little corn cakes. They looked like one of those Betty Crocker kid-sized layer cakes, but were actually a cross between corn bread and corn muffins. These are fabulous little breakfast breads, and there is nothing in recipe books, nor in the supermarket that comes close. The Pom originals are, alas, long gone, but those who remember them recall them served warmed in a toaster, plain or with a smear of butter. Don't you love it when nostalgia tastes so good?

Preheat the oven to 375°F. Position the oven rack in the middle of the oven. Line a baking sheet with parchment paper.

In the bowl of an electric mixer, cream together the shortening and sugar. Blend in the eggs. In a separate medium bowl, combine the cornmeal, flour, baking powder, baking soda, and salt. Fold the dry ingredients into the egg mixture, drizzling in the buttermilk as you do so to make a very thick batter.

Using a large ice-cream scoop, drop scoops of batter onto the prepared baking sheet. Flatten them slightly with wet fingertips.

Bake for 20 minutes or so, until the cakes are dry to the touch and the edges are barely starting to brown.

Meanwhile, for the glaze, whisk the honey, butter, and water together. Brush the glaze on the corn cakes as they come out of the oven.

For the uniform look of the original bakery corn cakes, use a 5-inch cookie cutter to cut the corn cakes, while still warm on the baking sheet, into perfect rounds (you can munch on the trimmings). These freeze well and can be reheated in a toaster oven.

SUGAR-CRUSTED VANILLA BUTTER SCONES

MAKES 1 DOZEN SCONES

4 cups all-purpose flour

⅓ cup plus ¾ cup sugar

4½ teaspoons baking powder

½ teaspoon baking soda

1 teaspoon salt

1 cup (8 ounces) cold unsalted
butter, cut into small pieces

1 egg

1½ teaspoons pure vanilla extract

¾ cup buttermilk

Rolling these scones in sugar before baking gives them a crisp, pastrylike finish. Originally called Better-for-the-Mistake Sugar Scones, these came about one day when I forgot to add sugar to the recipe. A good baker is always inventing and adapting, and this ambrosial scone is one of my all-time, go-to favorites, a happy result of improvisation.

~⋄~

Preheat the oven to 425°F. Stack 2 large baking sheets together and line the top one with parchment paper. Set aside.

In a food processor, combine the flour, the ⅓ cup sugar, the baking powder, baking soda, and salt. Process to blend. Add the butter and pulse for 15 seconds, or until the texture of coarse meal.

Pour the mixture into a large bowl. Make a well in the center and add the egg, vanilla, and buttermilk. Mix with a fork to make a soft dough.

Spread the remaining ¾ cup sugar on a work surface. Turn the dough out and knead gently on the sugared surface. Form the dough into two 8-inch disks, each about 1 inch thick. Turn the disks over once or twice to lightly coat with the sugar. Cut each disk into 6 wedges. Place the wedges on the prepared baking sheet.

Bake for about 18 minutes, or until golden brown. Transfer to wire racks to cool slightly or completely.

RAISIN OR CURRANT SCONES: When mixing in the wet ingredients, add 1 or 2 teaspoons ground cinnamon and about ½ cup raisins or dried currants, pressing them into the dough. Shape the disks and cut into wedges. Brush the tops with melted unsalted butter and sprinkle with white or coarse sugar.

B.B.
Test Kitchen
Notes

Cream Scones Make Lovely Shortcakes

If you wish, use heavy cream in place of the buttermilk and omit the baking soda. This will produce very delicate cream scones, which will do double duty as strawberry shortcakes.

JANE AUSTEN'S ROLLED OAT AND GOLDEN RAISIN SCONES

MAKES 12 TO 15 SCONES

2½ cups all-purpose flour

½ cup whole-wheat flour

2½ cups rolled oats (any type)

¾ cup sugar

5 teaspoons baking powder

¼ teaspoon baking soda

1 teaspoon salt

1½ cups (12 ounces) unsalted
    butter, in small chunks

½ cup whipping cream mixed with
    2 teaspoons lemon juice

1 cup half-and-half or light cream

½ cup golden raisins, plumped and
    patted dry (see page 18)

½ cup dried cranberries, plumped
    and patted dry (see page 18)

FINISHING TOUCHES

Melted butter for brushing

⅓ cup brown sugar for dusting

Tons of butter, golden raisins, cranberries, and cream make these the most tender, moist scones ever. They include a touch of whole-wheat flour for a rustic taste, but still sport a refined heritage. These are a tribute to one of my heros, Miss Jane Austen, who would no doubt have these with a cuppa' tea.

~❀~

Preheat the oven to 425°F. Stack 2 baking sheets together and line the top one with parchment paper. Position the oven rack in the upper third of the oven.

In the bowl of an electric mixer, combine both flours with the oats, sugar, baking powder, baking soda, and salt. Cut in the butter to make a grainy, mealy mixture. Then make a well in the center and add the whipping cream and lemon juice, then most of the half-and-half cream. Mix until just combined, adding more half-and-half until the mixture just holds together. Stir in the raisins and cranberries.

Turn the dough out onto a very well-floured surface. If the dough is very sticky, flour the top of the dough as well. Pat the mixture into a 1-inch-thick disk. Using a 2-inch diameter round cutter, cut out the scones, dipping the cutter into flour between each cut. Place each scone, as it is cut, onto the prepared baking sheet, leaving 2 to 3 inches between them. This should make 12 round scones. (You can also form the dough into a rectangular shape and cut it with a knife into 12 square- or triangle-shaped scones.) Brush the scones with melted butter and dust them with brown sugar.

Bake until just golden brown all over, 15 to 20 minutes.

CINNAMON APPLE DANISH CHEESECAKE SCONE STICKS

MAKES 8 TO 10 SCONES

APPLE FILLING

1 cup apple pie filling

¼ teaspoon ground cinnamon

Pinch of cloves

CREAM CHEESE FILLING

8 ounces cream cheese, softened

1 egg

¼ cup sugar

1 teaspoon pure vanilla extract

¼ teaspoon cinnamon

SCONE DOUGH

3 cups (approximately) all-purpose flour

¾ cup sugar

1 tablespoon baking powder

½ teaspoon baking soda

½ teaspoon salt

⅛ teaspoon ground cinnamon

¾ cup (6 ounces) unsalted butter, cut in 12 chunks

2 eggs

1½ teaspoons pure vanilla extract

½ to 1 cup buttermilk

FINISHING TOUCHES

Melted butter or cream

White sugar

Ground cinnamon

FONDANT

2 cups confectioners' sugar

2 to 3 tablespoons cream

½ teaspoon pure vanilla extract

A tender vanilla cinnamon scone is topped with spiced apple pie filling and a sweetened cream cheese filling. Even though these are scones, they taste just like an apple Danish with a dab of New York cheesecake tucked inside. They are finished with a luxurious drizzle of baker's fondant on top.

Preheat the oven to 400°F. Position the oven rack in the upper third of the oven. Stack 2 baking sheets together and line the top one with parchment paper. Have a third smaller baking sheet lined with parchment paper nearby.

In a small bowl, mix the apple pie filling with the cinnamon and cloves, cutting up larger wedges of apple with a knife. Set aside.

For the Cream Cheese Filling, place all the ingredients in the bowl of a food processor. Blend into a smooth paste by pulsing to start, then blending to make a creamy filling. Remove to a small bowl and refrigerate.

Without cleaning the food processor bowl prepare the scones. Place the flour, sugar, baking powder, baking soda, salt, and cinnamon in the bowl and blend briefly. Add the chunks of butter and pulse to make a grainy mixture.

Transfer the mixture to a large bowl. Make a well in the center and stir in the eggs, vanilla, and ½ cup of the buttermilk. Gather the mixture into a rough mass, adding in additional tablespoons of buttermilk as required to achieve a shaggy dough. Place the dough on a lightly floured work surface and knead it briefly, adding more flour if required to make a soft but cohesive dough.

Pat it into a 10- by 10-inch square and place it on the small parchment-lined baking sheet. Gently spread the Cream Cheese Filling on top of the dough. Then spoon on the Apple Filling. Gently fold the dough in half, pressing down on the edges to seal, and refrigerate for 30 minutes.

Using a sharp knife, cut the scone dough into small sticks, about 1 inch wide, and transfer the scone sticks to the larger stacked baking sheets. Gently twist each stick (the filling will ooze out a bit, which is okay). Brush each stick with melted butter or cream and dust with sugar and cinnamon.

Bake until the edges are golden, about 20 to 24 minutes. Let cool for 5 minutes and then top each stick with 1 to 2 tablespoons of Apple Filling.

Meanwhile, mix the confectioners' sugar with the cream and vanilla to make a soft fondant. Smear or drizzle it on the warm scone sticks. Alternatively, dust them with confectioners' sugar.

TOFFEE BAR CARAMEL SCONES

MAKES 8 SCONES

DOUGH

3¼ cups all-purpose flour

¾ cup (6 ounces) cold unsalted butter, cut into small pieces

⅓ cup white sugar

¼ cup firmly packed dark brown sugar

½ teaspoon salt

1 tablespoon baking powder

½ teaspoon baking soda

Tiniest pinch of ground nutmeg or cloves

¾ cup buttermilk

1 egg

1½ teaspoons pure vanilla extract

½ teaspoon butterscotch extract (optional)

½ cup caramel or butterscotch chips

½ cup chopped Heath bar or toffee bar

½ cup finely ground walnuts

TOPPING

1 egg white

⅓ cup butterscotch chips, finely chopped

Confectioners' sugar for dusting (optional)

These are a treasure of a scone, inspired by a visit to a coffee shop in downtown Toronto. Make them free-form with a large ice-cream scoop, or bake them in tuna cans (see page 195).

Preheat the oven to 425°F. Stack 2 baking sheets together and line the top one with parchment paper, or spray 8 tuna tins with nonstick cooking spray, line them with paper liners, and set on a parchment-lined baking sheet. Set aside.

In a food processor, combine the flour and butter and pulse for 10 to 20 seconds to break up the butter. In a medium bowl, combine both sugars, the salt, baking powder, baking soda, and nutmeg. Whisk to blend. Add to the food processor and pulse to combine.

Empty into a large bowl. Make a well in the center and add the buttermilk, egg, vanilla, and butterscotch extract. Stir to make a soft dough. Fold in the caramel or butterscotch chips, Heath bar bits, and nuts.

Using an ice-cream scoop or large spoon, scoop 8 mounds of batter onto the doubled baking sheets, or fill the prepared tuna cans at least three-fourths full.

For the topping, whisk the egg white in a medium bowl until foamy. Brush each scone with the egg white and distribute the butterscotch chips over each.

Bake the scones on the top shelf of the oven for 16 to 18 minutes, or until lightly browned. Lower the oven temperature if the scones appear to be browning too quickly. Let cool on the baking sheets or in the molds for 10 to 15 minutes. Transfer to wire racks to cool, then dust with confectioners' sugar.

MADISON AVENUE ORANGE AND LEMON FROSTED SCONES

MAKES 8 SCONES

DOUGH

3 cups all-purpose flour

⅓ cup sugar

4 teaspoons baking powder

½ teaspoon salt

2 teaspoons minced orange zest

⅔ cup (5 ounces) cold unsalted
    butter, cut into small pieces,
    plus melted butter for brushing

¼ teaspoon orange oil or extract

¼ teaspoon lemon oil or extract

1 teaspoon pure vanilla extract
    (optional)

1 egg

⅔ cup heavy whipping cream

¼ cup dried currants, plumped and
    patted dry (see page 18)

GLAZE

1½ cups confectioners' sugar

2 tablespoons frozen orange juice
    concentrate or water

⅛ teaspoon citric acid (see
    page 128), optional

¼ teaspoon orange oil or extract

Somewhere on Madison Avenue, there is yet another café with yet another scone that begged for an encore in the BB test kitchen. Here it is. These citrusy scones are nicely crusty, a perfect contrast to the tender, buttery interiors.

Preheat the oven to 450°F. Stack 2 baking sheets together and line the top one with parchment paper. Set aside.

In a food processor, combine the flour, sugar, baking powder, salt, and orange zest. Pulse to blend. Add the ⅔ cup (5 ounces) cold butter and pulse for 10 to 20 seconds, or until the texture of coarse meal. Add the orange and lemon oils, vanilla, egg, and cream. Process for 8 to 10 seconds to make a shaggy dough.

Turn out onto a lightly floured surface. Knead briefly to make a firm but soft dough. Gently press in the currants. Form the dough into 2 disks, each 1 inch thick. Cut each into 4 wedges. Place the wedges on the prepared baking sheets and brush them with melted butter.

Bake for 16 to 20 minutes, or until nicely browned. Transfer to wire racks and let cool for at least 10 minutes.

Meanwhile, make the glaze. In a medium bowl, whisk all of the ingredients together to make a very thick mixture. Add a teaspoonful or two of water if necessary to make a spreadable mixture.

Using a small metal spatula, glaze the scones once. Let stand for about 5 minutes, or until the glaze is set, then glaze them again.

Maple, Walnut, Oatmeal, and Brown Sugar Scones

MAKES 10 SCONES

DOUGH

3 cups all-purpose flour

4 teaspoons baking powder

⅓ cup firmly packed brown sugar

¾ teaspoon salt

¼ teaspoon ground cinnamon

¾ cup (6 ounces) cold unsalted butter, cut into small pieces

½ cup walnuts, lightly toasted (see page 17)

½ cup quick-cooking rolled oats

⅓ cup pure maple syrup

1 teaspoon pure vanilla extract

⅔ cup milk or half-and-half cream

TOPPING

3 tablespoons unsalted butter, melted

¼ cup pure maple syrup

¼ cup firmly packed brown sugar

¼ cup quick-cooking rolled oats

Pure maple syrup, a touch of brown sugar, butter, vanilla, and the heady aroma of toasted walnuts give these scones a country-inn flair. These are also good with chopped toffee, butterscotch chips, pecans or black walnuts, if you can find them.

Preheat the oven to 425°F. Stack 2 baking sheets together and line the top one with parchment paper. Set aside.

In a food processor, combine the flour, baking powder, brown sugar, salt, and cinnamon. Pulse for 15 to 30 seconds to blend. Add the butter and pulse for 10 to 20 seconds, or until the texture of coarse meal.

Empty into a large bowl. Stir in the walnuts and oats. Make a well in the center of the mixture and add the maple syrup, vanilla, and milk. Stir to make a soft dough.

Turn the dough out onto a lightly floured surface and knead briefly to make a cohesive mass. Form the dough into 2 disks, each about ¾ inch thick. Cut each into 5 wedges. Place on the prepared baking sheet. Brush each wedge with melted butter and drizzle with some maple syrup. Sprinkle on the brown sugar and oats.

Bake for 15 to 18 minutes, or until browned. Transfer to wire racks and let cool slightly or completely.

CHOCOLATE-STREAK SCONES

MAKES 8 TO 10 SCONES

CHOCOLATE STREAK MIXTURE

2½ ounces semisweet chocolate, coarsely chopped

⅓ cup sugar

3 tablespoons unsalted butter, softened

¼ teaspoon ground cinnamon

1 tablespoon unsweetened cocoa powder

1 teaspoon instant coffee powder

TOPPING

¼ cup unsweetened cocoa powder

¼ cup sugar

2½ ounces semisweet chocolate, very finely chopped

DOUGH

3 cups all-purpose flour

⅓ cup sugar

1 tablespoon baking powder

½ teaspoon salt

½ cup (4 ounces) cold unsalted butter, cut into small pieces

1 egg

1 teaspoon pure vanilla extract

1 cup heavy whipping cream, plus 6 to 8 tablespoons for brushing

Miniature pastries or scones? These are that delicate, an example of how versatile scones can be. A chocolate nut mixture is pressed into a scone dough to create a marbleized effect that offers a unique texture and taste. You can also make miniatures of these, drizzle on melted white chocolate after baking, and serve them up in confectionary cups as little sweets at the end of a meal.

Preheat the oven to 425°F. Stack 2 baking sheets together and line the top one with parchment paper. Set aside.

For the streaking mixture, in a food processor, combine all the ingredients and pulse for 10 to 20 seconds, or until crumbly. Set aside.

For the topping, stir all the ingredients together in a small bowl. Set aside.

For the dough, combine the flour, sugar, baking powder, and salt in a food processor. Pulse to blend. Add the butter and pulse for 10 to 20 seconds, or until the texture of coarse meal. Empty into a large bowl. Stir in the egg and vanilla, then the 1 cup cream to make a soft dough.

Turn out onto a lightly floured surface. Press the streaking mixture into the top of the dough and gently knead the mixture in. Form the dough into 2 disks, each ¾ to 1 inch thick. Cut each disk into 4 or 5 irregular wedges by turning the knife or dough cutter in alternating oblique cuts. Place the scones on the prepared baking sheet. Brush the scones with the remaining cream and sprinkle with the topping.

Bake for 12 to 15 minutes, or until the scones are dry to the touch and lightly browned on the edges. Transfer to wire racks and let cool slightly or completely.

DOUBLE-CHEDDAR SCONES

MAKES 8 TO 12 SCONES

3 cups all-purpose flour

4 teaspoons baking powder

1¼ teaspoons salt

1¼ teaspoons dry mustard

½ teaspoon baking soda

½ cup (4 ounces) cold unsalted
butter, cut into small pieces,
plus melted butter for brushing
(optional)

1½ cups shredded sharp cheddar
cheese

2 eggs

1 cup milk

½ cup shredded white cheddar
cheese for sprinkling

My friend Beryl Loveland of Beryl's Decorating Supply inspired these scones. They were tested with sharp, extra-sharp, pepper, and sun-dried tomato cheddar, all good choices. I first served these when I taught a course on Italian desserts (I had to get something going in the oven to warm up the class on a cold day). The results almost upstaged the fancy Italian dessert. I've served them at the start of every baking class ever since.

~❧~

Preheat the oven to 450°F. Stack 2 baking sheets together and line the top one with parchment paper. Set aside.

In a food processor, combine the flour, baking powder, salt, dry mustard, and baking soda. Pulse to blend. Add the butter and pulse for 10 to 20 seconds, or until the texture of coarse meal. Add three-fourths of the sharp cheddar and pulse just to mix.

Empty into a large bowl. Make a well in the center and add the eggs and milk. Stir to make a shaggy dough.

Turn out on a lightly floured surface and knead for 8 to 10 seconds to make a soft dough. Form the dough into 2 disks, each 1 inch thick. Cut each into 4 or 6 wedges. Place the wedges on the prepared baking sheets and brush them with melted butter.

Lower the oven temperature to 425°F and bake the scones for 8 to 12 minutes, or until lightly browned on the edges. For the last 5 minutes of baking, sprinkle the scones with the remaining sharp cheddar and the white cheddar. Transfer to wire racks and let cool slightly or completely.

ASIAGO CHEDDAR PANCETTA CHEESE SCONES

MAKES 8 TO 12 SCONES

3 cups all-purpose flour, plus more
    for dusting

4 teaspoons baking powder

½ teaspoon baking soda

1½ teaspoons salt

2¼ teaspoons dry mustard

½ cup (4 ounces) unsalted butter

1½ cups Wisconsin Asiago cheese,
    shredded

1 cup sharp white or orange
    cheddar cheese, in small
    chunks

2 eggs

1 cup milk

1 cup fried, drained, coarsely
    chopped pancetta (or bacon)

FINISHING TOUCHES

Melted butter for brushing

1 cup Asiago or shredded cheddar
    for topping

A hot, buttery scone that uses both zesty Wisconsin Asiago and sharp cheddar, and a hefty shower of crisp pancetta. This is a smoky, extravagant scone that is a just about a meal—it is so satisfying in a gourmet bistro sort of way.

Preheat the oven to 450°F. Stack 2 baking sheets together and line the top one with parchment paper.

In a food processor, whisk together the flour, baking powder, baking soda, salt, and dry mustard. Pulse in the butter to make a grainy mixture. Mix in both cheeses. Turn the whole mass out into a large bowl and make a well in the center. Stir in the eggs and milk to make a shaggy dough, and add most of the pancetta, reserving 1 to 2 tablespoons.

Turn out the dough onto a floured board and barely knead it to make a soft but cohesive mass. Shape into 2 rounds and cut each round into 4 or 6 wedges. Place the scones on the stacked baking sheets. Paint them with melted butter and/or dust with flour, sprinkle on more cheese, and garnish with the reserved pancetta. This is a somewhat wet dough. The wetter it is, the messier, but the more buttery and light the scone will be.

Put the scones in the oven, reduce the temperature immediately to 425°F, and bake until golden and cheesy looking, 13 to 18 minutes. You can also sprinkle them with more cheddar once they are about three-quarters done. Cool on a rack.

CHOCOLATE CHIP SCONES

MAKES 6 LARGE SCONES

DOUGH

3¼ cups all-purpose flour

⅔ cup sugar

4 teaspoons baking powder

¾ teaspoon salt

¾ cup (6 ounces) cold unsalted butter, cut into small pieces

1 egg

1 teaspoon pure vanilla extract

1 cup heavy whipping cream

1 cup semisweet chocolate chips

GARNISH

½ cup semisweet chocolate chips, melted

2½ ounces white chocolate, chopped and melted

Confectioners' sugar for dusting

On a trip to Phoenix, Arizona, for a food writer's conference, I stopped by a bagel shop where I saw some chocolate chip scones that looked as if they had been baked in tart shells, producing high sides and nicely mounded tops. They had been drizzled with melted white and dark chocolate, and dusted with confectioners' sugar. The effect was stunning. If you don't have tart shells, use tuna cans and bake them directly on a parchment paper–lined baking sheet.

~◊~

Preheat the oven to 425°F. Stack 2 baking sheets together and line the top one with parchment paper. Alternatively, spray six 4-inch tart pans with nonstick cooking spray and line a baking sheet with parchment paper. Set aside.

In a food processor, combine the flour, sugar, baking powder, and salt. Pulse to blend. Add the butter and pulse for 10 to 15 seconds, or until the texture of coarse meal. Empty into a large bowl. Make a well in the center and add the egg, vanilla, and cream. Stir to make a soft dough. Stir in the chocolate chips.

Using an ice-cream scoop or large spoon, scoop 6 mounds of dough onto the prepared baking sheets or into the tart pans. If using tart pans, place them on the prepared baking sheet.

Bake for 15 to 18 minutes, or until nicely browned. Transfer to wire racks to cool.

For the garnish, dip a fork in the semisweet chocolate and drizzle over the tops, and then dip another fork in the white chocolate and drizzle on the tops. Let set, then dust with confectioners' sugar.

WEEKEND IN NEW ENGLAND CRANBERRY SCONES

MAKES 1 DOZEN SCONES

DOUGH

3 cups all-purpose flour or 3¼ cups pastry flour

⅔ cup sugar

2 tablespoons baking powder

¾ teaspoon salt

¾ cup (6 ounces) cold unsalted butter, cut into small pieces

2 eggs

½ cup heavy whipping cream

1 cup frozen cranberries, whole or coarsely chopped

GLAZE

1 egg, beaten, or heavy whipping cream for brushing

White or coarse sugar for dusting

I came across these scones while on a lecture tour. At the New England Culinary Institute, fondly called NECI (or "Necki"), these were baked fresh each morning, and I quickly became addicted to them. One of NECI's chefs kindly obtained a copy of the large-scale recipe for me. I scaled it down for my website visitors to enjoy, and now here it is for you. The original recipe called for dried currants, but these are terrific with cranberries. If you use pastry flour, they will be even more tender, but the dough is a little more delicate to handle.

~✿~

Preheat the oven to 425°F. Stack 2 baking sheets together and line the top one with parchment paper. Set aside.

In a food processor, combine the flour, sugar, baking powder, and salt. Pulse to blend. Add the butter and pulse for 10 to 15 seconds or until the texture of coarse meal. Empty into a large bowl. Stir in the eggs and cream to make a soft, but firm dough.

Turn out onto a lightly floured surface. Knead briefly and then form into 2 disks, each about 1 inch thick. Using a dough cutter, cut into six 4-inch rounds, then cut each in half. Gather any scraps and cut out additional scones. Place the scones on the prepared baking sheet. For the glaze, brush beaten egg on each scone and dust with sugar.

Bake for 10 minutes, then lower the oven temperature to 400°F. Bake 8 to 10 minutes longer, or until golden brown. Transfer to wire racks and let cool slightly or completely.

HONOLULU HEALTH SCONES

MAKES 8 TO 12 SCONES

1 cup firmly packed dark brown
    sugar

⅓ cup honey

¼ cup vegetable oil

¼ cup orange juice or water

⅓ cup applesauce or banana puree

1 egg

2 egg whites

1 teaspoon pure vanilla extract

1 cup all-purpose flour

1 cup whole-wheat flour

2 teaspoons baking powder

½ teaspoon salt

½ teaspoon ground cinnamon

2½ cups quick-cooking rolled oats

2½ cups sweetened shredded
    coconut

1 cup dried cranberries, plumped
    and patted dry (see page 18)

1 cup raisins, plumped and patted
    dry (see page 18)

1½ cups pitted dates, plumped and
    patted dry (see page 18), and
    chopped

This scone recipe replicates a commercial scone from Hawaii that one of my website visitors asked me to duplicate. (She actually FedExed me a dozen of them!) It's a low-fat, multigrain scone that resembles the bites I see at health bars in training gyms. Have one of these, and you will feel very noble. It is a nutritious, delicious appetite-zapper.

Preheat the oven to 350°F. Stack 2 baking sheets together and line the top one with parchment paper. Set aside.

In a large bowl, combine the brown sugar, honey, oil, and orange juice. Beat until blended. Stir in the applesauce, egg, egg whites, and vanilla. In another large bowl, combine the flours, baking powder, salt, cinnamon, oats, and coconut. Stir to blend. Add to the wet ingredients and stir until smooth. Stir in the dried fruit. Blend well. The mixture will be sticky.

Turn the dough out onto a generously floured surface. Knead gently to make a smooth ball. Wrap the dough in plastic wrap and refrigerate it for 20 minutes.

Return the dough to the floured surface and divide it in half. Form each half into a disk about 1 inch thick. Cut into squares with a knife or into rounds using a 2½-inch biscuit cutter. Gather the scraps, re-form into a round, and cut out the remaining dough. Transfer to the prepared baking sheets.

Bake for 18 to 22 minutes, or until lightly browned. Transfer to wire racks and let cool slightly or completely.

B.B.
Test Kitchen
Notes

Honeybee Good

Honey is a terrific sweetener for baking. Some attribute special powers to honey, but essentially it is glucose and fructose, with some trace minerals and vitamins. Among the varieties available are alfalfa, buckwheat, blueberry, orange blossom, clover, and sage, sold in both liquid and whipped form. I recommend a mild-flavored liquid honey for my recipes, so that the honey flavor does not dominate.

ORANGE-OATMEAL SCONES

MAKES 8 TO 12 SCONES

2½ cups all-purpose flour

1 cup old-fashioned rolled oats

1 cup quick-cooking rolled oats

1 cup sugar, plus more for
   sprinkling

1 tablespoon baking powder

1 teaspoon salt

½ teaspoon baking soda

½ cup (4 ounces) cold unsalted
   butter, cut into small pieces

1 egg

½ cup fresh orange juice

¼ teaspoon orange or tangerine oil
   or extract

1 cup raisins, plumped and patted
   dry (see page 18)

½ cup minced dried peaches
   (optional)

Milk for brushing

Grated orange zest for sprinkling

I saved the best for last. These are dense, hearty, and perky with flavor and color. I found a version of these at a neighborhood café. I played with the recipe until they were every bit as good as the originals. Ironically, the store's scone supplier up and deserted them a couple of days later. I got to these scones just in time!

Preheat the oven to 425°F. Stack 2 baking sheets together and line the top one with parchment paper. Set aside.

In a food processor, combine the flour, both kinds of oats, 1 cup sugar, the baking powder, salt, and baking soda. Pulse to blend. Add the butter and pulse for 20 to 30 seconds, or until the texture of coarse meal. Empty into a large bowl. Add the egg, orange juice, and orange oil. Stir to make a soft dough. Stir in the raisins and peaches.

Turn out onto a lightly floured surface and knead until smooth. Roll or pat out the dough ½ inch thick. Using a 4-inch cookie cutter, cut out rounds. Gather the scraps, re-form into a round, and cut out the remaining dough. Place the scones on the prepared baking sheet, brush them with milk, and sprinkle with sugar and orange zest. Bake for 14 to 16 minutes, or until nicely browned. Transfer to wire racks and let cool slightly or completely.

B.B.
Test Kitchen
Notes

Orange Glaze

I often make a glaze for these oatmeal scones by stirring together 1 cup confectioners' sugar and 2 to 4 tablespoons orange juice, until the consistency of glaze. I spread a thin layer of it on the scones after they've cooled, and then I garnish the tops with grated orange zest. Heavenly. This luscious orange glaze is also a great topping on cranberry or maple-walnut scones.

Chapter 7

· ·

THE PASTRY SHOPPE

· ·

PASTRY MEANS MANY THINGS TO MANY PEOPLE.
I lean toward the French view and interpret it as
anything that is particularly buttery, and flakier or
lighter than a cake or muffin. There are four basic
types of pastry dough, and most pastries worthy of
their appellation are derived from one of them: *pâte
à choux*, or choux (pronounced "shoo") pastry; *pâte
feuilletée*, or puff pastry; *pâte brisée*, or pie dough; and
pâte sucrée, or tart dough.

Rich in eggs, choux, or cream puff, pastry dough is
piped in different shapes onto prepared baking sheets.
Once in the hot oven, the pastelike dough blooms
into a puffy, voluminous shape. After baking, the
choux pastries are split and filled with sweet or savory
preparations, such as whipped cream or custard,
to make classics like Paris Brest. I push the choux
envelope with my famed Cream Puff Cake (page 241),
which starts classically enough but ends with a
decidedly New World spin.

Many types of dough are labeled "puff pastry," but
the true *pâte feuilletée* is all butter, all delicious, and
quite distinct. Most home bakers shy away from the
challenges of puff pastry (the basis of croissants), but
once in a while, it is fun to give the butter arts a try
(see Breton Butter Galette, page 238).

Pie dough is both the home baker's and the pastry
chef's domain. In French, it is called *pâte brisée*, which
means "broken dough," referring to the shortness of
the crumb and flakiness of the crust. Pie dough can
be mastered, and I have taught more than one baker
the basics via the website. Around Thanksgiving, I am
deluged with pie and pie dough questions, and I spend
a lot of time creating new pies and troubleshooting
home bakers' own efforts. Similarly, *pâte sucrée*,
or sweet tart dough, forms the basis of many tasty
concoctions and is relatively easy to make. Either
dough is the gateway to unlimited creativity.

Cold hands and a warm heart mean great pastry.
Butter and other fats play an important role in the
construction of most types of pastry. The fat is best
incorporated while cold because it retains its integrity
and forms pockets in the dough. Once baking begins,
these pockets burst, forming the bubbles and layers
of a croissant or the flakes of a pie crust. If a pastry
breaks down due to overworking or warm conditions,
you can always stop and refrigerate the dough for a
short time to firm it up, or get the fat to firm up inside
the dough.

I highly recommend unsalted butter for all your
baking, but for pastry it's especially important. Find a
butter you like that performs well in your recipes; the
less water content, the better the butter will perform.

In Canada, the Lactantia brand has been popular for more than 50 years. In the United States, Cabot of Vermont produces some of the better butter I have tried, and I also am are partial to Land O' Lakes for its fine flavor and availability. Elsewhere, people swear by Irish butter, Belgian butter, Dutch butter, and especially French butter. In North America, the fat content in regular butter is approximately 80 percent. French butter contains at least 82 percent butterfat, and butters from regions such as Isigny and Échiré contain at least 84 percent butterfat. Some North American producers sell higher-fat "European style" or "ultrabutters." Some butters are "cultured," or fermented, during production (as most French butters are), which gives them a bit of a tangy taste. Butter that is not cultured is usually labeled as "sweet cream butter." In any event, it all comes down to your taste buds. Use what tastes good to you, but make sure you use unsalted butter for baking (unless indicated otherwise).

Finally, use flavorings sparingly in pastries, if at all. I exercise restraint with extracts, since even vanilla will compete with the pure taste of butter.

I offer an expansive range of pastries in this chapter, with an eye toward different occasions, tastes, sizes, and shapes. Most of these recipes are classics in the BB test kitchen. Even after baking these delights over and over, I still turn to them when I want something special.

CHOCOLATE BRIOCHE BUNS

MAKES 1 DOZEN BUNS

DOUGH

½ cup warm water

5 teaspoons instant yeast

1 cup warm milk

⅔ cup sugar

1¼ teaspoons salt

1 egg

2 egg yolks

½ cup (4 ounces) unsalted butter,
    softened

2 teaspoons pure vanilla extract

1 teaspoon grated lemon zest

2 cups all-purpose flour

2 to 3 cups bread flour

FILLING

10 ounces semisweet chocolate,
    coarsely chopped

⅓ cup sugar

¼ teaspoon ground cinnamon

GLAZE

1 egg beaten with a pinch of sugar

White or coarse sugar for
    sprinkling

This is a quick version of the French classic, pain au chocolat. *A rich dough hides a sweet cache of chocolate, the perfect foil for tea, coffee, or espresso.*

Stack 2 baking sheets together. Line the top one with parchment paper. Set aside.

For the dough, hand whisk the water and yeast together in the bowl of an electric mixer and let stand for 2 to 3 minutes to dissolve the yeast. Whisk in the warm milk, then the sugar, salt, egg, egg yolks, butter, vanilla, and lemon zest. Stir in the all-purpose flour, then 2 cups of the bread flour. Knead with the dough hook on the lowest speed of the mixer for 8 to 10 minutes, gradually adding more bread flour as required to form a soft, but firm dough.

Place the dough in a lightly greased bowl and place the bowl inside a large plastic bag. Close the bag loosely and let the dough rise for 45 minutes, or until almost doubled.

Gently deflate the dough. Turn the dough out onto a lightly floured surface and divide it into 12 equal portions. Let the dough rest for 10 minutes.

In the meantime, make the filling. Toss the chocolate, sugar, and cinnamon together in a small bowl.

Roll or press the dough into 12 ovals about ½ inch thick. Distribute the chocolate evenly among the ovals. Fold up the ends, then the sides of each oval to make a cylinder. Press the seams to seal. Place the buns on the prepared baking sheet and insert the sheet in the plastic bag. Close the bag loosely and let the buns rise for 30 to 45 minutes, or until puffy.

Preheat the oven to 350°F. Make 3 or 4 slits in the top of each bun. For the glaze, brush liberally with the egg mixture, then sprinkle with sugar. Bake for 18 to 22 minutes, or until golden brown. Transfer to a wire rack to cool.

Oh-So-Sticky Philadelphia Cinnamon Buns

MAKES 12 TO 14 LARGE BUNS

DOUGH

1½ cups warm water

2 tablespoons instant yeast

½ cup sugar

3 eggs

1 egg yolk

2 teaspoons pure vanilla extract

⅓ cup nonfat dry milk

2 cups all-purpose flour

3 to 4 cups bread flour

¾ cup (6 ounces) cold unsalted
    butter, shredded

2 teaspoons salt

FILLING

¾ cup firmly packed dark brown
    sugar

1½ teaspoons ground cinnamon

1 cup dried currants or raisins

1 cup chopped walnuts or pecans,
    or graham cracker crumbs

½ cup (4 ounces) unsalted butter,
    softened

PAN GLAZE

½ cup (4 ounces) unsalted butter

¾ cup firmly packed light brown
    sugar

¼ cup corn syrup

These coiled clouds of buttery dough are laced with cinnamon and coated with a brown sugar glaze. Light and moist, they resemble Danish without the work. For cinnamon bun fans who have nut allergies, I often substitute coarsely crushed graham crackers in the crunchy filling (a trick that also works for streusel topping). Another of my favorite BB test kitchen tricks is used here: shredding butter to make it easier to incorporate in the dough.

Coat a 12-inch square baking pan or two 10-inch round springform pans with nonstick cooking spray. Line a baking sheet with parchment paper. Set aside.

For the dough, hand whisk the warm water and yeast together in the bowl of an electric mixer and let stand for 2 to 3 minutes for the yeast to dissolve. Stir in the sugar, eggs, egg yolk, and vanilla, then stir in the dry milk, all-purpose flour, 3 cups of the bread flour, the butter, and salt. Knead with the dough hook on the lowest speed of the mixer for 8 to 10 minutes, adding more of the bread flour as required to make a smooth, elastic dough.

Turn the dough out onto a lightly floured surface and form it into a ball. Place the dough in a lightly greased bowl. Place the bowl inside a large plastic bag, close the bag loosely, and let the dough rise for 40 to 60 minutes, or until almost doubled in size.

Gently deflate the dough and let it rest for 20 minutes.

Meanwhile, make the filling and the glaze. For the filling, combine all the ingredients in a medium bowl and stir to blend. For the glaze, combine all the ingredients in a small bowl and stir to make a paste. Set aside.

Turn the dough out onto a lightly floured surface. Roll the dough out into a 14-inch square. Sprinkle liberally with the filling and press it in slightly. Roll the dough up into a log and refrigerate for 10 minutes. Cut the log into 1-inch slices.

Spread the glaze in the prepared square pan or divide it equally between the round pans. Arrange the dough slices in the square pan or divide between the round ones. Place the pan(s) inside a large plastic bag. Close the bag loosely and let the dough rise for 30 to 40 minutes, or until the slices are almost doubled in size.

Preheat the oven to 350°F. Place the pan(s) on the prepared baking sheet and bake for 30 to 35 minutes, or until browned. Let cool in the pan(s) for a few minutes, then invert onto a large tray or a parchment-lined baking sheet and serve immediately or glaze with fondant.

FONDANT-COVERED CINNAMON BUNS: Take these buns up a notch by applying a thick coat of Home Baker's Fondant (opposite) on each finished cinnamon bun. Sometimes I flavor my fondant with a touch of cocoa powder or cinnamon.

HOME BAKER'S FONDANT

MAKES ABOUT 1¼ CUPS

2 cups confectioners' sugar

1 teaspoon pure vanilla extract (optional)

3 to 6 tablespoons water, or as needed

This is a shortcut fondant. Real fondant is available from mail-order sources like The King Arthur Flour Company (see Source Guide, page 301).

Combine the confectioners' sugar and the vanilla in a small bowl. Whisk in the water and blend to make a soft, pourable glaze. Use immediately.

CREAM CHEESE–TOPPED MOCK STICKY BUNS

MAKES 1 DOZEN LARGE BUNS

DOUGH

¼ cup warm water

2 teaspoons instant yeast

¾ cup sugar

4 cups all-purpose flour

4 teaspoons baking powder

1 teaspoon salt

¾ cup (6 ounces) cold unsalted
   butter, cut into small pieces

¾ cup warm milk

FILLING

¾ cup firmly packed brown sugar

¼ cup white sugar

4 tablespoons (2 ounces) unsalted
   butter, softened

1 teaspoon ground cinnamon

Pinch each of ground nutmeg,
   ginger, and cloves (optional)

1½ cups raisins, plumped and
   patted dry (see page 18), then
   coarsely chopped

GLAZE

1 cup confectioners' sugar

½ teaspoon pure vanilla extract

1 teaspoon fresh lemon juice

¼ cup cream cheese at room
   temperature

2 to 4 tablespoons water

Quick and easy—that's the ticket! A rich scone dough, two leavening agents, tart molds, and a cream cheese glaze—even though there's a lot going on here, these buns are half the work of traditional sticky buns but with all the great taste.

Line 12 large muffin cups or twelve 4-inch tart molds with paper liners (spread them out to fit as required). You may also use empty 7-ounce tuna cans. Spray the molds generously with nonstick cooking spray. Line a baking sheet with parchment paper. Set aside.

In a small bowl, stir the warm water, yeast, and a pinch of the sugar together and let stand for 2 to 3 minutes to dissolve the yeast.

In a food processor, combine the sugar, flour, baking powder, and salt. Pulse to blend. Add the butter and process to the texture of coarse meal. Empty into a large bowl. Stir in the yeast mixture and the milk to make a soft dough.

For the filling, combine all the ingredients except the raisins in a small bowl. Stir to blend.

On a lightly floured surface, roll the dough out into a rectangle 14 to 16 inches long, 6 inches wide, and ½ to ¾ inch thick. Spread with the filling mixture and sprinkle on the raisins. Starting from a long side, roll up into a log. Cut into 1-inch slices and place each slice in a prepared mold. Let rise for 15 to 20 minutes, or until puffy.

Preheat the oven to 375°F. Place the molds on the prepared baking sheet and bake for 25 to 30 minutes, or until golden. Transfer to a wire rack to cool for 10 minutes before unmolding.

For the glaze, combine the confectioners' sugar, vanilla, lemon juice, and cream cheese in a small bowl. Stir in the water to make a spreadable mixture.

Using a small metal spatula, spread the rolls generously with the glaze.

CHOCOLATE SCHNECKEN

MAKES 2 DOZEN BUNS

DOUGH

⅓ cup warm water

5 teaspoons instant yeast

½ cup sugar

¾ cup warm milk

2 eggs

¾ cup (6 ounces) unsalted butter, softened

1 teaspoon salt

1 teaspoon pure vanilla extract

¼ cup sour cream

2 cups all-purpose flour

3 to 4 cups bread flour

FILLING

½ cup (4 ounces) unsalted butter, melted

2 cups firmly packed brown sugar

1 teaspoon ground cinnamon

1 teaspoon instant coffee, finely pulverized

2 tablespoons unsweetened cocoa powder

2½ ounces semisweet chocolate, ground in a food processor

¼ cup miniature chocolate chips

1 cup chopped pecans

½ cup dried currants (optional)

GLAZE

½ cup (4 ounces) unsalted butter, melted

1½ cups firmly packed brown sugar

1 teaspoon ground cinnamon

2 tablespoons unsweetened cocoa powder

These divine buns were part of a website salute to Valentine's Day, a holiday I make a big fuss about. A gift of Schnecken does its own romancing, subtly saying "I'd like to get to know you—and guess what? I can bake." But you don't have to wait for Valentine's Day to make or share these.

Schnecken translates as "snails" and refers to the tight, small, coils of these pastries. Schnecken are usually filled with cinnamon and sugar, but these also boast a sprinkling of semisweet chocolate. Use miniature chocolate chips in a pinch.

Spray 24 miniature muffin cups with nonstick cooking spray. Line 2 baking sheets with parchment paper. Set aside.

For the dough, hand whisk the water and yeast together in the bowl of an electric mixer and let stand for 2 to 3 minutes to dissolve the yeast. Stir in the sugar, milk, eggs, butter, salt, vanilla, and sour cream until blended. Stir in the all-purpose flour and 3 cups of the bread flour. Knead with the dough hook on the lowest speed of the mixer for 8 to 10 minutes, gradually adding more bread flour as required to make a smooth, elastic dough.

Turn the dough out onto a lightly floured surface and shape into a ball. Place the dough in a lightly greased bowl. Place the bowl in a large plastic bag, close the bag loosely, and let rise for 45 to 60 minutes, or until almost doubled.

For the filling, place all of the ingredients in a medium bowl in the order listed. Toss and stir lightly with a fork until combined into an even mixture.

Turn the dough out onto a lightly floured surface. Divide in half. Roll out one-half of the dough into a 12- by 14-inch rectangle. Cover evenly with half of the filling mixture. Starting from a short side, roll the dough up tightly. Repeat with the remaining dough. Refrigerate for 15 minutes. Cut the logs into 1-inch slices.

For the glaze, combine all the ingredients in a small bowl and stir to blend. Set aside.

Deposit 2 to 4 teaspoons of the glaze in the well of each muffin cup. Top with a dough slice. Place the pan in the plastic bag and close it loosely. Let the dough rise for 20 to 30 minutes, or until almost doubled.

Preheat the oven to 350°F. Place the pan on one of the prepared baking sheets. Bake for 25 to 30 minutes, or until golden brown. Remove from the oven and unmold onto the second prepared baking sheet, allowing the syrup to pour over the pastries. Recover the excess glaze and drizzle it over the pastries. Let stand for 5 minutes before removing. Serve warm or at room temperature.

COUNTRY PLUM TART

MAKES 1 TART; SERVES 8 TO 10

TART PASTRY

2½ cups all-purpose flour

1 cup (8 ounces) cold unsalted
    butter, cut into small pieces

¼ teaspoon cinnamon

½ cup cold heavy whipping cream

1 tablespoon sugar

¾ teaspoon salt

FILLING

2½ pounds small plums, quartered
    and pitted

¾ cup sugar

2 teaspoons fresh lemon juice

1 teaspoon raspberry or plum
    vinegar

1 teaspoon balsamic vinegar

⅛ teaspoon ground cinnamon

1 tablespoon all-purpose flour

1 tablespoon cornstarch

Confectioners' sugar for dusting
    (optional)

More of a pastry than a pie or tart, this treat impresses everyone and stays fresh looking and good tasting for days. If I had a country house in the south of France, this would be on the table all through the summer. Heavy cream makes for a lovely, rich tart crust.

Lightly grease a deep 9- or 10-inch quiche pan with a removable bottom, or a 10-inch pie pan or tart pan. Line a baking sheet with parchment paper. Set aside.

For the pastry, combine the flour, butter, and cinnamon in a large bowl. Using a pastry cutter or your fingers, cut or rub the butter into the flour until the mixture resembles a coarse meal. Make a well in the center and add the cream, sugar, and salt. Stir to make a rough mass. If the dough seems too dry, add 1 or 2 tablespoons of water. Transfer to a lightly floured surface and knead very gently for a few seconds to smooth out the dough. Divide the dough in half, form each half into a disk, and wrap well in plastic. Put one half in the refrigerator and the other in the freezer for at least 1 hour or as long as overnight.

For the filling, combine all the ingredients and toss to blend.

Remove both doughs from the refrigerator and freezer. Roll out the refrigerated dough into a 10-inch round to fit the bottom of the pan, then roll out and press the scraps into the sides of the pan and trim the edges. Mound the filling in the pastry shell.

Preheat the oven to 400°F. Using the large holes of a box grater, shred the remaining dough into a bowl. If the dough is too cold to work with, let it warm for 10 to 15 minutes. Sprinkle the shredded dough over the fruit.

Place the pan on the prepared baking sheet and bake for 15 minutes. Lower the oven temperature to 375°F and bake for another 20 to 30 minutes, or until the juices begin to bubble and the dough is lightly browned. Transfer the pan to a wire rack and let cool completely. If using a pan with a removable bottom, remove the pan sides and slide the tart onto a serving plate.

Before serving, dust with a generous amount of confectioners' sugar.

PIE DOUGH PRIMER
· ·

Can anyone bake a pie? Absolutely! I once feared pie dough until my very first pastry chef-teacher in hotel school demystified it for me. I learned that it was child's play, and great pies have been a part of my life ever since.

You can make your dough by hand or use my easy food processor method. Essentially, making pie dough is about working little pieces of fat (butter and/or shortening) into flour until you have a crumbly mixture. Then you add some cold water, you toss it around until it holds together, and you knead it a bit. You let it rest. You roll it out. At that point, you add prepared fillings, your own fillings, or even a combo of prepared and fresh. Extra dough freezes well, and when it emerges from the freezer, it's still homemade.

Pie Dough's Cast of Characters

ALL-PURPOSE FLOUR
Use unbleached all-purpose flour. All-purpose flour provides a nice balance for pie dough—neither too tender (and hard to handle), nor too resilient (and tough). Measure your flour carefully. However, if you use too little, that can be fixed when you roll out the dough.

BUTTER IS BEST, BUT . . .
. . . shortening makes a flakier texture. Therefore, I will often use half of each. Whipped margarines (salted or unsalted) are a crime against pie.

SALT
Without salt, pie pastry would taste flat. As for all baking, kosher salt is the best choice because it's additive free and has a clean taste.

LEMON JUICE
Lemon juice breaks down the gluten in the flour a bit, keeping the dough from getting tough. You may also use distilled white vinegar or cider vinegar.

ICE WATER
The liquid component in pie dough is usually ice water. Before you begin making pie dough, put a pitcher of water in the freezer. I use spring water, but tap water will do. Too little water, and the pastry will be hard to roll out. Too much, and you will lose that wonderful flakiness. Remember, you can always add more water, but it is hard to backtrack if you use too much.

Techniques

MEASURING
Make sure your flour, butter, eggs, shortening, and water are cold. Measure everything in advance and place it nearby. To measure flour, stir it in the canister first, then scoop it out with a metal measuring cup. Level it with a dinner knife.

MIXING
You can make pie dough by hand, but I recommend using a food processor. It's easy and fast, especially if you have big batches to make and freeze (pie dough freezes beautifully for up to 2 months). Use a good food processor (like a large-capacity KitchenAid). Start with flour, salt, and sugar, and run the machine for 10 seconds to mix. Add butter (or shortening and butter) in small chunks on top of the flour, then pulse to break up the fat into the flour. Stop the machine. Add most of the ice water and the lemon juice. Process for 15 seconds (no more!) to make a shaggy dough that just holds together (add more water at this point, if you think it's necessary). Turn the dough out onto a lightly floured surface and knead gently to make it all hold together. Form the dough into a disk. Place the dough in a self-sealing plastic bag and label it (especially if you are freezing in batches). Refrigerate the dough for at least 1 hour or up to 2 days, or freeze for up to 2 months.

ROLLING

Have your rolling pin on standby, a bowl of all-purpose flour for dusting, and a big, flat clean wood work surface. Roll the dough out gently, periodically lifting it and giving it a quarter turn. If the dough starts to resist (retracts as you roll), let it rest for a few minutes. Once it is large enough, fold it in quarters and deposit it in the pan. Gently unfold the dough and fit it into the pan. Repeat for the top (if preparing a double crust), allowing for a ¾-inch overhang. Trim the double-crust overhang with a paring knife to about ½ inch. Using your fingertips, press the edges together slightly to seal. Roll over to make an edge and press with fingertips to define the edge. Then, using three fingers—the first and third of one hand, and the index finger of your other hand—fashion a fluted border. There are a few ways to do this, and bakers often develop their own approach. The resulting look is different from pie to pie, but the important thing is to begin with a defined border and then manipulate it into a pretty, finished edge.

For fluted tart or quiche tins, the edge is easier to form. Simply roll a bottom crust to fit the tart or quiche pan, allowing enough dough to be gently pressed into the corners (where the fluted edge meets the pan bottom) and a ½-inch overhang. Then roll a rolling pin over the top of the pan, pressing slightly as you roll, and the pin will neatly trim away the excess pastry. If you are using a top crust, repeat this with top crust. When the excess is trimmed off, using your fingertips, lightly press the top crust onto the edges of the bottom crust to seal. Trim and crimp (press together with a fork).

For the best bets in rolling pins, see page 11.

BAKING

Fill your pie according to the recipe, and make sure your oven is preheated. (If the oven is not hot enough, the pie dough will melt instead of baking up fresh and flaky.) Glaze the top of a two-crust pie with some milk or a beaten egg, and cut a few air vents with a knife. Place the pie on a baking sheet. Place it in the oven and set a timer.

Bourbon and Cinnamon Bread-Pudding Tart

MAKES 1 TART; SERVES 12 TO 14

BREAD SHELL

1-pound loaf egg bread, brioche, or challah, cut into ½-inch slices and toasted

½ cup (4 ounces) unsalted butter, melted

½ cup sugar mixed with 1 teaspoon ground cinnamon

FILLING

¾ cup sugar

¼ cup cream cheese at room temperature

4 eggs

1 egg yolk

1 teaspoon pure vanilla extract

Tiny pinch of salt

¼ teaspoon ground cinnamon

2 tablespoons bourbon

1¼ cups heavy whipping cream

½ cup milk

This unique presentation of a buttery and rich bread pudding will have you thinking you are tasting cheesecake—it is that rich and that good. Using a springform pan (or a deep 9-inch quiche pan) dramatically changes the presentation. It is no longer a pudding, but a dense and lovely tart that looks like something you flew home from Paris.

~◊~

Preheat the oven to 350°F. Generously grease a 9- or 10-inch quiche pan or springform pan with 2½- to 3-inch sides. If using a pan with a removable bottom, line with aluminum foil to ensure there is no leakage between the bottom and the sides. Line a baking sheet with parchment paper. Set aside.

For the bread shell, cut the toasted bread slices on the diagonal. Dip the bread slices in melted butter on one side, then dip in the cinnamon sugar. Line the bottom and sides of the pan with the bread, cutting and fitting the pieces to fill all the gaps.

For the filling, combine the sugar, cream cheese, eggs, egg yolk, vanilla, salt, and cinnamon in a large bowl. Whisk briskly to blend, then stir in the bourbon, cream, and milk. Pour into the bread-lined pan. Place the pan on the prepared baking sheet.

Bake for 45 to 55 minutes, or until set. Remove from the oven and transfer to a wire rack. Let cool to room temperature. Refrigerate for at least 2 hours, or until chilled. Unmold onto a plate before serving.

BetterBaking.com Test Kitchen Master Pie Dough

MAKES ONE 9-INCH DOUBLE PIE CRUST OR TWO 9-INCH
SINGLE PIE CRUSTS

2 cups all-purpose flour

1 teaspoon sugar

½ teaspoon salt

¾ cup (6 ounces) cold unsalted
butter, cut into small pieces

4 to 6 tablespoons ice water

2 teaspoons fresh lemon juice

This is my workhouse pie crust recipe, and it comes together in a flash. Use it for any filling and any style, be it a traditional pie with crimped edges, a toney tart, or a pretty quiche. This makes one 9-inch double crust or two 9-inch single crusts. I use it for one double-crusted pie, or freeze one crust; or more often, I double the recipe and freeze the second batch. Pie dough freezes well for 2 months. For a somewhat flakier (but a little less buttery) pie crust I sometimes substitute ¼ cup vegetable shortening for ¼ cup of the butter.

In a food processor, combine the flour, sugar, and salt. Process for 10 seconds to combine. Add the butter and pulse until the texture of coarse meal.

Drizzle in the water and lemon juice. Process for exactly 15 seconds to make a rough ball of dough.

Turn the dough out onto a lightly floured surface. Knead very gently for a few seconds to smooth out the dough, dusting it lightly with flour as necessary to keep it from sticking. Divide the dough in half and form each half into a disk. Place the disks in a self-sealing plastic bag and refrigerate for at least 1 hour or overnight, or freeze for up to 2 months.

DUELING-DOUGH APPLE PIE

MAKES 1 PIE; SERVES 8

Pastry dough for a 9-inch pie crust
(page 225)

2 to 2½ pounds apples, peeled,
cored, and cut into ½-inch
wedges

1 cup sugar, plus more for
sprinkling

2 tablespoons all-purpose flour

½ teaspoon ground cinnamon

¼ teaspoon ground cloves
(optional)

4 sheets frozen filo dough, thawed

⅓ cup (3 ounces) unsalted butter,
melted

*Two kinds of dough give this classic apple pie a new spin: pastry dough for the
bottom, filo dough for the top. Testers proclaimed it a success: pretty to look at and
a delight with tea or coffee. Be sure to use McIntosh, Golden Delicious, or Cortland
apples, or some combination, but do not use Granny Smith.*

Preheat the oven to 400°F. Line a baking sheet with parchment paper.
Set aside.

On a lightly floured surface, roll the dough out into a 12-inch round. Fit
into a 9-inch pie pan, quiche pan, or tart pan and trim the excess dough (see
page 222).

Put the apples in a large bowl. In a small bowl, stir the 1 cup sugar, the
flour, cinnamon, and cloves together. Add to the apples and toss to coat.
Spoon into the pie pan.

Brush a sheet of filo with some of the melted butter and arrange on top of
the apples. Repeat with other sheets. Crimp the excess filo by rolling into a
decorative edge. Make slits in the top of the filo with a paring knife.

Drizzle with the remaining butter and sprinkle generously with sugar.
Place the pie pan on the prepared baking sheet. Bake for 25 minutes. Lower
the oven temperature to 350°F and bake for 15 to 20 minutes, or until the pie
is deeply browned and some apple juices are emitting through the slits. Let
cool on the baking sheet to room temperature.

VARIATION: To top the pie with shredded filo instead, use 2 to 3 cups loosely
packed shredded filo dough, or enough to cover the top of the pie. Sprinkle
the shredded filo on top of the apples.

APPLE-RASPBERRY PATCHWORK CROSTATA

MAKES 1 CROSTATA; SERVES 8 TO 10

PASTRY

2½ cups all-purpose flour

1 tablespoon sugar

½ teaspoon salt

¾ cup (6 ounces) cold unsalted butter, cut into small pieces

1 egg yolk

1 tablespoon fresh lemon juice

4 to 6 tablespoons ice water

FILLING

1½ to 2 pounds sweet apples, peeled, cored, and cut into ¼-inch-thick slices

2 cups fresh or frozen raspberries

1 cup sugar

⅛ teaspoon ground cinnamon

2 tablespoons all-purpose flour

2 tablespoons cornstarch

2 teaspoons balsamic vinegar or fresh lemon juice

1 egg

¼ cup heavy whipping cream

Milk for brushing

1 egg yolk beaten with 2 to 3 tablespoons milk or half-and-half cream

White or coarse sugar for sprinkling

This deep-dish tart features a rich pastry crust filled with mounds of apples and raspberries, then topped with a patchwork of dough. No fiddling with a top crust required, and it produces a unique finish. As in most of my recipes, sweet apples such as McIntosh, Golden Delicious, Pink Lady, and Cortland are best, especially when combined.

~⟨⟩~

Spray a 10-inch springform pan generously with nonstick cooking spray. Line a baking sheet with parchment paper. Set aside.

For the pastry, combine the flour, sugar, and salt in a food processor. Process for few seconds to blend. Add the butter and pulse to the texture of coarse meal. Add the egg yolk, lemon juice, and 4 tablespoons of the ice water. Process to make a soft mass of dough, adding more ice water as needed.

Turn the dough out onto a floured surface and knead briefly until smooth. Pat into a disk. Place in a self-sealing plastic bag and refrigerate for at least 1 hour or up to 3 days.

Preheat the oven to 425°F.

For the filling, combine the apples and raspberries in a large bowl. In a small bowl, stir the sugar, cinnamon, flour, and cornstarch together. Add to the fruit along with the vinegar. Toss to mix. In a small bowl, beat the egg and heavy cream together. Set aside.

On a lightly floured surface, roll the dough out to a 12-inch round. Fit the dough into the pan and trim the dough by using a paring knife or by rolling the rolling pin across the top (see page 222). Place the fruit mixture in the pan. Pour the egg-cream mixture evenly over the fruit.

Roll the excess dough out to ¼ inch thick. Using a serrated pizza cutter or pastry wheel, cut into 2- or 3-inch triangles, squares, or odd shapes.

Brush the edges of the pastry with some milk. Arrange the dough pieces in a patchwork fashion to cover the top surface of the tart completely. Brush with the egg-milk mixture. Sprinkle generously with sugar.

Place the tart on the prepared baking sheet and bake for 30 minutes. Lower the temperature to 375°F and bake for another 15 to 20 minutes, or until the pastry is golden brown and the juices are bubbling. Let cool on a wire rack for 2 to 3 hours before removing from the pan.

DULCE DE LECHE PECAN PIE

MAKES 1 PIE; SERVES 6 TO 8

Pastry dough for a 9-inch pie crust (page 225)

2 cups mixed whole and chopped pecans

1¼ cup homemade dulce de leche or one 14-ounce can prepared dulce de leche (see page 153)

1 cup firmly packed brown sugar

2 tablespoons unsalted butter, softened

3 eggs

¼ cup corn syrup

All you need is a prepared pie dough, dulce de leche filling, and a few pantry basics to create this new, luscious spin on pecan pie. I suggest using a small tart pan, rather than the usual pie plate, to make this gourmet-shop gorgeous.

Preheat the oven to 350°F. Line a baking sheet with parchment paper. Set aside.

On a lightly floured surface, roll the dough out into a 10-inch round. Line a 9-inch tart pan with the dough, trimming off any excess dough using a paring knife or the rolling pin (see page 222).

Distribute the pecans evenly across the tart shell. Combine the dulce de leche, brown sugar, butter, eggs, and corn syrup in a food processor and blend until smooth, about 30 seconds. Pour over the pecans in the pie shell.

Place the pie on the prepared baking sheet and bake for 30 to 35 minutes, or until just set. Transfer to a wire rack and let cool completely. Serve at room temperature or refrigerate for 2 hours to chill. Top with whipped cream or ice cream.

BROWNIE PIE À LA MODE

MAKES 1 PIE; SERVES 8 TO 10

Pastry dough for a 9-inch pie crust
(page 225)

FILLING

1 cup (8 ounces) unsalted butter,
melted

1¾ cups sugar

4 eggs

1 teaspoon pure vanilla extract

¾ cup unsweetened cocoa powder

1 cup all-purpose flour

¼ teaspoon salt

TOPPING

1 quart premium vanilla ice cream

Chocolate syrup or chocolate
sundae topping

Sprinkles or chocolate shavings

It's chocolate, it's ice cream, it's sensational: fudgelike brownie batter in a pie shell. For a shortcut, use brownie mix. This is a great barbecue finale or birthday pie. It stays fresh for days and can be frozen for up to 2 months. Don't you love it when simple is also delicious?

Preheat the oven to 375°F. Line a baking sheet with parchment paper. Set aside.

On a lightly floured surface, roll the dough out into a 12-inch round. Line a 9-inch pie pan or deep quiche pan with the dough. Trim off any excess dough and crimp the edges to form a decorative border (see page 222).

For the filling, combine the butter and sugar in a medium bowl. Whisk to blend. Whisk in the remaining ingredients. Spoon the filling into the pie pan.

Place the pan on the prepared baking sheet. Place in the oven and immediately lower the temperature to 350°F. Bake for 30 to 35 minutes, or until just set. Let cool to room temperature on the baking sheet.

Refrigerate for about 2 hours to chill. To serve, cut into thin wedges and top with ice cream, chocolate sauce, and some sprinkles.

Jenna the Waitress's Strawberry Chocolate Pie

MAKES 1 PIE; SERVES 6 TO 8

1 prebaked 9-inch pastry pie crust (or chocolate cookie crumb crust)

CHOCOLATE FILLING

1½ cups coarsely chopped semisweet chocolate (5 ounces)

¼ cup (2 ounces) unsalted butter

1 package (½ pound) miniature marshmallows

⅓ cup whipping cream

1 teaspoon pure vanilla extract

Extra whipping cream as required

FRESH STRAWBERRY FILLING

2 cups strawberries

4 tablespoons cornstarch

⅓ cup water

⅓ cup sugar

½ teaspoon strawberry or raspberry extract (optional)

1 tablespoon balsamic vinegar

2½ cups strawberries, diced if large, or halved if small

GARNISH

2 cups whipping cream whipped with 3 tablespoons confectioners' sugar

⅓ cup chocolate cookie crumbs

Diced strawberries

A dark and velvety chocolate experience. In the movie Waitress, written by Adrianne Shelley, this pie used a chocolate cookie crumb crust, but I went with a buttery, baked pastry pie crust. It's filled with a luscious, dark, silky chocolate filling and topped with a double strawberry filling. This is a sparkling romantic pie, decadent but with the fluttering of spring. You can make the elements a day ahead and then assemble a few hours before serving.

~•~

In a small saucepan over the lowest heat, slowly melt the chocolate and butter together. Remove from the heat and stir in the marshmallows to melt, then stir in the whipping cream and vanilla. Refrigerate while making the strawberry filling.

For the strawberry filling, crush or mash the 2 cups of strawberries. Combine the cornstarch and water in a small bowl and whisk. In a medium saucepan, heat the crushed berries with the sugar until they start to get a little liquidy. Add the cornstarch mixture and cook until lightly bubbling and thickened. Remove from the heat and stir in the strawberry extract (if using) and vinegar. Cool for 15 minutes, then fold in the fresh strawberries. Refrigerate for 2 hours.

To assemble the pie, spoon the chocolate filling into the pie shell. If the filling is too thick and cold, put it in a food processor and whiz it with some whipping cream drizzled in, until it is soft but not gloppy.

Top with the strawberry filling. Serve the pie with dollops of sweetened whipped cream and dust with chocolate crumbs and diced strawberries. Serve at once or chill for up to 2 days.

CREAM CHEESE–APRICOT TART

MAKES 1 TART; SERVES 8 TO 12

One 7-inch sponge or pound cake, sliced about ¾ inch thick and toasted

FIRST LAYER

1 pound cream cheese

2 eggs

1 (14-ounce) can sweetened condensed milk

1 teaspoon pure vanilla extract

1 tablespoon fresh lemon juice

2 tablespoons all-purpose flour

Pinch of salt

SECOND LAYER

2 cups sour cream

3 eggs

⅓ cup sugar

2 tablespoons all-purpose flour

½ teaspoon pure vanilla extract

TOPPING

1 large can apricot halves, drained

¼ to ⅓ cup apricot jam, warmed and sieved

This is a two-tiered cheesecake that calls for just 1 pound of cream cheese. Smooth, light, and pretty as a picture, it is as good plain as it is garnished with the apricots.

～⟨◊⟩～

Preheat the oven to 350°F. Line a baking sheet with parchment paper. Line a 9-inch springform pan or deep quiche pan with the cake slices, cutting and fitting as necessary. Set aside.

For the first layer, combine all the ingredients in a food processor and process until smooth, about 30 seconds. Pour into the cake-lined pan. Place the pan on the prepared baking sheet and bake for 20 minutes.

Meanwhile, for the second layer, combine all the ingredients in the food processor (no need to rinse) and process for 8 to 10 seconds, or until smooth.

Remove the cake from the oven and pour the second layer of the filling over the first. Return the cake to the oven and bake for 20 to 28 minutes, or until just set. Let cool in the oven for 30 minutes with the oven off and the oven door open completely. Refrigerate for at least 4 hours or as long as overnight.

For the topping, arrange apricot halves over the top, fitting them snugly together to cover the surface completely. Brush with the warmed jam. Let set for 5 to 10 minutes and repeat. Refrigerate for at least 2 hours before serving.

RUGALACH ROUNDUP

. . . .

Rugalach are made of a dough, a filling, and a finishing touch. You can mix and match all of these components, so feel free to experiment. I get a lot of email about rugalach. Someone is always raving about this one or that one, and I am constantly experimenting with ways to make this crescent-shaped pastry. Jewish and Eastern European delicatessens and bakeries all make their own rugalach, but homemade ones are always best. Not only are ingredients optimal, but freshness really counts. Here I offer a few of my favorite fillings and two of my best rugalach doughs. You can make rugalach in miniature crescent shapes or rolled into a jelly roll and then cut in hefty slices.

RUGALACH TIPS

Use a good unsalted butter, as butter is a huge part of what makes rugalach so luscious. Rugalach that are very rich with butter will leak as they bake. This is not a problem. As they cool and crisp, they will be fine.

Some rugalach recipes call for yeast. I have discovered that if you let these rugalach rise, they will taste like a flaky Danish. If you don't let them rise, they will be crisp and pastrylike. Fruit rugalach, for example, are good if you let the pastries rise a bit, whereas walnut or cinnamon ones are better without the rise.

My favorite appliance for making rugalach dough is a large food processor. Pulse to break up the butter, then add all the remaining ingredients to make a soft dough. If your food processor is small, you may have to make half of the dough at a time.

The dough must be refrigerated for at least 1 hour before using, and 2 to 3 hours is better. For pinwheel-style rugalach cut from a log, partially freeze the dough before cutting so that the log does not become misshapen from the force of the knife.

To roll out rugalach, work on a lightly floured surface. For a sugary crisp result, roll the dough on a work surface sprinkled with sugar. (If using this method, use a little less sugar in the filling.)

Rugalach dough can be frozen for 2 to 4 months, wrapped in waxed paper and placed in self-sealing plastic bags. Pastries can also be made up, frozen, and then popped in the oven. Glaze them just before baking. I prefer to bake pastries as required, unless I know I need a few dozen. I usually bake frozen pastries, as opposed to working with the frozen dough, as the former produces a lighter, better pastry.

These buttery pastries need to be baked on a nonstick surface for convenient clean up. Parchment paper seems to have been invented for the job; Silpats are another option (see page 10). Rugalach are very rich pastries, and they can "burn" on the bottom before they brown on the top. To reduce the possibility of overbrowning, bake rugalach on doubled-up baking sheets set on the bottom shelf of the oven.

For extra-flaky rugalach, preheat the oven to 375°F and lower the oven temperature to 350°F as soon as the pastries are slipped into the oven.

HOTEL SCHOOL CREAM CHEESE RUGALACH

MAKES ENOUGH DOUGH FOR 3 TO 4 DOZEN RUGALACH

DOUGH

3 cups all-purpose flour

⅜ teaspoon salt

¼ cup sugar

1 cup (8 ounces) cold unsalted
    butter, cut into small pieces

4 ounces cold cream cheese, cut
    into small pieces

1 egg

¼ cup sour cream

Filling of choice (page 234)

1 egg beaten with a pinch of sugar;
    or melted unsalted butter or
    half-and-half cream

White or coarse sugar for
    sprinkling, if using egg wash

I created this rugalach recipe when I was a pastry-chef-in-training at hotel school, and it is still my favorite. Three very competitive chefs in my class traded their own secret formulas for gâteau St. Honoré, Black Forest cake, and tarte Tatin for this recipe. You may add ½ to 1 teaspoon pure vanilla extract to this dough, but it is quite delicious without it.

For the dough, combine the flour, salt, and sugar in a food processor. Process to blend. Add the butter and cream cheese and pulse until lumpy. Add the egg and the sour cream and process to form a soft dough. Turn out onto a lightly floured surface. Divide into 3 equal portions and pat each portion into a disk.

Place in a self-sealing plastic bag and refrigerate for at least 1 hour or up to 3 days.

Preheat the oven to 375°F. Stack 2 baking sheets together and line the top one with parchment paper. Set aside.

Select a filling. Remove 1 dough disk from the refrigerator (reserve the others for additional batches). On a lightly floured surface, roll the dough out into a 10-inch round. If you are using the apricot-walnut filling, spread the round with the preserves. If you are using the chocolate chip filling, spread the round with the butter. Top with the remaining filling ingredients in the order given, covering the dough's surface as evenly as possible. Alternatively, you can toss the remaining ingredients together and distribute the mixture evenly over the dough. Using a pizza or pastry wheel, score the pastry in 12 wedges. Starting from the outside edge of a wedge, roll toward the center to make a small crescent. Repeat with the remaining wedges. Place the crescents on the prepared baking sheet.

Brush the tops with the egg-sugar wash and sprinkle with sugar. You can instead brush with butter or half-and-half cream—about ½ teaspoon per pastry—and omit the sugar topping.

Bake on the bottom shelf of the oven for 10 minutes. Lower the oven temperature to 350°F and bake for 10 to 14 minutes longer, or until nicely browned. Let cool on the pan for 10 minutes before transferring to wire racks to cool completely.

YEAST RUGALACH: For a buttery, Danish-like rugalach, whisk 1 tablespoon instant yeast with ¼ cup warm water. Make the rugalach dough, adding the yeast mixture after the flour, salt, and sugar are combined. Proceed with the recipe, allowing the 12 shaped crescents 15 to 20 minutes to rise before putting them in the oven.

RUGALACH FILLING WARDROBE

· ·

Here are two of my favorite rugalach fillings. Each recipe fills about one-third of a batch of rugalach dough, or about 12 pastries. Other fillings I use include minced gummi bears, raspberry jam, Nutella spread, sweetened shredded coconut, raisins, shredded apples, and slivers of almond paste. FILLS 12 PASTRIES

CLASSIC APRICOT-WALNUT FILLING

½ cup apricot preserves

⅔ cup ground walnuts

¼ cup sugar

½ teaspoon ground cinnamon

CHOCOLATE CHIP–PECAN FILLING

2 to 3 tablespoons unsalted butter, melted

⅔ (about 4 ounces) cup semisweet chocolate or miniature semisweet chocolate chips, ground in a food processor

¼ cup sugar

1 to 2 tablespoons unsweetened cocoa powder

¾ cup pecans, ground

CHEWY, STICKY CINNAMON STICKS

MAKES 12 LARGE STICKS

DOUGH

1¼ cups warm water

1 tablespoon instant yeast

2 eggs

¾ cup sugar

½ cup (4 ounces) unsalted butter, softened

1 teaspoon pure vanilla extract

⅓ cup nonfat dry milk

1 teaspoon salt

¼ teaspoon ground cinnamon

1 cup all-purpose flour

2 to 3 cups bread flour

FILLING

4 tablespoons (2 ounces) unsalted butter, softened

1 cup sugar

2 teaspoons ground cinnamon

2 cups raisins, plumped and patted dry (see page 18)

½ cup dried sour cherries, plumped and patted dry (see page 18)

1 egg white, beaten until foamy

White or coarse sugar for sprinkling

Take a baker to a bookstore and does she come home with a best-seller? No. Awhile ago, I stopped by a bookstore out west and was bowled over by their cafe's lovely cylinders of cinnamon and sugar, liberally dotted with raisins. They were chewy, dense, and delicious. Here's my version. If you want them puffier, just let them rise longer before baking.

Stack 2 baking sheets together and line the top one with parchment paper. Set aside.

For the dough, hand whisk the water and yeast together in the bowl of an electric mixer and let stand for 2 to 3 minutes for the yeast to dissolve. Whisk in the eggs, sugar, butter, vanilla, dry milk, salt, cinnamon, all-purpose flour, and 2 cups of the bread flour to make a thick dough. Knead with the dough hook on the lowest speed of the mixer for 8 to 10 minutes, gradually adding more bread flour as required to form a soft, elastic dough.

Turn the dough out onto a floured board and form it into a ball. Place in a lightly greased bowl. Place the bowl inside a large plastic bag, close the bag loosely, and let the dough rise for about 45 minutes, or until almost doubled in bulk.

Gently deflate the dough and let it rest for 10 minutes. Preheat the oven to 375°F.

On a lightly floured work surface, roll the dough out to a 20- by 10-inch rectangle. If the dough resists rolling out, let it rest for a few minutes. To add the filling, spread the butter over the dough, then sprinkle with the sugar, cinnamon, raisins, and cherries.

Starting from a short side, roll up the dough into a log and flatten it gently. Cut into 12 equal slices and place them on the prepared baking sheet. Brush with the egg white and sprinkle with sugar. You can also twist them before they rise for a decorative touch. Let rise for 15 minutes.

Bake for 25 to 30 minutes, or until browned. Transfer to wire racks to cool slightly before serving.

SOUR CREAM AND CINNAMON BABKA WITH CRUMB TOPPING

MAKES 2 MEDIUM CAKES OR 1 LARGE CAKE; SERVES 12 TO 16

DOUGH

1½ cups warm water

2 tablespoons instant yeast

3 eggs

1 teaspoon pure vanilla extract

2 drops almond extract

2 teaspoons fresh lemon juice

¾ cup sugar

1 teaspoon salt

⅓ cup nonfat dry milk

1 cup (8 ounces) unsalted butter,
    cut into small pieces and
    softened

3 cups all-purpose flour

2 to 3 cups bread flour

CINNAMON FILLING

4 tablespoons (2 ounces) unsalted
    butter, softened

1 cup firmly packed brown sugar

2 tablespoons corn syrup, maple
    syrup, or honey

2 to 4 teaspoons ground cinnamon

¾ cup chopped walnuts (optional)

CRUMB TOPPING

½ cup confectioners' sugar

½ cup all-purpose flour

4 tablespoons (2 ounces) cold
    unsalted butter

1 egg, beaten

White or coarse sugar for
    sprinkling

A yeasted coffee cake of Eastern European origins, babka is heaven to me because it strikes the right notes of sweet and bready. It's also relatively easy to make. I have a few babka recipes in my first cookbook, and they are among the most requested to this day. I often use my bread machine to make the dough, although I do a quick preliminary mix with a rubber spatula.

~❦~

Line a baking sheet with parchment paper. Generously grease two 9-inch springform pans or two 9- by 5-inch loaf pans. If making one large cake, generously butter a 10-inch tube pan. Set aside.

For the dough, hand whisk the water and yeast together in the bowl of an electric mixer and let stand for 2 to 3 minutes to dissolve the yeast. Stir in the eggs, vanilla and almond extracts, lemon juice, sugar, salt, and dry milk. Add the butter, the all-purpose flour, and 2 cups of the bread flour and continue to stir until the dough forms a rough ball. Let the dough rest for 12 minutes. Knead with the dough hook on the lowest speed of the mixer for 10 to 12 minutes, gradually adding more bread flour as required to make a smooth, elastic dough. Put the dough in a well-greased bowl. Place the bowl inside a large plastic bag, close the bag loosely, and let the dough rise for 45 to 90 minutes, or until puffy. (Or refrigerate the dough overnight, then let it stand at room temperature for 20 minutes before proceeding.) Turn the dough out onto a lightly floured board and divide it in half. Cover the dough with a tea towel and let rest for 10 minutes.

Meanwhile, for the filling, combine the butter, sugar, corn syrup, cinnamon, and walnuts in a food processor. Process to make a loose paste.

For the topping, combine the sugar and flour in a small bowl. Using a pastry cutter, cut in the butter to make a crumbly topping. Set aside.

To make 2 cakes, roll 1 dough piece out into a 16-inch square. Spread evenly with the filling. Roll the dough up into a cylinder and cut it in half crosswise. Place both halves beside each other in a prepared loaf pan or springform pan—it doesn't matter if they are a little squished. Repeat with the second half of the dough. To make 1 large cake, roll all of the dough out into a 20-inch square, spread evenly with the filling, and roll into a cylinder. Place in the prepared tube pan.

Brush with the beaten egg and sprinkle with white sugar. Place the pan(s) in a large plastic bag, close it loosely, and let the dough rise for 45 to 60 minutes, or until it is 1 inch above the top of the pan.

Preheat the oven to 350°F.

Place the pan(s) on the prepared baking sheet and bake for 40 to 55 minutes for 2 cakes, 50 to 70 minutes for 1 large cake, or until browned. Let cool in the pan for 15 minutes before unmolding onto a serving plate.

FLYING SAUCER PASTRIES

MAKES 6 TO 8 PASTRIES

1½ pounds frozen puff pastry,
    thawed

⅓ cup (3 ounces) unsalted butter,
    melted and cooled

½ cup sugar mixed with
    2 teaspoons ground cinnamon

Confectioners' sugar for dusting

Frozen puff pastry, a baker's best—and secret—friend, makes these instantly wonderful. You will need 2 packages of frozen puff pastry, or the equivalent of fresh pastry. For a special treat, drizzle these with melted white, semisweet, or milk chocolate or warmed maple syrup just before serving.

Preheat the oven to 425°F. Stack 2 baking sheets together and line the top one with parchment paper. Set aside

On a floured surface, roll the dough out ⅜ inch thick. Using a 6-inch metal mixing bowl as a template, cut out 5- or 6-inch rounds. Transfer to the prepared baking sheets. Brush each round with melted butter, and dust generously with the cinnamon sugar.

Bake for 15 minutes. Lower the oven temperature to 400°F and bake for 10 to 15 minutes longer, or until puffed and nicely browned.

Let cool on the baking sheet, then dust with confectioners' sugar.

Breton Butter Galette (Kouign Aman)

MAKES TWO 9-INCH GALETTES

1½ cups warm water

2¼ tablespoons instant yeast

1¾ cups sugar

¾ teaspoon salt

3½ cups bread flour

1½ cups (12 ounces) cold salted butter, cut into 1½-inch-thick slices

melted unsalted butter, for brushing

A slice of this galette makes a great breakfast or teatime treat. I had this for the first time at a little local pastry shop called Pâtisserie le Kouign Aman. The generous owner invited me into his production area and shared his method with me (for the complete story, see opposite page). I usually use unsalted butter for baking, but this recipe calls for salted butter in order to reproduce the original flavor. It takes practice to get this just right, but even your first effort will yield something remarkable.

Butter two 9-inch square pans or 9-inch pie pans. Stack 2 baking sheets together and line the top one with parchment paper. Set aside.

In the bowl of an electric mixer, hand whisk the water, yeast, and the 1 teaspoon sugar together and let stand for 2 to 3 minutes to dissolve the yeast. Briskly whisk in the sugar, salt and 3 cups of the flour. Knead with the dough hook on the lowest speed of the mixer for 5 to 8 minutes, adding as much of the remaining flour as required to make a soft dough. Transfer to a lightly floured surface. Form the dough into a ball and place in a lightly greased bowl. Place the bowl inside a large plastic bag, close the bag loosely, and let the dough rise for 45 to 60 minutes, or until about 40 percent puffier.

Turn out the dough onto a lightly floured surface. Roll the dough out into a 10-inch square. Arrange the butter slices over two-thirds of the dough. Fold the dough in thirds, like a letter. Wrap the dough in plastic wrap and refrigerate for 45 minutes.

Sprinkle ¼ to ⅓ cup of the sugar on the work surface. Roll the dough out to a 14- by 17-inch rectangle. Fold in thirds again. Turn the dough clockwise by one-quarter and add more sugar to the work surface. Roll the dough out again and fold in thirds again. Wrap the dough and refrigerate it for 30 minutes. Repeat the rolling and turning process 2 more clockwise turns. What you are doing is distributing the butter equally among several layers of dough. If butter leaks out, pinch the opening with your fingertips. Make sure you have enough sugar handy to keep the work surface well covered. The sugar will caramelize during baking.

Wrap the dough again and refrigerate it for 45 minutes. Divide the dough in half and place each in a prepared pan. Brush the tops with melted butter. Place the pans inside a large plastic bag, close the bag loosely, and let the dough rise for 1 to 2 hours, or until slightly puffy.

Preheat the oven to 400°F.

Place the pans on the prepared baking sheet, place in the oven, and immediately lower the oven temperature to 350°F. Bake for 30 to 40 minutes, or until golden and caramelized. Let cool in the pan or on the baking sheet to room temperature, then unmold and cut into serving pieces

KOUIGN AMAN

. . . .

One day, while strolling in a part of town that is
known for its vintage clothing shops, I happened
upon a vintage pâtisserie, tucked in between a tiny
restaurant and an art shop. There were few items for
sale: two croissants, a pie or two, and some bulbous
crusty rolls. Not much stock, but everything looked
special. The scent of butter permeated the air. On a
large baking sheet were slabs of what appeared to be
crisp crepes. I asked what they were. *"Kouign aman,*
Madame" was the quick reply. I had to ask three times
to get it right! In Breton, *kouign aman* apparently
means "butter bread" or "butter tart." The shop
owner/baker showed me day-old yeast dough. To
this he adds slabs of butter and rolls the dough much
the way you prepare puff pastry. The yeast dough
was combined with sugar to produce a crisp, chewy,
caramelized slab of thinly layered pastry. I asked
about proportions, and the baker kindly showed me
a flour-dusted notebook that contained his recipe. "A
pound of dough, a pound of butter, and some sugar."
Pastry shorthand for "simply delicious."

SWAN LAKE OR PIE DOUGH APPLE CHERRY STRUDEL

MAKES 2 STRUDELS; SERVES 8 TO 12

PIE DOUGH

2 cups all-purpose flour

1 tablespoon sugar

½ teaspoon salt

¼ cup shortening

½ cup (4 ounces) unsalted butter

4 to 6 tablespoons ice water

FILLING

6 cups fresh or frozen sliced apples

1¼ cups sugar

1 teaspoon apple pie spice or
cinnamon

1 tablespoon cornstarch

1 tablespoon fresh lemon juice

½ cup yellow raisins or pitted sour
cherries

TOPPING

1 egg with 1 tablespoon water or
milk

White or coarse sugar for
sprinkling

Confectioners' sugar for dusting

This makes big slabs of hold-together, portable strudel. Use frozen apple slices from the grocer, food-service supply, or Costco for a commercial bakery–style pastry that is homemade-good. Or use a mixture of fresh and frozen, or all fresh. This makes a great-tasting strudel that travels well if you're bringing dessert to an occasion.

~⟨◊⟩~

Prepare the pie dough by pulsing the dry ingredients to blend in a food processor. Add the shortening and butter and pulse to make a mealy mixture. Add the ice water (or more as required) and pulse to make a mass. Turn out the mixture and briefly knead and pat it into a dough. Cover and refrigerate for at least 1 hour, or overnight.

For the filling, toss all ingredients together in a large bowl.

Preheat the oven to 375°F. Stack 2 baking sheets together and line the top one with parchment paper.

For the strudel, divide the dough in half. Roll out a section at a time on a lightly floured board to a make a rectangle of 16 to 18 inches by 14 inches. Place half the apple filling on the end of the dough nearest you, leaving a 2-inch border. Roll up gently, flattening ever so slightly. Place the strudel on the doubled baking sheets. Repeat with the remaining dough and filling. Make slits on top of the strudel logs, brush them with egg wash or milk and sprinkle with sugar.

Bake for 20 minutes. Reduce the heat to 350°F and bake for another 20 to 25 minutes, or until the strudel is golden brown and the filling is beginning to bubble out of the slits. Cool to room temperature before serving. Dust with confectioners' sugar if desired.

CREAM PUFF CAKE

MAKES 1 LAYER CAKE; SERVES 8 TO 10

PASTRY

½ cup milk

½ cup water

1 tablespoon sugar

¾ teaspoon salt

½ cup (4 ounces) unsalted butter,
cut into pieces

1 cup all-purpose flour

4 eggs

1 egg beaten with 1 tablespoon
water

FILLING

1½ cups heavy whipping cream

3 tablespoons confectioners' sugar

½ teaspoon pure vanilla extract

1 package instant vanilla pudding,
prepared and chilled

TOPPING

1 cup confectioners' sugar

2 to 4 tablespoons water

4 ounces semisweet chocolate,
melted

This assembly of choux paste layers makes a giant éclair that looks like a cake but goes together like pastry. A filling of whipped cream and pudding is a shortcut for crème légère, which is usually made with homemade pastry cream. You may forego the topping and simply use melted chocolate.

~⟨०⟩~

Preheat the oven to 450°F. Line three 8-inch round cake pans with rounds of parchment paper. Line 2 baking sheets with parchment paper. Set aside.

For the pastry, combine the milk, water, sugar, and salt in a medium saucepan. Stir to blend. Place over medium heat, add the butter, and stir until melted. Increase the heat and bring to a rolling boil. Stir in all the flour at once. Blend well with a wooden spoon until the mixture forms a ball. Beat vigorously for 1 to 2 minutes. Empty into a bowl and let cool for 5 minutes.

Stirring vigorously with a wooden spoon, beat in the eggs one at a time until the mixture is smooth and glossy. Spoon the paste into a large pastry bag fitted with a ½-inch plain tip and pipe into each prepared pan in a spiral. Brush the paste with the egg mixture. (You may also spread the paste with a small metal spatula or a butter knife.)

Place the pans on the prepared baking sheets and bake for 15 minutes. Lower the temperature to 400°F and bake for another 15 minutes, or until lightly golden. Transfer to wire racks and let cool completely.

For the filling, beat the cream and confectioners' sugar together until soft peaks form. Fold the cream and vanilla into the chilled pudding.

Lay 1 choux paste base out on a platter. Spread with one-third of the filling. Top with the second pastry base and spread another third of the filling. Repeat with the final pastry base and remaining filling. Refrigerate for 2 to 3 hours.

For the topping, whisk the confectioners' sugar and water together in a small bowl to make a thick, but spreadable glaze. Pour or spread, using a metal spatula or knife, over top of cake. Let set. Drizzle the chocolate generously over the glazed cake.

To serve, cut into wedges with a serrated knife.

SIMPLY IRRESISTIBLE CARAMEL ÉCLAIRS

MAKES 3 TO 4 DOZEN SMALL ÉCLAIRS

CHOUX PASTE

1 cup water

½ cup (4 ounces) unsalted butter

1 cup all-purpose flour

1 teaspoon sugar

¼ teaspoon salt

4 eggs

PASTRY CREAM FILLING

½ cup sugar

6 egg yolks

2 tablespoons all-purpose flour

2 tablespoons cornstarch

⅛ teaspoon salt

2 cups milk

1 teaspoon pure vanilla extract

CARAMEL FONDANT

1 cup butterscotch or caramel
    chips

¼ cup (2 ounces) unsalted butter

3 to 4 cups confectioners' sugar

1 tablespoon brewed coffee

1 teaspoon pure vanilla extract

Warm water, as required

Inspired by the movie Simply Irresistible *(another food film on DVD you have to rent), these are luscious little éclairs: delicate but decadent, with a silken pastry cream filling and a unique caramel topping. Bakeries use either commercial coffee-flavored fondant or caramelized sugar. This novel approach gives you the ease of fondant, but with lovely notes of caramel. Make the éclairs small enough to serve two to three per person.*

This choux paste recipe makes about 1 pound of choux pastry (3 to 4 dozen puffs). If you are a novice, try making 1 batch to practice with. Use a ½-inch or ¾-inch plain tip to pipe out 4-inch logs of choux paste.

Preheat the oven to 425°F. Line 2 large baking sheets with parchment paper.

In a medium (3-quart) saucepan over medium heat, combine the water and butter. Once the butter has melted, bring the mixture to a full boil and immediately stir in the flour, sugar, and salt, using a wooden spoon. Stir until all the flour is blended in and the mixture leaves the sides of the saucepan to form a mass. Shuffle the pot briefly on the burner to dry the mixture somewhat. Remove from the heat and place the mixture in a large bowl (if mixing by hand) or in the mixing bowl of an electric mixer or food processor. Allow to cool for about 10 minutes. Then, with the mixer running or while stirring, add the eggs one at a time, blending well after each addition. The mixture should look smooth and glossy after the last egg is added.

Spoon the paste into a pastry bag fitted with a plain tip. Pipe out logs of choux paste onto the prepared baking sheets, about ½ inch thick and 4 inches long. Use a blunt knife dipped in water to separate the dough from the tip of the pastry bag.

Bake until golden brown (18 to 25 minutes). Remove from the oven and slit each cream puff just slightly on one side (to let steam out). Replace the baking sheets in the oven to dry the insides of the pastries. Remove from the oven and let cool in a draft-free place. Proceed with the recipe, or freeze the pastry for later use.

For the pastry cream, mix ¼ cup of the sugar with the egg yolks, flour, cornstarch, salt, and 1 cup of the milk in a small bowl.

In a medium saucepan, heat the remaining 1 cup milk and ¼ cup sugar. As it comes to a boil, whisk in the egg yolk mixture. Let the mixture resume boiling gently. Blend well with a whisk and stir briskly to avoid scorching. Once the mixture thickens, remove it from the heat. Let it stand for 2 or

3 minutes, then stir in the vanilla. Cool the mixture, then cover it tightly with plastic wrap (the wrap should lie directly on the surface of the custard to prevent a skin from forming). Store in the refrigerator until needed. Blend well with a wooden spoon before using to ensure it stays smooth.

For the Caramel Fondant, melt the butterscotch chips with the butter, either in 60-second increments in the microwave, or in a double boiler over simmering water. Stir to melt. Place in a food processor; add the confectioners' sugar, coffee, vanilla, and 2 tablespoons of warm water. Process to blend into a smooth, soft glaze, adding more water a bit at time to achieve the right consistency. You can add more confectioners' sugar if the mixture gets too soft.

To fill the éclairs, using a serrated knife, split the éclairs or cream puffs in half horizontally. Fill each bottom half with the pastry cream. Coat the tops of the éclairs with the Caramel Glaze, using a metal spatula or your fingers, and skimming off excess. Let the glaze set. You can also glaze these with melted chocolate.

VARIATION: Substitute softened ice cream for the pastry cream filling and freeze éclairs until ready to serve.

APPLE-CRANBERRY TART CAKE

MAKES 1 CAKE; SERVES 10 TO 12

Pastry Dough for a 9-inch crust
(page 225)

FILLING

2½ to 3 pounds apples, peeled,
cored, and cut into ¼-inch
slices

¾ cup raisins, plumped and patted
dry (see page 18), then coarsely
chopped (optional)

¼ cup sugar

¼ teaspoon ground cinnamon

½ cup cranberries, coarsely
chopped

VANILLA SAUCE

⅓ cup (3 ounces) unsalted butter,
melted

1 cup sugar

1½ teaspoons ground cinnamon

2 tablespoons all-purpose flour

3 eggs

1½ teaspoons pure vanilla extract

This is the perfect marriage of cake and pastry. Use a blend of soft, sweet apples such as McIntosh, Golden Delicious, or Cortland, and a tart, firm variety such as Granny Smith for the best flavor. This tart must be prepared a day ahead. You may replace the cranberries with blueberries.

Preheat the oven to 375°F. Brush a 10-inch springform pan or deep quiche pan generously with melted butter. Line a baking sheet with parchment paper. Set aside.

On a lightly floured surface, roll the dough out into a 12-inch round. Fit into the pan and, using a paring knife or the rolling pin, trim the excess dough (see page 222).

For the filling, combine all the ingredients in a large bowl. Toss to mix. Spoon into the pan. Cover the top loosely with aluminum foil.

Place the pan on the prepared baking sheet and bake the cake for 30 minutes. Lower the temperature to 350°F, remove the aluminum foil, and bake for 30 minutes longer, or until the apples are soft.

Meanwhile, for the vanilla sauce, combine all the ingredients in a medium bowl. Whisk to blend well.

When all the apples are soft, pour the sauce evenly over the cake, allowing it to permeate. Return the cake to the oven and bake for 20 to 22 minutes, or until deeply golden. Let cool completely on a wire rack, then refrigerate overnight. Remove the cake from the pan to serve.

VARIATION: If desired, the cake can be glazed with warmed apricot jam or dusted with confectioners' sugar.

BLUEBERRY AND SOUR CREAM CAKE

MAKES 1 CAKE; SERVES 8

PASTRY

1⅓ cups all-purpose flour

½ cup sugar

1½ teaspoons baking powder

¼ teaspoon salt

½ cup (4 ounces) cold unsalted
  butter, cut into small pieces

1 egg

FILLING

2 cups sour cream

½ cup sugar

2 egg yolks

½ teaspoon pure vanilla extract

2 cups fresh or frozen blueberries

Confectioners' sugar for dusting

This dessert cuts like a cake, tastes like a pastry, is as pretty as a tart, and is easy as pie. The pastry, because it has baking powder in it, tastes like a hybrid of pastry and cake. The filling is somewhere between cheesecake and custard pie. Sumptuous!

Lightly coat a 9-inch tart pan or deep quiche pan with nonstick cooking spray. Line a baking sheet with parchment paper. Set aside.

For the pastry, combine the flour, sugar, baking powder, and salt in a food processor. Process to blend. Add the butter and pulse to the texture of coarse meal. Add the egg and process until a soft dough forms. Pat the dough into a disk and place it in a self-sealing plastic bag. Refrigerate for 30 minutes.

Preheat the oven to 350°F. On a lightly floured surface, roll the dough out into a 12-inch round. If the dough breaks or is hard to roll, simply patch by hand as evenly as possible. Fit it into the prepared pan and, using a paring knife or the rolling pin, trim the excess dough (see page 222). Refrigerate the pan for 15 minutes.

For the filling, whisk the sour cream, sugar, egg yolks, and vanilla together in a medium bowl. Gently fold in the berries. Place the pan on the prepared baking sheet and pour the filling into the pan. Bake for 35 to 45 minutes, or until just set.

Let cool in the pan on a wire rack for 1 hour. Refrigerate for at least 4 hours or up to overnight. To serve, gently unmold the cake and set on a serving platter. Dust with confectioners' sugar.

MY BAKLAVA

SERVES 12 TO 16

PASTRY

2 packages (1 pound *each*) frozen
   filo dough, thawed

½ cup vegetable oil

1¼ cups (10 ounces) unsalted
   butter, melted

4 cups mixed ground almonds and
   walnuts

SYRUP

1 cup sugar

¾ cup water

½ cup honey

1 tablespoon fresh lemon juice

1 teaspoon ground cinnamon
   (optional)

Homemade baklava is usually much more flavorful than commercial versions, as it is generally fresher and more redolent with honey and butter. Either ground almonds or walnuts may be used; I often use a combination for the best flavor. Filo (or phyllo) dough is a pastry dough, but it is not easy to make at home. Keep a package or two in your freezer for a rainy day. It's extremely versatile, and commercial varieties yield great results.

Preheat the oven to 375°F. Brush a 9- by 13-inch baking pan with butter. Line a baking sheet with parchment paper and set aside.

Place the filo sheets near your work area and cover with a very damp kitchen towel. Stir the oil into the butter.

Using the 9- by 13-inch pan as your guide, cut the filo sheets to fit the pan. Begin layering the filo sheets, brushing each generously with the butter mixture as you go. After 6 to 8 sheets, sprinkle about ¼ cup ground nuts over the surface. Continue layering the sheets this way, sprinkling with nuts and ending with filo, until all the filo and nuts are used. Brush the final layer with the butter mixture. Make some steam vents in the top with a paring knife.

Place the baklava in the oven and bake for 20 minutes. Lower the oven temperature to 350°F and bake for 40 minutes longer, or until the pastry is golden brown.

Meanwhile, for the syrup, combine all the ingredients in a medium saucepan and cook, stirring, over medium heat until the sugar dissolves. Bring to a boil and cook for about 5 minutes, or until the mixture registers 220°F on a candy thermometer. Let cool to room temperature. Pour the cooled syrup evenly over the hot baklava. Let stand for 1 hour.

Using a very sharp knife, cut the pastry into diamond shapes by cutting 5 or 6 horizontal rows, then cutting diagonally across these rows.

Chapter 8

· ·

THE CAKE WALK

· ·

PEOPLE HAVE BEEN BAKING CAKES for millennia, and recipes from antiquity abound. Though cake may not have bread's wholesome reputation, it trades instead on its association with all things celebratory. Where there's a cake, there's likely to be a party close by.

Some people have a fear of cake and think it too rich, too filling, or across-the-board decadent, regardless of the recipe. But whether it's a simple pound cake or an elaborate chocolate layer cake, there are times when only cake will do—to mark an occasion, to end a perfect meal, or to reward yourself for almost any reason.

In this collection, I have an incredible range of cakes, from cheesecakes to a three-milk cake from Latin America to a unique twisted honey cake. Some are certainly extravagant, but they are all remarkably easy to make. Here are cakes for all the special occasions in your life, and all are guaranteed crowd pleasers.

CAKE TRICKS AND POINTERS

· ·

All ingredients should be at room temperature. A cold batter, made with cold eggs and cold butter, has to work harder to rise properly.

I use plain white granulated sugar for most test baking. If you want an even more tender crumb, try using superfine sugar for your cake baking. It is simply a more finely granulated white sugar, and is found in the baking aisles of supermarkets or through mail order. Superfine sugar dissolves more rapidly and keeps a cake moist and tender. If you can't find it, simply pulverize regular granulated sugar in your food processor for 20 to 30 seconds.

Generally, cake flour is not necessary, but you may wish to use it for very tender butter cakes. If you prefer cake flour, make sure you stir it before measuring to aerate it. This is how I measure all flour for my recipes, but it is especially important for cakes. Too much flour can change a delicate cake into a heavy one. You would not notice an extra bit of flour as much in a hearty, moist carrot cake, but you will in a lighter cake. Because flour is aerated, sifting is not necessary. Do whisk your dry ingredients together to make sure they are evenly combined before stirring them into the batter.

Cutting the fat into the flour before liquids are added (called the British method) coats the flour and helps prevent it from asserting its tougher nature. I don't typically use this procedure, but you may wish to experiment with it. To do so, cut the flour and butter together, as you would for making biscuits or pie dough, then continue with the recipe.

Use large, not extra-large, eggs. As for all baking, but particularly for delicately flavored cakes, use unsalted butter unless otherwise stated in the recipe.

Use pure vanilla extract. With cakes, I often resort to double-strength pure vanilla simply because I am partial to an assertive vanilla taste. You can experiment as you like. If you do not have double-strength on hand, double the amount of regular vanilla extract.

Always place your cake pan or pans on a parchment-lined baking sheet to protect the bottom and ensure even baking.

If your cakes rise unevenly, your oven's air flow might be erratic. To remedy this, turn the cake once during baking for more even results.

CHEESECAKE 101

Cheesecake is the belle of the ball, the cake with whom everyone wants to dance. Although it is a glamour puss with instant "wow" appeal, cheesecake is not difficult to make, but it does require special handling. Here are some tips.

Cheesecake can be made with ricotta cheese, cottage cheese, and even tofu, but the classic texture relies on pure cream cheese. Look for fresh cream cheese. Avoid commercial products that contain additives. Eggs, unless otherwise specified, should be large; in some recipes, but particularly with cheesecakes, extra-large eggs can upset the balance of the recipe. The sugar content can be reduced by 10 to 20 percent without compromising the final product. You can tailor cheesecakes to your taste by adding sour cream, whipping cream, preserves, nuts, or liqueurs in small amounts.

All ingredients should be at room temperature, especially the cream cheese and eggs. This allows for the proper incorporation of the eggs and will ultimately result in the best texture and volume. Properly creaming the cheese with the sugar and eggs is another must. Add the eggs one by one. The batter should be as homogenous as possible, and you should take care to scrape the sides and bottom of the container every so often during mixing to make

sure there are no thick globs of cream cheese stuck somewhere in the batter.

Springform or cheesecake pans with a removable bottom allow the chilled cake to be properly unmolded. Experience tells me that the cake rises higher if you allow the delicate batter to cling to ungreased sides.

You can use a food processor, hand beater, or hand whisk to make cheesecakes, but a stand mixer is best. A few cheesecakes are better made in a processor, but for the most part, I recommend stand mixers. A stand mixer is stable, and the bowl is ample for roomy mixing, whereas a food processor cannot always accommodate a large amount of batter. Cheesecake batters, especially, need sufficient blending, and stand mixers are up to the job. Stand mixers are powerful, but you should resist the temptation to mix on the highest speed, using the lowest instead.

There are three ways to avoid cracks in cheesecakes. The first method, and the one I prefer, involves cooling the cake gradually by turning off the oven after baking and letting the cake rest in the oven for 1 hour. The cake is then cooled further at room temperature. The second method involves refrigerating the baked cake immediately. Many bakers see this as heresy, but it works. The third method is to bake the cheesecake in a water bath: cover the outside of the pan twice over with aluminum foil to prevent leaks. Place a large roasting pan in the oven and add ¾ inch water. Place the filled cake pan in the water bath.

Regardless of baking technique, a cheesecake should be refrigerated for at least 8 hours and ideally 24 hours before a topping is added. Aside from canned fruit fillings, you can use fresh fruit, nut-crunch toppings, a chocolate glaze, and so on. Grand desserts need fine finishing touches.

Cutting should be performed carefully, using a long knife dipped in hot water and cleaned before each cut. You may also cut the cake using unwaxed dental floss held tautly across the cake. Simply lower the dental floss through the cake and pull it away, much like using a wire to cut through potter's clay. Either method yields perfect cake portions. Most cheesecakes freeze well, but they should be frozen without a topping. The topping is best applied just prior to serving.

BLACK TOP COOKIE CHEESECAKE

MAKES 1 CHEESECAKE; SERVES 16 TO 18

CRUST

1¼ cups finely chopped Oreo
    cookie crumbs (about
    8 cookies)

¼ cup firmly packed brown sugar

Pinch of ground cinnamon

4 tablespoons (2 ounces) unsalted
    butter, melted

CAKE

2 pounds cream cheese at room
    temperature

1¼ cups sugar

¼ cup all-purpose flour

4 eggs

2 egg yolks

⅓ cup heavy whipping cream

1½ teaspoons pure vanilla extract

1½ cups coarsely chopped Oreo
    cookies (about 10 cookies)

SOUR CREAM TOPPING

2 cups sour cream

¼ cup sugar

1 teaspoon pure vanilla extract

CHOCOLATE GLAZE

1 cup heavy whipping cream

8 ounces semisweet chocolate,
    chopped

1 teaspoon pure vanilla extract

6 Oreo cookies, pulled apart

This striking dessert features vanilla cheesecake studded with Oreo cookies and slathered with a smooth-as-silk chocolate ganache. No wonder it became famous (see accompanying story on page 252).

~⟨◊⟩~

Preheat the oven to 425°F. Line a baking sheet with parchment paper and set aside.

For the crust, combine all the ingredients in a 9- or 10-inch springform pan or cheesecake pan with a removable bottom. Toss with a fork to blend, then press into the bottom and slightly up the sides of the pan.

For the cake, in the bowl of an electric mixer fitted with the paddle attachment, blend the cream cheese on the lowest speed until smooth. One at a time, add the sugar, flour, eggs, egg yolks, cream, and vanilla, blending well after each addition and stopping occasionally to scrape the sides and bottom of the bowl.

Pour half of the batter into the prepared pan. Sprinkle with the coarsely chopped Oreos. Top with the remaining batter. Place the cake on the prepared baking sheet.

Bake for 15 minutes, then lower the oven temperature to 225°F and bake for another 50 minutes, or until just set. The cake will be wobbly in the center but set around the edges. Do not allow it to brown. Remove from the oven. Increase the oven temperature to 350°F.

For the sour cream topping, stir all the ingredients together in a medium bowl. Using a small metal spatula, gently spread the topping over the cake.

Return the cake to the oven and bake for 8 minutes to set the topping. Turn the oven off, open the oven door completely, and let the cake cool for 1 hour. Cover the cake loosely with aluminum foil and refrigerate for 8 hours or as long as overnight.

For the glaze, put the cream in a small saucepan and bring to a gentle boil. Stir in the chocolate, whisking constantly until smooth. Remove from the heat and stir in the vanilla. Let cool, then refrigerate.

To decorate the cake, unmold the cake onto a platter. Warm the chocolate glaze to a pourable consistency. Spread or pour the glaze onto the chilled cake. Let the excess pool around the bottom or scoop it off and reapply on the top.

Arrange 12 Oreo cookie halves around the outer perimeter.

OREO CHEESECAKE, OR MY TRIAL BY CHEESECAKE

Early on in the start of my culinary career, I ran my own business, Cuisine d'Or, and was a specialty cake caterer. One of my best clients, a local dessert restaurant aptly called Calories, implored me to make a cheesecake that no customer could resist and that would make them the talk of the town. I created an Oreo cheesecake, figuring the fusion of a commercial classic with cheesecake would prove a best-seller. I was right, and in time, I became known in the restaurant trade for this decadent cake. I invested in crates and crates of Oreo cookies to keep up with the demand, cursing all the while since the cakes cost almost as much to make as their sale price.

At the time, I had rented a bakery with another pastry chef, Jean-Claude Frappier, who was also providing specialty pastries for upscale hotels in the city. An accomplished and very competitive colleague, he came from the hallowed halls of French cuisine. I was self-trained at that point (I later graduated as a professional pastry chef), and suffice it to say, we were an odd pairing. Jean-Claude often viewed my work with a combination of envy and disdain. I viewed his with envy and disbelief.

"How could she make Oreo cheesecake? How gauche," I would hear him say under his breath. "How many cream puffs can anyone eat?" I would quietly mutter back. It was a war of the whisks, a collision of cultures in the kitchen.

One day, exhausted from having baked day in, day out for five days, I wearily placed Oreo cakes and plain vanilla cheesecakes in the oven. I neglected to sprinkle cookie "dust" (Oreo crumbs) on the Oreo versions (in order to distinguish them from my classic California and New York cheesecakes). Once the cakes were cooled and chilled, I realized I didn't know which to garnish with chocolate cream and cookies, and which to adorn with strawberries. There were 60 cakes! I was aghast, reeling from the lost effort and ingredients. There was no way I could put fresh berries on a cake chock full of chopped-up chocolate sandwich cookies!

Jean-Claude casually glanced up from his choux pastry station, sipped his espresso (which he carefully brewed every day), and actually offered to help me. "*Tiens*, mademoiselle," he said, as he skewered a cake tester into the cakes, bringing out a cake-crumb laden stick smeared with dark and cheesy crumbs. "When it comes out white, that's a plain *gâteau*. When you see these dirty crumbs, that's your *affaire* Oreo." He returned to his espresso, and I resisted hugging him in relief.

I was grateful to Jean-Claude for his rescue and ingenious tactic, but he really had no use for my *affaire* Oreo, and he wasn't too gracious about it. Nevertheless, the Oreo cakes always sold out very quickly, as did his Black Forest tortes, and my colleague and I retained a grudging respect for each other in the days that followed the incident. We never did become the long-lost sister-and-brother act of pastrydom, but in time he even forgave me (though he may not have forgotten) for having jammed his 60-quart Hobart mixer on my first day in the bakery, breaking the unit and forcing him to whip some 80 quarts of heavy whipping cream for his napoleons by hand. I did manage to have the mixer rewelded at an overnight garage, but not before Jean-Claude suffered a bad case of tendonitis (and I learned some choice French expletives).

A couple of months after that fateful day, the owner of Calories informed me that *Bon Appétit* magazine had requested my Oreo cheesecake recipe. I was in heaven. Fame and fortune were at my door! Good-bye dirty dishes, hello Hollywood! I thought. (Not really, but it was a thrill.) When the recipe ran in the magazine, I framed the column, and later, I went on to be a contributor to *Bon Appétit*. My first feature was, fittingly, a collection of my 12 favorite recipes for cheesecake. I was very proud of that article and remember it vividly. I was newly pregnant at the time with my first son, and testing cheesecake was making me rather queasy. Nonetheless, I made it through, and the cakes were lovely, but of course, none was as memorable as the Oreo.

One day, I received a letter from the Nabisco people, who asked me to stop using the name Oreo unless it was clearly identified as a registered trademark. I was known in the food press, and now I was known in the biscuit boardroom! I complied with the request, of course, and I was flattered to see that Nabisco eventually produced their own recipes for consumer and commercial versions of Oreo cheesecake. It may not seem so exotic now, but it's an inspired creation than I'm proud of, and it still makes me smile each time I make the recipe or see versions of my first prototypes in restaurants.

TUXEDO JUNCTION CHEESECAKE

MAKES 1 CHEESECAKE; SERVES 12 TO 18

CRUST

1½ cups graham cracker crumbs

¼ teaspoon ground cinnamon

¼ cup firmly packed brown sugar

4 tablespoons (2 ounces) unsalted butter, melted

CAKE

2 pounds cream cheese at room temperature

1¼ cups sugar

3 tablespoons all-purpose flour

Tiny pinch of salt

2 teaspoons pure vanilla extract

1 teaspoon grated lemon zest

¼ teaspoon lemon oil or extract (optional)

5 eggs

2 egg yolks

⅓ cup heavy whipping cream

SOUR CREAM TOPPING

2 cups sour cream

½ teaspoon pure vanilla extract

2 tablespoons sugar

CHERRY TOPPING

1 (19-ounce) can sour cherries

2 tablespoons cornstarch

½ cup sugar

¼ teaspoon almond extract

2 teaspoons fresh lemon juice

1 cup slivered almonds, toasted, for garnish (see page 17), optional

One of my favorite website features honored Ken Burns's PBS series on jazz in America. For one of the photos I used my elder son's tenor saxophone as a prop to highlight a plate of New Orleans–style beignets, a pot of chicory-infused coffee, and my tasty Tuxedo Junction Cheesecake, which takes its name from the jazz standard. I had so much fun just naming the recipes! Everyone needs one classic cheesecake, and this is mine. It calls for a water bath, a technique that makes for an exceptionally creamy texture.

Preheat the oven to 450°F. Line a baking sheet with parchment paper. Place a roasting pan on the baking sheet and add up to ¾ inch water. Place this in the oven. Wrap 2 layers of aluminum foil around the outside of a 10-inch springform pan or cheesecake pan with a removable bottom.

For the crust, combine all the ingredients in the prepared pan. Toss to blend, then press into the bottom and slightly up the sides of the pan.

For the cake, in the bowl of an electric mixer fitted with the paddle attachment, blend the cream cheese with the sugar on the lowest speed until smooth. One at a time, add the flour, salt, vanilla, lemon zest, lemon oil, eggs, egg yolks, and cream, mixing until smooth after each addition and stopping occasionally to scrape the sides and bottom of the bowl.

Pour into the prepared pan. Place the pan in the water bath in the preheated oven. Bake for 15 minutes, then lower the temperature to 300°F and bake for another 35 to 40 minutes. The cake should jiggle only in the center, and it should barely be browned.

Meanwhile, for the sour cream topping, combine all the ingredients in a small bowl and stir to blend. Set aside.

Remove the cake from the oven and increase the oven temperature to 350°F. Spread the sour cream topping over the cake and bake the cake for another 8 minutes. Turn the oven off and leave the oven door partially open. Let the cake sit in the oven for 1 hour. Cover the cake loosely with aluminum foil and refrigerate for at least 8 hours or as long as overnight.

For the cherry topping, drain the cherries and reserve the liquid. In a small bowl, stir 4 tablespoons of the cherry liquid into the cornstarch. In a small saucepan, combine the remainder of the reserved cherry liquid, the sugar, almond extract, and lemon juice. Cook over medium heat until it begins to bubble. Whisk in the cornstarch mixture and cook until the mixture thickens. Remove from heat, stir in the cherries, and let cool. Refrigerate for at least 45 minutes, or until needed.

To decorate the cake, unmold it onto a serving platter. Brush some of the cherry topping liquid onto the cake sides to use as a glue. Press the slivered almonds onto the sides. Spread the remaining cherry topping on top of the cake.

Taking a Stand on Mixers

When it comes to mixers, I am unabashedly fond of KitchenAid stand, or heavy-duty, mixers. They have stood the test of time, and they are simply the best you can buy. The KitchenAid family line goes back to the founding of the Hobart Manufacturing Company in the early 1920s. Hobart, a leading commercial food-service equipment supplier, introduced an 80-quart commercial dough mixer in 1915. A few years later, the company introduced a domestic mixer: the KitchenAid model H (H for *hefty*, perhaps? It weighed 65 pounds). Several other models followed, and the one we know best today is the model K. It was introduced in the mid-1930s, and its exterior design, recognized by the Industrial Designers Society of America, has remained virtually unchanged since then. The innards are another story, of course; many improvements have been made, and the mixer's capacity, as well as its powerful motor, make it a solid investment for any baker. Even the pros usually have a domestic-sized KitchenAid in their bakeshops. Incidentally, the original model K retailed for $55, which is about the price of one of its attachments today! Other superb mixer choices include the Viking, Cuisinart, or Kenwood Rival mixers.

RASPBERRY SUNDAE CHEESECAKE

MAKES 1 CHEESECAKE; SERVES 14 TO 20

CRUST

1¼ cups shortbread cookie crumbs

¼ cup sugar

Pinch of ground cinnamon

¼ cup (2 ounces) unsalted butter, melted

CAKE

2½ pounds cream cheese at room temperature

1 (14-ounce) can sweetened condensed milk

⅔ cup sugar

¼ cup all-purpose flour

6 eggs

⅓ cup whipping cream

2½ teaspoons pure vanilla extract

1 cup raspberry preserves, preferably seedless

2 cups miniature marshmallows

1 cup white chocolate chunks

SOUR CREAM TOPPING

1¼ cups sour cream

1 teaspoon pure vanilla extract

3 tablespoons confectioners' sugar

FINISHING TOUCHES

½ cup raspberry preserves, preferably seedless, warmed

1 pint fresh raspberries

Apricot jam, warmed, to glaze

½ cup marshmallow fluff or white chocolate, warmed, for drizzling

I love marshmallows with anything and raspberries anytime. This is a gorgeous, creamy, New York–style cheesecake, with hunks of white chocolate, marshmallow cream, and a ribbon of raspberry preserves floating through a cheesecake dream. It's finished with yet more raspberries and a stippling of white chocolate and/or warm marshmallow fluff. It's like a raspberry sundae, only better—it's pretty enough to serve as a knockout dessert. It also won't melt away like a sundae, but it does vanish pretty quickly.

~❖~

Preheat the oven to 375°F. Mix together the crust ingredients and pat into a 10-inch springform pan.

Cream the cheese in an electric mixer on the lowest speed until smooth. Blend in the condensed milk, then the sugar and flour. Add the eggs, cream and vanilla and blend on slow speed until smooth, scraping the bottom and sides of the bowl often.

Pour half of the batter into the pan. Spread on half of the raspberry preserves and swirl a bit with a knife or fork. Add half of the marshmallows and swish them around. Cover with the remaining batter, white chocolate chunks, and add the remaining preserves and marshmallows, swirling with a fork again to marbleize the batter and immerse the marshmallows in the cheesecake.

Place the cheesecake carefully in the water bath. Bake for 15 minutes at 375°F, then lower the oven temperature to 350°F and bake another 50 minutes.

Meanwhile, for the Sour Cream Topping, combine the sour cream, vanilla, and confectioners' sugar. Spread on the cake and bake another 12 minutes.

Turn the oven off. Open the oven door and let the cake cool in the oven for 1 hour before removing. Cover the cake lightly with plastic wrap and refrigerate overnight.

For the Finishing Touches, before serving (or several hours earlier), warm the raspberry preserves and brush them on the cake surface. Then place fresh raspberries in concentric circles and brush them with warmed apricot preserves. Drizzle or stipple with warmed marshmallow fluff or melted white chocolate.

DULCE DE LECHE CHEESECAKE

MAKES 1 CHEESECAKE; SERVES 14 TO 16

CRUST

1½ cups ground shortbread cookies

¼ cup firmly packed brown sugar

2 tablespoons blanched almonds, toasted and finely ground (see page 17)

4 tablespoons (2 ounces) unsalted butter, melted

CAKE

2¾ pounds cream cheese

1 cup plus 3 tablespoons homemade dulce de leche (page 153) or 1 (14-ounce) can prepared dulce de leche

½ cup firmly packed brown sugar

2 teaspoons pure vanilla extract

1 or 2 drops almond extract

1 tablespoon rum (optional)

4 eggs

¼ cup heavy whipping cream

Tiny pinch of salt

3 tablespoons all-purpose flour

TOPPING

1½ cups sour cream

½ teaspoon pure vanilla extract

2 tablespoons confectioners' sugar

⅓ cup homemade or prepared dulce de leche for garnish

With its luscious caramel flavor, this is perfect party fare. If you are as fond of dulce de leche as I am, also check out Tango Cookies (page 153) and Dulce de Leche Pecan Pie (page 228).

Preheat the oven to 350°F. Line a baking sheet with parchment paper and set aside.

For the crust, combine all the ingredients in a 10-inch springform pan or a cheesecake pan with a removable bottom. Toss to blend, then press into the bottom of the pan.

For the cake, in the bowl of an electric mixer fitted with the paddle attachment, blend the cream cheese on the lowest speed until smooth. One at a time, add the dulce de leche, brown sugar, vanilla and almond extracts, rum, eggs, cream, salt, and flour, blending well after each addition and stopping occasionally to scrape down the sides and bottom of the bowl.

Pour into the prepared pan and place pan on the prepared baking sheet. Bake for 20 minutes, then lower the oven temperature to 325°F. Bake 15 to 20 minutes longer, or until set all over. Remove from the oven. Increase the temperature to 350°F.

For the sour cream topping, stir all the ingredients together in a medium bowl. Spoon gently over the cake.

Return the cake to the oven and bake for 5 to 7 minutes. Turn the oven off, open the oven door completely, and let the cake cool for 1 hour. Refrigerate for 30 minutes, then cover the pan with aluminum foil and refrigerate for at least 8 hours or as long as overnight.

To garnish, heat the dulce de leche in a small saucepan over low heat until warmed. Pour in a spiral design on top of the cake. Using a wet paring knife, pull lines from the innermost point of the spiral to the sides to create a spiderweb design.

APPLE-DAPPLE DUTCH CHEESECAKE

MAKES 1 CHEESECAKE; SERVES 12

CRUST

1 cup graham cracker crumbs

¼ cup ground walnuts

⅓ cup firmly packed brown sugar

1 teaspoon ground cinnamon

4 tablespoons (2 ounces) unsalted
butter, melted

CAKE

2 pounds cream cheese at room
temperature

1 cup firmly packed brown sugar

⅓ cup all-purpose flour

4 eggs

2 egg yolks

1½ teaspoons pure vanilla extract

Pinch of ground nutmeg

Pinch of ground cinnamon

⅓ cup heavy whipping cream

SOUR CREAM TOPPING

2 cups sour cream

2 tablespoons firmly packed brown
sugar

APPLE TOPPING

½ cup firmly packed brown sugar

4 tablespoons (2 ounces) unsalted
butter

1½ pounds Golden Delicious or
Braeburn apples, peeled, cored,
and cut into ¼-inch-thick slices

¼ cup apple cider or juice

4 teaspoons cornstarch mixed with
¼ cup water

This is a luxurious apple cheesecake I made for a local dessert store called Calories. It is especially nice at Thanksgiving when you are pied-out, or serve it at a midwinter Sunday brunch, or just any old time apples are ripe and plentiful.

Preheat the oven to 425°F. Line a baking sheet with parchment paper. Set aside.

For the crust, combine all the ingredients in a 10-inch springform pan or a cheesecake pan with a removable bottom. Toss to blend, then press into the bottom and slightly up the sides of the pan.

For the cake, in the bowl of an electric mixer fitted with the paddle attachment, blend the cream cheese on the lowest speed until smooth. One at a time, add the brown sugar, flour, eggs, egg yolks, vanilla, nutmeg, cinnamon, and cream, blending well after each addition and stopping to scrape the sides and bottom of the bowl.

Pour into the prepared pan and place the pan on the prepared baking sheet. Bake for 15 minutes, then lower the oven temperature to 225°F and bake for 50 minutes longer, or until the cake is slightly wobbly in the center but set and not browned on the edges. Remove from the oven. Increase the temperature to 350°F.

For the sour cream topping, stir the sour cream and brown sugar together in a medium bowl until smooth. Using a small metal spatula, gently spread the topping over the cake.

Return the cake to the oven and bake for 8 minutes. Turn the oven off, open the oven door completely, and let the cake cool for 1 hour. Cover the cake loosely with aluminum foil and refrigerate for at least 8 hours, or preferably overnight.

For the apple topping, combine the brown sugar and butter in a large pot. Cook over medium heat to melt the butter and dissolve the sugar a bit, about 3 minutes. Stir in the apples and cook for 3 to 5 minutes, or until soft. Stir in the apple cider and then the cornstarch mixture and cook over low to medium heat for about 2 minutes, or until the topping has thickened and is the consistency of apple pie filling. Remove from the heat and let cool for 30 minutes, or refrigerate until needed.

Unmold the cake onto a platter and spread with the apple topping.

CHEESECAKE ON A STICK

GRAHAM CRACKER CRUST

1½ cups graham cracker crumbs

½ cup firmly packed light brown sugar

⅓ cup (3 ounces) unsalted butter, melted

1 teaspoon pure vanilla extract

CHEESECAKE

5 (8-ounce) packages cream cheese at room temperature

¾ cup sugar

1 (14-ounce) can sweetened condensed milk

¼ cup all-purpose flour

Pinch of salt

5 eggs

2 egg yolks

¼ cup whipping cream

1 tablespoon pure vanilla extract

Wooden Popsicle or lollipop sticks, as required

MELTED CHOCOLATE COATING

1 to 2 pounds chocolate, finely chopped (see sidebar)

Shortening or unsalted butter, as required

FINISHING TOUCHES

Graham cracker crumbs, chopped nuts, colored sprinkles, crushed peppermints, mini chocolate chips, sanding sugars

These extra-creamy cheesecake wedges with their chewy, buttery-sweet graham crust get the cold shoulder in the freezer. This recipe can also be made into cheesecake "pops" or truffle-sized cheesecake sweets, which are perfect for a party or anytime you need to impress on a smaller scale. For variations, you could use a dulce, chocolate, or marble cheesecake as your base, and vary the coatings and finishing touches. Not only is this recipe easy, it lasts in the freezer for many months, so you'll have a creamy treat whenever you need it.

~◊~

Preheat the oven to 325°F and position the oven rack in the middle of the oven.

If you are making wedges, make the graham cracker crust by combining all the ingredients in a 9- or 10-inch springform pan. Toss to blend, then press into the bottom of the pan.

If you are making cheesecake "pops" instead of wedges, make only half the graham mixture and set it aside to roll the pops in. To prepare the pan for the cheesecake, simply spray a 9- or 10-inch springform pan with nonstick baking spray. Line the bottom with a circle of parchment paper

In the bowl of an electric mixer or a large food processor, blend the cream cheese, sugar, condensed milk, flour, and salt until smooth. Add the whole eggs and the egg yolks, one at a time, beating well at low speed after each addition. Beat in the cream and vanilla.

Spoon the batter into the cake pan. Bake until the cheesecake is firm and slightly golden on top, 65 to 90 minutes.

Let the cheesecake cool in the oven with the door open for 1 hour. Then allow it to come to almost room temperature. Cover the cheesecake with plastic wrap and refrigerate it until very cold, at least 6 hours or overnight.

For wedges, cut the cheesecake into 12 to 16 wedges and stick a Popsicle stick two-thirds of the way into each wedge. Freeze the cake a few hours or overnight. For cheesecake pops or truffles, when the cheesecake is cold and very firm, scoop the cheesecake into 2-ounce balls and place them on a parchment paper–lined baking sheet. Carefully insert a lollipop stick into each cheesecake ball. Freeze the cheesecake pops, uncovered, until very hard, at least 1 to 2 hours.

CONTINUED ON NEXT PAGE

CONTINUED FROM PREVIOUS PAGE

When the cheesecake wedges or pops are frozen and ready for dipping, melt the chocolate in a double boiler set over simmering water, or in 1-minute increments in the microwave. For every 8 to 12 ounces of chocolate, stir in 1 to 2 tablespoons of shortening or unsalted butter.

Dip a frozen cheesecake wedge or pop in the melted chocolate, swirling quickly to coat it completely. Shake off any excess. While the chocolate is still wet, sprinkle on the nuts or other finishing touches. Once the chocolate sets a bit, you can re-dip half the wedge or pop into another sort of melted chocolate (white into dark, or milk chocolate into white or dark), or drizzle it with another melted chocolate.

Gently place the cheesecake sticks on a baking sheet, lined with parchment paper. Before storing the cheesecake wedges or pops, spread out a paper muffin liner to create a pastry holder and place the cheesecake wedge or pop on it. Refrigerate for up to 3 days or freeze for up to 3 to 4 months. If the cheesecake is frozen, remove it from the freezer about 30 minutes before serving.

MELTING CHOCOLATE

The chocolate for the coating can be white, milk, or dark chocolate, or a combination, but all should be excellent-quality melting chocolate. Don't use coating, couverture, or confectioners' chocolate. These come in wafers or disks and melt but do not offer adequate chocolate taste (since they are not pure chocolate). For white chocolate, Callebaut melts well (in a double boiler or a bowl over steaming water). If it seizes up, add a few teaspoons of vegetable shortening.

TIRAMISU CHEESECAKE

MAKES 1 CHEESECAKE; SERVES 12 TO 14

ESPRESSO SYRUP

4 teaspoons instant espresso
   powder or finely ground
   instant coffee

⅓ cup water

¼ cup sugar

2 tablespoons coffee liqueur

CAKE

12 to 16 ladyfingers

1 pound cream cheese at room
   temperature

8 ounces mascarpone cheese at
   room temperature

⅔ cup sugar

1 teaspoon pure vanilla extract

1 tablespoon orange liqueur
   (optional)

4 eggs

2 egg yolks

⅓ cup heavy whipping cream

TOPPING

½ cup (4 ounces) unsalted butter

½ cup sugar

2 teaspoons brewed espresso or
   double-strength brewed coffee

16 to 20 ladyfingers, quartered
   crosswise

Confectioners' sugar or ⅓ cup
   semisweet chocolate shavings
   for dusting

Tiramisu, also known as Tuscan trifle, was created in the Siena region of Tuscany. Like many Italian dishes, it was created in honor of an illustrious fellow, in this case the Grand Duke Cosimo de'Medici III. The original recipe called for custard, but Italian triple-cream cheese now stands in.

If you like tiramisu, you'll love my Tiramisu Cheesecake. I created it because it is more stable than most tiramisu, which last only a day or so in the refrigerator. This cake has the character of the classic that inspired it, but can be prepared a few days in advance for a party. Espresso powder is available in some gourmet shops, or you can pulverize regular instant coffee to a fine texture. Use ladyfingers that are thick, not thin and crisp. If you do not have mascarpone on hand, you can substitute an equal amount of cream cheese or Neufchâtel.

~⟨◊⟩~

Preheat the oven to 350°F. Lightly spray a 9-inch springform pan or a cheesecake pan with a removable bottom with nonstick cooking spray. Line a baking sheet with parchment paper. Set aside.

For the espresso syrup, stir the coffee, water, and sugar together in a small saucepan. Heat just to dissolve the sugar, about 2 minutes. Remove from heat and let cool to room temperature. Stir in the liqueur.

For the cake, arrange the ladyfingers in the prepared pan, cutting or trimming as needed to line the bottom. Brush the espresso syrup over the cookies and allow it to soak in. Reapply until all the syrup is used. In the bowl of an electric mixer fitted with the paddle attachment, blend the cheeses and sugar together on low speed until smooth. One at a time, add the vanilla, orange liqueur, eggs, egg yolks, and cream, blending well after each addition and stopping occasionally to scrape the sides and bottom of the bowl. Pour over the prepared crust.

For the topping, melt the butter with the sugar over low heat in a small saucepan. Briskly whisk in the coffee. Pour into a medium bowl. Toss the quartered ladyfingers with this mixture. Arrange the coffee-infused ladyfingers on top of the cake.

Bake for about 35 to 40 minutes, or until just set all over. Let cool partially and refrigerate for at least 6 hours or as long as overnight. Unmold and dust with confectioners' sugar or shaved chocolate.

STICKY TOFFEE CHEESECAKE

MAKES 1 CHEESECAKE; SERVES 14 TO 18

STICKY TOFFEE TOPPING

¾ cup (6 ounces) unsalted butter

2 cups firmly packed light brown
sugar

1½ cups whipping cream

CRUST

1½ cups shortbread cookie crumbs

5 tablespoons unsalted melted
butter

¼ cup firmly packed dark brown
sugar

¼ cup dates

Tiny pinch each of ground cloves,
nutmeg, and cinnamon

CHEESECAKE FILLING

2½ pounds cream cheese, softened

1½ cups sugar

¾ cup whipping cream

⅓ cup sour cream

6 eggs

1 tablespoon pure vanilla extract

3 tablespoons all-purpose flour

As if cheesecake wasn't over the top already! Why not add sticky toffee sauce and whole chunks of Sticky Toffee Cake? (See page 266 for the variation, pictured.) For a chilled cake, this is one hot number. Although sticky toffee cakes hail from Down Under, the gooey toffee flavor atop creamy cheesecake is too good to keep from this hemisphere.

For the Sticky Toffee Topping, place the butter, brown sugar, and cream in a small saucepan. Simmer for 20 to 30 minutes, until thickened and sticky. Cool to room temperature or refrigerate until needed.

Meanwhile, for the crust, place the cookie crumbs, butter, brown sugar, dates, and spices in a food processor and pulse to mince the dates finely and create a clumpy mixture. Press into a 9-inch springform pan.

Preheat the oven to 425°F. Line a baking sheet with parchment paper and place the pan on it.

For the filling, in the bowl of an electric mixer, blend the cream cheese and sugar until smooth. Add the whipping cream, sour cream, eggs, vanilla, and flour and blend well until the mixture is smooth and no unmixed bits of cream cheese are stuck in the bottom.

Drizzle a few tablespoons of the Sticky Toffee Topping on the crust, spreading it thinly to coat the bottom. Spoon the cheesecake batter on top. Refrigerate the remainder of the topping. Bake for 45 to 55 minutes, or until the top is just set. Remove from the oven and refrigerate for at least 8 hours, or overnight.

To serve, unmold the cake onto a serving platter. Spoon on the reserved sticky toffee topping (if it is very thick, warm it up on low heat). Offer additional sauce on the side.

VARIATION: This is the simpler approach to this cake—this filling doesn't include the chunks of Sticky Toffee Cake. If you want to include them, the recipe is on the next page along with the directions to make this a Sticky Toffee Chunk Cheesecake (pictured). The choice is yours.

STICKY TOFFEE CAKE

MAKES 1 SMALL CAKE TO USE IN THE STICKY TOFFEE CHEESE-
CAKE (PAGE 265), OR SERVES 6 TO 8 AS A CAKE ON ITS OWN

¾ cup pitted dates

¾ cup water

¼ teaspoon baking soda

⅓ cup (3 ounces) unsalted butter

½ cup firmly packed light brown
    sugar

2 tablespoons white sugar

1½ teaspoons pure vanilla extract

1 egg

1 cup all-purpose flour

½ teaspoon baking powder

Pinch of salt

If you want to make the over-the-top version of Sticky Toffee Cheesecake (page 265), you will need one batch of this Sticky Toffee Cake. This is baked and then cut into small chunks and folded into the Sticky Toffee Cheesecake. It's up to you; the cake is divine with or without it, but I personally am partial to chunks of good things in cheesecake—it makes for added visual impact. Of course, if you forget the cheesecake and just want a great snacking cake, stop at this recipe and go no further.

Preheat the oven to 350°F. Line a baking sheet with parchment paper. Spray an 8- or 9-inch square cake pan or an 8- by 11-inch brownie pan with nonstick cooking spray and line the bottom with parchment paper. Place the pan on the baking sheet.

In a medium saucepan, simmer the dates in the water until they are softened and almost dissolved into a mush. Remove from stove and stir in the baking soda (the mixture will foam a bit). Cool well.

In a medium mixing bowl, cream the butter with both sugars and the vanilla until well blended. Blend in the egg, and then fold in the flour, baking powder, and salt. Turn into the prepared pan and bake until the cake is just set and springs back when touched, about 35 to 40 minutes. Once it is cooled, freeze it while preparing the cheesecake. When ready to use, cut into medium-sized chunks. Fold into the cheesecake batter (see page 265) after the vanilla is folded in.

TENDER 'N' GOLD BUTTER CAKE

MAKES 1 LOAF CAKE; SERVES 8

¾ cup sugar

½ cup (4 ounces) unsalted butter, softened

1 tablespoon corn syrup

2 tablespoons fresh lemon juice

1 teaspoon pure vanilla extract

3 eggs

1 cup cake flour, or 1 scant cup all-purpose flour

2 tablespoons nonfat dry milk

½ teaspoon baking powder

¼ teaspoon salt

Pinch of ground nutmeg

This recipe is a favorite from a feature I did about my spins on popular commercial foods. I also call this my nobody-doesn't-like-this cake, which is a nod to an ad campaign the Sara Lee Company ran years ago. This is as delicate a pound cake as you are likely to find. The sugar is pulverized in a food processor to make it superfine.

Preheat the oven to 325°F. Line the bottom and sides of a 7- by 3-inch foil loaf pan or 8- by 4-inch metal loaf pan with parchment paper and then spray with nonstick cooking spray. Line a baking sheet with parchment paper. Set aside.

Put the sugar in a food processor and process for 20 to 30 seconds. Add the butter and process until fluffy. With the machine running, add the corn syrup, lemon juice, vanilla, and the eggs one at a time. Blend until smooth. In a medium bowl, combine the flour, dry milk, baking powder, salt, and nutmeg. Whisk to blend. Gradually add to the wet ingredients and blend until smooth, stopping the machine to scrape down the sides of the container as necessary.

Spoon the batter into the prepared pan and place the pan on the prepared baking sheet. Bake for 50 to 60 minutes, or until the cake is lightly browned and springs back when lightly touched. Let cool in the pan on a wire rack for 10 minutes, then unmold onto the wire rack and let cool completely.

B.B.
Test Kitchen Notes

Don't Judge an Egg by Its Cover

As long as I can remember, there has been a popular belief that brown eggs are more nutritious than white eggs. Not so. It simply comes down to a matter of pigment. Lately, the choice among eggs has become more complicated. There are free-range eggs, high-omega-3 eggs, hand-raised eggs, happy eggs, and even green eggs (see page 304). If you make frequent use of egg whites, try the Eggology product or Burnbrae Farm products (see page 300), which I use often to make egg-white omelets, macaroons, and amaretti.

GUYS AND DOLLS THREE-MILKS CAKE

MAKES 1 SHEET CAKE OR ROUND CAKE; SERVES 8 TO 10

CAKE

½ cup (4 ounces) unsalted butter, softened

1 cup sugar

5 eggs

1 teaspoon pure vanilla extract

1½ cups all-purpose flour

1¼ teaspoons baking powder

¼ teaspoon salt

⅓ cup milk

SYRUP

1 cup sweetened condensed milk

1 cup evaporated milk

1 cup whole milk

1 tablespoon light rum (optional)

Whipped cream and kiwifruit, peach, and strawberry slices for garnish

I explored variations on milk ingredients for my Alfajores cookies (page 153), and now I'm hooked. Tres leches cake is popular with Costa Ricans and Nicaraguans, among others. It's a rich yellow cake that is soaked after it's baked. The result is like a combination cake, pudding, and cheesecake. One slice of this rum-kissed delight will remind you of the line from Guys and Dolls *that refers to a milk and rum drink: "What a wonderful way to get children to drink their milk!"*

Preheat the oven to 350°F. Lightly butter a 9- by 13-inch cake pan or a 10-inch springform pan. If using a springform pan, wrap the outside tightly with 2 sheets of aluminum foil to prevent any leakage. Line a baking sheet with parchment paper. Set aside.

In the bowl of an electric mixer fitted with the paddle attachment, cream the butter and sugar together on low speed until light and fluffy. Beat in the eggs and vanilla. In a medium bowl, combine the flour, baking powder, and salt. Whisk to blend. Add to the wet ingredients and blend well. Then beat in the milk until smooth, stopping to scrape the sides and bottom of the bowl.

Spoon the batter into the prepared pan and place the pan on the prepared baking sheet. Bake for 28 to 32 minutes, or until the cake springs back when gently touched. Let cool in the pan on a wire rack for 20 minutes, then unmold onto the wire rack and let cool completely.

For the syrup, combine all the ingredients in a medium bowl. Stir to blend. Pour the syrup evenly over the cake. Refrigerate for at least 3 hours or as long as 3 days. To serve, cut into squares or slices and top with a dollop of whipped cream and sliced fruit.

BANANA CAKE WITH CHOCOLATE FROSTING

MAKES 1 BUNDT OR TUBE CAKE; SERVES 12 TO 16

CAKE

½ cup (4 ounces) unsalted butter, softened

½ cup oil

1¾ cups sugar

4 eggs

1½ teaspoons pure vanilla extract

1 tablespoon very strong brewed coffee

3¼ cups all-purpose flour

1 tablespoon baking powder

½ teaspoon baking soda

½ teaspoon salt

Pinch of ground cinnamon

1 cup buttermilk

1½ cups banana puree (about 3 ripe bananas)

FROSTING

4 ounces milk chocolate, chopped

⅓ cup half-and-half cream

2 tablespoons unsalted butter, softened

½ teaspoon pure vanilla extract

2 to 3 cups confectioners' sugar

3 to 6 tablespoons water

If you are attracted by this recipe, you're probably one of those people who is always on the lookout for a better banana cake. (Did you know that bananas can be frozen, whole and unpeeled, until needed?) This cake is fine-grained, light, and moist, not the typical heavy, hearty banana cake meant for the lunch box (though, of course, you can tuck a slice in one). I also make banana muffins out of this batter.

Preheat the oven to 350°F. Generously spray a 12-cup Bundt pan or a 10-inch tube or angel food cake pan with nonstick cooking spray. Line a baking sheet with parchment paper and set aside.

In the bowl of an electric mixer fitted with the paddle attachment, cream the butter, oil, and sugar together on low speed until light and fluffy. Add the eggs one at a time, then the vanilla and coffee. In a medium bowl, combine the flour, baking powder, baking soda, salt, and cinnamon. Whisk to blend. Set aside. Add the buttermilk to the butter mixture, then gradually add the dry ingredients and banana puree. Mix for 2 to 3 minutes, or until smooth, stopping occasionally to scrape the sides and bottom of the bowl.

Spoon the batter into the prepared pan and place it on the prepared baking sheet. Bake for 70 to 80 minutes, or until the cake springs back when gently pressed. Let cool in pan on a wire rack for 15 minutes, then unmold onto the wire rack or a serving plate and let cool completely.

For the frosting, combine the chocolate and cream in a small saucepan. Place over low heat to melt the chocolate, stirring until smooth. Pour into the bowl of an electric mixer fitted with the whisk attachment and beat in the butter, vanilla, and confectioners' sugar on low speed. Add the water, a tablespoon at a time, as needed to reach a spreadable consistency. Spread on the top and sides of the cooled cake.

THE UNDERGROUND BAKER'S SECRET-FORMULA CARROT CAKE

MAKES 1 CAKE; SERVES 10 TO 12

CAKE

1¼ cups vegetable oil

2¼ cups sugar

4 eggs

2 teaspoons vanilla extract

1 tablespoon fresh lemon juice

¼ teaspoon orange oil

2½ cups all-purpose flour

2½ teaspoons baking powder

½ teaspoon baking soda

¼ teaspoon salt

1½ teaspoons ground cinnamon

¾ cup walnuts, coarsely chopped

1 tablespoon grated orange zest

½ cup sweetened shredded
    coconut

2 cups firmly packed shredded
    carrots (about 3 carrots)

½ cup canned crushed pineapple,
    drained

½ cup golden raisins, plumped and
    patted dry (see page 18)

ICING

8 ounces cream cheese at room
    temperature

1 tablespoon unsalted butter,
    softened

1 tablespoon fresh lemon juice

½ teaspoon vanilla extract

1 teaspoon grated lemon zest

1 teaspoon grated orange zest

3 to 4 cups confectioners' sugar

Shredded carrot, ground walnuts,
    and ground cinnamon for
    garnish

At one time, I was baking 200 of these cakes every week and delivering them to cafes and restaurants around Montreal. This is the cake that launched the baker who is behind BB. So, for me, it will never be "just another carrot cake." If you're using off-season carrots (which likely have sat in storage), add a grated apple to the mixture for a bit more moisture and flavor.

Preheat the oven to 350°F. Generously spray a 10-inch tube pan or a 9-inch angel food cake pan with nonstick cooking spray. Line a baking sheet with parchment paper and set aside.

For the cake, whisk the oil, sugar, and eggs together in a large bowl. Stir in the vanilla, lemon juice, and orange oil. In a medium bowl, stir the flour, baking powder, baking soda, salt, and cinnamon together. Stir into the wet ingredients until blended. Stir in the nuts, orange zest, coconut, carrots, pineapple, and raisins until well blended.

Spoon into the prepared pan and place the pan on the prepared baking sheet. Bake for 60 to 70 minutes, or until the cake springs back when gently pressed. Let cool in the pan on a wire rack for about 30 minutes, then unmold onto the wire rack and let cool completely.

For the icing, whisk the cream cheese and butter together in a medium bowl. Stir in the lemon juice, vanilla, and both zests. Stir in enough confectioners' sugar to make a thick icing.

Spread the icing over the cake. Sprinkle the center with shredded carrot and then sprinkle ground walnuts and a touch of cinnamon over the carrot.

VARIATION: To layer the cake (as pictured at right), slice the cake horizontally into 4 equally thick disks. Spread icing between each of the layers and garnish the top with shredded carrot and ground walnuts and dust with cinnamon.

MOIST AND MELLOW YELLOW BIRTHDAY CAKE OR CUPCAKES

MAKES 1 LAYER CAKE OR SHEET CAKE, OR 24 CUPCAKES;
SERVES 8 TO 10

2 cups sugar

¾ cup (6 ounces) unsalted butter, softened

3 eggs

1 teaspoon pure vanilla extract

½ cup warm water

½ cup warm milk

2¾ cups all-purpose flour

2 tablespoons cornstarch

1 tablespoon baking powder

⅜ teaspoon salt

Master Brownie Frosting (page 118) or Pastry Chef's Trade-Secret Buttercream (opposite) for icing

At the BB website, I receive many requests for the perfect birthday cake. We always want to bake something special for those we love. This one comes pretty close to perfection: moist, light, golden, and wonderful when iced.

Preheat the oven to 350°F. Generously spray two 8- or 9-inch round cake pans with nonstick cooking spray. Line the bottom of each pan with a round of parchment paper. You can also use a 9- by 13-inch pan, or line 2 dozen muffin cups with paper liners and grease the tops of the pans. Line 2 baking sheets with parchment paper. Set aside.

Put the sugar in a food processor and process for 20 to 30 seconds. Add the butter and process until fluffy. Add the eggs one at a time, processing in between, then add the vanilla, water, and milk and process to blend. In a medium bowl, combine the flour, cornstarch, baking powder, and salt. Whisk to blend. Gradually add the dry ingredients to the wet ingredients and process until smooth, stopping occasionally to scrape the sides of the container. Blend for 2 to 3 minutes, or until smooth.

Pour the batter into the prepared pan(s) and place on the prepared baking sheets. Bake the round cakes for 25 to 35 minutes, the large cake for 35 to 45 minutes, and the cupcakes for 18 to 25 minutes, or until the cakes spring back when gently pressed. Let cool in the pan(s) on a wire rack for 15 minutes, then unmold onto the wire rack and let cool completely. Ice the top and sides of the cooled cake or the tops of the cupcakes.

B.B. Test Kitchen Notes

Secret Tip for Extra-Moist Cake

All white or yellow birthday-style cakes profit from being brushed with a simple syrup before they are frosted. Simmer ½ cup water with ½ cup sugar for 2 to 3 minutes, and then cool. Brush over exposed cake surfaces and let set before icing. This will guarantee an extra-moist birthday cake.

PASTRY CHEF'S TRADE-SECRET BUTTERCREAM

MAKES 2 TO 3 CUPS, ENOUGH TO FROST 2 TO 3 DOZEN
CUPCAKES, DEPENDING ON SIZE; 1 LARGE LAYER CAKE; OR
2 SHEET CAKES

1 pound white fondant

1½ cups (12 ounces) unsalted
butter, softened

½ cup vegetable shortening

1 to 2 teaspoons pure vanilla
extract

½ to 1 teaspoon coffee liqueur,
orange oil, or almond, lemon,
or maple extract to taste

Food coloring of choice (optional)

Don't you just loathe gritty confectioners' sugar–based icing? Nothing is so cloyingly sweet and as troublesome to spread on a cake. Pastry chefs rely on a fondant-based buttercream that is a lovely change from typical icings. Ask your neighborhood baker or pastry chef for fondant (beg, plead, promise scones), check a cake decoration store, or try a mail-order source (fondant lasts forever)—see the Source Guide, page 301. This is the silky icing that everyone loves and associates with store-bought cupcakes. You can also use warmed fondant to drizzle or smear on homemade cinnamon buns.

~⟨◊⟩~

In the bowl of an electric mixer fitted with the paddle attachment, combine the fondant, butter, and shortening. Blend on low speed for 3 to 4 minutes, or until smooth.

Switch to the whisk attachment and whip on the highest speed for 5 to 7 minutes, or until light, fluffy, and voluminous. Add the vanilla, liqueur, and food coloring and whip on medium speed for 1 minute to combine.

Use immediately, cover and refrigerate for up to 1 week, or freeze for up to 2 months. Before using chilled buttercream, let sit at room temperature for 30 minutes, then beat for 2 to 3 minutes, or until fluffy.

MAJESTIC CINNAMON-RIPPLE YELLOW CAKE

MAKES 1 TUBE CAKE; SERVES 14 TO 16

1½ cups (12 ounces) unsalted butter, melted

2½ cups sugar

6 eggs

1 tablespoon pure vanilla extract

¼ teaspoon orange oil or extract

4 cups all-purpose flour

5 teaspoons baking powder

½ teaspoon baking soda

½ teaspoon salt

1¼ cups fresh orange juice or milk

2 to 2½ teaspoons ground cinnamon for sprinkling

2 to 4 tablespoons white or coarse sugar for sprinkling

2 to 4 tablespoons confectioners' sugar for dusting

In my first cookbook, you will find Majestic Honey Cake, so named because it stands high in size and in flavor. Visitors to the website often implore me to create other cakes with a similar lofty attitude. Yellow and rippled with cinnamon, this one is just as majestic. The inspiration came from a cake I tasted at a high-school bake sale. A Greek grandmother had made about a dozen of these high-standing cakes, and I had to have one. Price tag: $6. Taste: priceless.

Preheat the oven to 350°F. Generously spray a 9-inch tube pan or angel food cake pan with nonstick cooking spray. Line a baking sheet with parchment paper. Set aside.

In the bowl of an electric mixer fitted with the paddle attachment, combine the butter, sugar, eggs, vanilla, and orange oil. Blend on low speed until smooth. In a medium bowl, combine the flour, baking powder, baking soda, and salt. Whisk to blend. Gradually add the dry ingredients to the wet ingredients and process until smooth. Add the orange juice and blend, stopping occasionally to scrape the sides and bottom of the bowl.

Spoon one-third of the batter into the prepared pan and sprinkle with some of the cinnamon. Repeat the layering. Finish the top of the cake with cinnamon and white sugar. Place on the prepared baking sheet. Bake for 65 to 75 minutes, or until the cake springs back when gently pressed. Let cool completely in the pan on a wire rack, then unmold. Dust with confectioners' sugar.

BUTTERSCOTCH BREAD

MAKES 1 CAKE; SERVES 8 TO 10

CAKE

½ cup (4 ounces) unsalted butter

1⅓ cups firmly packed brown sugar

2 eggs

2 teaspoons pure vanilla extract

2 cups all-purpose flour

1 teaspoon baking powder

½ teaspoon baking soda

¼ teaspoon salt

1 cup buttermilk

PENUCHE FUDGE FROSTING

½ cup (4 ounces) unsalted butter

1 cup firmly packed brown sugar

⅓ cup whipping cream

This is really more of a brown sugar cake than a bread, but butterscotch bread sounds far more interesting. It is a light, moist cake tasting deeply of caramel, with a thin sludge of brown butter fudge topping. This is a one-layer pan cake that makes a nice change from chocolate. It keeps well but never lasts a day.

Preheat the oven to 350°F. Line a 9-inch layer cake pan with a circle of parchment paper. Spray with nonstick cooking spray and place on a parchment paper–lined baking sheet.

In the bowl of an electric mixer, cream the butter and brown sugar until light and fluffy. Add the eggs and vanilla and blend well. Fold in the flour, baking powder, baking soda, and salt and, as it mixes, add the buttermilk. Blend to make a smooth batter and then spoon into the prepared pan.

Bake for 30 minutes, then reduce the oven temperature to 325°F and bake until done, another 15 to 20 minutes. The cake should spring back when gently pressed and peak in the middle. Cool in the pan.

For the penuche frosting, gently simmer the butter, brown sugar, and whipping cream together until the mixture thickens and reaches the soft ball stage, about 7 to 12 minutes. Remove from the stove and beat with a wooden spoon for 2 to 4 minutes, until it loses its luster and thickens. Spread on the cake while the frosting is still warm. It will set like a coating of fudge.

WORLD'S BEST CLASSIC DEEP-DISH APPLE CAKE

MAKES 1 CAKE; SERVES 12 TO 16

FILLING

18 to 24 large McIntosh apples, peeled, cored, and quartered

⅓ cup sugar

2½ –3 tablespoons ground cinnamon

1 tablespoon fresh lemon juice

BATTER

1 cup corn oil or canola oil

2½ cups sugar

5 eggs

4 teaspoons pure vanilla extract

3 cups all-purpose flour

3¼ teaspoons baking powder

½ teaspoon salt

Confectioner's sugar for dusting

For years, my mother-in-law made a deep-dish apple cake. She gave me the recipe and although I followed it to the letter, my cake, while good, never looked like hers. I overhauled it from the bottom up—and voilà! I now have the apple cake of my dreams, and you can too. This apple cake is big and bold and exploding with apples (in fact, the batter is almost an afterthought). The recipe takes an impossibly large amount of apples—they should overflow the pan before you add the batter. It also takes ages to bake through—about 90 minutes—but just bake it slowly and let it brown nicely, keeping an eye on it.

Preheat the oven to 350°F. Spray a 9- by 13-inch baking pan with nonstick cooking spray. Line a baking sheet with parchment paper.

Prepare the apples and place them in a large bowl. Toss with the sugar, cinnamon, and lemon juice and set aside. In a large bowl, hand whisk the oil and sugar, then add the eggs and vanilla. Fold in the flour, baking powder, and salt to make a very gloppy batter that is thick but not firm.

Place the apples in the prepared baking pan. They should cover the pan quite generously, and pretty well overflow it—apples should be just about falling out of the pan. If you find you need more apples, now is the time to prepare and add more to the pan. Pour the batter as evenly as you can over the apples. Shuffle the pan a few times. The batter will settle more during baking.

Place the pan on the prepared baking sheet and bake for 60 to 90 minutes (it varies, depending on how juicy the apples are), or until the cake is set and slightly browned on top. The cake may be a bit mushy, with so many apples in it, but there should not be raw batter in the center. If you are concerned about the outer edges burning, lower the oven temperature to 325°F for the last third of the baking time.

Let the cake cool well before cutting. Dust with confectioners' sugar if you like. This cake can be made 2 to 3 days ahead, but it does not freeze well.

TRIPLE TWISTED HONEY CAKE

MAKES 2 TUBE CAKES

YELLOW BATTER

1¼ cups vegetable oil

2½ cups white sugar

6 eggs

2 teaspoons vanilla extract

¼ teaspoon orange oil

1 cup milk or water

4 cups all-purpose flour

4 teaspoons baking powder

½ teaspoon salt

CHOCOLATE BATTER

1 cup (8 ounces) unsalted butter, melted

1½ cups white sugar

¾ cup firmly packed brown sugar

3 eggs

2 teaspoons vanilla extract

1¾ cups warm brewed coffee

¾ cup unsweetened cocoa

3 cups all-purpose flour

2½ teaspoons baking powder

1 teaspoon baking soda

½ teaspoon salt

HONEY BATTER

1 cup vegetable oil

1 cup honey

1½ cups white sugar

½ cup firmly packed brown sugar

4 eggs

1 cup strong brewed tea

½ cup fresh orange juice

3½ cups all-purpose flour

4 teaspoons baking powder

½ teaspoon baking soda

4 teaspoons ground cinnamon

½ teaspoon each salt, ground cloves, and ground allspice

This recipe is a twist on the honey cake tradition, combining three classic concepts—yellow cake, fudge cake, and honey spice cake—to produce a new but instant classic cake that always brings raves. The recipe yields 2 cakes, each with a terrific tiger-stripe swirl. Freeze one for later use, or give it to a friend. You can also keep it wrapped on the counter for up to a week, for easy slicing.

Preheat the oven to 350°F. Generously spray two 9- or 10-inch angel food cake pans with nonstick cooking spray. Set aside.

For the yellow batter, combine the oil, sugar, eggs, vanilla, and orange oil in a food processor. Process to blend. Add the milk and process for 30 to 45 seconds, until smooth. In a medium bowl, combine the flour, baking powder, and salt. Whisk to blend. Gradually add the dry ingredients to the wet ingredients and process until smooth, stopping to scrape the sides of the container as necessary. Transfer the batter to a large bowl.

Without cleaning the food processor, repeat the process to make the chocolate batter and the honey cake batter and put each in a separate bowl.

In the prepared cake pans, layer the chocolate, then the yellow, and then the honey cake batter. You can swirl the batters slightly with a butter knife or leave as is. Dust the tops with sugar. Bake for 65 to 75 minutes, or until the cakes spring back when gently touched. Let cool in the pans on wire racks for 20 to 30 minutes, then unmold and let cool completely.

COLA CUPCAKES

MAKES 2 DOZEN CUPCAKES

1¾ cups all-purpose flour

2 cups sugar

¾ cup unsweetened cocoa powder

1 teaspoon baking soda

2 teaspoons baking powder

⅛ teaspoon salt

1 teaspoon pure vanilla extract

2 eggs

½ cup vegetable oil

1 cup flat cola

1 cup buttermilk or warm brewed coffee

Master Brownie Frosting (page 118) or Pastry Chef's Trade-Secret Buttercream (page 273) for frosting

These terrific dark chocolate cupcakes, based on a vintage chocolate cake recipe, are perfect for any occasion. No creaming is required, and they are easily made by hand. The recipe can be doubled and tripled with perfect results. I often freeze bags of these, unfrosted. When I want to serve the cupcakes, I frost them while they are still frozen; the airy cake thaws very quickly, in about 20 minutes.

Preheat the oven to 350°F. Line two 12-cup muffin pans with paper liners and grease the tops of the pans. Line 2 baking sheets with parchment paper. Set aside.

In a large bowl, combine the flour, sugar, cocoa, baking soda, baking powder, and salt. Whisk to blend. Whisk in the vanilla, eggs, oil, cola, and buttermilk until thoroughly smooth. This is a thin batter.

Pour into the prepared muffin cups, filling them three-fourths full. Place the pans on the prepared baking sheets and bake for 25 to 30 minutes, or until the cupcakes are slightly puffed in the center and spring back when gently touched. Let cool in the pans on wire racks for 15 minutes, then unmold onto the wire racks and let cool completely before frosting.

OLD-FASHIONED PIE TIN CRUMB CAKE

MAKES 1 CAKE; SERVES 6 TO 8

1½ cups all-purpose flour

¾ cup white sugar

⅓ cup firmly packed brown sugar

1½ teaspoons baking powder

½ teaspoon baking soda

⅛ teaspoon salt

½ cup (4 ounces) unsalted butter

1 teaspoon ground cinnamon

⅛ teaspoon grated fresh nutmeg

2 eggs

1 teaspoon pure vanilla extract

1 cup plain yogurt or soured milk*

* Put 1 tablespoon of lemon juice in a measuring cup and then pour in milk to measure 1 cup. Allow it to stand while assembling the recipe. The milk will curdle or sour.

A little crumb cake that is meltingly tender (the yogurt helps) and full of pure vintage goodness. The crumb topping is made as part of the batter (you'll see; it all works out!) for a quick coffee cake that is just the right size to disappear in two days or less. It's baked in a pie tin and slices into neat wedges of wholesome cake, perfect for tea and coffee time.

Preheat the oven to 350°F. Line a baking sheet with parchment paper and spray a 9-inch pie tin with nonstick cooking spray. Place the tin on the baking sheet.

In a food processor, blend the flour, both sugars, baking powder, baking soda, and salt together briefly. Add the butter and pulse to make fine crumbs. To make the topping, remove ½ cup of the crumbs to a small bowl and stir in the cinnamon and nutmeg. Set aside.

To the remaining crumbs in the food processor bowl, add the eggs, vanilla, and yogurt and blend to make a thick batter.

Spoon the batter into the prepared pie tin and sprinkle on the reserved crumb topping. Bake for 40 to 50 minutes, or until the cake seems firm when gently touched. Cool well in the pan before cutting into wedges to serve.

VARIATION: Swirl in a few tablespoons of blueberry or raspberry jam, once the batter is spread in the prepared pie tin.

THE "M" LIST
KEY LIME BUNDT CAKE

MAKES 1 CAKE; SERVES 12 TO 16

CAKE

2 cups sugar

Zest of 2 limes, finely minced

1 cup (8 ounces) unsalted butter, almost at room temperature

4 eggs

2 yolks

2 teaspoons pure vanilla extract

2 tablespoons lime juice

½ teaspoon lime oil*

¼ teaspoon lemon oil*

1⅓ cup evaporated milk

¼ to ½ teaspoon citric acid* (optional)

3¾ cups all-purpose flour

4 teaspoons baking powder

½ teaspoon baking soda

⅜ teaspoon salt

LIME SYRUP

¾ cup water

½ cup lime juice

1½ cups sugar

½ teaspoon lime oil*

½ teaspoon citric acid (optional) (see page 128)

LEMON LIME CREAM CHEESE GLAZE

2 cups confectioners' sugar

4 ounces cream cheese, softened

2 to 3 tablespoons lime or lemon juice, or a combination

2 tablespoons unsalted butter

Oprah Winfrey has her "O" list, a list of the most inspiring items in beauty, books, and food. Years ago, I caught an Oprah show where she touted her "favorite things," one of which was a glorious lemon-lime Bundt cake. It looked fabulous and I knew I had to create my own (but, of course, better). This is an "M" list specialty—a delicate crumbed cake that sings with fresh lemon and lime. Just the fragrance of this cake as it cools is pure paradise. If you have a large food processor, you can use it to mix the batter for a quick and easy cake. The recipe calls for three special ingredients—lemon oil, lime oil, and citric acid, all of which are easily found in stores or online. You'll still have great results if you omit them, but they make this cake totally awesome.

~(o)~

Preheat the oven to 350°F. Spray a 12-cup Bundt pan or large angel food cake pan (not a pan with a removable bottom!) liberally with nonstick cooking spray. Place the Bundt pan on a parchment paper–lined baking sheet.

In a food processor (a large one, otherwise use your mixer), pulverize the sugar and lime zest for 2 minutes. Add the butter and cream it into the sugar, then add the eggs, yolks, and vanilla and blend well. Add the remaining ingredients and blend into a smooth batter. Pour the batter into the prepared cake pan, and place the pan on the prepared baking sheet.

Bake for 1 hour or longer until the cake tests done. It should be light golden brown, puffed up, and firm to the touch. Invert the cake onto a serving platter.

Meanwhile, for the lime syrup, in a small saucepan, bring all ingredients to a boil. Let simmer for 5 minutes. Cool. Poke holes all over the cake with a cake tester. Drizzle on some of the syrup. Let it set. Then, using a pastry brush, brush on another coat of the syrup and let dry for 10 minutes or so. Repeat until the syrup is used up.

For the glaze, blend the ingredients in a medium bowl, either with a whisk or in a food processor, to make a drippy glaze. Put the glaze in a measuring cup and drizzle it over the cake. Garnish with lime zest and fresh flowers. You can also forgo the glaze and dust the cake with confectioners' sugar just before serving.

* Lemon and lime oil are both available through Boyajian of Boston. Check online or in the Source Guide, page 299.

Swiss Chocolate Strawberry Scone Cake

MAKES 2 SMALL CAKES OR 1 LAYER CAKE; SERVES 8 TO 10

BUTTERY SCONE SHORTCAKE

3 cups all-purpose flour

1 cup sugar

4 teaspoons baking powder

½ teaspoon baking soda

¼ teaspoon salt

¾ cup (6 ounces) unsalted butter

2 eggs

¾ cup cream, plus more as needed

2 teaspoons lemon juice

2 teaspoons pure vanilla extract

1 cup semisweet miniature chocolate chips or finely chopped Swiss chocolate

1 egg white, beaten (optional)

White sugar (optional)

TOPPING

1 cup whipping cream

1 teaspoon pure vanilla extract

3 tablespoons confectioners' sugar

2 baskets fresh strawberries, washed, hulled, and sliced

Chocolate shavings (preferably Swiss chocolate)

Store-bought fudge sauce, warmed

Nothing, but nothing, is as fresh, inviting, easy, and crowd-pleasing as this cake. With luscious berries and a coating of Swiss chocolate on a rich, buttery shortcake base, it's like a Black Forest Cake taken to the country fair. It's no wonder this recipe has been downloaded some 2,500 times from the BetterBaking.com website. This makes two small cakes or one double-decker. You can make the cake part a day ahead and then assemble it just before serving. It can also be topped with warm fudge sauce.

Preheat the oven to 400°F. Stack 2 baking sheets together and line the top one with parchment paper. Line two 8-inch layer cake pans with parchment paper and spray with nonstick cooking spray. Place the pans on the stacked baking sheets. (Instead of using cake pans, you can also simply trace 2 circles in pencil on the parchment paper, using a bowl, and then pat the dough into the circles.)

In a food processor, place the flour, sugar, baking powder, baking soda, and salt and process to blend briefly. Add the butter in chunks and pulse to create a mealy mixture. Remove to a large bowl. Make a well in the center and stir in the eggs, cream, lemon juice, and vanilla. Add more cream a tablespoon at a time, if needed, to make the mixture hold together. Let it stand for a minute. Stir to make a soft dough, and then remove to a lightly floured work surface. Knead gently to make a dough that just holds together. Divide into 2 parts and place in the prepared pans or pat into the circle outlines. Press half the chocolate into the top of each round of dough. If you want a slightly shiny, sugared top to show through the chocolate covering, you can brush the tops with a beaten egg white and dust with white sugar before topping with the chocolate.

Bake until nicely browned, 22 to 26 minutes. Cool.

Meanwhile, beat the whipping cream with the vanilla and 2 tablespoons of the confectioners' sugar until soft peaks form. Crush half the berries and then toss them with the diced berries in a bowl with the remaining confectioners' sugar. (You want some of it to be saucy.)

On each scone shortcake, smear on half of the whipped cream, then half of the berries, and dust with the chocolate shavings. Alternatively, make a 2-layer shortcake by sandwiching the shortcake circles with the whipped cream and berries. This makes a heavier, thicker cake, but it will be nice and tall. Another option is to make individual scones or round biscuits, split them before serving, and smear with whipped cream and berries.

Garnish with a bit of warm fudge sauce.

BEN'S BISTRO
CHOCOLATE FUDGE CAKE

MAKES 1 CAKE; SERVES 8 TO 10

CAKE

½ cup hot water

4 ounces semisweet chocolate, melted and cooled

1¾ cups all-purpose flour

1 teaspoon baking soda

½ teaspoon salt

½ cup (4 ounces) unsalted butter, softened

1⅓ cups sugar

3 eggs

1 teaspoon pure vanilla extract

¾ cup milk or half-and-half cream, warmed

FROSTING

3 ounces semisweet chocolate, melted and cooled

3 tablespoons unsalted butter

2 cups confectioners' sugar

1 teaspoon pure vanilla extract

2 to 6 tablespoons warm water

This is named for my youngest son, Benjamin, an avid chocolate cake eater. "Put it in the book!" was Ben's enthusiastic response to his first bite of this cake. This makes a single-layer cake. Bake it in a deep fluted tart pan to gussy it up.

Preheat the oven to 350°F. Generously spray a 10-inch springform pan or a deep, 10-inch fluted tart pan with nonstick cooking spray. Line a baking sheet with parchment paper. Set aside.

For the cake, stir the hot water into the cooled chocolate. In a medium bowl, combine the flour, baking soda, and salt. Whisk to blend.

In the bowl of an electric mixer fitted with the paddle attachment, cream the butter and sugar together on the lowest speed until light and fluffy. Beat in the eggs, then the vanilla. Beat in the chocolate mixture, then the flour mixture. With the machine running, add the warm milk. Scrape the sides and bottom of the bowl and mix again.

Spoon the batter into the prepared pan and place it on the prepared baking sheet. Bake for 40 to 45 minutes, or until the cake springs back when lightly pressed. Let cool in the pan on a wire rack for 15 minutes, then unmold onto the wire rack and let cool completely before frosting.

For the frosting, combine the chocolate, butter, confectioners' sugar, and vanilla in a food processor and process for about 1 minute to make a soft, smooth frosting. Add 2 tablespoons warm water if needed to achieve the right consistency. Spread the frosting on the cake with a small metal spatula, swirling with a fork afterward in a decorative fashion.

Refrigerate the cake for 20 to 30 minutes to let the frosting set.

CHOCOLATE–SOUR CREAM BUNDT CAKE

MAKES 1 TUBE OR BUNDT CAKE; SERVES 8 TO 12

1 cup (8 ounces) unsalted butter, melted and cooled

2¾ cups sugar

4 eggs

2 teaspoons pure vanilla extract

3 cups all-purpose flour

¾ cup unsweetened cocoa powder

1 tablespoon baking powder

½ teaspoon salt

½ teaspoon baking soda

2 cups sour cream

⅓ cup milk

5 ounces semisweet chocolate, coarsely chopped

Confectioners' sugar for dusting

This cake came about when I had some extra sour cream on hand. The cake improves with age—if you can manage to keep snackers away from it. The chocolate chunks melt inside, and the top develops a sweet, tender crust.

Preheat the oven to 350°F. Generously spray a 10-inch tube pan or a 12-cup Bundt pan with nonstick cooking spray. Line a baking sheet with parchment paper. Set aside.

In the bowl of an electric mixer fitted with the paddle attachment, cream the butter and sugar together on the lowest speed until light and fluffy. Beat in the eggs and vanilla until smooth.

In a medium bowl, combine the flour, cocoa, baking powder, salt, and baking soda. Whisk to blend. Gradually blend the flour mixture into the batter. Mix in the sour cream and milk until thoroughly blended, stopping occasionally to scrape down the sides and bottom of the bowl.

Spoon half of the batter into the prepared pan. Top with half of the chocolate. Add the remaining batter and top with the remaining chocolate. Place the pan on the prepared baking sheet. Bake for 60 to 70 minutes, or until the cake springs back when lightly pressed. Let cool in the pan on the wire rack for 10 minutes, then unmold onto the wire rack and let cool completely. Dust with confectioners' sugar.

B.B.
Test Kitchen
Notes

The Pan That Launched Millions of Cakes

The Bundt pan celebrated its fiftieth anniversary in 2000. The Nordic Ware Company of Minneapolis, Minnesota, which invented the pan and owns the name, estimates that there are more than 45 million Bundt pans in American kitchens today. In 1966, a baker from Texas set off a Bundt frenzy when she won second prize at the Pillsbury Bake-Off for her Tunnel of Fudge Cake. (I featured my own version of this recipe on the website.) At the time, Nordic Ware had to keep its operations running around the clock to meet the demand.

WOOLWORTH'S FUDGE CAKE

MAKES 1 CAKE; SERVES 10 TO 14

CAKE

4 ounces unsweetened chocolate, melted

¾ cup (6 ounces) unsalted butter

2 cups firmly packed brown sugar

⅓ cup white sugar

3 eggs

2 teaspoons pure vanilla extract

2⅓ cups all-purpose flour

3 tablespoons unsweetened cocoa powder

2 teaspoons baking soda

⅜ teaspoon salt

1 cup sour cream

1 cup boiling water

FUDGE FROSTING

3 cups miniature marshmallows

¼ cup (2 ounces) unsalted butter

¾ cup semisweet chocolate chips

1 to 2 cups confectioners' sugar

¼ cup (2 ounces) cold butter, in small pieces

1 teaspoon pure vanilla extract

Light cream, as required

The Woolworth's I grew up with used to have its own in-store bakery, which made old-fashioned cupcakes, blueberry pie, corn muffins, and brownies all from scratch. They also made a diner-style, lofty fudge cake that sliced like a dream. It wasn't too sweet—the icing was just sweet enough—but it was so good! Woolworth's is now gone but the memory of its homey baking remains. It's yours for the enjoyment with this wonderful vintage-style, yet contemporary recipe, created from my memory.

Preheat the oven to 350°F. Generously spray a 9- by 13-inch rectangular pan with nonstick cooking spray and place on a large baking sheet lined with parchment paper.

In a double-boiler or in the microwave, on low, melt the chocolate and let it cool. In a mixer bowl or food processor, cream the butter with both sugars. Add the eggs and vanilla and blend until smooth. Fold in the flour, cocoa, baking soda, and salt and mix very slightly. Then fold in the sour cream, boiling water, and melted chocolate. Blend well and make sure no batter is stuck in the well of the mixer bowl. Spoon into the prepared pan.

Bake until the cake springs back when gently pressed, 42 to 52 minutes.

For the frosting, in a medium saucepan, slowly melt the marshmallows with ¼ cup of the butter. Remove from the stove and mix until smooth. Let cool for 5 minutes. In a microwave, melt the chocolate chips. Then place both the marshmallow mixture and the melted chocolate in a food processor and blend with the confectioners' sugar, remaining ¼ cup butter, vanilla, and a little cream to make a thick, glossy frosting (it will seem almost shiny). Spread on the cooled cake. Let set for 1 to 2 hours, until quite firm. This cake also freezes well.

DEEP, DARK FUDGE CONFECTION CAKE

MAKES 1 CAKE; SERVES 8

CREAM CHEESE PART

4 ounces cream cheese at room temperature

¼ cup sugar

2 tablespoons all-purpose flour

1 egg

1 cup miniature semisweet chocolate chips

CHOCOLATE-COCONUT PART

½ cup chocolate chips

½ cup finely chopped walnuts

1 tablespoon sugar

3 tablespoons unsweetened shredded coconut

BATTER

¼ cup unsweetened cocoa powder

1½ cups all-purpose flour

1 cup firmly packed brown sugar

1 teaspoon baking powder

½ teaspoon baking soda

⅛ teaspoon salt

1 cup warm brewed coffee

⅓ cup vegetable oil

2 tablespoons distilled white vinegar

Confectioners' sugar for dusting (optional)

None of my BB visitors can get enough of chocolate cakes of any sort. Call it the quirk, or the magic, of baking, but each recipe tester who tried this one got different results and yet, happily, each version was, by all accounts, great. It is a moist cake with a sticky, chewy, chocolaty ripple running through that you can't see, but that you can taste—and exult in.

Preheat the oven to 350°F. Line a 9-inch springform pan or a 9-inch round cake pan with a round of parchment paper. Spray the pan and paper with nonstick cooking spray. Line a baking sheet with parchment paper. Set aside.

For the cream cheese part, in the bowl of an electric mixer fitted with a paddle attachment, combine all the ingredients and beat on the lowest speed until smooth.

For the chocolate-coconut part, stir all the ingredients together in a small bowl and set aside.

For the batter, combine the cocoa, flour, brown sugar, baking powder, baking soda, and salt in a medium bowl. Whisk to blend. Make a well in the center and whisk in the coffee, oil, and vinegar. Blend well to make a smooth batter.

Spoon the batter into the prepared pan, and then spoon on the cream cheese mixture, depositing it in dollops over the surface. It does not have to be even. Sprinkle the chocolate-coconut part over the top. The 2 mixtures will sink into the cake during baking.

Place the pan on the prepared baking sheet. Bake for 25 to 35 minutes, or until the cake springs back when gently touched. This cake is quite moist due to the cream cheese part, but it should be set in the center. Let cool in the pan on a wire rack for at least 45 minutes, then unmold onto the wire rack and let cool completely. (The cake is a little fragile until it sets up.) Dust with confectioners' sugar, if desired.

KILLER CHOCOLATE LAYER CAKE

MAKES 1 LAYER CAKE; SERVES 10 TO 12

CAKE

2 cups sugar

1 cup (8 ounces) unsalted butter, melted and cooled

¼ cup vegetable oil

3 eggs

2 teaspoons pure vanilla extract

2½ cups all-purpose flour

1 teaspoon baking soda

2 teaspoons baking powder

½ teaspoon salt

⅛ teaspoon ground cinnamon

1 cup unsweetened cocoa powder

1½ cups warm flat cola or brewed coffee

ICING

½ cup chocolate chips, melted

¾ cup (6 ounces) unsalted butter, softened

1 teaspoon pure vanilla extract

¾ cup unsweetened cocoa powder

4 cups confectioners' sugar

½ cup brewed coffee

1 cup chocolate shavings for garnish

1 candied or maraschino cherry

You don't see cakes like this one every day: easy to make, moist, high, and a good keeper. I call it one of my "little black dress" cakes. If you don't have cola on hand, you can substitute warm mild coffee. For some reason, the cherry in the center reminds me of Saturday morning cartoons, and I always think of this as a Minnie Mouse Cake.

Preheat the oven to 350°F. Lightly grease two 9-inch round cake pans and line the bottoms with parchment-paper rounds. Line 2 baking sheets with parchment paper. Set aside.

For the cake, combine the sugar, butter, and oil in a large bowl. Whisk until blended. Beat in the eggs and vanilla. In a medium bowl, combine the flour, baking soda, baking powder, salt, cinnamon, and cocoa. Whisk to blend. Stir into the wet ingredients, then continue to stir while drizzling in the cola to make a thin batter.

Pour the batter into the prepared cake pans and place the pans on the prepared baking sheets. Bake for 35 to 40 minutes, or until the cakes spring back when gently touched. Let cool in pans on a wire rack for 15 minutes, then unmold gently onto the rack and let cool completely.

For the icing, combine the chocolate, butter, vanilla, cocoa, and 1 cup of the confectioners' sugar in a food processor. Process to blend, then add the remaining confectioners' sugar and process until light and fluffy, drizzling in the coffee as needed to achieve the right consistency.

To decorate, place 1 cake layer on a cardboard circle, cake board, or round platter. Spread the top with icing about ½ inch. Place the second layer on top and ice the cake, sides first, then the top with the rest of the icing. Garnish with chocolate shavings and place the cherry in the center.

Sweet Potato Pecan Caramel Bourbon Pound Cake

MAKES 1 CAKE; SERVES 14 TO 18

PECAN CARAMEL MARSHMALLOW STREUSEL

½ cup (4 ounces) unsalted butter

1 cup pecans

½ cup butterscotch chips

1 cup miniature marshmallows

1 cup firmly packed light brown sugar

CAKE

1 cup (8 ounces) unsalted butter

2½ cups sugar

5 eggs

1 cup whipping cream, half-and-half, or evaporated milk

1 tablespoon pure vanilla extract

2 cups mashed sweet potatoes

4½ cups all-purpose flour

4 teaspoons baking powder

1 teaspoon baking soda

½ teaspoon salt

½ teaspoon ground cinnamon

½ teaspoon pumpkin pie spice

BOURBON BROWN SUGAR GLAZE TOPPING

⅓ cup (3 ounces) unsalted butter

¾ cup firmly packed brown sugar

⅓ cup confectioners' sugar

3 tablespoons bourbon

1 teaspoon pure vanilla extract

FINISHING TOUCHES

½ cup toasted chopped pecans

½ cup warmed marshmallow sauce or fluff, or melted white chocolate

A moist, tall sweet potato cake with caramel pecan streusel and a warmed marshmallow glaze atop a sticky brown sugar bourbon topping. This is an extravagant holiday or special occasion cake that will become an instant new tradition. Hint: the darker the sweet potatoes, the prettier the interior crumb and hue of this cake will be. If you don't want to bother with the streusel, leave it out. This cake rocks no matter what. It's . . . yummy. Seriously, it's one for the ages.

Preheat the oven to 350°F. Line an angel food cake pan with parchment paper cutouts, held in place with nonstick cooking spray. Spray the pan interior again to ensure no sticking. Line a baking sheet with parchment paper and place the cake pan on it.

For the streusel, in a food processor, grind the ingredients together to make a coarse mixture and set aside.

For the cake, in the bowl of an electric mixer, cream the butter and sugar until well blended. Blend in the eggs, whipping cream, and vanilla, then blend in the sweet potatoes. Fold in the flour, baking powder, baking soda, salt, and spices and blend well. Spoon into the prepared cake pan. If using the streusel, spoon in two-thirds of the batter, distribute the streusel on top, and top with the remaining batter.

Bake until the cake springs back when gently touched, about 80 to 90 minutes. If the cake needs further baking, reduce the oven temperature to 325°F to ensure that the top and bottom do not get too browned or dry. When it is baked, let cool for 30 to 45 minutes and then invert on a serving platter.

For the topping, heat the butter and brown sugar in a small saucepan and let it cook, bubbling gently, for about 5 to 8 minutes, until slightly thickened. Remove from the stove and briskly stir in the confectioners' sugar. Stir in the bourbon and vanilla. Drizzle the topping over the cake, then sprinkle on the chopped pecans.

Let cool for 30 to 60 minutes, then drizzle on the melted white chocolate or warmed marshmallow sauce. This cake keeps well, gently covered, and can be frozen.

SOUR CREAM STREUSEL COFFEE CAKE

MAKES 1 TUBE CAKE; SERVES 12 TO 14

FILLING

⅓ cup firmly packed dark brown
    sugar

2 teaspoons unsweetened cocoa
    powder

2 ounces semisweet chocolate,
    coarsely chopped

1 teaspoon ground cinnamon

⅓ cup dark raisins, plumped and
    patted dry (see page 18)

⅓ cup golden raisins, plumped and
    patted dry (see page 18)

1 cup walnuts, toasted and
    chopped (see page 17)

CAKE

3¼ cups all-purpose flour

1 tablespoon baking powder

½ teaspoon baking soda

¼ teaspoon salt

¾ cup (6 ounces) unsalted butter,
    softened

½ cup firmly packed brown sugar

1⅓ cups white sugar

4 ounces cream cheese at room
    temperature

5 eggs

1½ teaspoons pure vanilla extract

1 cup sour cream

Memories of deli coffee cakes were the inspiration for this recipe. Put on some coffee or make some tea, settle back, and share this with friends. Without the filling, it makes a lovely pound cake.

Preheat the oven to 350°F. Generously spray a 9- or 10-inch tube pan or angel food cake pan with nonstick cooking spray. Line a baking sheet with parchment paper and set aside.

For the filling, combine all the ingredients in a small bowl and stir to blend.

For the cake, combine the flour, baking powder, baking soda, and salt in a medium bowl. Whisk to blend. In the bowl of an electric mixer fitted with the paddle attachment, cream the butter with both sugars on low speed until light and fluffy. Beat in the cream cheese until blended. Beat in the eggs and vanilla, then the sour cream. Gradually add the flour mixture and mix well for 3 to 4 minutes, stopping occasionally to scrape the sides and bottom of the bowl.

Spread one-third of the batter in the prepared pan. Top with a generous ⅓ cup of the filling mixture. Repeat layering, ending with the filling. Place the pan on the prepared baking sheet. Bake for 55 to 70 minutes, or until the cake is set and springs back when gently pressed. You can also use a cake tester as a guide. Let cool in the pan on a wire rack for 10 minutes, then unmold onto the wire rack and let cool completely.

St. Louis Gooey Butter Cake

MAKES 2 CAKES; SERVES 10 TO 12

DOUGH

¼ cup warm water

4½ teaspoons instant yeast

½ cup milk, warmed

⅓ cup sugar

1 egg

4 tablespoons (2 ounces) unsalted butter, softened

2 teaspoons pure vanilla extract

¼ teaspoon salt

2½ cups all-purpose flour

TOPPING

2½ cups sugar

1 cup (8 ounces) unsalted butter, softened

Pinch of salt

¼ cup corn syrup

2⅓ cups all-purpose flour

¼ cup warm water

2 teaspoons pure vanilla extract

Confectioners' sugar for dusting

This cake is for sale in nearly every pastry shop, bakery, and supermarket in St. Louis. I contacted fellow food writer Barbara Gibbs Ostmann, and she said that the recipe for this cake was published in the St. Louis Post Dispatch well before 1975, when she joined the paper. She agreed with me that it's an unusual recipe. "If you're not from St. Louis, you'll wonder exactly what you did wrong the first time you make this cake," she said. The first time I tried the recipe, it didn't work for me, but I have since tweaked it, with wonderful results. Shame on St. Louis for not sharing this sooner! It's a yeasty, sweet bread base, topped with a caramelized, gooey delight. There's nothing else quite like it.

~·❦·~

Generously spray two 9-inch round cake pans with nonstick cooking spray. Line 2 baking sheets with parchment paper. Set aside.

For the dough, hand whisk the water and yeast together in the bowl of an electric mixer and let stand for 2 to 3 minutes to dissolve the yeast. Stir in the milk, sugar, egg, butter, vanilla, salt, and 2 cups of the flour. Knead with the dough hook on the lowest speed of the mixer for 5 to 8 minutes, gradually adding more flour as required to make a smooth dough. Place the bowl inside a large plastic bag, close the bag loosely, and let rise for about 45 minutes, or until almost doubled.

Meanwhile, prepare the topping. In a food processor, combine all the ingredients and process for 20 to 30 seconds, or until blended into a smooth paste.

Turn out the dough onto a lightly floured surface and divide in half. Press each half into the bottom and sides of a prepared pan, pressing lightly to fit. Crimp the edges to make a border. With a small knife, make some slits in the dough. Spread half the topping on each cake. Let rise, uncovered, for 25 minutes, or until puffy.

Preheat the oven to 375°F. Place the pans on the prepared baking sheets. Bake for 20 minutes. Lower the temperature to 350°F and bake for 15 minutes longer, or until bubbly and lightly browned. Let cool on a wire rack until the topping settles down, about 15 minutes. Cut into wedges in the pan and serve warm or at room temperature.

APRICOT-BRANDY FRUITCAKE

MAKES 2 LOAF CAKES OR 1 TUBE CAKE; SERVES 12 TO 16

4 cups dried apricots (preferably Californian), coarsely chopped

2 cups golden raisins

½ cup dark raisins

½ cup candied orange peel

¼ teaspoon lemon oil or extract

¼ teaspoon orange oil or extract

2 teaspoons grated lemon zest

2 teaspoons grated orange zest

2 tablespoons orange liqueur

½ cup canned crushed pineapple, drained

¾ cup brandy, heated

1 Granny Smith or other tart apple, peeled, cored, and shredded

2 cups pecans

¾ cup walnuts, toasted and chopped (see page 17)

1 cup (8 ounces) unsalted butter, softened

1¾ cups sugar

4 eggs

1 teaspoon pure vanilla extract

3 cups all-purpose flour

1½ teaspoons baking powder

½ teaspoon salt

1 teaspoon ground cinnamon

¼ teaspoon ground cloves

¼ teaspoon ground nutmeg

⅛ teaspoon ground ginger

⅛ teaspoon ground allspice

Brandy, orange liqueur, or apple cider (or a mixture of each) for soaking

A mail-order company called 1812 Matthews House is the inspiration behind this one-of-a-kind fruitcake. It showcases California apricots, golden raisins, and mellow walnuts all set in a buttery pound cake foundation, creating a cake symphony. Because it is uncomplicated, it's a good starter fruitcake for beginners, and it's a cake that works well year-round. The best part about this cake is the textured surface of golden apricots poking their way through. This is one for both fruitcake fans and protesters. It is simply sublime (and no candied green and red cherries!).

Combine the apricots, both types of raisins, candied orange peel, citrus oils and zests, orange liqueur, and pineapple in a large bowl. Toss with the hot brandy. Cover lightly with plastic wrap and let stand at room temperature for 1 hour or as long as 2 days.

Just before making the cake, stir the apple and nuts into the soaked fruit mixture. Preheat the oven to 325°F. Line the bottom of two 9- by 5-inch loaf pans or a 9- or 10-inch tube pan with parchment paper. Spray nonstick cooking spray on the parchment paper. Line a baking sheet with parchment paper. Set aside.

In the bowl of an electric mixer fitted with the paddle attachment, cream the butter and sugar together on the lowest speed until light and fluffy. Beat in the eggs and vanilla. In a medium bowl, combine the flour, baking powder, salt, and spices. Whisk to blend. Add to the wet ingredients and blend until smooth. Add the fruit mixture and blend to make a thick batter.

Spoon into the prepared pan(s) and place the pan(s) on the prepared baking sheet. Bake for 2½ to 3 hours, or until the cake is firm, but not too brown and springs back when gently touched. It is dense, however, and will not spring back quite like a lighter pound cake. If the top is baking too quickly, cover it loosely with aluminum foil and lower the oven temperature to 300°F. Let cool in the pan(s) on a wire rack for 15 minutes, then unmold onto the wire rack and let cool completely.

Sprinkle or lightly soak a large piece of clean cheesecloth (or 2 pieces if you have made 2 cakes) with brandy. Using a cake tester or small, sharp knife, poke holes all over the surface of the cake. Wrap the cake(s) in the soaked cheesecloth. Wrap in plastic wrap, then in a clean tea towel, or place in a cake tin.

Refresh the cheesecloth once a week by sprinkling with more soaking liquid. Rewrap and age for at least 3 days or as long as 6 months.

THE FRUITCAKE PROJECT

If you're reading this, you must be intrigued by fruitcake. Perhaps you're curious to see if there is such a thing as a good fruitcake. Absolutely! Perhaps you would like to recapture some of the flavor and memories that go along with a good fruitcake (as opposed to the specimens that inspire lame jokes that circulate, much like inferior fruitcakes, every year). If you have a trusted family formula, my recipes may give you some ideas for new spins. I make a definitive Traditional Holiday Fruitcake (page 297) in the BB test kitchen, but I also embrace more unusual flavors, such as sour cherry and chocolate, in my seasonal cakes. If you're inspired, preheat the oven and roll up your sleeves. It doesn't have to be holiday time to enjoy one of these cakes, nor do you have to bake them well in advance of the holidays to age them.

VINTAGE FRUIT COCKTAIL CAKE

MAKES 1 CAKE; SERVES 10

CAKE

1½ cups sugar

2 eggs

½ cup corn or canola oil

1½ teaspoons pure vanilla extract

2 cups all-purpose flour

¼ teaspoon salt

1½ teaspoons baking powder

¼ teaspoon baking soda

1 (14- to 16- ounce) can fruit cocktail, not drained

BUTTER GLAZE TOPPING

¾ cup sugar

½ cup (4 ounces) unsalted butter

½ cup evaporated milk

This is vintage baking at its best. This cake turned up in a supermarket frozen food section: a low-slung pound cake with a buttery glaze, made with fruit cocktail. Too weird—I figured it had to have been a classic somewhere to pop up in this fashion. Indeed, I found versions of Fruit Cocktail Cake in many cookbooks, often with no measurements for the canned fruit and too much baking soda. I tweaked and perfected, and the result is this toothsome little cake that whips up in seconds. It is almost a bastardized baba au rhum or savarin cake, but done American style: easy and great.

Preheat the oven to 350°F. Generously spray a 12-cup Bundt pan or tube cake pan with nonstick cooking spray. Place it on a parchment paper–lined baking sheet.

In a mixing bowl, whisk together the sugar, eggs, oil, and vanilla. Fold in the remaining ingredients to make a thick but gloppy batter. Pour into the prepared pan.

Lower the oven temperature to 325°F as soon as you put the cake in the oven and bake, for 55 to 60 minutes, or until the cake springs back when gently touched and its edges are just browned. Cool for 10 minutes in the pan and then unmold.

Meanwhile, make the glaze. Put all the ingredients in a 2-quart saucepan. Over low to medium heat, stir and gently bubble for 5 to 10 minutes, until the mixture thickens to a light custard or thick sauce consistency. Pour the glaze over the cake while still hot and let the excess ooze down around the cake (it should be sitting in a puddle of this delicious sticky sauce).

TRADITIONAL HOLIDAY FRUITCAKE

MAKES 2 LOAF CAKES OR 1 TUBE CAKE; SERVES 16 TO 24

CAKE

1½ cups dark raisins

1¼ cups golden raisins

½ cup dried currants

1 cup mixed candied orange and lemon peel

1 cup candied cherries

1 cup packed pitted dates, chopped

¾ cup brandy, dark rum, or whiskey, heated

1 cup (8 ounces) unsalted butter, melted

1¾ cups white sugar

½ cup firmly packed brown sugar

4 eggs

2 teaspoons pure vanilla extract

2 tablespoons honey or corn syrup

3 cups all-purpose flour

1½ teaspoons baking powder

½ teaspoon salt

1 teaspoon ground cinnamon

½ teaspoon ground nutmeg

½ teaspoon ground cloves

1½ cups walnuts, toasted and chopped (see page 17)

Candied cherries for garnish (optional)

Brandy, orange liqueur, or apple cider (or a mixture or both) for soaking

Gently spiced, not too dark, not too light, this fruitcake is wonderful fresh, but improves greatly with aging. My fruitcakes are especially good aged at least 1 month or as long as 6 months.

~⟨◊⟩~

For the cake, at least 2 hours or up to 2 days before making the cake, combine the dark raisins, golden raisins, currants, candied peel, cherries, and dates in a large bowl. Toss with the hot brandy and set aside to soak.

Preheat the oven to 325°F. Line the bottom of two 9- by 5-inch loaf pans or one 9- or 10-inch tube pan with parchment paper and spray the paper with nonstick cooking spray. Line a baking sheet with parchment paper. Set aside.

In the bowl of an electric mixer fitted with the paddle attachment, cream the butter and both sugars together on the lowest speed until fluffy. Beat in the eggs, vanilla, and honey. In a medium bowl, combine the flour, baking powder, salt, and spices. Whisk to blend. Gradually add to the wet ingredients and stir to blend. Stir in the fruit and nuts until well blended.

Spoon into the prepared pans. At this point, you may garnish the top of the cake with extra cherries. Place the pan(s) on the prepared baking sheet. Bake for 2½ to 3 hours, or until the cake is firm, lightly browned, and springs back when gently pressed. If the top is baking too quickly, cover it loosely with aluminum foil and lower the temperature to 300°F. Let cool in the pan(s) on the wire rack for 15 minutes, then unmold onto the wire rack and let cool completely.

Sprinkle or lightly soak a large piece of cheesecloth (or 2 pieces if you have made 2 cakes) with brandy. Using a cake tester or a small knife, poke holes all over the surface of the cake(s). Wrap the cake(s) in the soaked cheesecloth. Wrap in plastic wrap, then in a clean tea towel, or place in a cake tin.

Refresh the cheesecloth once a week by sprinkling with more soaking liquid. Rewrap and age for at least 3 days or as long as 6 months.

½ cup oil

1⅓ cup bu......

3 eggs

½

Source Guide

· ·

INGREDIENTS

· ·

American Spoon Foods

1668 Clarion Avenue
P.O. Box 566
Petoskey, MI 49770-0566
Phone: 231.347.9030 or 888.735.6700 (US only)
Fax: 800.647.2512
www.spoon.com

American Spoon Foods of Michigan has long been a favorite supplier of dried fruits, preserves, and sauces. Their product line is always evolving. You may order online, or request their colorful catalog.

Barbours

165 Stewart Avenue
Sussex, NB
Canada E4E 3H1
Phone: 506.432.2323
www.barbours.ca

In Atlantic Canada and elsewhere in the world, one tea rings the bell: Maritime's King Cole orange pekoe tea, which is still wrapped in real gauze tea sachets. It's a cult item with many folks.

Bella Viva Orchards

3019 Quincy Road
Denair, CA 95316
Phone: 800.552.8218
www.bellaviva.com

Best-ever dried fruit, especially varieties of California dried apricots, plums, and pluots (a cross between a plum and an apricot).

Boyajian

144 Will Drive
Canton, MA 02021
Phone: 800.965.0665
Fax: 781.828.9922
www.boyajianinc.com

Boyajian of Boston manufactures a unique line of pure citrus oils, flavored oils, vinegars, and natural flavorings. No extract can approach the fresh flavor that Boyajian citrus oils add to foods. Boyajian is a family company operated by people who know and love food. You may order their products online or purchase them at finer gourmet shops.

Burnbrae Farms

R.R. #1 Lyn, ON
Canada KoE 1Mo
Phone: 800.666.5979
www.naturegg.com

A Canadian company that produces omega-3 eggs and other fine egg and egg white products.

Cabot Creamery

1 Home Farm Way
Montpelier, VT 05602
Phone: 888.792.2268
www.cabotcheese.com

Cabot Creamery of Vermont produces some of the most impressive dairy products around. Their butters and cheeses (particularly their cheddar) are world class. You will find Cabot products in supermarkets in the Northeast, and in finer shops elsewhere. You may also order their cheeses online.

Callebaut Chocolate

www.callebaut.be

If you like Belgian chocolate, Callebaut is the name to remember. The company manufactures a wide range of products for both home bakers and professionals.

Canadian Favourites

1525 Parent Avenue
Windsor, ON
Canada N8X 4J8
Phone: 519.253.7171 or 877.335.2372
Fax: 519.253.7927
www.canadianfavourites.com

This online store offers a broad variety of Canadian products for baking, snacking, and cooking. Great for expat Canucks or Americans wanting to try favorites like Fry's Cocoa, King Cole Tea, Dad's Cookies, Magic Baking Powder, and Canadian flour and cereals such as Red River.

Eggology

6728 Eton Avenue
Canoga Park, CA 91303-2813
Phone: 818.610.2222 or 888.669.6557
Fax: 818.610.2223
www.eggology.com

If you use egg whites a lot in baking, or if you prefer them to whole eggs, try Eggology bulk egg whites. This 100 percent pure, pasteurized product is sold in 16-ounce and 64-ounce containers. Order by phone.

Fleischmann's Yeast

www.breadworld.com

Fleischmann's literally revolutionized baking in North America when it introduced its yeast products more than 130 years ago, and it has since become synonymous with quality and reliability. No other yeast company provides as much support to home bakers as Fleischmann's. For recipes, baking advice, and more, visit their website. Fleischmann's yeast products are available in stores nationwide.

Ghirardelli Chocolate Company

www.ghirardelli.com

There's something about San Francisco and chocolate. Ghirardelli has been in business for 150 years, and their chocolates include bars, chips, and cocoa for baking, as well as boxed treats and specialty products for the trade.

Giusto's Specialty Foods, Inc.

344 Littlefield Avenue
South San Francisco, CA 94080
Phone: 866.972.6879
Fax: 650.873.2826
www.giustos.com

Giusto's is a family-run company that specializes in organic grains and flours.

Hammons Products Company

105 Hammons Drive
P.O. Box 140
Stockton, MO 65785
Phone: 888.429.6887
Fax: 417.276.5187
www.black-walnuts.com

The Hammons Company sells black walnuts that are native to the central and eastern United States. Black walnuts have a more pronounced, earthy flavor than the more widely known English walnuts. I like them in muffins and especially in oatmeal cookies.

Harney & Sons Fine Teas

P.O. Box 665
Salisbury, CT 06068
Phone: 518.789.2100 or 888.427.6398 (US only)
Fax: 518.789.2100
www.harney.com

Harney & Sons offers a wide array of traditional herbal and organic teas, as well as samplers and accessories. You may order online or request a catalog.

Hodgson Mill

1100 Stevens Avenue
Effingham, IL 62401
Phone: 800.347.0105
Fax: 217.347.0198
www.hodgsonmill.com

Fine producers of all-natural grain-based foods.

Hulman & Company/Clabber Girl

P.O. Box 150
Terre Haute, IN 47808
Phone: 812.232.9446
www.hulman.com

Baking powder seems like a simple ingredient, but not all products are alike. I go through baking powder like some households go through laundry detergent. I've tried them all, and Hulman's Clabber Girl baking powder is the queen of the ball. Hulman also sells (non-GMO) cornstarch, and other products.

The King Arthur Flour Company

58 Billings Farm Road
White River Junction, VT 05001
Phone: 800.827.6836
Fax: 800.343.3002
www.kingarthurflour.com

King Arthur Flour is a baker's mecca. For malt powder, fondant, coarse sugar, baker's caramel, special tools, and much more, turn and face Vermont. You may order online or from their printed catalog.

Magic Baking Powder

Kraft Canada
Phone: 888.572.3806
www.kraftcanada.com

In Canada, we use Magic Baking Powder, sold in the familiar brown and yellow canister.

McCormick

Phone: 800.632.5847
www.mccormick.com

McCormick is the largest spice and flavoring company in the world. When it comes to quality, variety, and availability, they are unmatched. From spices and extracts, to dressings, dips, and Old Bay Seasoning, you'll find McCormick products on a store shelf near you. In Canada, look for the Club House brand, which is made by McCormick.

Nielsen-Massey Vanillas

1550 Shields Drive
Waukegan, IL 60085-8307
Phone: 847.578.1550 or 800.525.PURE (7873; US only)
Fax: 847.578.1570
www.nielsenmassey.com

Nielsen-Massey Vanillas has been supplying my test kitchens with pure vanilla for several years. The company has been in the business for nearly a century, and their products have set the standard for professional bakers and an increasing number of home bakers.

Penzeys Spices

Phone: 414.760.7337 or 800.741.7787 (US only)
Fax: 414.760.7317
www.penzeys.com

Penzeys Spices is my preferred mail-order source for vanilla, spices, herbs, and seasonings. Bill Penzey and his colleagues know their business, and the quality of the products they sell is second to none. You may order online or via their catalog, or you may shop in one of their growing number of retail stores.

Red Star Yeast and SAF Gourmet Yeast

P.O. Box 737
Milwaukee, WI 53201
Phone: 887.677.7000 or 800.445.4746
www.redstaryeast.com or
www.safyeast.com

Red Star and SAF yeasts are solid performers. SAF is popular among professional bakers, and I like it for its reliability in yeasted sweet breads such as cinnamon buns. Red Star is an excellent general-purpose yeast. The company's website is very informative (for wheat-free bakers as well).

Robin Hood Multifoods, Inc.

80 Whitehall Drive
Markham, ON
Canada L3R OP3
Phone: 800.268.3232
www.robinhood.ca

In Canada, Robin Hood is the name for flour. They produce organic flours, as well as various all-purpose and bread flours. The familiar yellow Robin Hood packages are available in most supermarkets. Robin Hood also manufactures and distributes the legendary Red River Cereal, a wheat and flax mix that is a staple in many Canadian homes.

Saco Foods

P.O. Box 620707
Middleton, WI 53562
Phone: 800.373.SACO (7236; US only)
www.sacofoods.com

Saco Buttermilk Blend has been a staple in my test kitchens for years. It is pure powdered buttermilk, and it tenderizes and flavors baked goods like nothing else. Saco Foods also manufactures chocolate chunks that are perfect for Toll House–style cookies, and a premium cocoa that is a flavorful blend of Dutch processed and natural cocoas.

Schapira Coffee and Tea company

Pine Plains, NY
Phone: 518.398.7100
www.schapira.com

Schapira's Coffee and Tea Company is a small coffee-roasting operation in the Hudson Valley region of New York State. Their coffee is distinctly delicious for drinking and as an ingredient in recipes that call for brewed joe. Schapira sells mostly to the trade, but consumers may order some of their legendary blends through their website.

Scharffen Berger

Chocolate Maker
2000 Folsom Street
San Francisco, CA 94110
Phone: 800.930.4528
Fax: 415.626.7991
www.scharffenberger.com

In a few short years, Scharffen Berger has risen to become what many consider the leading chocolate maker in the United States. You may order online or contact them directly.

Spices Etc.

P.O. Box 2088
Savannah, GA 31402
Phone: 800.827.6373
www.spicesetc.com

Fine spices and natural extracts of all flavors from vanilla to mango and from cococut to caramel. Also a supplier of dried fruit, quality teas, dry cheese powder, and buttermilk powder.

Sultan's Delight

P.O. Box 090302
Brooklyn, NY 11209
Phone: 800.852.5046
Fax: 718.745.2563

Based in Brooklyn, Sultan's Delight stocks all manner of Mediterranean and Middle Eastern foods.

Valrhona Chocolate

www.valrhona.com

France's Valrhona manufactures fine chocolate products for home and professional use. Their cocoa in particular is full-bodied and sharp with intense chocolate flavor.

White Lily Flour

4740 Burback Road
Memphis, TN 38118
Phone: 800.742.6729 or 800.599.1380 (US only)
www.whitelily.com

White Lily Flour is made from soft winter wheat that is ground and sifted to produce a very delicate product, wonderful for quick breads. The company produces cornmeal and mixes as well.

Zabar's

2245 Broadway
New York, NY 10024
Phone: 212.787.2000
Fax: 212.580.4477 or 800.697.6301
www.zabars.com

Zabar's is a favorite New York destination for gourmet foods and housewares. Some items are available for sale online.

EQUIPMENT AND SUPPLIES

All-Clad Metalcrafters

424 Morganza Road
Canonsburg, PA 15317
Phone: 800.255.2523
www.allclad.com

I've been a fan of All-Clad cookware for years. The company manufactures a superb line of stainless-steel pots, pans, roasters, and kitchen tools. Their unique line of professional-grade stainless-steel bakeware (with a gorgeous champagne finish) is virtually indestructible and featured on many TV cooking shows. You will find All-Clad products in finer kitchen supply shops.

Anchor Hocking

519 Piece Avenue
Lancaster, OH 43130
Phone: 740.681.6478
www.anchorhocking.com

Anchor Hocking manufactures a nice line of large commercial-style cookie jars and storage containers.

Ares Kitchen and Baking Supplies

2355 A Trans Canada Highway
Pointe-Claire, QC
Canada H9R 5Z5
Phone: 514.695.5225
Fax: 514.695.0756
www.arescuisine.com

Canada's leading baking and cooking supplies store.

BetterBaking.com

www.betterbaking.com

My website is your gateway to exclusive baking products and tools. Visit my online shop, especially for custom rolling pins, the pride of my test kitchen.

Cooking Enthusiast

www.cookingenthusiast.com

For a terrific online selection of knives (including knife storage cases), rasp or microplane zesters, and other tools, visit Cooking Enthusiast on the web.

Beehive Kitchenware

One West Street
Fall River, MA 02720
Phone: 508.678.7700
www.beehivekitchenware.com

Beehive makes quality pewter cookware, as well as copper and silver baking tools. I recommend their copper and silver measuring cups, their heart-shaped pewter measuring spoons, and their whale-bone-facsimile, carved-handle pastry wheel. A husband-and-wife team designs and manufactures these one-of-a-kind "useful" artworks.

Beryl's Cake Decorating and Pastry Supplies

P.O. Box 1584
North Springfield, VA 22151
Phone: 800.488.2749
Fax: 703.750.3779
www.beryls.com

Beryl's Cake Decorating and Pastry Supplies is operated by a generous and talented baker named Beryl Loveland. Beryl was born in England, and when she moved to the United States, she found that many of the materials she had used in her craft back home were not available. She has since remedied that. You may order imported British and French supplies online or request a catalog.

Big Green Egg

3417 Lawrenceville Highway
Tucker, GA 30084-5802
Phone: 800.559.8852 (Canada) or 800.939.3447 (US)
Fax: 404.321.0330
www.biggreenegg.ca (Canada)
or www.biggreenegg.com (US)

I like to bake on the barbecue, and one of the more impressive grills I have seen for baking (never mind grilling) is the Big Green Egg (yes, it's green, and it looks like an egg). This ceramic wonder retains heat and moisture like nothing I have ever seen. It burns lump charcoal, and it costs more than a conventional grill, but if you're really fond of barbecue cooking, crack open an Egg.

Bridge Kitchenware Corp.

49 Eagle Rock Avenue
East Hanover, NJ 07936
Phone: 973.240.7364
www.bridgekitchenware.com

Bridge Kitchenware of New York has been serving the trade and retail customers since 1946. They sell tools from the major lines and hard-to-find items like professional-grade food slicers and mills. You may order by phone or online.

Chantal Cookware

5425 North Sam Houston Parkway West
Houston, TX 77086
Phone: 800.365.4354
www.chantalcookware.com

For terrific teakettles, look for the Chantal line (equipped with harmonica whistles). Chantal also manufactures fine cookware, bakeware, and kitchen tools. You may purchase online or contact the company for retail information.

Chefs

5070 Centennial Boulevard
Colofado Springs, CO 80919
Phone: 800.338.3232
Fax: 800.967.2433
www.chefscatalog.com

Chef's Catalog of Dallas, Texas, has been in business since 1979. They carry many of my favorite lines, including All-Clad, KitchenAid, and Le Creuset.

Chicago Metallic

Phone: 800.323.3966
www.cmbakeware.com

Chicago Metallic is among the leading North American manufacturers of commercial and retail bakeware. Consult a restaurant supply store or order through Golda's Kitchen or King Arthur Flour Company.

Component Design NW

P.O. Box 10947
Portland, OR 97296
Phone: 800.338.5594
Fax: 800.879.2364
www.cdn-timeandtemp.com

For timers and thermometers, check out the Component Design Northwest line. CDN manufactures an excellent line of digital and analog instruments, including thermometers that are designed to check oven and freezer temperatures. Look for CDN products in kitchen supply stores.

Cuisinart

www.cuisinart.com

Cuisinart has long been synonymous with food processors, but their product lines extend to great stand mixers, cookware, scales, ice cream makers, and much more.

Cumberland General Store

P.O. Box 4468
Alpharetta, GA 30023
Phone: 800.334.4640
www.cumberlandgeneral.com

Cumberland General Store supplies everything from spinning wheels to barrels to butter molds to pea shellers. A treasury of homestead products.

Danesco

18111 Trans-Canada Highway
Kirkland, QC
Canada H9J 3K1
Phone: 877.DANESCO (877.316.3726)
Fax: 800.363.6595
www.danescoinc.com

Danesco is the brand to look for if you're tracking down a Danish dough whisk. You can also find this item via Golda's Kitchen and King Arthur Flour Company.

Doughmakers

1650 E. Industrial Drive
Terre Haute, IN 47802
Phone: 888.386.8517
Fax: 812.299.7788
www.doughmakers.com

Doughmakers manufactures aluminum and steel bakeware that has a patented natural pebbled finish that promotes even browning and won't wear off. If you're a cookie hound, check out these pans. And, if you can find one, buy a cheesecake pan—they're incredibly durable.

Edlund Company

159 Industrial Parkway
Burlington, VT 05401
Phone: 802.862.9661
Fax: 802.862.4822
www.edlundco.com

Edlund of Vermont makes commercial food-service quality kitchen scales. Look for Edlund products in restaurant supply stores.

Emile Henry

www.emilehenry.com

Emile Henry offers a vast and colorful array of bowls, pie plates, cooking dishes, and much more. Look for their very large line in a good kitchen supply store.

Golda's Kitchen

2885 Argentia Road
Mississauga, ON
Canada L5N 8G6
Phone: 905.712.1475 or
866.GOLDA99 (866.465.3299)
Fax: 905.816.9997
www.goldaskitchen.com

Golda's Kitchen retail store is also Canada's largest online cooking and baking mail-order supplier. They carry all the items I use in my test kitchens, as well as BB's custom rolling pins. They also carry Red River Cereal and other Canadian products.

Hearth Kitchen Company

226 Selleck Street, Suite B
Stamford, CT 06902
Phone: 203.325.8800
Fax: 203.323.1771
www.hearthkitchen.com

Hearth Kitchen Company makes an outstanding hearth baking stone kit, perfect for pizzas (see page 89).

J. K. Adams Company

P.O. Box 248
1430 Route 30
Dorset, VT 05251
Phone: 800.451.6118
Fax: 802.362.5472
www.jkadams.com

J. K. Adams Company of Dorset manufactures rolling pins, prep boards, and other wooden items, as well as tableware made of Vermont slate.

James Sloss

3705 SE Locks Road
Dayton, OR 97114
Phone: 503.864.3423
www.frenchbutterdish.com

James Sloss produces lovely French butter dishes that keep butter at a spreadable temperature. The dishes are wheel-thrown, high-fired stoneware, and no two are alike. Sloss also makes bowls, mugs, vases, and terrific pie plates.

Jessica's Biscuit

www.ecookbooks.com
Phone: 800.878.4264

This Massachusetts company has been selling cookbooks since 1980. If it's in print and about food, Jessica's Biscuit will procure it for you.

John Borin

Fine Hand Made Clocks
1508 Nevada Drive
Plano, TX 75093
Phone: 469.467.7454 or 888.284.6348
www.johnborin.com

The clock pictured on page vi was custom made for me by this fine artist.

Kenwood Mixers

www.kenwood.co.uk

Kenwood mixers, manufactured in England, are solidly built and offer 5- and 7-quart bowls. They are available in North America in finer kitchen supply stores.

KitchenAid

P.O. Box 218
Street Joseph, MI 49085
Phone: 800.422.1230
www.kitchenaid.com

If you're going to invest in a mixer (or a food processor), invest in a KitchenAid. You've seen them in stores, you've seen them on cooking shows, you've pined, you've wondered. Yes, a KitchenAid is worth it. Yes, you can leave it to a loved one in your will. It's built like a tank, and it will handle any and all mixing and food processing jobs. They also manufacture great dishwashers, refrigerators, and stoves. Watch for new product lines like cutlery.

La Cuisine

323 Cameron Street
Alexandria, VA 22314-3219
Phone: 800.521.1176
www.lacuisineus.com

La Cuisine is a retail store in Alexandria, Virginia. They stock many tools and ingredients from France, including Matfer molds and mandolines. La Cuisine publishes a regular newsletter called A la Carte that contains recipes and news about new ingredients and tools.

Lamson & Goodnow

45 Conway Street
Shelburne Falls, MA 01370
Phone: 800.872.6564
Fax: 413.625.9816
www.lamsonsharp.com

For knives, look for LamsonSharp forged cutlery. Lamson & Goodnow sells online, and they have the best bread knives, dough cutters, and apple-paring knives available.

Le Creuset of America

Phone: 877.273.8738 (US) or 866.666.6162 (Canada)
www.lecreuset.com

Le Creuset of France manufactures porcelain-enameled cast-iron cookware that is as beautiful to look at as it is durable. You will find Le Creuset products in finer kitchen stores.

Lee Valley Tools Ltd.

P.O. Box 6295, Station J
Ottawa, ON
Canada K2A 1T4
Phone: 800.267.8735 (US) or 800.267.8761 (Canada)
www.leevalley.com

For a unique zesting and grating tool, visit Lee Valley Tools and check out their stainless-steel rasp (also known as a microplane). Lee Valley also sells their own private-branded knives made by Sabatier of France. You may order from Lee Valley online or by catalog.

Lehman's

One Lehman Circle
P.O. Box 270
Kidron, OH 44636
Phone: 888.438.5346
www.lehmans.com

Lehman's is a uniquely American enterprise. It was established in 1955, and its catalog has always been known as Lehman's Non-Electric. The company has been supplying the Amish of Ohio, and others, with "roots" products that do not require electricity. Kitchen appliances, homesteading tools, and an amazing selection of wood-burning stoves are just a few examples of what Lehman's carries. They can supply everything from graniteware bake- and cookware to a circa-1800 milk separator to a modern line of steel and enamel homestead-style appliances.

Lockwood Manufacturing, Inc.

84 Easton Road
Brantford, ON
Canada N3P 1J5
Phone: 519.756.2800 or 800.265.8445
Fax: 519.756.1541
www.lockwoodmfg.ca

Lockwood Manufacturing has been supplying professional bakers in Canada with commercial-grade bakeware for more than 40 years. Commercial pans, robust as they are, get so much use that Lockwood provides a reglazing service for its customers. For home use, Lockwood pans will last a lifetime.

Lodge Manufacturing Company

Phone: 423.837.7181
www.lodgemfg.com

Lodge has been pouring cast iron in Tennessee for more than a century. They manufacture skillets, griddles, and Dutch ovens in several sizes, as well as many other accessories, including those triangular dinner bells you see in the movies. Look for Lodge accessories in stores or online.

Magic Mill International

105 Pleasant Avenue
Upper Saddle River, NJ 07458
Phone: 201.785.8840
Fax: 201.885.8841
www.magicmillusa.com

Manufactured by Electrolux of Sweden, Magic Mill mixers are unique in their construction and how they work dough. Many home bakers like these units for their capacity (up to 24 cups of flour) and swear by their design.

Matfer Bourgeat

16300 Stagg Street
Van Nuys, CA 91406
Phone: 800.766.0333
Fax: 818.782.0799
www.matferbourgeatusa.com

Matfer does not sell directly to consumers, but they can direct you to a source in your area that represents their products. I especially recommend their nested, Exoplast cookie cutter sets, which come in both fluted and plain edges. They're hard to get, but worth sleuthing out.

Nordic Ware

5005 Highway 7
Minneapolis, MN 55416-2274
Phone: 952.920.2888 or 877.466.7342
Fax: 952.924.8561
www.nordicware.com

Nordic Ware manufactures a wide range of aluminum and steel bakeware, including several models of their trademark Bundt pans. They also make crepe pans, microwave ware, and other assorted kitchenware. Nordic Ware is a family-owned company that has been in business for more than 50 years.

Oster

www.oster.com

Oster is known for its excellent blenders, and the same quality can be found in many of their other products.

Padinox

P.O. Box 201606
RPO Sherwood
489 Brackley Point Road
Winsloe, PEI
Canada C1A 9E3
Phone: 902.629.1500
Fax: 902.629.1502
www.paderno.com

Located on beautiful Prince Edward Island, Padinox is Canada's only cookware manufacturer. The company produces the Paderno and Chaudier lines of stainless-steel cookware, as well as a line of utensils, kettles, and bakeware. Their products are available at better retailers and online.

Pepper Mill Imports, Inc.

P.O. Box 775
Carmel, CA 93921
Phone: 831.393.0244
Fax: 831.393.0801
www.peppermillimports.com

Pepper Mill Imports are makers and importers of famed Atlas mills used for coffee, spices, salt, and pepper.

Primo Grills and Smokers

5999 Goshen Springs Road
Norcross, GA 30071
Phone: 770.729.1110
Fax: 770.729.1111
www.PrimoGrill.com

Outdoor grills and barbecues, perfect for grilled pizzas, breads, and homemade naan.

Rochow Swirl Mixer Company

P.O. Box 10405
1900 University Avenue
Rochester, NY 14610-0405
Phone: 585.244.1120
Fax: 585.244.7931
www.rochowcutters.com

Rochow Swirl Mixer Company is a family-owned company that supplies many restaurants and bakeries. They carry cookie, scone, and doughnut cutters. Each item is heavy-duty and meant to last a few generations. Their biscuit cutters and Christmas teddy-bear cutters are the best, bar none.

Rycraft

9234 E. Valley Road, Suite D
Prescott Valley, AZ 86314
Corvallis, OR 97333
Phone: 800.479.2723
Fax: 800.479.7911
www.rycraft.com

Rycraft manufactures wonderful terra-cotta cookie stamps, sugar keepers, and other ceramic items.

Seafoam Wood Turning Studio

3178 Route 6, Seafoam
RR# 4 River John, NS
Canada B0K 1N0
Phone: 902.351.3886
www.seafoamwoodturning.com

Sunrise Woodcrafts of Nova Scotia produces some neat wooden items like oatmeal spurtles, dibbers (for planting seeds in the garden), letter openers, and other items. You may order online or contact them by telephone.

Snow River Wood Products

809 N Central Avenue
Crandon, WI 54520
Phone: 812.238.5000
Fax: 812.232.8504
www.snowriverwood.com

Snow River Wood Products manufactures great bowls out of walnut and rock maple. They're perfect for mixing and kneading dough, or tossing salads. Snow River also makes pastry, cutting, and utility boards.

Sur La Table

P.O. Box 840
Brownsburg, IN 46112
Phone: 800.243.0852
Fax: 317.858.5521
www.surlatable.com

Sur La Table is a kitchen-supply house that originated in Seattle. They've been in business since 1972, and their catalog reaches nearly 9 million consumers. Sur La Table is known for its selection and customer service.

Thorpe Rolling Pins

336 Putnam Avenue
P.O. Box 4124
Hamden, CT 06514
Phone: 203.787.0281
Fax: 203.230.2753

Thorpe manufactures excellent rolling pins. Look for them in finer kitchen supply stores.

Vic Firth Gourmet

77 High Street
Newport, ME 04953
Phone: 800.894.5970
www.vicfirthgourmet.com

Banton Vic Firth specializes in outstanding rolling pins—all hardwood with metal ball bearings, as well as pepper mills of all descriptions. You can order directly or contact them for a retailer in your area.

Victorinox

www.victorinox.com

Victorinox's fine knives and accessories can be found in better kitchen supply stores.

Viking Range

111 Front Street
Greenwood, MS 38930
Phone: 662.455.1200 or 888.VIKING1 (888.845.4641)
Fax: 662.455.3127
www.vikingrange.com

For commercial ranges and cookware, as well as commercial style home stand mixers.

Weber-Stephen Products Co.

200 East Daniels Road
Palatine, IL 60067-6266
Phone: 800.446.1071 (US) or 800.265.2150 (Canada)
www.weber.com

I'm always trying new things, but when it comes to gas grills, my heart belongs to Weber. There is a reason why grill owners who have discovered this brand refer to their grills as "my Weber" (instead of "my barbecue"), and there is a reason why these grills show up in divorce settlements. A Weber grill is not so much a grill as it is an appliance, well designed and solidly built. Why pollute the environment by tossing out inferior grills every couple of years? Invest in a Weber, and you'll never look back.

Williams-Sonoma

Phone: 405.717.6131 or 877.812.6235 (US only)
www.williams-sonoma.com

Williams-Sonoma is a premier retailer of fine ingredients, appliances, and furnishings for the cook with discerning tastes. You may order online, by phone, or visit one of their retail stores.

Wilton Industries

2240 West 75th Street
Woodridge, IL 60517
Phone: 800.794.5866 (US) or 800.387.3300 (Canada)
Fax: 888.824.9520 (US) or 416.679.0798 (Canada)
www.wilton.com

Wilton Industries stocks all manner of supplies for cake decorating, conventional bakeware and pans in special shapes, candy-making equipment, and much more. Wilton supplies are available at finer kitchen retailers and online. Their annual catalogs are great for inspiration (especially for special-occasion baking).

Zojirushi

Phone: 310.769.1900 or 800.733.6270
www.zojirushi.com

Zojirushi makes well-engineered bread makers.

Zyliss USA Corporation

One Post Suite 100
Irvine, CA 92618
Phone: 888.794.7623
www.zylissusa.com

When you're shopping for kitchen "gadgets," look for Zyliss. Swiss quality and design are evident even in their simplest tools.

ASSOCIATIONS AND ORGANIZATIONS

The American Institute of Baking

1213 Bakers Way
P.O. Box 3999
Manhattan, KS 66505-3999
Phone: 800.633.5137
Fax: 785.537.1493
www.aibonline.org

The Bread Bakers Guild of America

670 West Napa Street, Suite B
Sonoma, CA 95476
Phone: 707.935.1468
Fax: 707.935.1672
www.bbga.org

International Association of Culinary Professionals

1100 Johnson Ferry Road
Suite 300
Atlanta, GA 30342
Phone: 404.252.3663 or 800.928.4227 (US only)
Fax: 404.252.0774
www.iacp.com

Index

Metric Conversions

. . . .

Weight

¾ oz	21 g
1 oz	28 g
1¼ oz	35 g
1½ oz	43 g
2 oz	57 g
2½ oz	70 g
3 oz	85 g
4 oz	113 g
5 oz	140 g
6 oz	170 g
7 oz	200 g
½ lb/8 oz	225 g
10 oz	285 g
¾ lb/12 oz	340 g
1 lb/16 oz	454 g
1¼ lb	570 g
1½ lb	680 g
1¾ lb	790 g
2 lb	900 g
2½ lb	1.1 kg
3 lb	1.4 kg
3½ lb	1.6 kg
4 lb	1.8 kg
5 lb	2.2 kg
6 lb	2.7 kg
7 lb	3.15 kg
8 lb	3.5 kg
10 lb	4.5 kg
20 lb	9 kg

Length

⅛ inch	3 mm
¼ inch	6 mm
½ inch	1 cm
¾ inch	2 cm
1 inch	2.5 cm
1½ inches	4 cm
2 inches	5 cm
3 inches	8 cm
4 inches	10 cm
5 inches	12 cm
6 inches	15 cm
7 inches	18 cm
8 inches	20 cm
9 inches	23 cm
10 inches	25 cm
11 inches	28 cm
12 inches	30 cm
13 inches	33 cm
14 inches	35 cm
15 inches	38 cm
16 inches	40 cm
18 inches	46 cm
20 inches	50 cm
24 inches	60 cm

Volume

⅛ tsp	0.5 mL
¼ tsp	1 mL
½ tsp	2 mL
¾ tsp	4 mL
1 tsp	5 mL
1½ tsp	7.5 mL
2 tsp	10 mL
1 Tbsp	15 mL
4 tsp	20 mL
2 Tbsp	30 mL
3 Tbsp	45 mL
4 Tbsp	60 mL
¼ cup	60 mL
5 Tbsp	75 mL
⅓ cup	80 mL
½ cup	125 mL
⅔ cup	160 mL
¾ cup	185 mL
1 cup	250 mL
1¼ cups	310 mL
1½ cups	375 mL
1¾ cups	435 mL
2 cups/1 pint	500 mL
3 cups	750 mL
4 cups/1 quart	1 L
5 cups	1.25 L
6 cups	1.5 L
7 cups	1.75 L
8 cups	2 L
9 cups	2.25 L
10 cups	2.5 L
11 cups	2.75 L
12 cups	3 L
1 quart	1 L

Temperature

100°F	38°C
110°F	43°C
200°F	95°C
225°F	105°C
250°F	120°C
275°F	140°C
300°F	150°C
325°F	160°C
350°F	180°C
375°F	190°C
385°F	196°C
400°F	200°C
425°F	220°C
450°F	230°C
475°F	240°C
500°F	260°C

Can and jar sizes

12 oz jar	355 mL jar
14 oz can	398 mL can
19 oz can	540 mL can
28 oz can	796 mL can